Macintosh® C Programming Primer Volume II

Mastering the Too[ls]
Using THINK C®

Dave Mark

Addison-Wesley P[ublishing]

Reading, Massachusetts Men[lo Park, California]
Don Mills, Ontario Wokingh[am, England]
Sidney Singapore Tokyo M[adrid San Juan Paris]
Seoul Milan Mexico City Taipei

Library of Congress Cataloging-in-Publication Data
(Revised for vol. 2)

Mark, Dave.
      Macintosh programming primer.

      Includes index.
      Bibliography: p.
      Vol. 2 has title: Macintosh C programming primer.
      Contents: [1] Inside the toolbox using THINK's
Lightspeed C — v. 2. Mastering the toolbox using
THINK C.
          1. Macintosh (Computer) — Programming.
2. C (Computer program language). I. Reed,
Cartwright. II. Title.
III. Title: Macintosh C programming primer.
QA76.8.M3M368 1989   005.265   88-34992
ISBN 0-201-15662-8
ISBN 0-201-57016-5

ISBN 0-201-57016-5
 4 5 6 7 8 9 10 - MW - 94939291
Fourth printing, November 1991

To Deneen and my father,
both of whom reached milestones this year.

Contents

Foreword

Scott Knaster

Back in 1984, just after the end of the Pleistocene Era, it was actually possible for one person to know just about everything there was to know technically about a Macintosh. There was, after all, just one model, the venerable but not venerated Macintosh 128K. In fact, calling the Macintosh 128K the first member of a product line was pretty much wishful thinking; after all, they didn't say "World War I" until the sequel came out.

But I digress (or just think of it as hypertext). For all its 64K of ROM, several hundred routines, and many storage options (you could connect an external $3\frac{1}{2}$ inch disk drive, or not), the Macintosh programmer's world was well-defined, and by today's standards, it was graspable—you could get your head around it, as they used to say here in California.

Things around here are a little bit different now, of course. Chances are your Macintosh knows how to talk to one or two across the room, and if you're really cool, probably a few hundred more located somewhere between here and Indonesia. There are now well over a thousand routines defined in the many versions of the ROMs that Apple's genius engineers have cranked out over the past few years in between cans of Jolt cola and occasional minutes of sleep. It's a rich and complex world for programmers of all stripes, both professional and hobby varieties.

And that, at last, is where this book comes in. Not too long ago, I was wondering (electronically) aloud why no one had written a practical, up-to-date book about programming the Macintosh in C, currently the most popular language among Macintosh programming gurus. The answer, of course, was that there was a book like that. Hiding behind the innocent guise of a primer was just such a volume, with friendly presentation, thoroughness, and fun. That was Volume I of the *Macintosh Programming Primer,* predecessor of this book.

(Digression again: as you probably know, the folks who invented the Macintosh planned on programmers using Pascal or assembly language. At that time, C was for UNIX hackers and employees of huge telephone companies. Pretty soon, though, the clamor for C started, and the rest is history. If you have practical reasons for avoiding C, such as the need for features available in another language, you probably have no reason to switch. To those of you who resist C for religious reasons, I'll point out that Pascal and C really aren't so different. It's a little like those two guys with black and white faces on Star Trek; they hated each other, but nobody else could tell them apart. Language religion wars don't really help anyone, but writing great software does.)

Anyway, Dave Mark sees all the neat new stuff in the Macintosh world as his playground, and he invites us to play, too. In this wonderful volume, we get to go exploring with Dave as he takes us on a tour of many of the things that our new and improved Macintoshes can do. Some of my favorite discussions include the ones about cdevs, object programming, and the world of living color with Color QuickDraw, but they're all entertaining. By choosing THINK C as the learning tool, we can all easily sing along with Dave as we go.

This book is full of fun and good learning. With the vast landscape of Macintosh programming as your goal and Dave Mark as your friend, you'll soon feel the awe and mystery of commanding your Macintosh to do great things.

Scott Knaster

Preface

From the sounds of it, *Macintosh Programming Primer, Volume I* was well received. Cartwright Reed and I got lots of letters, phone calls, and AppleLinks, and all were much appreciated. People also sent us personal letters relating their own programming experiences. We even got Christmas cards!

We also received a bunch of letters from people with suggestions for Volume II of the *Primer*. These letters were the primary factor in determining the table of contents for this book. Color QuickDraw, Object Programming, and TextEdit all made the cut—you asked for it, you got it!

I am very interested in hearing from you. Feel free to send me your comments on Volume II, good or bad. I'd also love to see examples of your work. Has anyone built an application that's on the market, or being regularly used? Keep in touch. As always, send all letters, comments, and cards (especially baseball cards—I love those!) to:

Mac Primer Comments
2534 North Jefferson Street
Arlington, VA 22207

One more thing. Please join me and millions of others in the campaign to save our planet's natural resources. Recycling, conservation of water and gasoline, and reduced consumption of non-biodegradable products are vital to that goal. I believe that together we *can* make a difference.

D.M.
Arlington, VA

Acknowledgments

Macintosh Programming Primer, Volume II is the result of much hard work by many people. I am truly grateful to all of them for sharing in my dream.

First and foremost, I'd like to thank my wife and best friend, Deneen Melander, for all her patience and understanding. YMBFITWWOK?

Thanks to Dave Allcott, Mark Geschelin, Greg Howe, Darrell LeBlanc, Philip Borenstein, Guillermo Ortiz, Jim Reekes, Phil Shapiro, Forrest Tanaka, and Jon Zap for all the time and energy they put into the technical review process. These guys made all the difference in the world (and kept my imagination from taking complete control of the facts). Thanks to Wayne Correia for getting me in touch with such great tech reviewers!

A special thanks to my brother, Stu Mark, for all of his help in getting this book off the ground (especially for typing in and testing all the programs).

I'd also like to thank Julie Stillman (my wicked editor), Elizabeth Grose, and Diane Freed, the folks at Addison-Wesley who dragged this book, kicking and screaming, out of me. They made the process a true pleasure (well, most of the time!).

Finally, thanks to Steve Baker and Cartwright Reed, there for me through thick and thin.

1

Welcome Back

The first volume of the Macintosh Programming Primer *presented the fundamental concepts involved in programming the Macintosh using THINK C and the Macintosh Toolbox. Ready for more?*

Welcome Back!

The *Macintosh Programming Primer* is a tutorial in the art of Macintosh programming. In Volume I you learned the basic skills for creating your own Macintosh applications. Volume II, *Mastering the Toolbox Using THINK C* builds on those skills, covering more advanced topics. By the time you finish this book you will understand the fundamental toolbox concepts such as memory management using handles and pointers. You'll be able to write specialized code such as MDEFs, INITs, cdevs, and filter procedures. You'll have mastered the intricacies of Color QuickDraw and TextEdit. You'll even have your first object oriented program under your belt.

Volume I in Review

Before moving on to new topics, it may be useful to review some of the key areas covered in Volume I. Being relatively comfortable with these topics will really make a difference in your understanding of Volume II.

Volume I of the *Macintosh Primer* started off with a discussion of Macintosh programming tools. By now, you should be an old hand at using THINK C, Symantec's excellent development environment. You should also be pretty comfortable with the THINK C source level debugger. The programs in this volume were all developed using THINK C version 4.02, but they should work with any version of THINK C.

Volume I also spent a considerable amount of time discussing ResEdit, Apple's graphical resource editor. For the most part, this volume assumes that you know how to create all the standard resource types, how to change a resource, and how to change a resource's ID. All of the resources in this book were created with ResEdit version 1.2.

You should definitely understand the major differences between C and Pascal, which were covered in Volume I. For example, you should know when to use the & operator when passing arguments to a Toolbox function. You should know the size of all the popular C types as well (you know, shorts and ints are 2 bytes, but longs are 4 bytes).

You should also feel pretty comfortable with the process of looking things up in *Inside Macintosh*. Many of the topics covered in Volume

II of the *Macintosh Programming Primer* are described only in Volume V of *Inside Macintosh*, so you might want to buy a copy. Having the complete set of *Inside Macintosh* volumes (including the *XRef*) definitely will enhance your coding experience.

The first actual Mac programming topics covered in Volume I were QuickDraw and window management. Volume I presented several programs that created windows based on `WIND` resources, drawing both text and graphics in the windows. You should be an old hand with routines such as `GetNewWindow()`, `ShowWindow()`, and `SetPort()`.

The first book introduced event processing along with Toolbox routines like `GetNextEvent()` and `WaitNextEvent()`. You should understand the process of calling these routines to retrieve events, as well as the steps involved in processing each of the basic event types once you've retrieved events.

Volume I introduced the concepts of pull-down and pop-up menu-handling. The creation of menu bars from `MBAR` resources was discussed, as well as the addition of individual menus built from `MENU` resources. You should understand how to add command-key equivalences to your menus, as well as the general mechanism of enabling, disabling, and allowing selection from your menus and menu items. You should be able to add special characters (such as check marks) to your menu items.

Volume I introduced the Dialog Manager and the Control Manager, using Toolbox routines such as `ModalDialog()`, `GetDItem()`, and `GetCtlValue()`. You should feel comfortable creating dialog and alert templates using resource types such as `ALRT`s, `DLOG`s, and `DITL`s. You should understand the basic concept of controls and control values.

Volume I also discussed the basics of scrap (clipboard) management, printing, file access, scroll bars, pictures (and `PICT` resources), sounds (and `'snd'` resources), and basic error handling. A chapter on ResEdit and the creation of custom application icons was also presented.

Each of these topics is important. If you feel a little fuzzy on one of them, review that material in Volume I. One skill that you'll definitely want to have is the ability to read the descriptions of the Toolbox routines found in *Inside Macintosh* and translate those descriptions from Pascal into C.

Volume II Topics

Volume I of the *Macintosh Programming Primer* generated a lot of mail. Most of the mail was positive (thanks!), and chock-full of suggestions for a second volume. Many of the suggestions involved fundamental programming concepts such as pointers, handles, and memory allocation. People asked questions about the proper usage of Toolbox routines such as `HLock()` and `HUnlock()`. Several people asked for a discussion on the best way to connect window-related information to the parent window, so that the information could be accessed directly from the `WindowPtr`. Two of the most popular topics were Color QuickDraw and object-oriented programming.

You'll find every one of these topics inside this book. Here's a bird's-eye view of Volume II.

Chapter 2 — Toolbox Techniques

This chapter contains a potpourri of Toolbox tidbits. For starters, the Macintosh memory model is presented, with special emphasis on addresses and pointers. The roles of the compiler and the Macintosh Memory Manager are discussed, and the Mac's mechanism for allocating space is described.

Next, the difference between relocatable and nonrelocatable memory is covered, leading up to an explanation of handles. Although handles were used in many of the programs found in Volume I, they never were covered in much detail. If you are going to make effective use of handles in your own programs, you'll need a thorough understanding of them. Chapter 2 should do the trick.

Chapter 2 also includes a section on memory management under MultiFinder. Although your application will never know if it's running under MultiFinder, it is important that you have a basic understanding of MultiFinder. This section also discusses your application's interface with the Finder.

The remainder of the chapter is dedicated to miscellaneous tips that will make your life a little easier. Concepts such as 32-bit clean Macintosh programming and issues specific to THINK C, such as the use of routine and variable prototypes, are discussed. The difference between C and Pascal's calling conventions are covered, as well as the aforementioned `WindowPtr` piggybacking techniques.

There's something for everyone in Chapter 2. You'll probably want to read it once to get familiar with the contents, then refer back to it as the concepts come up in subsequent chapters.

Chapter 3 — Code Resources

Chapter 3 introduces alternatives to the world of double-clickable applications. The chapter starts with a description of several different code forms, from the cdev that makes the modular Control Panel possible to the filter procedures that allow you to customize and expand Toolbox entities such as the Dialog Manager, TextEdit, and the List Manager.

Chapter 3's first program takes the form of an **INIT**, a code resource that gets executed at system start-up. This particular INIT loads a font number from a resource and sets the default application font to that font. The INIT makes use of a special piece of code that plots the INIT's icon (see Figure 1.1) while the INIT is running. You can use this special code when you write your own INITs.

Chapter 3's second program is a **cdev** designed to work with the INIT. A cdev is a special file that contains resources recognized by the Control Panel. When you open the Control Panel, all the cdevs in your system folder will appear in a scrolling list on the left-hand side. The cdev developed in this chapter (pictured in Figure 1.2) allows you to set the default application font from a pop-up menu drawn in the Control Panel's window.

Chapter 3's third program is an **MDEF** that allows you to create menus made up of pictures instead of text. An MDEF is the menu definition procedure used by the toolbox to create and allow selection from pull-down and pop-up menus. Your MDEF (see Figure 1.3) will create its menu from a set of PICT resources you'll provide in the calling application's resource fork.

Figure 1.1   Chapter 3's INIT icon.

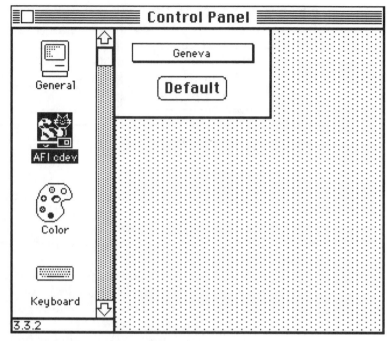

Figure 1.2   Chapter 3's cdev in action.

Figure 1.3   PICT MDEF in action!

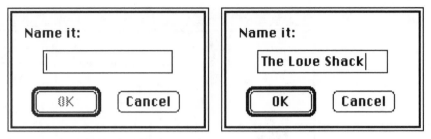

Figure 1.4   A dialog box, with the OK button disabled and enabled.

Chapter 3's final program shows you how to use a filter procedure with the Dialog Manager to filter events as they occur in a dialog box. Figure 1.4 shows a dialog box with an editable text field. Notice that the OK button is dimmed when the text field is empty. That's the work of the filter procedure.

Chapter 3 gives you four specific instances of specialized code that you can use in your own programs. More importantly, these examples will give you a leg up on creating any stand-alone code. For example, you can use the techniques presented here to create your own CDEF (control definition procedure), WDEF (window definition procedure), or LDEF (list definition procedure, for use with the List Manager).

Chapter 4 — Color QuickDraw

None of the programs presented in Volume I were written to take advantage of the fantastic color capabilities of the Macintosh. Because of the Mac's black-and-white screen, you may not be aware that even the first Macintoshes supported color via QuickDraw calls such as ForeColor() and BackColor(). These calls are part of Classic QuickDraw, which supports only eight colors (including black and white).

When the Macintosh II was introduced (along with *Inside Macintosh, Volume V*) the world of **Color QuickDraw** was born. Chapter 4 covers the data structures and Toolbox routines you'll use to program with Color QuickDraw and its cousin, **32-Bit QuickDraw**. There's a section on the **Palette Manager**, a set of Toolbox routines that allows you to build and draw with your own custom palette of colors. There's even a section on off-screen drawing environments.

Chapter 4's first program starts by checking to see whether Color QuickDraw is currently installed. If not, it puts up the alert shown in Figure 1.5.

If Color QuickDraw is installed, the program steps through each of the currently installed graphic devices and, if the device represents an active screen, displays the color table for that device, centered on the devices screen. Figure 1.6 shows the color table for a monochrome screen.

Figure 1.5　The "I don't support Color QuickDraw" Alert.

Figure 1.6　Color table for a monochrome device.

Chapter 4's second program demonstrates the Palette Manager. The program creates three palettes, one made up entirely of shades of red, one made up of shades of gray, and one composed of a variety of bright colors. Next, three windows are created and one of the three palettes is assigned to each window. When a window receives an updateEvt, its update routine draws a series of concentric rectangles, using all the colors of that window's palette. If the program is run on an 8-bit display, only 256 different colors can be displayed at a single time. If each window requires 100 colors (for a total of 300), somebody's going to lose! The Palette Manager makes sure that the frontmost window gets what it needs, even to the detriment of some of the other windows. This program will give you a real feel for the Palette Manager.

Chapter 4's third program, **ColorTutor**, is perhaps the most useful program in the chapter. ColorTutor uses CopyBits() to demonstrate the 16 transfer modes available under Color QuickDraw. Figure 1.7 shows the ColorTutor window in glorious black and white.

The source code used to create ColorTutor may be interesting, but the program itself will prove more useful yet. ColorTutor provides a

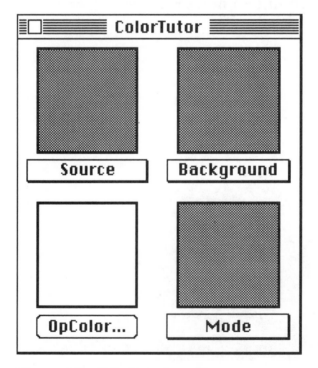

Figure 1.7   ColorTutor in action.

color lab, enabling you to try out the different color transfer modes in the comfort and privacy of your own home.

Chapter 4's final program demonstrates 32-Bit QuickDraw's off-screen drawing environments (also know as **gworlds**). You'll create a gworld, then draw a gray ramp and a color ramp inside the gworld. You'll then use CopyBits() to copy the gworld's pixels to windows of varying sizes. Gworlds are invaluable for producing flicker-free color animation.

Chapter 5 — TextEdit

It's hard to imagine a Mac scenario that doesn't include some form of TextEdit. When you change the name of an icon in the Finder or type in a dialog's text field, you're using TextEdit. There have been lots of requests for a comprehensive TextEdit application. Well, here it is!

Chapter 5 starts with a thorough examination of the TextEdit Toolbox routines. Chapter 5 then presents **FormEdit**, a complete TextEdit application. FormEdit is chock-full of special features. As you can see in Figure 1.8, FormEdit consists of two fields, a Name field and a Misc field. Both fields support all the usual TextEdit features (such as cut, copy, and paste). The Misc field supports automatic scrolling when its scroll bar is active. This means that if

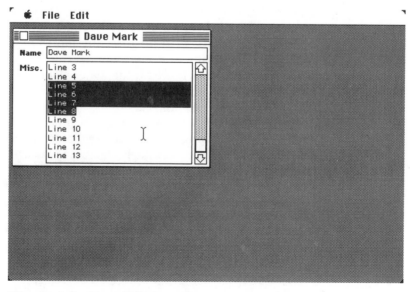

Figure 1.8   FormEdit in action.

you click the mouse in the middle of the Misc field and then drag the mouse, extending the selection above (or below) the top (or bottom) of the window, the scroll bar will scroll automatically.

FormEdit will provide you with a good TextEdit reference when you build your own TextEdit applications. You can reuse as much of FormEdit's code as you like.

Chapter 6 — Object Programming

One of the most requested topics for Volume II of the *Macintosh Programming Primer* was that of object programming (formerly known as object-oriented programming, or just plain OOP). Apple has gone to great lengths to get its developers up to speed on object programming, calling it "the future of Macintosh development." Apple's MacApp development environment is a completely object-oriented development environment. The commitment and the direction is there. The future of Macintosh development definitely lies with object programming.

The people at Symantec have built their own object programming environment. THINK C (version 4.0 and later) comes with a set of libraries that enable you to create and manipulate objects within your own programs. The Think Class Library (or TCL) contains all the objects you'll need to build powerful Macintosh programs. The TCL contains scroll bar objects, push-button objects, even window objects. These objects will greatly simplify your development cycle and make your code much more maintainable.

Chapter 6 starts with an introduction to object programming, explaining the major concepts you'll need to use the TCL and to design your own objects. Next, the major elements of the Think Class Library are presented, along with some pointers on how to get started with your own projects.

Finally, Chapter 6 presents an object program that you can use as a starter kit. The program creates rectangular objects that you can drag around in a window. Each object has its own set of properties (such as pattern, size, and stacking depth) and will be redrawn automatically when an updateEvt occurs. The window can be scrolled using either a horizontal or a vertical scroll bar (see Figure 1.9).

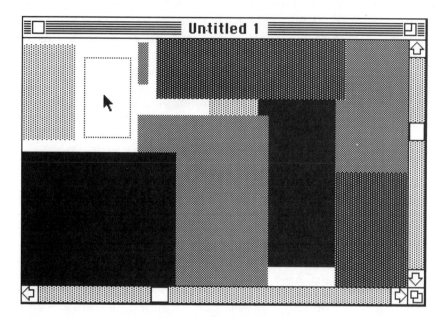

Figure 1.9 Chapter 6's object program in action.

Appendix A — Glossary of Terms

The glossary of terms presented in Volume II is a superset of the one in Volume I. Most of the terms presented come from the glossary found in *Inside Macintosh X-Ref* and have been reprinted with permission.

Appendix B — Source Code Listing

The source code of every program presented in this book is listed for reference in Appendix B. Several of the programs listed in this appendix are somewhat different than their chapter counterparts. For example, the source code to the MDEF listed in Chapter 3 does not perform scrolling or pop-up functions. Both the scrolling and the pop-up code have been added to the source code listing found in the appendix. If you notice a discrepancy between the code listed in a chapter and the code in Appendix B, use the version in Appendix B. In addition, several source code listings provided in Appendix B are not found anywhere else in the book. For example, the ShowINIT code that displays icons at INIT time is found only in Appendix B.

Volume II follows Volume I's method of presentation pretty closely. Each topic is presented as a whole, with descriptions of all the important Toolbox routines as well as related tips and techniques. Once the topic is laid out, an example program is presented from stem to stern. The resource file is created (if necessary), as well as the THINK C project and source code files. The process of compiling and running the program is described, with screen shots included wherever possible.

How to Use This Book

Each *Macintosh Programming Primer* chapter is made up of the main text and **tech blocks**. The main text is the narrative portion of this text. Read this first. It contains the information you need to input and run the example programs. Because we've placed a premium on getting you going immediately, we have you run the program before discussing how the code works. Impatient programmers are invited to go directly to Appendix B, which contains commented listings of all the programs discussed in the book. If you have questions after typing in the programs, refer to the chapter in which the program is discussed. If you prefer a more sedate pace, read a chapter at a time, type in the programs and test them as you go. Try the variants to the program if they sound interesting.

At some points, the narrative is expanded with a tech block, indicated by a distinctive gray background. It's OK to ignore them during your first read-through.

There are several important terms and conventions used throughout the *Macintosh Programming Primer*.

> Tech blocks will have this appearance in the main text. If you feel comfortable with the subject discussed in the main text, read the tech blocks for more detail. Otherwise, come back to them later.

All of the source code is presented in a special font. For example:

```
while ( i < 20 )
    PassTheParameters();
```

Toolbox routines and C functions are also in the code font when they are described in the text. Code should be typed in the same case as presented in the text. C is a case-sensitive language. Please note the similarity between the upper case `L` and the lower case `l`, and be careful to type in the correct choice.

Whenever we refer to a function or procedure call, a pair of parentheses is placed at the end of the procedure or function name. `GetNewWindow()` is an example of a function call.

Finally, boldface type is used to point out the first occurrence of new terms and file names.

Ready, Set . . .

At this point, you should be ready to go. Make sure you at least skim through Chapter 2 before you dive into your favorite subject. You'll probably want to refer to Chapter 2 a time or two as you read through the rest of the book. Oh, yes, one more thing. If you like, you can send in the coupon found in the back of the book for a floppy disk containing all the source code found in this volume.

Go!

2

Toolbox
Techniques

This chapter discusses some of the techniques that are fundamental to Macintosh software development. It covers issues ranging from basic memory management to the differences between C and Pascal calling conventions.

After the publication of the first volume of the *Macintosh Programming Primer*, many people sent suggestions regarding topics they wanted to see covered in the second volume. This chapter covers some of the most requested topics, which also happen to be among the most important. The Macintosh memory model is discussed, as is the importance of being 32-bit clean. Pointers and handles are covered, and strategies for dealing with each are presented. Also included is a tips and techniques section full of useful tidbits, such as piggybacking techniques for tying your window's data to your windows.

There's something for everyone in Chapter 2. You'll probably want to read it once to get familiar with the contents, then refer back to it as the concepts come up in subsequent chapters.

To start off, the next section discusses pointers and handles.

All About Pointers

Those of you who are already pointer masters might want to skip ahead to the next section while the topic of pointers is addressed briefly.

The Macintosh's random access memory (or RAM) is arranged as a contiguous series of address locations, starting with the address 0 and ending with an address one less than the total number of bytes of RAM. The RAM on a 1-megabyte Mac Plus ranges from 0 to 1,048,575 in decimal, or from 0 to 0x000FFFFF in hex.

The notation 0xFFFF is standard C syntax for the hex number FFFF. The 0x tells the C compiler that the rest of the number should be interpreted as hex.

The Macintosh uses 32-bit (4-byte) addresses. The highest number that can be represented in 32 bits is 0xFFFFFFFF (hex) or 4,294,967,296 (that's four *billion*) in decimal. This means that the Macintosh architecture is limited to a maximum of 4,294,967,296 bytes (4 gigabytes) of RAM. That's 4,096 megabytes. Wow!

Figure 2.1 shows a memory layout for a 4,096-megabyte machine. The address of each byte appears to its left.

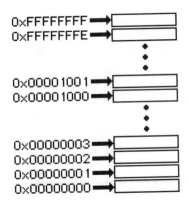

Figure 2.1   Memory layout for 32-bit machine.

Pointers are nothing more than addresses. A pointer to a specific byte of memory is the 4-byte address of the byte. For example, a pointer to the very first byte of memory has a value of 0L.

Here's another conventional tidbit for you to try at home. When the compiler encounters the letter L immediately following a decimal constant, the compiler treats that constant as a long int, taking up 4 bytes. Thus, the constant 0L is equivalent to the constant 0x00000000.

When you think of a byte, think of a constant like 0xE3. Two hex digits represent a number ranging from 0 to 255 (or from -128 to 127, in the case of a signed byte). When you think of two bytes, think of a short or an int, or a constant like 0xA287.

Because addresses are always 4 bytes long, pointers are always 4 bytes long. Consider the following code:

```
Ptr myPtr;
int num;

myPtr = &num;
*myPtr = 42;
```

When the MacOS runs this code, 4 bytes will be allocated for myPtr (because it's a pointer/address) and 2 bytes will be allocated for num (because it's an int). Take a look at Figure 2.2.

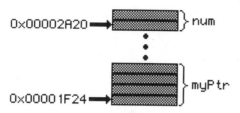

Figure 2.2   A pointer and its variable.

In this drawing, myPtr's 4 bytes start at 0x00001F24 and num's 2 bytes start at 0x00002A20. Why were they allocated so far apart? They could well have been allocated in 6 consecutive bytes. The point is, you shouldn't count on a particular memory configuration, and you shouldn't really care whether or not your variables are close together.

In C, the notation &num represents the 4 byte address of num, also known as a pointer to num. Thus, the statement:

```
myPtr = &num;
```

is the same as saying:

```
myPtr = 0x00002A20;
```

The notation *myPtr represents the memory locations pointed to by myPtr. Because myPtr was declared as a pointer to an int, *myPtr represents an ints worth of memory (2 bytes). The statement:

```
*myPtr = 42;
```

will write the number 42 in the two bytes starting at 0x00002A20, just as if we had said:

```
num = 42;
```

Get used to thinking of pointers as 4-byte numbers. When you pass a parameter with an & in front of it, you are actually passing a pointer to the parameter. For example:

```
PaintRect( &myRect );
```

passes exactly 4 bytes to PaintRect(). Specifically, it passes a pointer to the 8-byte data structure myRect (a.k.a, the address of the first byte of myRect).

Pointers Are Never Relocatable

When you pass the address of a data structure to a routine, you had better make sure that the data structure stays in the same place in memory at least until that routine returns. In the previous example, if you pass 0x00002A20 to PaintRect() as the address of myRect, myRect had better stay at 0x00002A20 until PaintRect() returns.

Why would anyone ever move things around in memory? This is a good question, and it forms the basis for our explanation of handles. For now, just remember that pointers are always 4 bytes long and are never relocatable.

The Macintosh Memory Layout

Before discussing handles, let's step through a bird's-eye view of the Mac's memory layout. Look at Figure 2.3, the Macintosh memory map.

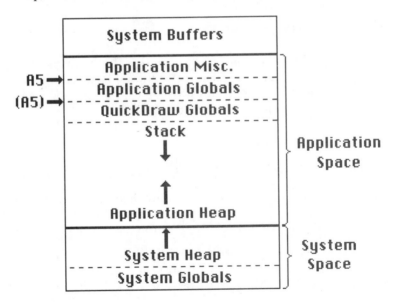

Figure 2.3   Macintosh memory map.

The System Space

The **system space** starts at address 0x00000000 and is dedicated to the Macintosh operating system. The beginning of the system space is dedicated to system globals. These globals are described in Appendix C of the *Inside Macintosh X-Ref*. For example, the global CaretTime defines TextEdit's caret blink interval in ticks (60ths of a second). CaretTime is a long and takes up the 4 bytes starting at 0x000002F4.

> Take a look at the *X-Ref's* Appendix C. If you need access to one of these globals, chances are good that Apple provides a Toolbox routine specifically designed to return (and possibly to change) that global's value. Conversely, if no access routine exists, you should think long and hard before you manipulate that global. Although Apple tries not to change the meaning and location of the system globals, sometimes circumstances force such changes to be made. When the Mac II was introduced, the global GhostWindow (0xA84) was no longer supported. Several major applications that had taken advantage of this global no longer worked properly on the Mac II.

Above the system globals lies the **system heap**. The system heap is a block of memory used by the system for its own memory allocation. For the most part, you won't need to worry about the system heap. The memory used by your application will reside in the application space.

The Application Space

When an application is launched, the MacOS allocates a block of memory called the **application space.** Under MultiFinder, several application spaces exist at the same time. Even though an application is in the background, it may still be active, accessing memory in its own application space.

As shown in Figure 2.3, near the top of your application's space, directly above the stack, lies your application's copy of the QuickDraw globals. The QuickDraw globals include a pointer to the current port (thePort), a set of patterns (white, black, gray, ltGray, and dkGray), the standard arrow cursor (arrow), the bitmap of the main screen (screenBits), and the seed for the random number generator (randSeed).

At the heart of every Mac is a central processing unit (CPU). All Mac CPUs are members of the Motorola 68000 family. Mac Pluses, SEs, and portables sport a 68000, Mac IIs a 68020, and SE/30s, IIXs, IIci's, IIcx's and IIfx's a 68030. Every 68000 family CPU has 16 32-bit registers. Eight of these registers are called address registers (known as A0 through A7) and eight are called data registers (known as D0 through D7).

Several of the CPU's registers play well-defined roles for the MacOS. For example, the address in the A5 register contains a pointer to the boundary between the current application's copy of the QuickDraw globals and the application's own globals. Applications use this pointer (known in assembly language as (A5)) to access their copies of the QuickDraw globals by decrementing (A5). Applications access their own globals by incrementing (A5). Figure 2.4 shows a sample MultiFinder layout with two applications open.

Under MultiFinder, applications take turns being **active**. Even if an application is in the background, it can still get its share of CPU time. When the MacOS makes an application active, it updates A5 to point into that application's space, allowing the application to find its QuickDraw globals.

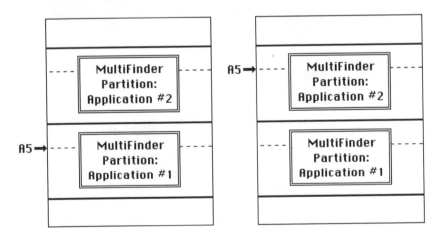

Figure 2.4 The A5 register points to application #1's globals when it is active and to application #2's globals when it is active.

In addition to the QuickDraw globals, copies of some of the system globals are also stored in the application's space. One example is the global `MenuList`, which contains a handle (don't worry, we'll get to handles in a minute) to the list of menus available to the current application. Because each application has its own set of menus, MultiFinder makes sure that the official `MenuList` is a duplicate of the current foreground application's local `MenuList` handle.

In addition, any parameters passed into the application by the launching application are stored here. For example, when you double-click a HyperCard stack in the Finder, the Finder launches HyperCard, passing the name of the stack as a parameter (for more info on Finder parameters, see *Inside Macintosh, Volume I*, pages 57–58).

The Stack

Every data structure and variable used by your program has a size, and thus takes up space in memory. A `short` and an `int` both take up 2 bytes of memory. A `long` takes up 4 bytes. A pointer to a `short` (or to anything for that matter) also takes up 4 bytes.

When your application is active, register A7 holds a pointer to the first free byte of stack space. Figure 2.5a shows an empty stack, with

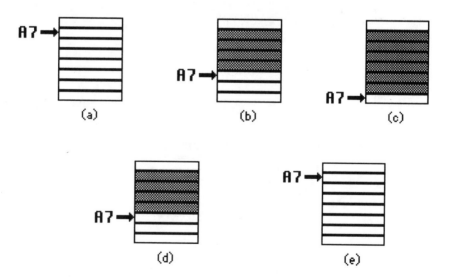

Figure 2.5 An empty stack (a), a `long` pushed on the stack (b), an `int` pushed on top of the `long` (c), the `int` popped off (d), and, finally, the `long` popped off (e).

A7 pointing to the first available byte on the stack. Figure 2.5b shows a long pushed on the stack, A7 being decremented by 4 bytes to make room for the long. The reason A7 gets decremented is that the stack grows down, from higher memory towards lower memory.

Figure 2.5c shows another two bytes (the size of an int) pushed on the stack. In Figure 2.5d, the int has been popped off the stack and A7 has been incremented by two bytes. Finally, the long is popped off the stack (Figure 2.5e), and A7 again points to the first available byte on the stack.

When your application is first loaded, space for your application's globals is allocated on your application's stack.

> When THINK C compiles your application, it replaces references to your globals with the appropriate offset from A5. Under normal circumstances (when you are writing an application), this information is not that important to you. However, when you write stand-alone code (such as an INIT or an MDEF), A5 will point to the calling application's globals (which have no relation to the stand-alone code's globals). If you want to use globals in your stand-alone code, THINK C has just the thing! Basically, when you use THINK C to build a stand-alone code resource, you can access your globals off of register A4 instead of A5. This technique is described in the THINK C *User's Manual* (at least in the one that came with v4.0), starting at the bottom of page 86.

When a routine is called, each of its parameters is pushed on the stack. Next, each of the local variables in the routine is pushed on the stack. For example, consider the following code:

```
MakeWindow( resID )
int resID;
{
    WindowPtr         w;

    w = GetNewWindow ( resID, NIL_POINTER,
                       MOVE_TO_FRONT );
}
```

Before MakeWindow() is called, the stack is set up as pictured in Figure 2.6a, with the space needed by any nested calls leading up to the call to MakeWindow() at the base of the stack. When

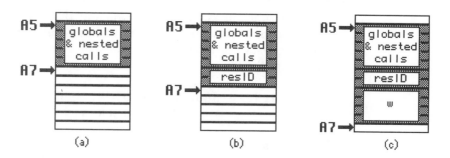

Figure 2.6   Parameters and local variables allocated on the stack.

MakeWindow() is called, the parameter resID is pushed onto the stack, as shown in Figure 2.6b. Notice that A7 is decremented by 2 because resID is a 2-byte int. Next, the local variables are pushed on the stack. In this case, A7 is decremented by 4 to make room for the 4 byte local variable w (see Figure 2.6c).

> • When a routine is called, the parameters and then the local routine variables are pushed onto the stack.
>
> • When the routine exits, the locals and the parameters are popped off the stack and the return value (if any) is pushed onto the stack.

The Application Heap

A critical part of your application's space is your application's heap. The heap starts out as a big block of contiguous memory. As you need it, you make requests for this space.

> When you declare a variable, you're using stack space. When you allocate space with a call to NewPtr() or NewHandle(), you're using heap space. You are also using heap space when you call a Toolbox routine that allocates memory for you. Check out the three different calls to GetNewWindow() that follow and see if you can predict where the new WindowRecord is allocated.

Sometimes memory requests come in the form of explicit calls to Toolbox routines such as `NewPtr()` and `NewHandle()`. Sometimes the requests are made as the result of a call to a Toolbox routine. Consider the following code:

```
w = GetNewWindow ( resID, NIL_POINTER,
                MOVE_TO_FRONT );
```

By passing `NIL_POINTER` as the second parameter, this code asked `GetNewWindow()` to allocate a non-relocatable block the size of a `WindowRecord` on the application's heap. The nice thing about this approach is that it is easy. The disadvantage is that you have no control over where in the heap that memory is allocated. Why is this important? Suppose you had a heap that was 10 bytes in size. Now, allocate 3 bytes on the heap, as shown in Figure 2.7a. Next, allocate a second block, this time 4 bytes in size (Figure 2.7b). You now have 3 bytes free in the heap, right at the top. Now deallocate the first block, leaving your heap looking like Figure 2.7c. You have a nonrelocatable block of 4 bytes locked smack-dab in the middle of your heap. Now suppose you need a contiguous block of 4 bytes from the heap. Although you have 6 bytes of unused heap space, there is no way to allocate a block bigger than 3 bytes. You are the unwitting victim of heap fragmentation!

Before talking about handles (Apple's antiheap fragmentation device) let's look at two alternative methods of `WindowRecord` allocation.

```
Ptr wStorage;

wStorage = NewPtr( sizeof( WindowRecord ) );
w = GetNewWindow ( resID, wStorage,
                MOVE_TO_FRONT );
```

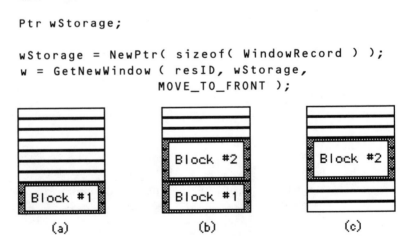

Figure 2.7 The horror of heap fragmentation.

This piece of code accomplishes almost exactly the same thing as the previous example. The space for the `WindowRecord` is still allocated on the application heap. This time, however, the code allocated the space in a specific location. If you know your application will need only a single window, you could make your call to `NewPtr()` at the very beginning of your program, while the heap is still relatively empty, thus keeping the nonrelocatable block all the way at the bottom of the heap, minimizing fragmentation. This technique is even more important if you know you'll be making use of lots of nonrelocatable blocks.

> The more sophisticated your application, the more likely you'll be hit by heap fragmentation and the more important your own approach to memory management becomes!

The third approach to window allocation is extremely simple:

```
WindowRecord    wRecord, *w;

w = GetNewWindow( resID, &wRecord,
              MOVE_TO_FRONT );
```

This example declares `WindowRecord` as a local variable. This means that the space gets allocated on the stack instead of on the heap. Although this approach promises never to fragment the heap, it promotes unsightly stack build-up. The stack was not intended for dynamic memory allocation. That's the heap's job!

Handles, At Last!

Handles were invented to give programmers an alternative to heap-fragmenting, nonrelocatable blocks. The basic concept is simple. When your application starts up, a block of 64 **master pointers** is allocated at the base of the heap. Although these master pointers are nonrelocatable pointers, because they are at the base of the heap, they do not fragment the heap.

A handle is a pointer to one of these master pointers. When you allocate a relocatable block on the heap, a master pointer is set to point to the block and a handle is set to point to the master pointer.

The memory manager can now move the data block, updating its master pointer with the new address of the block. Throughout this process, the block's handle remains valid because it remains pointing to the same exact address, that of the nonrelocatable master pointer.

Here's an example that should make this a little clearer:

```
Handle      handleTo8, handleTo16;

handleTo8 = NewHandle( 8 );
handleTo16 = NewHandle( 16 );
```

Figure 2.8 shows the memory layout after this code is executed. When the application started up, 64 master pointers were allocated at the base of the heap. One of these will become handleTo8's master pointer. The next master pointer will become handleTo16's master pointer. The first call to NewHandle() allocates a block of 8 bytes and makes handleTo8 a handle to that block. This is the same thing as saying that handleTo8's master pointer now points to this 8-byte block.

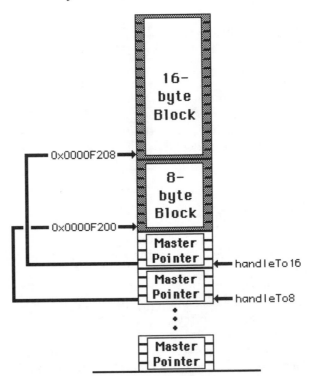

Figure 2.8   Two handled blocks on the heap.

The second call to `NewHandle()` allocates a block of 16 bytes (right on top of the 8-byte block) and makes `handleTo16` a handle to this block. This means that `handleTo16` points to its master pointer and `handleTo16`'s master pointer points to the 16-byte block.

The next piece of code releases the 8-byte block, creating a hole in the heap:

```
DisposHandle( handleTo8 );
```

`DisposHandle()` frees up the handled block but does not change the value in the master pointer. It's up to the program to remember that `handleTo8` is no longer valid. Figure 2.9 shows the result of the call to `DisposHandle()`. Notice the 8-byte hole in the middle of the heap.

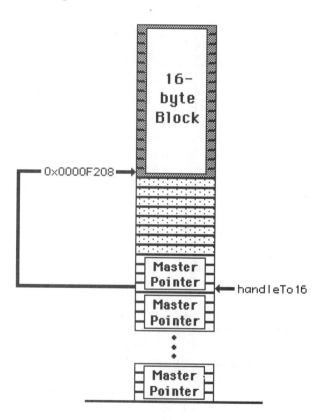

Figure 2.9   Deallocating the first handled block.

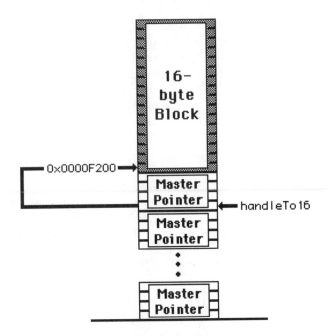

Figure 2.10   The Memory Manager compacts the heap.

Now comes the interesting part. At certain well-defined times, the Memory Manager will attempt to compact the heap. Basically, this means moving all relocatable blocks as far toward the base of the heap as they will go and updating their master pointers. Figure 2.10 shows the sample heap after compaction.

Even though the value of `handleTo16`'s master pointer has changed (it was decremented by 8 bytes), `handleTo16` remains the same. It still points to the same location in memory and is still a handle to the same 16 bytes of data.

Careful With That Handle, Eugene!

A little while ago it was said that the Memory Manager compacts the heap at well-defined times. Appendix A in *Inside Macintosh X-Ref* contains a list of Toolbox routines that may move or purge memory. Anytime you call one of these routines, your heap is a candidate for compaction.

Why should you care? Take a look at this piece of code:

```
Handle    myRectHandle;

myRectHandle = NewHandle( 8 );
SetRect( *myRectHandle, 10, 10, 50, 50 );
PaintRect( *myRectHandle );
```

This code allocates an 8-byte block of memory using NewHandle(), placing the handle in myRectHandle.

> Normally, when you want a Rect, you declare one as a local variable. This piece of code accomplishes the same thing (almost) by allocating 8 bytes (the size of a Rect) directly on the heap. Why almost? The difference is this. This code allocated the memory on the heap. When you declare a local variable, you're allocating the memory on the stack (remember?). Although this technique works, it is not recommended. It is shown here purely for demonstration.

When the code just shown called SetRect(), it passed the master pointer to the 8-byte block instead of a pointer to a Rect. Hey! A pointer to an 8-byte block is a pointer to an 8-byte block, isn't it? As it turns out, SetRect() is not on the list of routines that may move memory, so this call is perfectly valid. The call to PaintRect() is a different story entirely.

Suppose the heap were compacted in the middle of the call to PaintRect(). The code passed a specific 4-byte value to PaintRect(). When the heap moves, this value remains the same. The pointer that was passed in does not change, but the data has just moved in memory. The pointer is no longer valid and PaintRect() is likely to crash or at least start acting a little funny.

This problem is a real show-stopper. Luckily, there is an easy solution. Enter HLock() and HUnlock(). HLock() locks a handle, so that the handled block becomes nonrelocatable. HUnlock() makes the handled block relocatable again. Take a look at this code:

```
Handle    myRectHandle;

myRectHandle = NewHandle( 8 );
SetRect( *myRectHandle, 10, 10, 50, 50 );
HLock( myRectHandle );
PaintRect( *myRectHandle );
HUnlock( myRectHandle );
```

HLock() and HUnlock() give you all the power and efficiency of handles with the protection of nonrelocatable blocks. Although it's tempting, try not to submit to the lock-it-always syndrome. Minimize your calls to HLock(), because a locked handle is a heap-fragmenting handle. Remember, you need to lock a handle only if you are going to dereference it in a routine that moves memory. If you pass a handle as a parameter, there is no need to lock it. If you are unsure, go ahead and call HLock(). Just remember to call HUnlock() as soon as possible.

When To Use Handles

In general, you should use handles instead of pointers for your dynamic memory allocation. The overhead for master pointers is relatively small compared to the benefits of relocatable blocks. Sometimes, however, you have to use pointers. WindowRecords, for example, must always be nonrelocatable. They were designed that way by Apple from the very beginning. For this reason, if you allocate your own WindowRecords, you'll do it with a call to NewPtr().

Resources, for the most part, are relocatable. Routines like GetResource(), GetPicture(), and GetString() return handles to their respective resources. Remember, if you pass the address of a handled block (i.e., a dereferenced handle) to a routine that may move memory, you'd better lock it first. The address of a field in a handled struct must follow the same rules:

```
PicHandle   pic;

pic = GetPicture( 400 );
HLock( pic );
FrameRect( &((**pic).picFrame) );
HUnlock( pic );
```

The address of the picFrame field will not be valid anymore if the entire pic moves while we're in FrameRect().

Miscellaneous Tips and Techniques

The remainder of this chapter is dedicated to tips and techniques that will make your life a lot easier. It starts off with a discussion of the memory management routines MoreMasters() and

`MoveHHi()`. These routines are described in *Inside Macintosh, Volume II*, Chapter 1. Read this section. You'll be glad that you did.

MoreMasters( ) and MoveHHi( )

When your application starts up, its heap is created with a block of master pointers at the base of the heap. The routine `MoreMasters()` allocates an additional block of master pointers. Call `MoreMasters()` during the initialization phase of your program. You will get 64 master pointers per call.

`MoveHHi()` moves a handled block as high in the heap as it can until the block hits either the top of the heap or a nonrelocatable (or a locked relocatable) block. Call `MoveHHi()` immediately before you call `HLock()`. This will help minimize the fragmentation of your heap while the handle is locked.

Purgeable Blocks

All handles are marked as either purgeable or nonpurgeable. When you create a block with `NewHandle()`, the handle is automatically marked as nonpurgeable. When you load a resource with `GetResource()` or a similar routine, however, the block created for the resource may be purgeable (depending on a flag set in the resource itself).

If the Memory Manager needs to allocate a block of memory and there is not a big enough block of free space available on the heap, the Memory Manager tries to compact the heap. It starts by moving relocatable blocks around, trying to create bigger blocks of free space. If the Memory Manager still cannot fulfill its request, it starts purging purgeable blocks, until it has enough room.

If a block is purged, its handle is said to be empty. Before you work with the handle to any purgeable resource, call `LoadResource()`. `LoadResource()` will reload the resource if it was purged. You can mark a handle as nonpurgeable and purgeable with the routines `HNoPurge()` and `HPurge()`.

Keeping Your Applications 32-bit Clean

Though addresses are commonly thought of as 4-byte values, they are actually much more complex. For example, several of the 32 bits that make up a handle are actually flags that mark the handle as purgeable, locked, or as belonging to a resource.

> Most Macintoshes run in 24-bit mode. This means that every 4 byte address dedicates 3 bytes to the actual address with 1 byte remaining free for use as flags. Some Macs (the Mac IIci, for one) can switch between 24 and 32-bit modes. In 32 bit mode, all 32 bits are used as addresses. A/UX, Apple's version of the Unix operating system, always runs in 32-bit mode.

Don't make any assumptions about the internal structure of an address. If you need access to a handle's purge bit, use the routines provided by the Toolbox, HPurge() and HNoPurge(). Don't access raw data structures when the Toolbox provides a way to access the information via a routine. Apple provides these access routines so that your programs will not break when Apple changes the format of a field or data structure.

Piggybacking Data on Your Windows

Suppose you have an application that supports multiple windows, each window having two scroll bars and two pop-up menus (remarkably like the window in Figure 2.11). When you detect a mouseDown in a particular window, how do you tell if the mouseDown was in one of the controls or in one of the menus? You could keep a linked list of all the ControlHandles and MenuHandles, but that would be cumbersome. If only there were a simple way to link a window's data right to the window, so the data could be accessed directly from the WindowPtr. Hmmm...

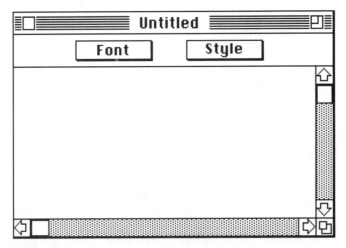

Figure 2.11   Piggyback window.

There are several ways to solve this problem. This book uses something called the **piggyback technique**. This technique is used in Chapter 5's TextEdit program and in most of the real-world applications in the book.

Here's the piggyback technique for allocating the example window shown in figure 2.11.

```
typedef struct
{
    WindowRecord            theWindow;
    int                     windowType;
    MenuHandle              fontMenu, styleMenu;
    ControlHandle           vScroll, hScroll;
}
MyWindRecord, *MyWindPeek;

WindowPtr       piggyWindow;
Ptr             wStorage;

wStorage = NewPtr( sizeof( MyWindRecord ) );

piggyWindow =   GetNewWindow( 400,
                wStorage, MOVE_TO_FRONT );
```

This chunk of code starts by creating a piggyback window struct. The struct includes room for a type field (in case several different types of windows are needed in the application), two menus, and two scroll bar handles.

Instead of allocating just enough room for a window, the code allocates the extra room for the piggyback information. When the program returns from `GetNewWindow()`, `piggyWindow` will point to this bigger block of space, whose first 156 bytes look exactly like a regular `WindowRecord`. This means `piggyWindow` can be passed to routines like `SetPort()` with the expected results. If an `updateEvt` for `piggyWindow` is received, the program can retrieve `piggyWindow` by casting `gTheEvent.message` to a `WindowPtr` as usual. In this case, however, the program will also have access to the menus and scroll bars:

```
ControlHandle  aScrollBar;

aScrollBar =  ((MyWindPeek)
              gTheEvent.message)->vScroll;
```

The `windowType` field can be accessed the same way. This field is used when multiple window types are used in an application. A `#define` is created for each window type and the `windowType` field is set to the appropriate `#define` as soon as the window is created. When a program wants to check the type of a window, it first must check whether it's a desk accessory or a normal window. This technique is illustrated in Chapter 5's FormEdit program.

Because part of every `WindowRecord` is a linked list of controls belonging to that window, there is an alternative to the piggyback technique. If the only data you are trying to piggyback is a set of `ControlHandles`, you can place some #defined constant in the control's `contrlRfCon` field. Then, when you want to retrieve a window's data, walk through the window's control list until you find a control whose `contrlRfCon` field is the one you're looking for.

Calling Them, So They Can Call You

Sometimes you will provide a pointer to one of your routines (a procPtr) as a parameter to a Toolbox routine so that the Toolbox routine can call your routine. Your routine (the one the procPtr points to) is called a **callback routine**. Callbacks provide hooks into normally unreachable processes. A common callback is the filter proc, used by `ModalDialog()`. You pass a filter proc to `ModalDialog()` and `ModalDialog()` calls your filter proc every time it handles an event.

Filter procs (as well as other types of callbacks) are discussed in Chapter 3. That chapter also presents a complete filter proc (code and all) that gets called from `ModalDialog()`. The important point here is that sometimes you write code that you want to be called by the Toolbox. The Toolbox expects all routines it calls to follow the Pascal calling conventions.

The Pascal calling conventions work like this. The calling routine pushes the arguments on the stack from left to right, then calls the routine. When the routine returns, any return value can be found on the stack. Because most C programmers do not particularly care about details like this, the THINK C programmers provided an alternative. If you declare your functions and procedures to be of type pascal, THINK C will automatically generate code that meets Pascal calling conventions. Here's an example of a function that returns a `BOOLEAN`:

```
pascal Boolean myFunc( myArg )
int myArg;
{
}
```

Here's the declaration of a procedure with no parameters:

```
pascal void myProc()
{
}
```

On the other hand, suppose you have a pointer to a Pascal routine that you'd like to call yourself. In Chapter 3, a standalone piece of code is built into a resource of type `PROC`. Next, a program is written that loads the resource (with `GetResource()`) and calls the standalone code with a call to the THINK C routine `CallPascal()`. `CallPascal()` is used to call a procedure (a `void` function). Pass to `CallPascal()` the parameters that you want passed to the function, passing the function pointer as the very last parameter.

> If `CallPascal()` is still a little fuzzy to you, take a look at the `INIT` presented in Chapter 3.

THINK C provides additional routines to call other types of Pascal functions. Use `CallPascalB()` to call a function that returns a `BOOLEAN`. Use `CallPascalW()` to call a function that returns either an `INTEGER` or a `CHAR`. Finally, use `CallPascalL()` to call a function that returns a `LONGINT`, a `Ptr`, or a `Handle`.

In Review

A lot of important topics were covered in this chapter. Every concept presented here will come up again later on in the book. If you like, take some time now and review some of the referenced *Inside Macintosh* chapters. This stuff really is important, especially if you're planning on writing applications that will be used by other people or that will be sold for big profits.

Look out! You're about to burst out of the world of double-clickable applications. Chapter 3 digs into stand-alone code design and development and presents lots of examples.

Code Resources

*Every program developed in
Macintosh Programming Primer,
Volume I has taken the form of a
double-clickable application. This
chapter shows you how easy it is to use
the same programming techniques
to create specialized chunks of code
such as INITs, cdevs, MDEFs and
filter procs.*

Specialized Code

Not all useful Macintosh software comes in the form of a double-clickable application. How many of these types do you recognize?

INITs are also known as **Startup documents**. They are usually found in your System folder. At startup (or boot) time, the Macintosh operating system checks each file in the System folder for a resource of type INIT. Every time an INIT resource is found, it is loaded into memory, locked, and executed. INITs can be used to launch a piece of standalone code that will run in the background (like an alarm clock or a screen dimmer). They can also allocate and initialize some memory to be used later by an application.

cdevs are more commonly known as **Control Panel documents**. When the Control Panel desk accessory starts up, it looks through the System folder for files of type cdev. The Control Panel displays a scrolling list of each cdev file's icon, as pictured in Figure 3.1. When you click on a cdev's icon, the Control Panel looks in the cdev file for a resource of type cdev with a resource ID of -4064 (in order for a cdev to run properly, it must have this resource). When the cdev resource is found, it is loaded into memory, locked, and executed. The

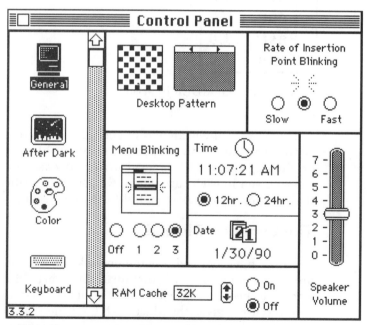

Figure 3.1   Some scrolling cdevs.

43

cdev uses the area to the right of the scroll bar to put up its own TextEdit fields, buttons, scroll bars, etc. As you enter text and change settings, the cdev writes the changes to its resource fork and/or makes whatever other adjustments are needed.

MDEFs, **WDEF**s, and **CDEF**s are examples of code resources you use all the time. They implement custom menus, windows, and controls. Figure 3.2 shows an MDEF in action. Every Macintosh menu has a `procID` associated with it. This `procID` determines which MDEF will be used to implement the menu. Most Macintosh menus have a `procID` of 0. This means that when the Menu Manager wants to draw and allow selection from that menu, it must look for an MDEF resource with an ID of 0. Once it finds the appropriate resource, it (guess what!) loads the resource, locks it, and executes it. Later on in the chapter, you'll write your own MDEF and call it from within an application.

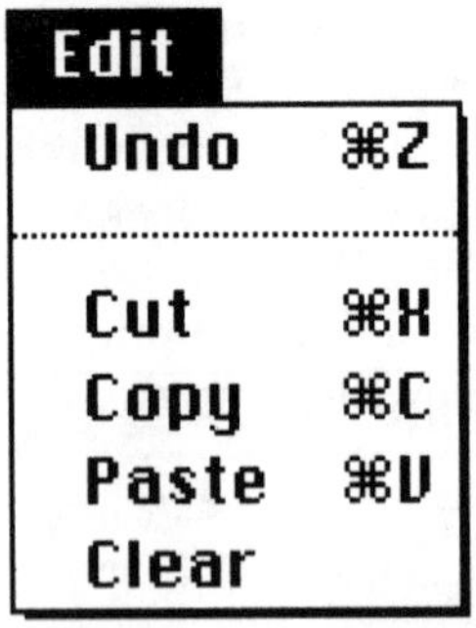

Figure 3.2   An MDEF in action.

There are many examples of specialized Macintosh code. The goal of this chapter is to make you comfortable with the process of producing your own. Several different examples are presented, showing you in each case where we got the specifications for writing the code and exactly how we built the final product.

The Common Thread

You may have noticed a common link among the examples in the previous section. In each instance, some form of code resource was loaded, locked, and executed. The support of standalone, executable code resources gives the Macintosh (and the Macintosh programmer) a great deal of power and flexibility. Just imagine. You can write an MDEF that builds a color menu, based on the number of colors available on that particular machine. You can then use that MDEF in all five of your brand new, best-selling color applications, just by copying and pasting the MDEF resource using ResEdit. Better still, once you build the MDEF, you can reuse it again and again, without ever having to muck with its source code.

Chapter Programs

Every program in this chapter will explore a new alternative to the rigid world of double-clickable applications:

- **AFI** (pronounced affy) — AFI, or Application Font INIT, sets the default application font. The application font determines the default applications used by most applications. For example, if AFI sets the default application font to Monaco, the next time you run MacPaint and select the text tool, you'll be drawing in Monaco. The AFI demonstrates the use of an icon at INIT time, painting it on the screen in line with all the other INIT icons.

- **AFI cdev** — AFI cdev provides a Control Panel interface for AFI. When the AFI icon is selected, a pop-up menu of available fonts is displayed in the Control Panel. When a font is selected, the low-memory global that stores the default application font is updated, and a resource within the cdev file is updated as well, saving the value for next time.

- **MDEF** and **MDEF Tester** — This pair of programs represents an MDEF and a program that tests the MDEF. The MDEF takes a specified set of PICT resources and builds a menu from them. The menu is as wide as the widest picture, and each cell is as tall as the tallest picture.

- **DLOG Filter Proc** — Several of the Toolbox managers offer special **filter procs** or **callbacks** built into the Toolbox routines. Using these callbacks can sometimes make your programming infinitely easier. For example, you can pass a pointer to a procedure to `ModalDialog()` and `ModalDialog()` will call your procedure every time it gets an event. We'll demonstrate a filter proc that dims a dialog's OK button as long as the TextEdit field has no text in it.

Feel free to use these programs as shells for your own INITs, cdevs, MDEFs, and filter procs. In addition, you are welcome to use the PICT MDEF in your own applications.

AFI, the Application Font INIT

AFI actually consists of two separate pieces of code. The first, ShowINIT, displays an icon on the screen at INIT time. This piece of code is the standard used by most Macintosh INITs. ShowINIT.c will be compiled into a code resource of type `PROC`. Within the INIT, `GetResource()` is used to load the `PROC` into memory. Next, the `PROC` is locked then executed via a call to `CallPascal()`.

> Although routines like `GetPicture()` and `GetNewWindow()` are limited to a single resource type (`PICT` and `WIND`), `GetResource()` can be used to load any resource. The relocatable code resource was given the name `PROC`, but it could have been called `WIZZ` or even `X9i].`
>
> As was discussed in Chapter 2, `CallPascal()` is used to call a routine using the Pascal calling conventions. Because `PROC` will have no inherent association with either C or Pascal, it is important to make sure the correct calling conventions are used.

Start by building a project for the ShowINIT `PROC`.

Create a folder in your development folder called **ShowINIT ƒ**. Remember, you can create the **ƒ** character (which is used here as a substitute for the word *files*) by typing Option-f. Inside this folder, create a new project called **ShowINIT.π** (the π is actually an Option-p). Then, add MacTraps to the project.

> This is a strategy change from Volume I's naming convention. In Volume I, the source code file is called **xxx.c**, the project is called **xxx Proj** and the resource file is called **xxx Proj.Rsrc**. The folks who developed THINK C used a different strategy, which is used in this volume. From now on, if the source code file is named **xxx.c**, the project file will be named **xxx.π** (you type the π by holding down the Option key and typing p), and the resource file will be named **xxx.π.rsrc**. THINK C is case-insensitive regarding the name of the resource file.

Next, select Set Project Type... from the Project menu. Set the parameters in the Project Type dialog box as they appear in Figure 3.3. First, click the Code Resource radio button. Then, change the

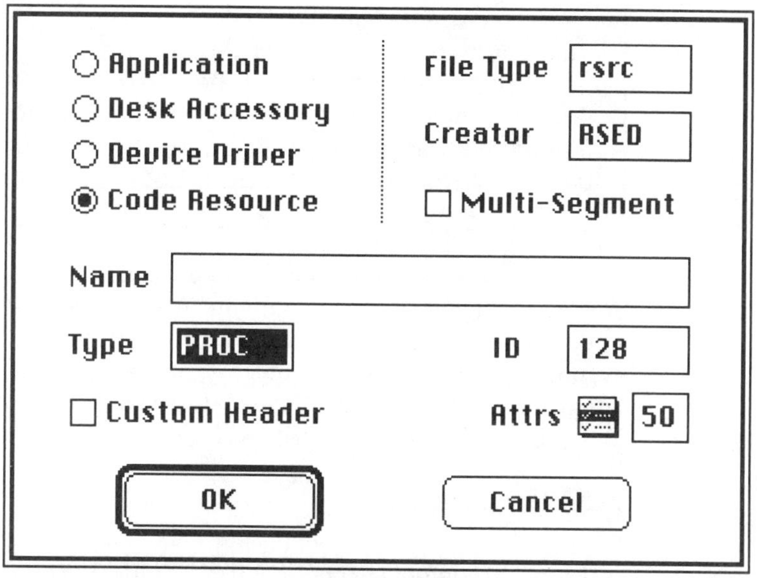

Figure 3.3   Set Project Type dialog box for ShowINIT.

File Type to `rsrc` and the Creator to `RSED`. This will force the
Finder to launch ResEdit when you double-click on the file you create
when you build this project. Change the `Type` field to `PROC` and the
ID field to `128`. When you build the code resource, you want to create
a `PROC` resource with an ID of `128`. There's nothing special about the
number 128. You can use any resource ID you like. Finally, change
the `Attrs` field to `50`. This forces the space for the resource to be
allocated on the System Heap and makes sure the resource gets
locked after it is loaded into memory. Because this resource is needed
at INIT time, you have no choice but to allocate space on the System
Heap. No applications (such as the Finder) have been launched yet,
so there are no application heaps from which to steal space.

   Click OK to save the Project Type dialog box settings. Next, you'll
enter the ShowINIT source code. Create a new file by selecting New
from the File menu. Enter the source code for ShowINIT.c (you can
find it at the beginning of Appendix B). Save the file as **ShowINIT.c**.
Add the file to the project.

This chapter does not walk through ShowINIT's source code. Some of the concepts it uses are pretty advanced and are really not appropriate to this section. This is the *only* program that will be treated this way, however. It is included in the book as a project because there was no other way to get you the ShowINIT P R O C.

Now you're ready to build the code resource. Select Build Code Resource... from the Project menu. Answer Yes when asked to Bring the project up to date?. THINK C will try to compile the code resource. If you run into problems, check for typos. Once you get the program to compile, the Save code resource as: dialog will appear. Save the code resource as **ShowINIT**.

AFI Resources

Great! Now you're ready to create **AFI,** your INIT. Create a new folder in your development folder called **AFI ƒ**. Launch ResEdit and open windows until the AFI ƒ window is open. Select New from the File menu to create a new file in the AFI ƒ folder. Name the file **AFI.π.rsrc** (see Figure 3.4).

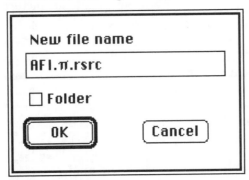

Figure 3.4   Creating AFI's resource file.

The first resource you will place in AFI's resource file is the P R O C you created earlier. Keeping the AFI.π.rsrc window open, open the resource file ShowINIT you created earlier. You should see the single resource type P R O C in ShowINIT's resource type window. Select P R O C (it should be highlighted) and then select Copy from the Edit menu. Bring the AFI.π.rsrc window to the front and select Paste from the Edit menu. The resource type PROC should appear in the AFI.π.rsrc window.

Next, you will create some ICN#s. These will ultimately be plotted on the screen by the ShowINIT PROC. You will create a total of nine ICN# resources. The first eight (numbers 128 through 134, and -4064) represent an animation sequence. You create the illusion of animation by plotting several icons, one right after the other, each one slightly different than the one before it. Your animation sequence will indicate that AFI is changing the default application font to something other than Geneva.

You may be wondering about the unusual choice of the ICN# resource ID number -4064. A more logical resource ID (such as 135) could have been used, but because this resource will be shared with a cdev in the next project, it made sense to pick a resource ID that falls within the range of those recognized by cdevs. More on this later.

ICN# 136 is the icon you will plot if the default application font is to be left as Geneva. Figure 3.5 shows the ICN#s used in this example. Create all nine. You can change the pictures, but make sure you keep the same resource IDs.

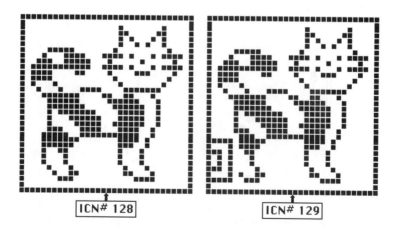

Figure 3.5   AFI's ICN#s.

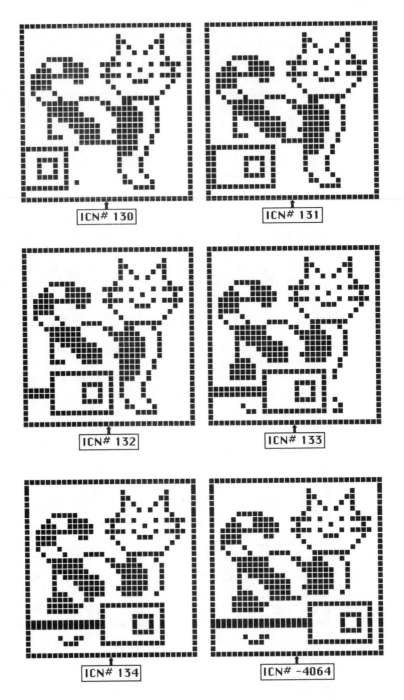

Figure 3.5   *(continued)*

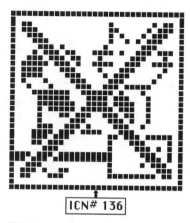

ICN# 136

Figure 3.5 *(continued)*

If you create color icons (cicn resources) with the same ID as the ICN# resources, ShowINIT will attempt to plot the color icons on Macintoshes that sport Color QuickDraw. You must provide the black and white ICN#s in any case. Several public domain cicn editors are available on the bulletin boards. As of this writing, ResEdit doesn't support graphic editing of color icons. You can try to create cicn resources in hexadecimal using ResEdit, but we wouldn't recommend it (unless, of course, you're the kind of person who gets a kick out of doing 10,000-piece, monochromatic jigsaw puzzles).

Finally, you will create a resource to keep track of the current application font. Create a new resource type with the name of word (see Figure 3.6).

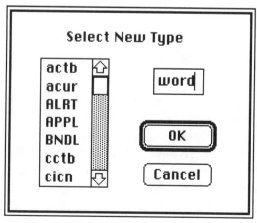

Figure 3.6 Creating a word resource.

Select New from the File menu to create a new word resource. The
general resource editor will appear. You will use this editor in a
second. First, select Get Info from the File menu and give this new
resource a resource ID of −4048.

> Once again, a resource ID like 128 could have been used, but the
> word resource will be shared with the cdev as well.

Now, use the general (or hexadecimal) resource editor to specify
the word resource. Make sure you click on the left side of the editor
(just to the right of the line number reading 000000) before you
start typing. Enter the four hexadecimal digits 0001. Your window
should look like Figure 3.7.

Excellent! The file AFI.π.rsrc should now contain three different
resource types: nine ICN#s, one PROC, and one word. You are now
ready to create the project and enter the source code for your INIT.

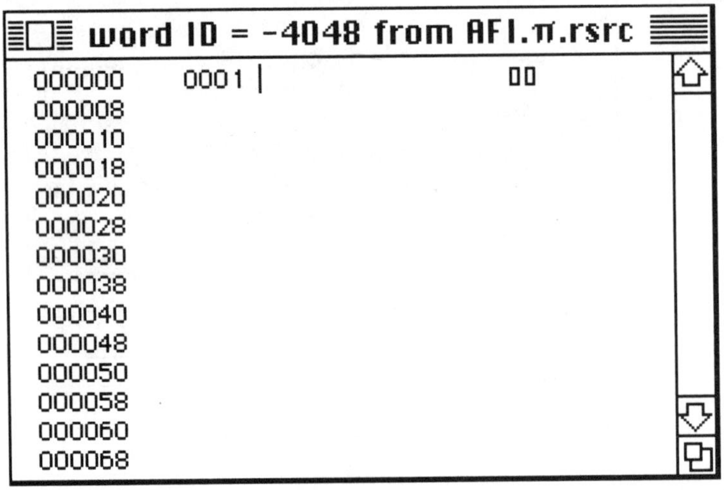

Figure 3.7   Entering the word resource.

> ATTENTION!! IMPORTANT NOTICE!!!
> The programs in this book were tested using version 4.0 of THINK C.
> If you are using THINK C 5.0 or later, you'll need to make a few
> changes to your code. These changes are completely described
> starting on page 508.

Creating the AFI Project

Inside the AFI *f* folder, create a new project named (what else?) **AFI.π**. Add MacTraps to the project. Next, select Set Project Type from the Project menu and change the settings to reflect the specifications in Figure 3.8.

First click the Code Resource radio button. Change the File Type to INIT and the Creator to RSED. The RSED will allow you to double-click the INIT file and go right into ResEdit. The type of INIT tells the MacOS to open this file at start-up time and to execute any INIT resources found in the file. Because the MacOS will open any INIT resource it finds in the file, you could use any resource ID for the INIT; 0 is used here by convention. Just as you did for your PROC resource, set the Attrs field to 50.

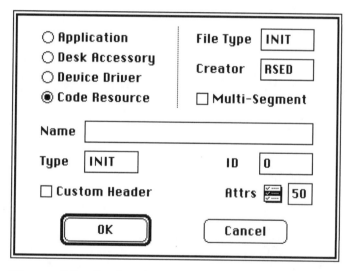

Figure 3.8   Setting the Project Type.

Next, create a new source code file, save it as **AFI.c**, and add it to the project. Type the following source code into AFI.c:

```
#define  BASE_ICON_ID         128
#define  LAST_ICON_ID         -4064
#define  PROC_ID              128
#define  WORD_RES_ID          -4048
#define  NUM_ICONS            8
#define  NORMAL_APP_FONT      applFont
#define  DELAY                30L
```

```
main()
{
      Handle      procH, wHandle;
      int         i, fontNumber;
      long  dummy;

      if ( ( wHandle = GetResource( 'word', WORD_RES_ID ) ) !=
            OL )
      {
            fontNumber = *( (short *)(*wHandle) );

            *( (short *) 0x0204 ) = fontNumber - 1;

            WriteParam();

            if ( ( procH = GetResource( 'PROC', PROC_ID ) ) !=
                  OL )
            {
                  HLock(procH);

                  if ( fontNumber == NORMAL_APP_FONT )
                  {
                        CallPascal( BASE_ICON_ID + NUM_ICONS, -
                              1, *procH);
                  }
                  else
                  {
                        CallPascal( BASE_ICON_ID, O, *procH);

                        Delay( DELAY, &dummy );

                        for ( i=1; i<NUM_ICONS-1; i++ )
                              CallPascal( BASE_ICON_ID + i, O,
                              *procH);

                        CallPascal( LAST_ICON_ID, -1, *procH);
                  }

                  HUnlock(procH);
            }
      }
}
```

OK. Now comes Miller time. Select Build Code Resource... from the Project menu. Click Yes when prompted to Bring the project up to date?. Once the code compiles, you'll be prompted for a file name for your code resource. Save the INIT as **AFI**. The messages Linking AFI and Copying AFI.π.rsrc should appear as the INIT is built. The message Copying AFI.π.rsrc is especially important because it means that THINK C found the resource file. If in doubt, open the newly created AFI using ResEdit. The three resource types you created should be there. In addition, you should also find an INIT resource with the name AFI and a resource ID of 0.

In ResEdit, close the file AFI so you are looking at the list of files in the folder AFI *f*. Select the file AFI and select Get Info from the File menu. Make sure that AFI has a type of INIT and a creator of RSED.

Quit ResEdit. Now, copy the file AFI into your System folder and reboot.

Danger, Will Robinson!!! Before you go too far, you might want to create an INIT tester. Because of cosmic human frailty (screw-ups), your INIT might not work properly (it might even crash). The trouble is, if the INIT is in your System folder, every time you reboot, you'll bail out before you can get to the Finder to remove the INIT from the System folder.

Enter the INIT tester. Originally invented in 1926 by Carlo Quatious, the INIT tester is simply a floppy copy of a standard System disk (preferably the same System version as that of your boot disk). Instead of placing your INIT in the System folder on your hard drive, gently slide the INIT into the System folder on the floppy disk (be sure to grasp it firmly on both sides). If the INIT fails, simply reboot, hold down the mouse button, and the brain-damaged System disk will eject, leaving your hard drive pure and clean. Thanks, Carlo!

If your INIT went kablooey, open the INIT resource using ResEdit and select Get Info from the File menu. Make sure the locked checkbox is checked (THINK C should have done this for you). If all went well, the ICN# with the big X through it should have appeared underneath the **Welcome To Macintosh** window. The X indicates that AFI will leave the application font at its normal setting, Geneva. When you created the word resource, you entered a 2-byte integer

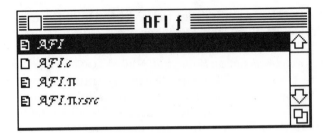

Figure 3.9   Zapf Chancery as application font.

with a value of 1. Your INIT retrieves this integer and compares it with the predefined constant, `applFont` (which happens to be 1). The constant `applFont` is defined as a member of an enumerated set in the Mac #include Quickdraw.h.

Try editing the AFI's `word` resource using ResEdit (edit the copy of AFI in the INIT tester's System folder). Make sure you leave it at 2 bytes. Change the 1 to a 4. This represents the font `monaco`. Save your changes and reboot your INIT tester. You should see some animation this time. If not, are you sure you edited the correct AFI file? Did you reboot from the floppy?

The animation indicates that the application font has been changed. Fire up ResEdit. Do you notice anything different? The lists should all be displayed using Monaco instead of Geneva. Figure 3.9 shows a ResEdit window with the application font set to 0012 (Zapf Chancery).

Note that if you set the `word` resource to an undefined font, Geneva will appear as the application font. Experiment.

Walking Through the AFI Source Code

This section takes a look at the source code for AFI. `BASE_ICON_ID` is the resource ID of the first `ICN#` in the animation sequence. The program draws the first seven `ICN#`s, one on top of the other, leaving the INIT icon-drawing cursor in the same place. Finally, it draws the `ICN#` with resource ID `LAST_ICON_ID`. This time, however, it moves the INIT icon drawing cursor to the next icon position. Doing this ensures that when the next INIT draws its icon, it won't appear on top of this INIT's icon.

```
#define BASE_ICON_ID 128
#define LAST_ICON_ID -4064
```

PROC_ID is the resource ID of the PROC. WORD_RES_ID is the resource ID of the word resource. NUM_ICONS determines the number of ICN#s (including LAST_ICON_ID) to be used in the animation sequence. NORMAL_APP_FONT is the normal application font. If the word resource designates this font, the ICN# with the big X through it will be drawn in place of the animation sequence. Finally, DELAY indicates the number of ticks (60ths of a second) the program waits between drawing the first ICN# in the animation, and drawing the last seven. Increasing the delay gives the viewer more time to realize that an animation is going on.

```
#define  PROC_ID            128
#define  WORD_RES_ID        -4048
#define  NUM_ICONS          8
#define  NORMAL_APP_FONT    applFont
#define  DELAY              30L
```

AFI consists of a single routine, named main(). Any number of routines could have been used, as long as main() was the first one in the file. procH will be used as a handle to the PROC when it is loaded with GetResource(). Similarly, wHandle will handle the word resource.

```
main()
{
    Handle     procH, wHandle;
    int        i, fontNumber;
    long  dummy;
```

The word resource is loaded first. If this loading is successful, the program locks the resource and dereferences it to get at the first two bytes addressed by the handle, placing the results in the int fontNumber. After unlocking the handle, the program writes fontNumber −1 out to the two bytes that start at memory location 0x0204. Then, the program writes this change to Parameter-RAM via a call to WriteParam().

Important notice! Do not disregard!

Parameter-RAM (P-RAM) is a chunk of 20 bytes of memory on the Macintosh clock chip that is backed up by your Mac's battery. Because of the battery, this memory stays around even if your Mac is powered down.

At boot time, the 20 bytes of P-RAM are copied into low memory, at the location pointed to by the global `SysParam`. To change P-RAM, change the appropriate low memory byte, then call `WriteParam()`. `WriteParam()` copies all 20 bytes back to the clock chip.

The two bytes starting at `0x0204` are the low memory copy of the default application font. Because this copy is −1 based instead of 0 based, always subtract 1 before writing to this location. This means that Geneva, known as 3 to the rest of the world, is stored in P-RAM as a 2.

Now comes the important notice. **Don't mess with Parameter RAM**. Although P-RAM is well documented (*Inside Macintosh*, *Volume II*, pp. 380–382), Apple is likely to change the functionality of individual bytes within P-RAM without telling anyone. This means that any application built around P-RAM is likely to break in the near future. P-RAM is included in this book's examples for demonstration purposes only. *Caveat Programmus*.

```
if ( ( wHandle = GetResource( 'word', WORD_RES_ID ) ) !=
    0L )
{
    fontNumber = *( (short *)(*wHandle) );

    *( (short *) 0x0204 ) = fontNumber - 1;

    WriteParam();
```

Once the application font is set, the program is ready to draw its icons. First, it loads the PROC. Once the PROC has been loaded, the program locks it so that it won't move around during execution. If the font is set to Geneva, the program draws the ICN# with the big X through it. The program calls the `PROC` by passing its pointer to `CallPascal()`. The first two parameters to `CallPascal()` will be passed on to the `PROC`. The first parameter specifies the resource ID of the `ICN#`, and the second parameter specifies the number of pixels to move the INIT icon cursor after the icon is drawn. Passing 0 tells the `PROC` to leave the cursor in place. This results in the next icon being drawn on top of this one. Passing –1 tells the `PROC` to move to the beginning of the next icon space. This results in the next icon appearing to the right of the current icon.

```
if ( ( procH = GetResource( 'PROC', PROC_ID ) ) != 0L )
{
    HLock(procH);

    if ( fontNumber == NORMAL_APP_FONT )
    {
        CallPascal( BASE_ICON_ID + NUM_ICONS, -1,
        *procH);
    }
```

If the font is anything but `applFont` the INIT performs the animation sequence. It draws the first icon, then delays about half a second. The `dummy` parameter is not used. Next, all but the last icon are drawn in place. Then the program draws the last icon, moving the INIT icon cursor as a courtesy to the next INIT. Finally, the INIT unlocks the `PROC` and exits.

```
    else
    {
        CallPascal( BASE_ICON_ID, 0, *procH);

        Delay( DELAY, &dummy );

        for ( i=1; i<NUM_ICONS-1; i++ )
            CallPascal( BASE_ICON_ID + i, 0,
            *procH);

        CallPascal( LAST_ICON_ID, -1, *procH);
    }

    HUnlock(procH);
}
}
}
```

The AFI cdev

The next program is a **cdev**, or Control Panel device. This cdev will appear in the Control Panel's scrolling list of icons. When you click on the icon, a pop-up menu label and a push button will appear in the body of the Control Panel (see Figure 3.10).

The pop-up menu lets you select the new default application font. The **Default** button sets the font back to `applFont`. Pretty straight-forward, right? Let's get started.

Create a new folder in your development folder called **cdev ƒ**. Now you'll create the project resources.

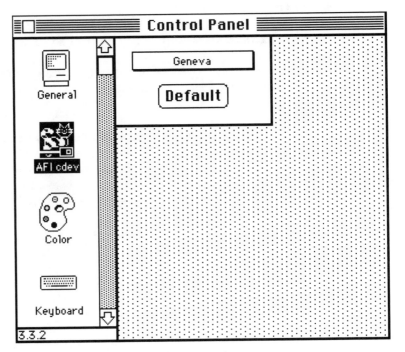

Figure 3.10 The AFI cdev in action.

AFI cdev Resources

You will create seven different resources for this project, as well as borrowing the INIT, ICN#, word, and PROC resources from your INIT project. Start by copying the file AFI.π.rsrc into the cdev *f* folder. Rename the copy to **cdev.π.rsrc**. Open the file in ResEdit. You should see something like Figure 3.11.

Now, open up the file AFI (your INIT, probably in the System folder). Copy the INIT and paste it into cdev.π.rsrc. You should now see something like Figure 3.12. Now you're ready to create some new resources.

cdevs are required to provide the following seven resources:

- **DITL –4064** — The dialog items that will appear when your cdev icon is clicked.

- **mach –4064** — A description of the types of machines on which your cdev will run (for example, Mac IIs with Color QuickDraw only).

- **nrct –4064** — The rectangle, in Control Panel local coordinates, that will be dedicated to your cdev. The area outside this area will be painted gray.

Figure 3.11   A copy of AFI.π.rsrc.

Figure 3.12   cdev.π.rsrc with the INIT resource from AFI.

- **ICN# –4064** — The icon that will appear in the Control Panel's scrolling icon list.

- **BNDL –4064** — The BNDL resource linking the FREF and the ICN#, allowing the icon to appear in both the Control Panel and the Finder.

- **FREF –4064** — The FREF links the file to the BNDL.

- **cdev –4064** — The cdev resource is the code resource that implements the cdev. THINK C will create this resource by compiling your source code.

In addition to these resources (and the ones that have already been copied into the resource file), you will need a creator resource (so that the Finder will display your icon) and a MENU resource (for the font pop-up). The creator 'FNT?' is registered with MacDTS.

cdev resource IDs are limited to the range –4033 through –4064. The Control Panel reserves the resource IDs from –4049 through –4064. Resource IDs from –4033 through –4048 are available for use by your cdev.

Return to the window associated with the file cdev.π.rsrc. Create a DITL with a resource ID of –4064. Create two DITL items according to the specifications in Figure 3.13.

Next, create a BNDL resource according to the specifications in Figure 3.14. Make sure you change the BNDL's resource ID to –4064.

Next, create an FREF according to the specifications in Figure 3.15. Change the FREF resource ID to –4064.

Now create an FNT? resource with a resource ID of 0. The sample program's FNT? 0 resource is shown in Figure 3.16. If you need a refresher course on creator resources, go back to Chapter 8 in *Macintosh Programming Primer, Volume I*. Edit the first byte (the size byte) using the hexadecimal (left) side of ResEdit's general editor. The sample program's size byte is set to hex 14 (which, as you know, is equal to decimal 20). Following the size byte, the sample program has 20 bytes of text. Remember, if you change the message, change the size byte accordingly.

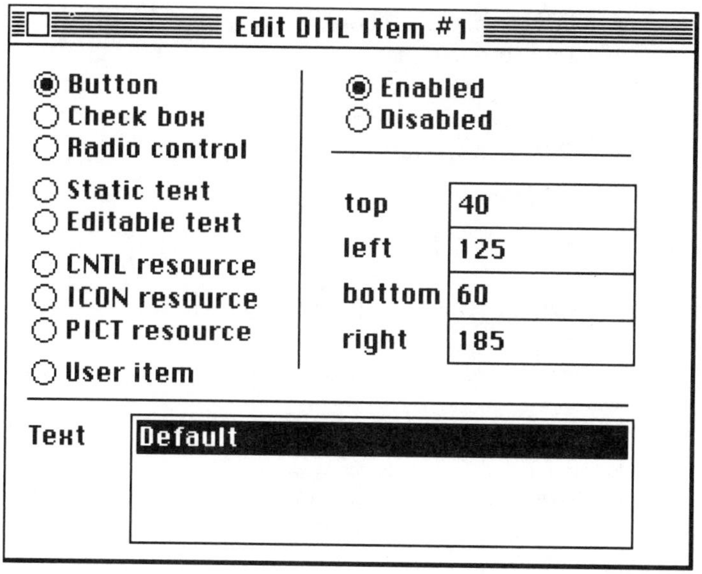

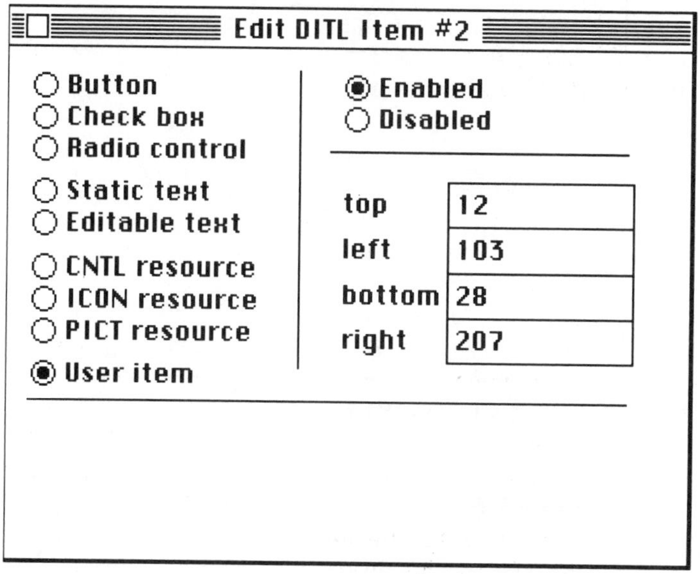

Figure 3.13 DITL item specifications.

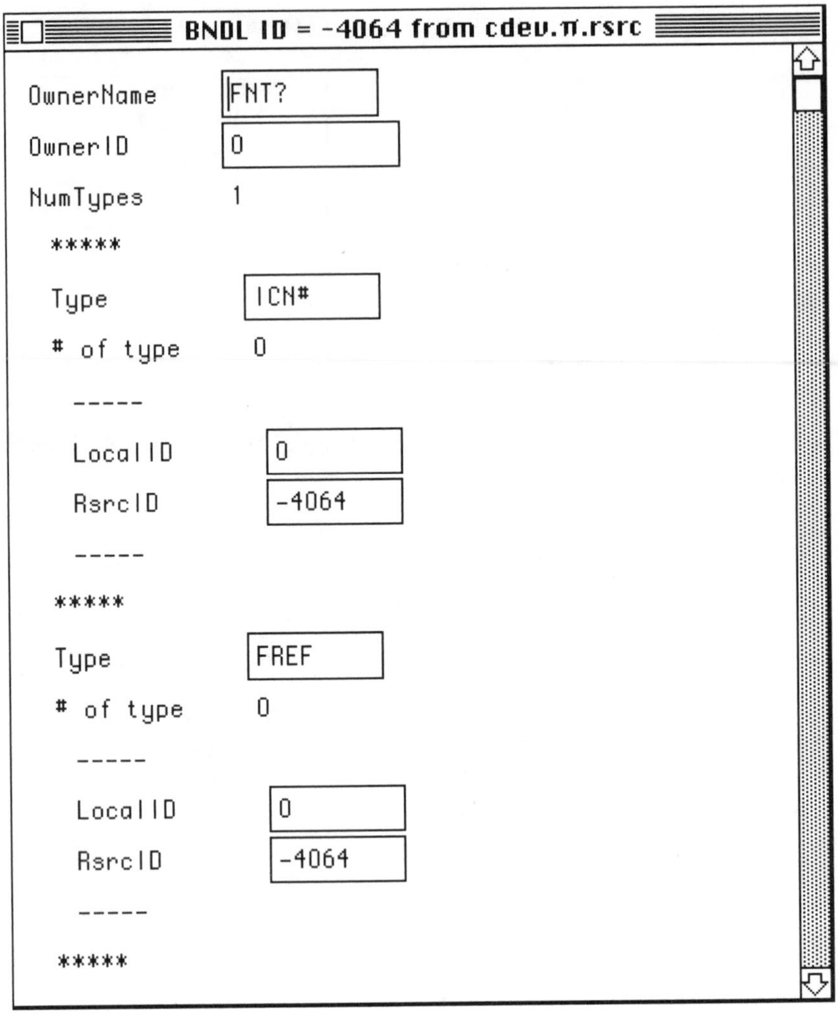

```
▤□▤▤▤▤ BNDL ID = -4064 from cdev.π.rsrc ▤▤▤        ⇧
 OwnerName     │FNT?        │
 OwnerID       │0           │
 NumTypes       1
   *****
   Type        │ICN#       │
   # of type    0
    -----
    LocalID     │0          │
    RsrcID      │-4064      │
    -----
   *****
   Type        │FREF       │
   # of type    0
    -----
    LocalID     │0          │
    RsrcID      │-4064      │
    -----
   *****                                            ⇩
```

Figure 3.14 BNDL specification.

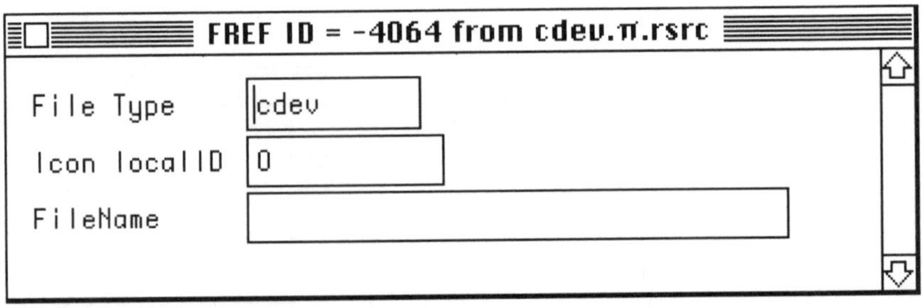

```
▤□▤▤▤▤ FREF ID = -4064 from cdev.π.rsrc ▤▤▤        ⇧
 File Type    │cdev       │
 Icon localID │0          │
 FileName     │                      │               ⇩
```

Figure 3.15 FREF specifications.

```
 ▤☐▤ FNT? ID = 0 from cdeu.π.rsrc ▤▤▤
 000000    |1459 6F75 7220 6D65   DYour me    ⬆
 000008     7373 6167 6520 6865   ssage he
 000010     7265 2121 21          re!!!
 000018
 000020
 000028                                       ⬇
 000030                                       ⬕
```

Figure 3.16   The sample creator resource.

Next, create a `mach` resource with an ID of –4064 according to the specs in Figure 3.17. A table of legal `mach` specifications appears at the bottom of page 328 of *Inside Macintosh, Volume V.* The specifications used in this sample indicate that this cdev should be made available on all machines.

Create a `MENU` resource for the Font pop-up. Use the specifications in Figure 3.18. Notice that this resource ID should be set to –4048. Because the `MENU` is not a required cdev resource, its resource ID is limited to the range –4033 through –4048.

```
 ▤☐▤ mach ID = -4064 from cdeu.π.rsrc ▤
 000000    FFFF 0000          0000       ⬆
 000008
 000010
 000018
 000020
 000028                                  ⬇
 000030                                  ⬕
```

Figure 3.17   mach specifications.

```
 ▤☐▤▤ MENU "Font" ID = -4048 from cdeu.π.rsrc ▤▤▤
                                                    ⬆
  MenuID        |-4048
  ProcID         0
  EnableFlgs     $FFFFFFFF
  Title          Font
  *****          0                                  ⬇
```

Figure 3.18   MENU specifications.

Finally, create an `nrct` with a resource ID of –4064. The `nrct` specifies the top, left, bottom, and right of a `Rect`. Figure 3.19 shows the sample program's `nrct` in both the template format and in the general, hexadecimal format (for those of you with older versions of ResEdit). Notice that the left coordinate is set at 87. This will place the left edge of the cdev rectangle just to the right of the Control Panel scroll bar.

Well, that's it for resources! Your list of resources should look like the one in Figure 3.20. Save that resource file and move on.

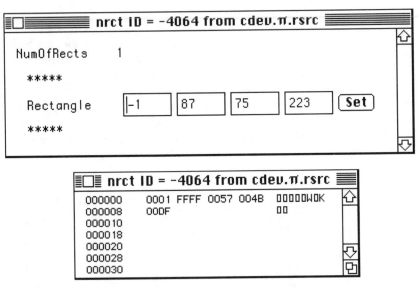

Figure 3.19 nrct specifications, in template and in general format.

Figure 3.20 The resources in cdev.π.rsrc.

The cdev Source Code

Create a new project in the cdev ƒ folder. Call the project **cdev.π**.
Next, add MacTraps to the project. Select New from the File menu to
create a new source code file and save the file as **cdev.c**. Add cdev.c
to the project. Here's the source code for cdev.c. Type it in and then
save it:

```c
#define DEFAULT_ITEM              1
#define USER_ITEM                 2

#define RUN_ON_ALL_MACHINES       1L
#define ERROR_STATE               0L
#define WORD_RES_ID               -4048
#define FONT_MENU_ID              -4048

#define NORMAL_APP_FONT           applFont

typedef struct
{
    short    curFontNum;
} FontNumInfo, **FontNumH;


pascal long main( message, item, numItems, cPanelID, e,
            cDevValue, cpDialog )
int             message, item, numItems, cPanelID;
EventRecord     *e;
long            cDevValue;
DialogPtr       cpDialog;
{
    int         itemType, fontNumber, choice;
    Handle      itemH, tempHandle;
    Rect        itemRect;
    MenuHandle  fontMenu;
    Str255      tempStr;

    if ( message == macDev )
        return( RUN_ON_ALL_MACHINES );
    else if ( message == initDev )
    {
        tempHandle = NewHandle( sizeof( FontNumInfo ) );
        fontNumber = FindFontNumber();
        (**((FontNumH)tempHandle)).curFontNum = fontNumber;
```

```
        return( (long)tempHandle );
}


if ( (cDevValue != cdevUnset) && (cDevValue !=
    ERROR_STATE) )
{
    switch( message )
    {
        case hitDev:
            if ( item == DEFAULT_ITEM + numItems )
            {
                GetDItem( cpDialog, USER_ITEM + numItems,
                        &itemType, &itemH, &itemRect );
                fontNumber = NORMAL_APP_FONT;
                SetAppFont( fontNumber );
                DrawFontName( fontNumber, &itemRect );
                (**((FontNumH)cDevValue)). curFontNum =
                    fontNumber;
                FixResource( fontNumber );
            }
            else if ( item == USER_ITEM + numItems )
            {
                GetDItem( cpDialog, USER_ITEM + numItems,
                        &itemType, &itemH, &itemRect );
                fontMenu = GetMenu(FONT_MENU_ID );
                InsertMenu( fontMenu, -1 );
                AddResMenu( fontMenu, 'FONT' );
                itemRect.right += 1;
                choice = DoPopup( &itemRect, fontMenu );

                if ( choice != 0 )
                {
                    GetItem( fontMenu, choice,&tempStr );
                    GetFNum( tempStr, &fontNumber );
                    SetAppFont( fontNumber );
                    DrawFontName( fontNumber, &itemRect );
                    (**((FontNumH)cDevValue)).curFontNum =
                        fontNumber;
                    FixResource( fontNumber );
                }

                DeleteMenu( FONT_MENU_ID );
                ReleaseResource( fontMenu );
            }
```

```
                    break;
            case closeDev:
                DisposHandle( (Handle)cDevValue );
                break;
            case nulDev:
                break;
            case updateDev:
                GetDItem( cpDialog, USER_ITEM+numItems,
                        &itemType, &itemH, &itemRect );
                FrameRect( &itemRect );
                MoveTo( itemRect.left + 1, itemRect.bottom );
                LineTo( itemRect.right, itemRect.bottom );
                LineTo( itemRect.right, itemRect.top + 1 );
                fontNumber = (**((FontNumH)cDevValue)).curFontNum;
                DrawFontName( fontNumber, &itemRect );
                break;
            case activDev:
                break;
            case deactivDev:
                break;
            case keyEvtDev:
                break;
            case macDev:
                return( 1L );
                break;
            case undoDev:
                break;
            case cutDev:
                break;
            case copyDev:
                break;
            case pasteDev:
                break;
            case clearDev:
                break;
        }
    }
    return( cDevValue );
}
```

```
/*****************************FixResource*******/

FixResource( fontNumber )
short   fontNumber;
{
    Handle  wHandle;

    if ( ( wHandle = GetResource( 'word', WORD_RES_ID ) ) !=
        OL )
    {
        *( (short *)(*wHandle) ) = fontNumber;
        ChangedResource( wHandle );
        WriteResource( wHandle );
    }
}

/*****************************DoPopup *******/

int         DoPopup( popupRectPtr, theMenu )
Rect        *popupRectPtr;
MenuHandle theMenu;
{
    Point   popupUpperLeft;
    long    theChoice = 0x0000;

    popupUpperLeft.h = popupRectPtr->left + 2;
    popupUpperLeft.v = popupRectPtr->bottom;

    LocalToGlobal( &popupUpperLeft );

    InvertRect( popupRectPtr );
    theChoice = PopUpMenuSelect( theMenu, popupUpperLeft.v,
                              popupUpperLeft.h, 0 );
    InvertRect( popupRectPtr );
    return( LoWord( theChoice ) );

}

/*****************************  FindFontNumber   */

short FindFontNumber()
{
    Handle  wHandle;
    short   fontNumber;
```

```
    if ( ( wHandle = GetResource( 'word', WORD_RES_ID ) ) !=
    OL )
    {
        fontNumber = *( (short *)(*wHandle) );
        return( fontNumber );
    }
    else
        return( NORMAL_APP_FONT );
}

/*********************************** SetAppFont */

SetAppFont( fontNum )
short   fontNum;
{
    *( (short *) 0x0204 ) = fontNum - 1;

    WriteParam();
}

/*********************************** DrawFontName */

DrawFontName( fontNum, rPtr )
short   fontNum;
Rect    *rPtr;
{
    Str255      tempStr;
    int         w;
    Rect        tempRect;

    tempRect = *rPtr;
    InsetRect( &tempRect, 2, 2 );
    EraseRect( &tempRect );
    if (fontNum == 1)
        GetFontName (geneva, & tempStr);
    else
        GetFontName( fontNum, &tempStr );
    w = rPtr->right - rPtr->left - StringWidth( tempStr );
    MoveTo( rPtr->left + w/2, rPtr->bottom - 4 );
    DrawString( tempStr );
}
```

Next, set the project type parameters to settings appropriate for a cdev. The sample program's Set Project Type dialog box is shown in Figure 3.21. Click the Code Resource radio button. Set the File Type to cdev. This tells the Control Panel that this file contains resources that make up a c d e v. In addition, at boot time the MacOS will open files of type cdev and execute any INIT resources it finds. That's why the AFI INIT resource was copied into the resource file. If you stick the cdev file in the System folder, you no longer need the AFI INIT file.

Set the Creator to FNT?. You'll use this information to BNDL an icon to your cdev in both the Control Panel and the Finder. Set the Type to cdev and the ID to -4064. Finally, set the Attrs field to 20. Click the OK button to save your changes.

Now you are ready to build the cdev. Select Build Code Resource... from the Project menu. When prompted to Bring the project up to date?, click Yes. Once you get cdev.c to compile, save the cdev as **AFI cdev**. Now try it out!

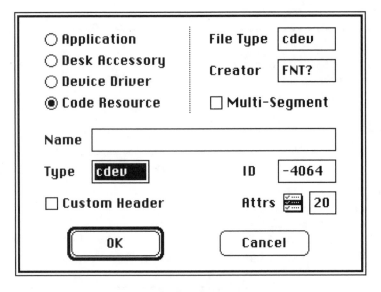

Figure 3.21 Set Project Type dialog box.

Checking Out the AFI cdev

Copy the AFI cdev to your System folder. Before you go any further, see if the Finder recognizes your cdev. Go back to the Finder, open the System folder, and select by Name from the View menu (see Figure 3.22).

Figure 3.23 shows the sample System folder viewed by name. The Kind field associated with AFI cdev should say Control Panel doc. If yours doesn't say this, your file type is not set correctly. The file type should be cdev.

Figure 3.22   View by Name.

System Folder			
Name	Size	Kind	Last M
AFI cdev	6K	Control Panel doc...	We
After Dark	74K	Control Panel doc...	Fri
After Dark Files	--	folder	Tue
AppleLink Out Basket	--	folder	Tue

Figure 3.23   The sample Control Panel document.

Now verify that the INIT still works. Make sure that AFI cdev is in the System folder, and that AFI (the INIT you built earlier in the chapter) has been removed from the System folder. Reboot your Mac. Depending on the setting of the `word` resource within AFI cdev, you should see either the animation sequence or the icon with the big X through it. If not, use ResEdit to make sure the INIT resource is inside AFI cdev.

Now take a deep breath and compose yourself. Slowly (savoring the moment), select the Control Panel from the menu. Did your cdev icon appear in the scrolling list? If not, carefully check your `BNDL`, `FREF`, and `FNT?` resources. If these look good, drag the cdev file onto the desktop. Did its icon appear? If not, check your resources again. Once you get the icon to appear on the desktop, your icon will probably appear in the Control Panel.

Next, click on the AFI icon in the Control Panel's scrolling icon list. Your Control Panel should look something like Figure 3.9. Click on the pop-up font menu. Select a new application font. Close the Control Panel and open ResEdit. ResEdit's lists should be drawn in the selected font.

Walking Through the cdev Source Code

This section takes a look at the source code for this cdev. It starts off with some #defines. `DEFAULT_ITEM` is the `DITL` item number of the reset button. `USER_ITEM` is the `DITL` item number of the user item. The user item determines where the pop-up font menu will appear.

```
#define DEFAULT_ITEM                1
#define USER_ITEM                   2
```

The sample cdev introduces the concept of code resource messages. Unlike normal applications or even INITs, which run from start to finish and then exit, cdevs are called repeatedly. Each time a cdev gets called, one of its parameters (message) gets set to a value, telling the cdev what action to take. For example, when the Control Panel first calls the cdev, it will pass initDev in the message parameter, asking the cdev to allocate any private storage it may need, and to initialize the settings of any controls. A complete list of all legal cdev messages can be found in *Inside Macintosh, Volume V*, page 333.

RUN_ON_ALL_MACHINES is a response to the macDev message. Actually, the sample cdev will never receive a macDev message, because macDev messages are sent only to cdevs with a mach resource set to 0000FFFF. The code is included here just as an example.

One of the cdev parameters is cDevValue. cDevValue serves several purposes. If it is set to a value of ERROR_STATE when the cdev is called, there is a problem, possibly the result of a lack of memory. When you allocate your private data structure (see FontNumInfo, below), you'll return a handle to the data structure. On subsequent calls of the cdev, the Control Panel will pass the handle back in the parameter cDevValue.

```
#define  RUN_ON_ALL_MACHINES              1L
#define  ERROR_STATE                      0L
#define  WORD_RES_ID                      -4048
#define  FONT_MENU_ID                     -4048

#define  NORMAL_APP_FONT                  applFont
```

The data structure FontNumInfo holds the current font number setting. Instead of going to all the trouble of allocating (and keeping around) a data structure, the program could have just checked the location 0x0204, or the contents of the word resource. This method was used here to illustrate the technique of allocating and retrieving a data structure in a cdev, because most of your cdevs will need this technique.

```
typedef struct
{
    short curFontNum;
} FontNumInfo, **FontNumH;
```

The specifications for main() and its parameters were obtained from *Inside Macintosh, Volume V* at the bottom of page 329. Remember, whenever you write a routine that will get called by the Toolbox, the routine must be declared as pascal. Because the calling sequence in *Inside Macintosh* specified main() as a function returning a long, the sample program declares main() as a pascal long.

item tells you the DITL item number that was hit, when you receive a hitDev message. Because the DITL in the sample program is appended to the Control Panel's DITL, numItems (the number of items in the Control Panel's DITL) must be subtracted from item before it can be used.

cPanelID is the base resource ID of the Control Panel's own resources. It is not used here. e is a pointer to the EventRecord associated with a hitDev, nulDev, activDev, deActivDev, updateDev, and keyEvtDev.

Finally, cpDialog is the Control Panel's DialogPtr.

```
pascal long main  ( message, item, numItems,cPanelID, e,
                    cDevValue, cpDialog )
int               message, item, numItems, cPanelID;
EventRecord       *e;
long              cDevValue;
DialogPtr         cpDialog;
{
        int          itemType, fontNumber, choice;
        Handle       itemH, tempHandle;
        Rect         itemRect;
        MenuHandle   fontMenu;
        Str255       tempStr;
```

If the program gets a macDev message, it tells the Control Panel to go ahead and use this cdev. When an initDev message is received, the program allocates a FontNumInfo struct, gets the current font number, updates the curFontNum field, and returns the handle to the Control Panel, so the program gets it back in cDevValue.

```
if ( message == macDev )
      return( RUN_ON_ALL_MACHINES );
else if ( message == initDev )
{
      tempHandle = NewHandle( sizeof( FontNumInfo ) );
      fontNumber = FindFontNumber();
      (**((FontNumH)tempHandle)).curFontNum = fontNumber;
      return( (long)tempHandle );
}
```

cdevUnset is passed continually in cDevValue until the program responds to an initDev message. Once it has processed an initDev message, assuming that no error state exists, the program can process all messages.

```
if ( (cDevValue != cdevUnset) && (cDevValue != ERROR_STATE) )
{
    switch( message )
    {
```

On a `hitDev` of the reset button, the program sets the font to NORMAL_APP_FONT, redraws the pop-up label, updates its private storage, and writes the new font value into its `word` resource.

```
        case hitDev:
            if ( item == DEFAULT_ITEM + numItems )
            {
                GetDItem( cpDialog, USER_ITEM + numItems,
                        &itemType, &itemH, &itemRect );
                fontNumber = NORMAL_APP_FONT;
                SetAppFont( fontNumber );
                DrawFontName( fontNumber,
                        &itemRect );
                (**((FontNumH)cDevValue)).curFontNum =
                fontNumber;
                FixResource( fontNumber );
            }
```

On a `hitDev` in the USER_ITEM, the program loads the menu, adds all the current fonts to it, and implements the pop-up.

```
            else if ( item == USER_ITEM + numItems )
            {
                GetDItem( cpDialog, USER_ITEM + numItems,
                        &itemType, &itemH, &itemRect );
                fontMenu = GetMenu( FONT_MENU_ID );
                InsertMenu( fontMenu, -1 );
                AddResMenu( fontMenu, 'FONT' );
                itemRect.right += 1;
                choice = DoPopup( &itemRect, fontMenu );
```

If a choice was made from the menu, the program converts the item to a `Str255`, then converts the `Str255` to a `fontNumber`. Next, it sets the application font to that font number, redraws the pop-up label, updates its private storage, and writes the `word` resource.

```
                    if ( choice != 0 )
                    {
                        GetItem( fontMenu, choice, &tempStr );
                        GetFNum( tempStr, &fontNumber );
                        SetAppFont( fontNumber );
                        DrawFontName( fontNumber, &itemRect );
                        (**((FontNumH)cDevValue)).curFontNum =
                            fontNumber;
                        FixResource( fontNumber );
                    }
```

Whether or not a choice was made from the pop-up, the program
still must delete the menu from the menu list, as well as free up the
storage held by the MENU resource.

```
                    DeleteMenu( FONT_MENU_ID );
                    ReleaseResource( fontMenu );
                }
                break;
```

On a closeDev message, the program frees up the memory that
was allocated at initialization.

```
        case closeDev:
            DisposHandle( (Handle)cDevValue );
            break;
        case nulDev:
            break;
```

On an updateDev message, the program draws the outline of the
button label and then draws the font name in the label.

```
        case updateDev:
            GetDItem( cpDialog, USER_ITEM+numItems,
                    &itemType, &itemH, &itemRect );
            FrameRect( &itemRect );
            MoveTo( itemRect.left + 1, itemRect.bottom );
            LineTo( itemRect.right, itemRect.bottom );
            LineTo( itemRect.right, itemRect.top + 1 );
            fontNumber = (**((FontNumH)cDevValue)).
                        curFontNum;
            DrawFontName( fontNumber, &itemRect );
            break;
        case activDev:
```

```
            break;
    case deactivDev:
            break;
    case keyEvtDev:
            break;
    case macDev:
            return( 1L );
            break;
    case undoDev:
            break;
    case cutDev:
            break;
    case copyDev:
            break;
    case pasteDev:
            break;
    case clearDev:
            break;
    }
}
```

No matter what the message was, the program always returns cDevValue. This keeps the handle to the program's private storage around for the next call.

```
    return( cDevValue );
}
```

FixResource() loads the word resource. Next, the resource data (the first two bytes) is set to the fontNumber passed as a parameter. The call to ChangedResource() marks the resource as having been changed. The call to WriteResource() checks the resource's changed flag and, if the resource was changed, writes out its new value to the resource fork.

This technique is fundamental to Macintosh software development. Read the description of ChangedResource() on page 123 of *Inside Macintosh, Volume I.*

```
/***************************** FixResource *******/

FixResource( fontNumber )
short   fontNumber;
{
```

```
    Handle  wHandle;

    if (( wHandle = GetResource( 'word', WORD_RES_ID )) != OL)
    {
        *( (short *)(*wHandle) ) = fontNumber;
        ChangedResource( wHandle );
        WriteResource( wHandle );
    }
}
```

DoPopup() implements a pop-up menu using theMenu. The
label inside the Rect pointed to by popupRectPtr will be inverted
and the pop-up will be hung right below the label. Once a selection is
made, the label is reinverted and the selected item number returned.

```
/****************************** DoPopup ******/

int     DoPopup( popupRectPtr, theMenu )
Rect        *popupRectPtr;
MenuHandle theMenu;
{
    Point    popupUpperLeft;
    long     theChoice = 0x0000;

    popupUpperLeft.h = popupRectPtr->left + 2;
    popupUpperLeft.v = popupRectPtr->bottom;

    LocalToGlobal( &popupUpperLeft );

    InvertRect( popupRectPtr );
    theChoice = PopUpMenuSelect( theMenu, popupUpperLeft.v,
                popupUpperLeft.h, 0 );
    InvertRect( popupRectPtr );
    return( LoWord( theChoice ) );
                }
```

FindFontNumber() loads the word resource. If it was loaded
successfully, the first two bytes of the resource are returned. If the
resource could not be loaded, NORMAL_APP_FONT is returned.

```
/***************************** FindFontNumber */

short FindFontNumber()
{
```

```
Handle   wHandle;
short    fontNumber;

if (( wHandle = GetResource( 'word', WORD_RES_ID )) != OL)
{
    fontNumber = *( (short *)(*wHandle) );
    return( fontNumber );
}
else
    return( NORMAL_APP_FONT );
}
```

SetAppFont() writes the specified fontNum to the two bytes starting at location 0x0204. WriteParam() updates Parameter-RAM.

> Remember, if you work directly with Parameter-RAM your applications are likely to break in the near future.

```
/*********************************  SetAppFont  */

SetAppFont( fontNum )
short fontNum;
{
    *( (short *) 0x0204 ) = fontNum - 1;

    WriteParam();
}
```

DrawFontName() erases the pop-up menu label (the call to InsetRect() ensures that the lines of the label are not erased, just the text). Then, the current font name is calculated and drawn, centered in the label.

> Because Geneva is the Macintosh default application font, the font name Geneva is displayed when fontNum is equal to 1. Note that this setting will cause ShowINIT to display the INIT icon with an X drawn across it, while the normal Geneva setting will cause ShowINIT to animate the startup icon.

```
/******************************* DrawFontName */

DrawFontName( fontNum, rPtr )
short    fontNum;
Rect     *rPtr;
{
    Str255       tempStr;
    int          w;
    Rect         tempRect;

    tempRect = *rPtr;
    InsetRect( &tempRect, 2, 2 );
    EraseRect( &tempRect );
    if (fontNum==1)
    GetFontName ( geneva,&tempStr).
    else
    GetFontName( fontNum, &tempStr /);
    w = rPtr->right - rPtr->left - StringWidth( tempStr );
    MoveTo( rPtr->left + w/2, rPtr->bottom - 4 );
    DrawString( tempStr );
}
```

Wasn't that fun? cdevs and INITs were made for each other. Well, on to the next topic, MDEFs . . . .

Writing Your Own MDEF

The next project involves the Menu Manager. You are going to create a custom menu definition procedure (MDEF) that displays pictures instead of text. This is one of my favorites.

PICT MDEF takes a series of PICT resources and uses their picFrames to calculate the size of a pop-up menu. The widest of the PICTs determines the width of the pop-up, and the tallest of the PICTs determines the height of each cell of the pop-up. Figure 3.24 shows the PICT MDEF in action.

Figure 3.24   PICT MDEF in action.

The MDEF Project and Source Code

First, you'll create the MDEF resource. Later on, you'll build an MDEF tester.

Create a folder in your development folder called **MDEF ƒ**. Create a new project inside the MDEF ƒ folder called **MDEF.π**. Add MacTraps to the project.

Next, select Set Project Type... from the Project menu. Figure 3.25 shows the sample program's Set Project Type... dialog box. Click the Code Resource radio button. Set the File Type to rsrc and the Creator to RSED. This asks the Finder to start up ResEdit when you double-click on the resource file. Set the Name to PICT (not really needed—for readability in ResEdit only) and the Type to MDEF. Set the ID to 400 and the Attrs to 20.

Next, select New from the File menu to create a new source code file. Save the file as **MDEF.c** and add the file to the project. Here's the source code. Start typing....

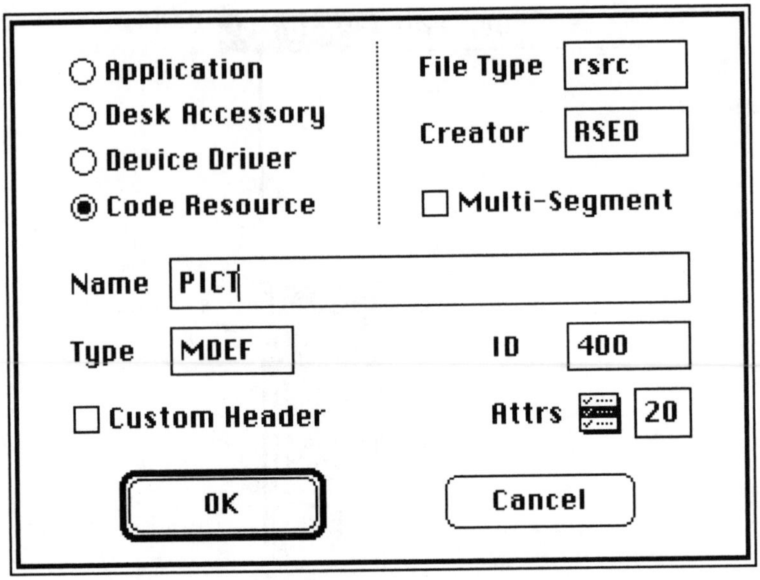

Figure 3.25   The MDEF Set Project Type dialog box.

```
#define MARGIN          2


/******************************************** main ***/

pascal voidmain( message, theMenu, menuRectPtr, hitPt,
            whichItemPtr )
int          message;
MenuHandle   theMenu;
Rect         *menuRectPtr;
Point        hitPt;
int          *whichItemPtr;
{
    short     PICTResID, numPicts, maxH, maxV, i;
    PicHandle myPicture;
    Rect      r, tempRect;
    int       newItem;

    switch( message )
    {
        case mDrawMsg:
            GetNumPicts( theMenu, &PICTResID, &numPicts );
            CalcMaxHV( PICTResID, numPicts, &maxH, &maxV );
```

```
        r.top = menuRectPtr->top + MARGIN/2;
        r.left = menuRectPtr->left + MARGIN;
        r.bottom = r.top + maxV;
        r.right = r.left + maxH;

        for ( i=0; i<numPicts; i++ )
        {
            myPicture = GetPicture( PICTResID + i );
            tempRect = r;
            CenterPict( myPicture, &tempRect );
            DrawPicture( myPicture, &tempRect );
            OffsetRect( &r, 0, maxV + MARGIN );
        }
        break;
    case mChooseMsg:
        GetNumPicts( theMenu, &PICTResID, &numPicts );
        CalcMaxHV( PICTResID, numPicts, &maxH, &maxV );

        if ( PtInRect( hitPt, menuRectPtr ) )
        {
            newItem = ( (hitPt.v - menuRectPtr->top) /
                        (maxV + MARGIN) ) + 1;
            if ( ( *whichItemPtr > 0 ) && ( *whichItemPtr
                != newItem ) )
            {
                r = *menuRectPtr;
                r.top += ( (*whichItemPtr-1) * (MARGIN +
                           maxV) );
                r.bottom = r.top + maxV + MARGIN;
                InvertRect( &r );
            }

            if ( *whichItemPtr != newItem )
            {
                *whichItemPtr = newItem;
                r = *menuRectPtr;
                r.top += ( (*whichItemPtr-1) * (MARGIN +
                           maxV) );
                r.bottom = r.top + maxV + MARGIN;
                InvertRect( &r );
            }
        }
        else if ( *whichItemPtr > 0 )
        {
```

```
            r = *menuRectPtr;
            r.top += ((*whichItemPtr-1) * (MARGIN + maxV));
            r.bottom = r.top + maxV + MARGIN;
            InvertRect( &r );
            *whichItemPtr = 0;
        }
        break;
    case mSizeMsg:
        GetNumPicts( theMenu, &PICTResID, &numPicts );
        CalcMaxHV( PICTResID, numPicts, &maxH, &maxV );
        (**theMenu).menuWidth = maxH + 2 * MARGIN;
        (**theMenu).menuHeight = (maxV + MARGIN) *
                                    numPicts;

        break;
    }
}


/***************************** CenterPict ********/

CenterPict( thePicture, myRectPtr )
PicHandle   thePicture;
Rect        *myRectPtr;
{
    Rect    windRect, pictureRect;

    windRect = *myRectPtr;
    pictureRect = (**( thePicture )).picFrame;
    myRectPtr->top = (windRect.bottom - windRect.top -
                    (pictureRect.bottom - pictureRect.top))
        / 2 + windRect.top;
    myRectPtr->bottom = myRectPtr->top + (pictureRect.bottom -
                                        pictureRect.top);
    myRectPtr->left = (windRect.right - windRect.left -
                    (pictureRect.right - pictureRect.left))
        / 2 + windRect.left;
    myRectPtr->right = myRectPtr->left + (pictureRect.right -
                                        pictureRect.left);
}
```

```
/********************************************  CalcMaxHV  ***/

CalcMaxHV( PICTResID, numPicts, hPtr, vPtr )
short       PICTResID, numPicts, *hPtr, *vPtr;
{
    short       i;
    Rect        r;
    PicHandle   myPicture;

    *hPtr = 0;
    *vPtr = 0;
    for ( i=0; i<numPicts; i++ )
    {
        myPicture = GetPicture( PICTResID + i );
        r = (**myPicture).picFrame;

        if ( r.bottom - r.top > *vPtr )
            *vPtr = r.bottom - r.top;
        if ( r.right - r.left > *hPtr )
            *hPtr = r.right - r.left;
    }
}



/********************************************  GetNumPicts  ***/

GetNumPicts( theMenu, baseIDPtr, numPictsPtr )
MenuHandle  theMenu;
short       *baseIDPtr, *numPictsPtr;
{
    *baseIDPtr = HiWord((**theMenu).enableFlags);
    *numPictsPtr = LoWord((**theMenu).enableFlags);
}
```

Building Your MDEF

Once the source code is typed in and saved, it's time to build the MDEF code resource. Select Build Code Resource... from the Project menu. Click Yes to Bring the project up to date?, and fix any bugs picked up by the compiler. Once your code compiles, save it in the MDEF ƒ folder as **PICT MDEF**.

Building the MDEF Tester

Before walking through the MDEF source code, let's create an application to test the MDEF. This application, **MDEF Tester**, is a simple application with a main event loop, a single window with no close box, and a menu bar consisting of menus entitled , File, Edit, and Pictures. The File menu supports a single item, Quit. The **Pictures** menu uses the newly created MDEF (as opposed to MDEF 0, the standard MDEF) to display and allow selection from a series of PICT resources.

Start by creating a resource file for the MDEF tester project. Launch ResEdit and create a new file within the MDEF ƒ folder. Call the file **Tester.π.rsrc**.

Next, open the file PICT MDEF, select the MDEF resource, and select Copy from the Edit menu. Close the PICT MDEF window and open the newly created Tester.π.rsrc window. Select Paste from the Edit menu to add the MDEF resource to the MDEF tester's resource file.

The next step is to create an MBAR resource and set its resource ID to 400. Click on the asterisks, then select New from the File menu to add a MENU resource ID to the MBAR. The sample program's MBAR is shown in Figure 3.26.

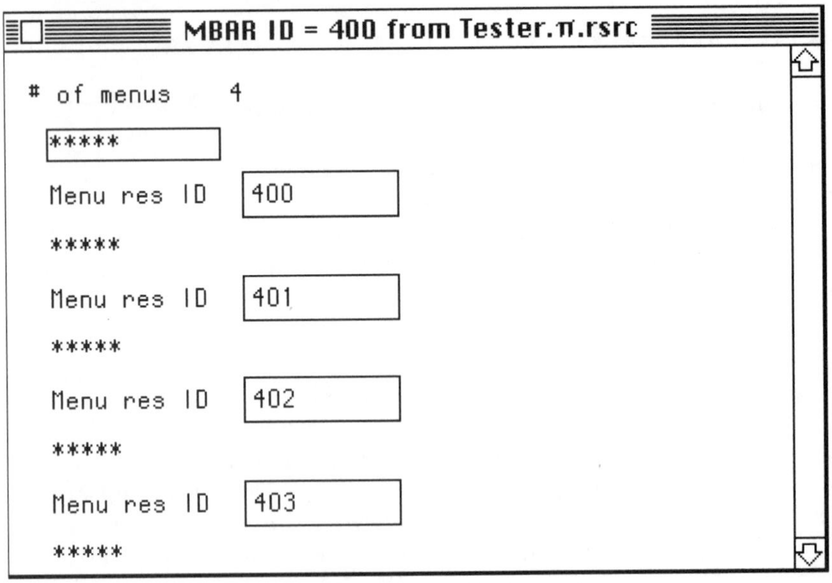

Figure 3.26   MBAR resource for MDEF Tester.

Next, you'll create the four MENU resources. Create a MENU resource with a resource ID of 400, according to the specs in Figure 3.27. The title of this menu should be the character.

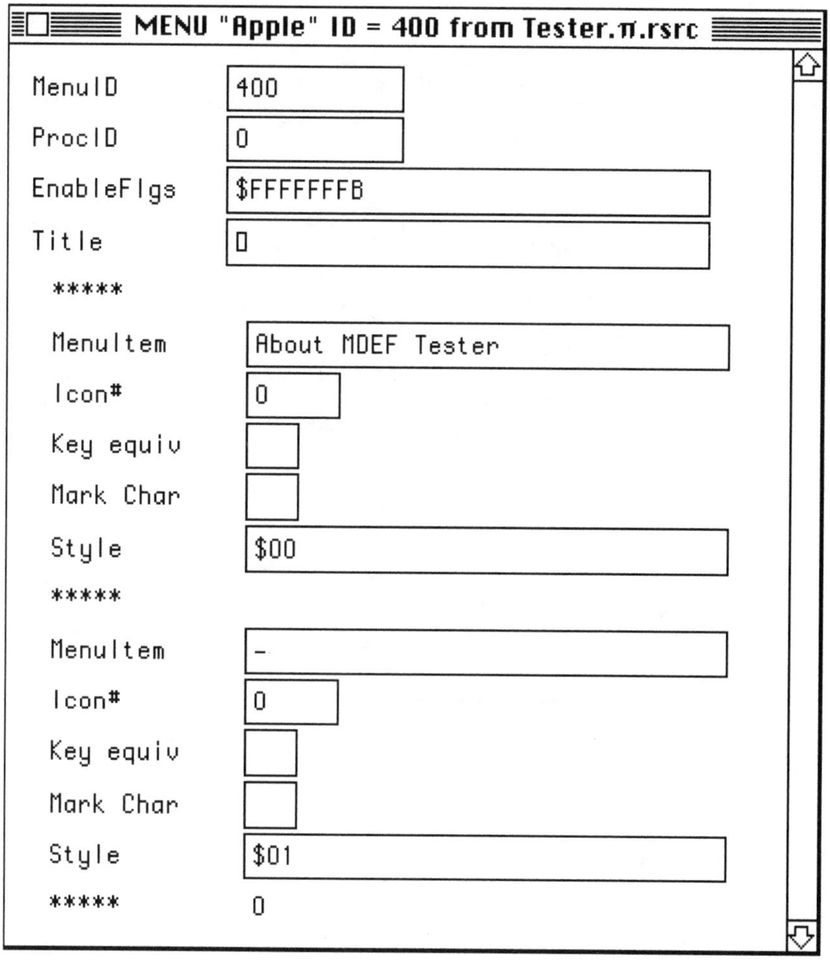

```
┌────────────────────────────────────────────────────────────┐
│ ▤☐▤▤▤   MENU "Apple" ID = 400 from Tester.π.rsrc ▤▤▤      │
├────────────────────────────────────────────────────────────┤
│  MenuID          ┌──────────────────┐                   ⬆   │
│                  │ 400              │                       │
│  ProcID          ┌──────────────────┐                       │
│                  │ 0                │                       │
│  EnableFlgs      ┌────────────────────────────────────┐     │
│                  │ $FFFFFFFB                          │     │
│  Title           ┌────────────────────────────────────┐     │
│                  │                                  │     │
│     *****                                                   │
│     MenuItem     ┌────────────────────────────────────┐     │
│                  │ About MDEF Tester                 │     │
│     Icon#        ┌──────────────────┐                       │
│                  │ 0                │                       │
│     Key equiv    ┌────┐                                     │
│                  │    │                                     │
│     Mark Char    ┌────┐                                     │
│                  │    │                                     │
│     Style        ┌────────────────────────────────────┐     │
│                  │ $00                                │     │
│     *****                                                   │
│     MenuItem     ┌────────────────────────────────────┐     │
│                  │ -                                  │     │
│     Icon#        ┌──────────────────┐                       │
│                  │ 0                │                       │
│     Key equiv    ┌────┐                                     │
│                  │    │                                     │
│     Mark Char    ┌────┐                                     │
│                  │    │                                     │
│     Style        ┌────────────────────────────────────┐     │
│                  │ $01                                │     │
│     *****          0                                    ⬇   │
└────────────────────────────────────────────────────────────┘
```

Figure 3.27 Specifications for MENU 400.

Next, create the File MENU according to the specifications in Figure 3.28.

Next, create the Edit MENU according to the specifications in Figure 3.29.

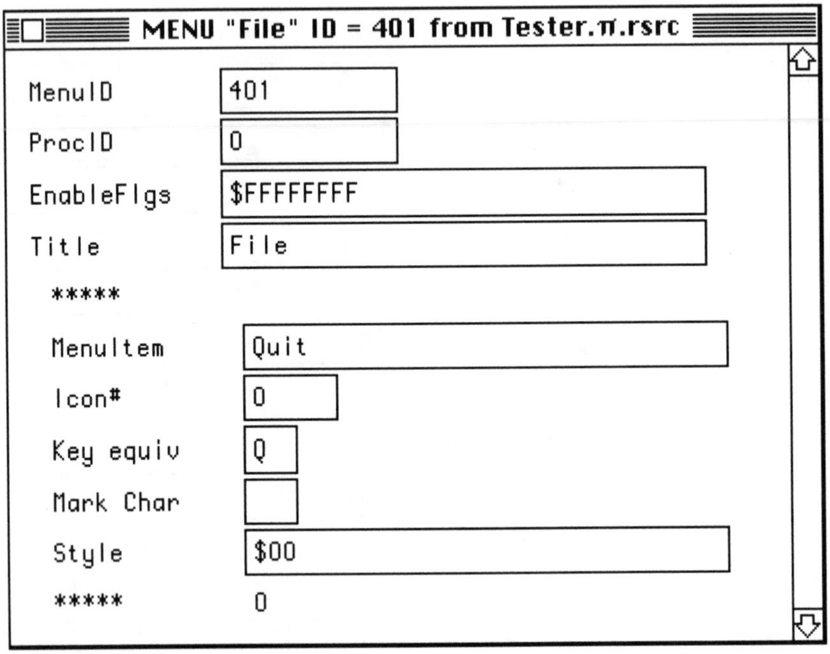

```
┌────────────────────────────────────────────────────┐
│▤□▭▭▭ MENU "File" ID = 401 from Tester.π.rsrc ▭▭▭   │⇧
│ ┌──────────────────────────────────────────────┐   │
│   MenuID          ┌────────────┐                │
│                   │401         │                │
│   ProcID          │0           │                │
│   EnableFlgs      ┌──────────────────────────┐  │
│                   │$FFFFFFFF                 │  │
│   Title           │File                      │  │
│     *****                                        │
│   MenuItem        ┌──────────────────────────┐  │
│                   │Quit                      │  │
│   Icon#           │0           │                │
│   Key equiv       │Q  │                         │
│   Mark Char       │   │                         │
│   Style           │$00                       │  │
│     *****            0                           │⇩
└────────────────────────────────────────────────────┘
```

Figure 3.28   Specifications for MENU 401.

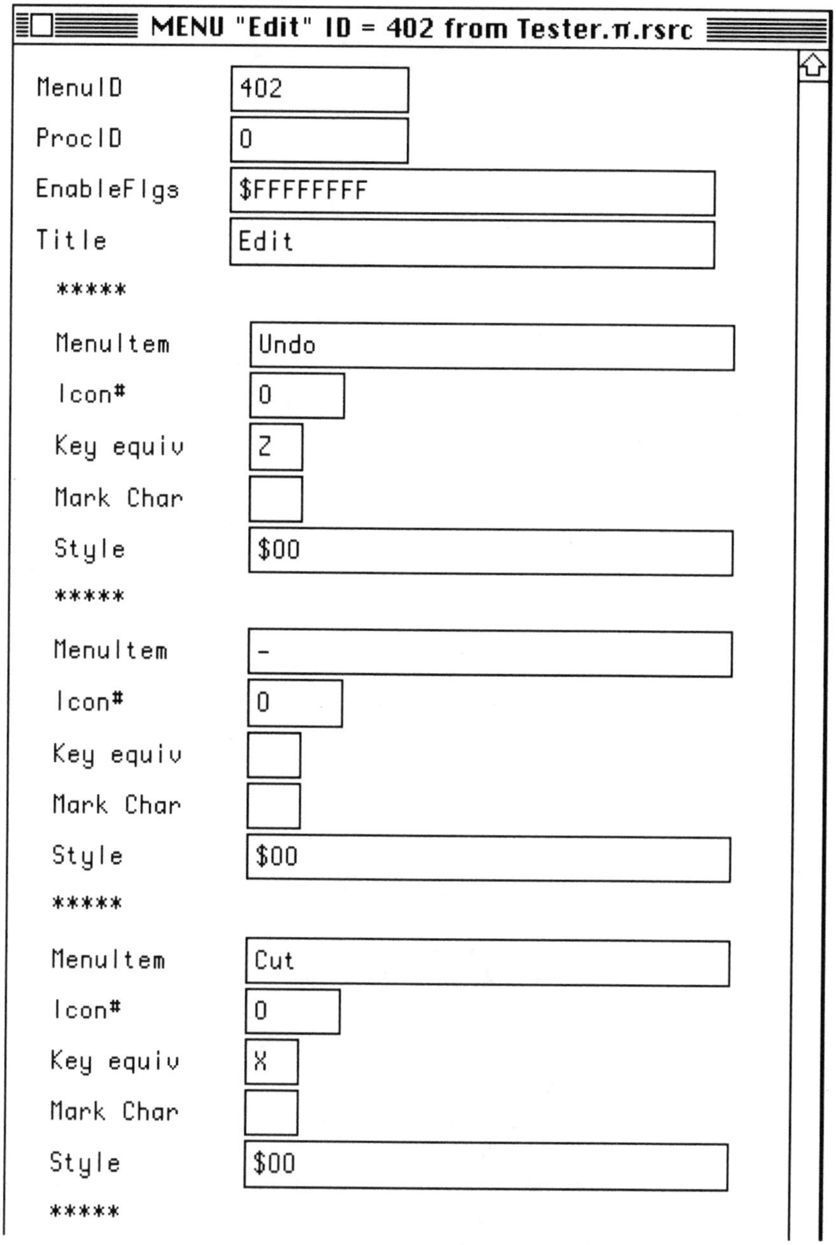

```
▤☐▤▤▤  MENU "Edit" ID = 402 from Tester.π.rsrc ▤▤▤

  MenuID          402

  ProcID          0

  EnableFlgs      $FFFFFFFF

  Title           Edit
    *****
    MenuItem      Undo

    Icon#         0

    Key equiv     Z

    Mark Char

    Style         $00
    *****
    MenuItem      –

    Icon#         0

    Key equiv

    Mark Char

    Style         $00
    *****
    MenuItem      Cut

    Icon#         0

    Key equiv     X

    Mark Char

    Style         $00
    *****
```

Figure 3.29   Specifications for MENU 402.

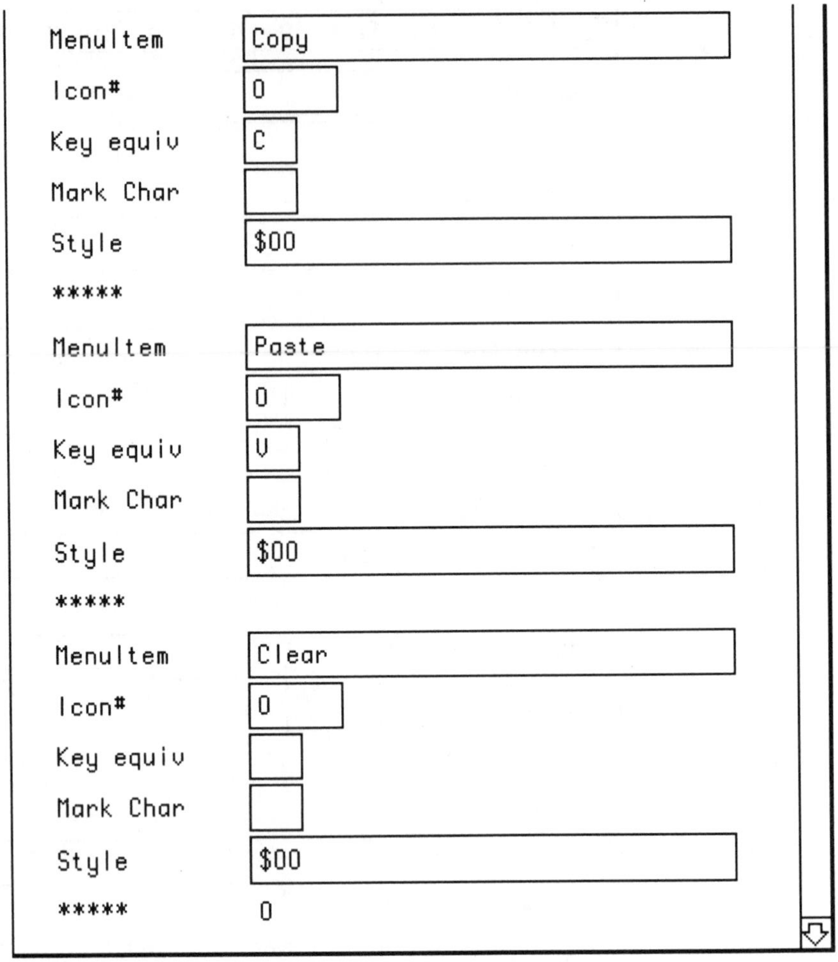

MenuItem	Copy
Icon#	0
Key equiv	C
Mark Char	
Style	$00

*****

MenuItem	Paste
Icon#	0
Key equiv	V
Mark Char	
Style	$00

*****

MenuItem	Clear
Icon#	0
Key equiv	
Mark Char	
Style	$00

***** 0

Figure 3.29   *(continued)*

Next, create the Pictures MENU according to the specifications in Figure 3.30. This MENU holds the key to interfacing a MENU with the custom MDEF. The ProcID field normally holds the value 0. This tells the Menu Manager to implement this menu by calling MDEF 0. Setting the ProcID field to 400 tells the Menu Manager to call your MDEF (MDEF 400).

The MDEF shown here uses the **EnableFlgs** field to specify which PICT resources to include in the pull-down menu. The first two bytes of the EnableFlgs specify the resource ID of the first PICT in the menu. In Figure 3.30, the first two bytes are set to 0x0190 in hexadecimal, or 400 in decimal.

The second two bytes specify the number of PICTs to include in the menu. In Figure 3.30, the second two bytes are set to 0x0005 in hexadecimal, or 5 decimal. This means you'll include 5 PICTs in the menu. The PICTs to be loaded are those with resource IDs 400, 401, 402, 403, and 404.

One final point about the sample MDEF. Because the EnableFlgs field is used to specify the PICTs, it can't be used to turn on and off specific menu items. Consider this point when you are designing your own MDEFs.

If you are using ResEdit 2.0 or later, you'll have to use the hex editor to get at the Pictures menu's Enable Flags field. Create a Pictures MENU with no menu items. Select Get Resource Info from the Resource menu and set the resource ID of the menu to 403. Close the Get Info window and close the MENU window. Now comes the tricky part.

In the list of MENUs, single-click on the newly created MENU 403. Select Open Using Hex Editor from the Resource menu. The resource will open using the hex editor instead of the normal MENU editor. The hex portion of the window should show 3 lines, each with 4 sets of digits. Edit the hex side (don't mess with the ASCII digits on the right side) so the three lines read:

```
0193 0000 0000 0190
0000 0190 0005 0850
6963 7475 7265 7300
```

This procedure will also set the MDEF field to 400. For more info, check out IM:364 for a complete description of the MENU resource format.

Next, create five PICT resources, with IDs of 400, 401, 402, 403, and 404. Figure 3.31 shows the five PICTs created for this example. The floppy disk is 404, the Mona Lisa is 403, the house 402, the dog-cow (Moof ™!) is 401, and the musical note is 400.

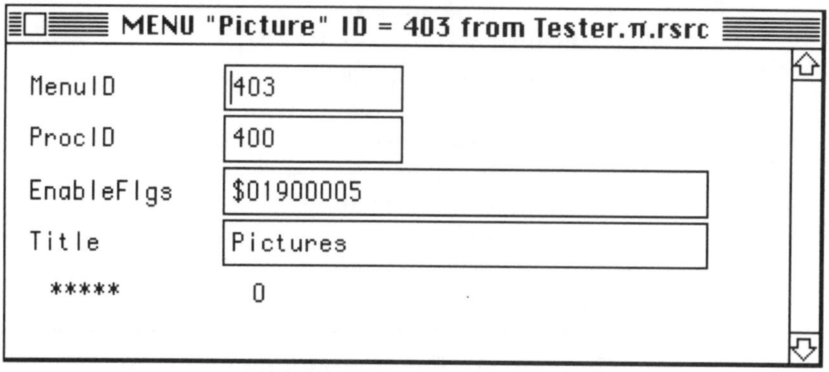

Figure 3.30 Specifications for MENU 403.

The final resource is the `WIND` that will be used as a template for the picture window. Create a `WIND` according to the specifications in Figure 3.32.

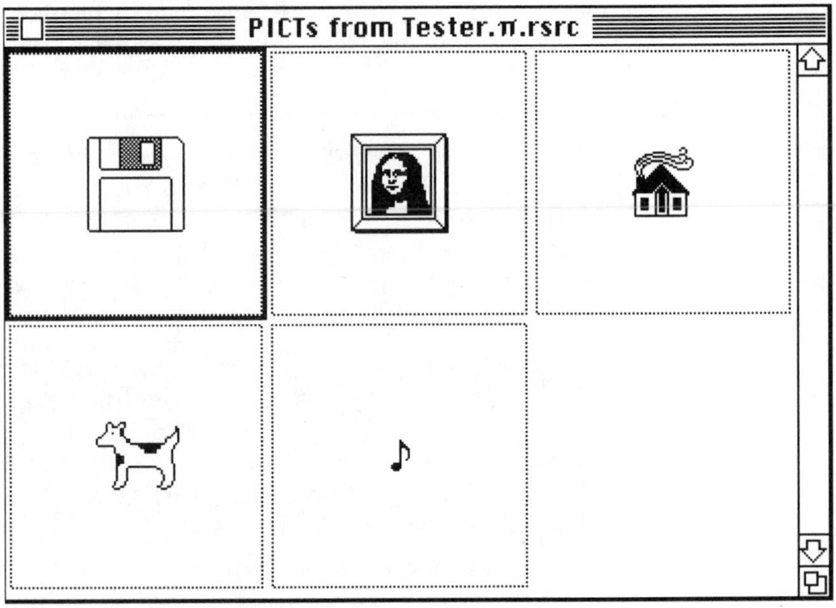
PICTs from Tester.π.rsrc

Figure 3.31 Sample `PICT` resources.

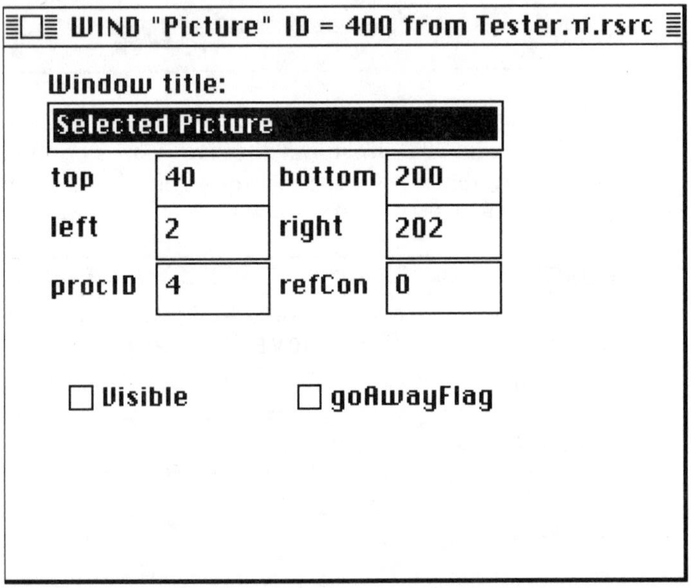
WIND "Picture" ID = 400 from Tester.π.rsrc
Window title:
Selected Picture
top
40
bottom
200
left
2
right
202
procID
4
refCon
0
Visible
goAwayFlag

Figure 3.32 Specifications for `WIND 400`.

Now that you've created all the resources for the MDEF test[ ], create a new project in the MDEF *f* folder called **Tester.π**. Add MacTraps to the project. Select New from the File menu to create a new source code file. Save the file as **Tester.c** and add the file to the project. Enter the following source code in Tester.c.

```
#define BASE_RES_ID          400
#define APPLE_MENU_ID        400
#define NIL_POINTER          0L
#define MOVE_TO_FRONT        -1L
#define REMOVE_ALL_EVENTS    0

#define WNE_TRAP_NUM         0x60
#define UNIMPL_TRAP_NUM      0x9F
#define MIN_SLEEP            60L
#define NIL_MOUSE_REGION     0L

#define FILE_MENU_ID         401
#define F_QUIT_ITEM          1

#define PICT_MENU_ID         403


Boolean        gDone, gWNEImplemented;
EventRecord    gTheEvent;
MenuHandle     gAppleMenu;
PicHandle      gCurPicture;
WindowPtr      gTheWindow;


main()
{
    ToolBoxInit();
    MenuBarInit();

    gTheWindow = GetNewWindow( BASE_RES_ID, NIL_POINTER,
                               MOVE_TO_FRONT );
    SetPort( gTheWindow );
    ShowWindow( gTheWindow );

    gCurPicture = GetPicture( BASE_RES_ID );

    MainLoop();
}
```

```
/********************************* ToolBoxInit */


ToolBoxInit()
{
    InitGraf( &thePort );
    InitFonts();
    FlushEvents( everyEvent, REMOVE_ALL_EVENTS );
    InitWindows();
    InitMenus();
    TEInit();
    InitDialogs( NIL_POINTER );
    InitCursor();
}



/********************************* MenuBarInit*/


MenuBarInit()
{
    Handle      myMenuBar;

    myMenuBar = GetNewMBar( BASE_RES_ID );
    SetMenuBar( myMenuBar );
    gAppleMenu = GetMHandle( APPLE_MENU_ID );
    AddResMenu( gAppleMenu, 'DRVR' );
    DrawMenuBar();
}



/******************************* MainLoop ********/


MainLoop()
{
    gDone = FALSE;
    gWNEImplemented = ( NGetTrapAddress( WNE_TRAP_NUM,
                        ToolTrap ) !=
                        NGetTrapAddress( UNIMPL_TRAP_NUM,
                        ToolTrap ) );
    while ( gDone == FALSE )
    {
        HandleEvent();
    }
}
```

```
/************************************** HandleEvent   */

HandleEvent()
{
    char    theChar;

    if ( gWNEImplemented )
        WaitNextEvent( everyEvent, &gTheEvent, MIN_SLEEP,
                    NIL_MOUSE_REGION );
    else
    {
        SystemTask();
        GetNextEvent( everyEvent, &gTheEvent );
    }

    switch ( gTheEvent.what )
    {
        case mouseDown:
            HandleMouseDown();
            break;
        case keyDown:
        case autoKey:
            theChar = gTheEvent.message & charCodeMask;
            if (( gTheEvent.modifiers & cmdKey ) != 0)
                HandleMenuChoice( MenuKey( theChar ) );
            break;
        case updateEvt:
            BeginUpdate( gTheEvent.message );
            DrawMyPicture( gCurPicture, gTheWindow );
            EndUpdate( gTheEvent.message );
            break;
    }
}


/************************************** HandleMouseDown */

HandleMouseDown()
{
    WindowPtr   whichWindow;
    short int   thePart;
    long int    menuChoice, windSize;
```

```
        thePart = FindWindow( gTheEvent.where, &whichWindow );
        switch ( thePart )
        {
            case inMenuBar:
                menuChoice = MenuSelect( gTheEvent.where );
                HandleMenuChoice( menuChoice );
                break;
            case inSysWindow :
                SystemClick( &gTheEvent, whichWindow );
                break;
            case inDrag :
                DragWindow( whichWindow, gTheEvent.where,
                            &(screenBits.bounds) );
                break;
        }
}


/*********************************** HandleMenuChoice */

HandleMenuChoice( menuChoice )
long int    menuChoice;
{
    int theMenu;
    int theItem;

    if ( menuChoice != 0 )
    {
        theMenu = HiWord( menuChoice );
        theItem = LoWord( menuChoice );
        switch ( theMenu )
        {
            case FILE_MENU_ID :
                if ( theItem == F_QUIT_ITEM )
                    gDone = TRUE;
                break;
            case PICT_MENU_ID :
                EraseRect( &gTheWindow->portRect );
                InvalRect( &gTheWindow->portRect );
                gCurPicture = GetPicture( BASE_RES_ID + theItem
                                          - 1 );
                break;
        }
        HiliteMenu( 0 );
    }
}
```

```
/****************************** DrawMyPicture *********/

DrawMyPicture( thePicture, pictureWindow )
PicHandle   thePicture;
WindowPtr   pictureWindow;
{
    Rect     myRect;

    myRect = pictureWindow->portRect;
    CenterPict( thePicture, &myRect );
    DrawPicture( thePicture, &myRect );
}


/****************************** CenterPict *********/

CenterPict( thePicture, myRectPtr )
PicHandle   thePicture;
Rect        *myRectPtr;
{
    Rect     windRect, pictureRect;

    windRect = *myRectPtr;
    pictureRect = (**( thePicture )).picFrame;
    myRectPtr->top = (windRect.bottom - windRect.top -
                    (pictureRect.bottom - pictureRect.top))
        / 2 + windRect.top;
    myRectPtr->bottom = myRectPtr->top + (pictureRect.bottom -
                                          pictureRect.top);
    myRectPtr->left = (windRect.right - windRect.left -
                    (pictureRect.right - pictureRect.left))
        / 2 + windRect.left;
    myRectPtr->right = myRectPtr->left + (pictureRect.right -
                                          pictureRect.left);
}
```

Save your code and then select Run from the Project menu. Once you get the code to compile, you should see something similar to Figure 3.24 when you click on the Pictures menu. Select a picture from the menu. MDEF Tester should draw the selected PICT in the window.

MDEF Tester is basically a combination of the ShowPICT program and the basic approach to event loop programming found in most of the applications in Volume I of the *Macintosh Primer*. Because the

techniques presented in MDEF Tester have already been presented
many times, this section will focus on the MDEF source code only.

Walking Through the PICT MDEF Source Code

`MARGIN` defines the number of pixels that should be left on each side
of each menu item.

```
#define    MARGIN                    2
```

The calling sequence for an MDEF is defined on page 362 of *Inside
Macintosh, Volume I*. Because the Macintosh Toolbox will be calling
this code resource, its entry point must be defined to be of type
`pascal`. The call is defined as a `Procedure`, not as a `Function`
returning a specific type, so `main()` will be declared as a `void`. This
yields the definition of `main()` as a `pascal void`.

The `message` parameter specifies which message this MDEF is
reacting to. The `mDrawMsg` asks the program to draw the menu
within the `Rect` specified by `menuRectPtr`. The `mChooseMsg` asks
the program to use the current mouse location (specified by `hitPt`),
the menu's `Rect` (`menuRectPtr`), and the last selected item
(`whichItemPtr`) to draw the menu appropriately and implement a
selection. The `mSizeMsg` asks the program to specify the menu's
height and width (used by the Menu Manager to calculate the menu's
`Rect`).

```
/*********************************************** main ***/

pascal voidmain( message, theMenu, menuRectPtr, hitPt,
          whichItemPtr )
int          message;
MenuHandle   theMenu;
Rect         *menuRectPtr;
Point        hitPt;
int          *whichItemPtr;
{
    short      PICTResID, numPicts, maxH, maxV, i;
    PicHandle  myPicture;
    Rect       r, tempRect;
    int        newItem;
```

When the program receives the mDrawMsg, it calls GetNumPicts() to retrieve the first PICT resource ID, as well as the total number of PICTs from the menu's EnableFlgs field. That information is then passed on to CalcMaxHV() to calculate the height and width of each cell of the menu.

```
switch( message )
{
    case mDrawMsg:
        GetNumPicts( theMenu, &PICTResID, &numPicts );
        CalcMaxHV( PICTResID, numPicts, &maxH, &maxV );
```

Because the Menu Manager has already drawn the shadowed menu rectangle, all the program has to do is draw each item. It uses the routine CenterPict() to calculate a Rect the size of the current PICT that's centered in the Rect provided as an input parameter. For more on CenterPict(), see ShowPICT from *Macintosh Programming Primer, Volume I*.

```
r.top = menuRectPtr->top + MARGIN/2;
r.left = menuRectPtr->left + MARGIN;
r.bottom = r.top + maxV;
r.right = r.left + maxH;

for ( i=0; i<numPicts; i++ )
{
    myPicture = GetPicture( PICTResID + i );
    tempRect = r;
    CenterPict( myPicture, &tempRect );
    DrawPicture( myPicture, &tempRect );
    OffsetRect( &r, 0, maxV + MARGIN );
}
break;
```

When the program receives the mChooseMsg, it calls GetNumPicts() to retrieve the first PICT ID and the number of PICTs. It then calls CalcMaxHV() to calculate the height and width of each menu item.

> The program has to call `GetNumPicts()` and `CalcMaxHV()` each time the MDEF is called with a message, because no global variables are provided in this code resource to use as long-term storage. Because these routines are pretty fast, they don't affect performance. If you need to, however, you can use the techniques described in Chapter 2 to add globals to your MDEF.

```
case   mChooseMsg:
    GetNumPicts( theMenu, &PICTResID, &numPicts );
    CalcMaxHV( PICTResID, numPicts, &maxH, &maxV );
```

If the mouse cursor is inside the menu rectangle, the program first figures out which item the cursor is in. If there is a currently selected item and it is not the current item, the previous item must be deselected using a call to `InvertRect()`.

```
if ( PtInRect( hitPt, menuRectPtr ) )
{
    newItem = ( (hitPt.v - menuRectPtr->top) /
            (maxV + MARGIN) ) + 1;
    if ( ( *whichItemPtr > 0 ) && ( *whichItemPtr
        != newItem ) )
    {
        r = *menuRectPtr;
        r.top += ( (*whichItemPtr-1) * (MARGIN +
                maxV) );
        r.bottom = r.top + maxV + MARGIN;
        InvertRect( &r );
    }
```

After the program has taken care of any needed deselection, it's time to select the current item. Again, `InvertRect()` is used to select the appropriate item.

```
    if ( *whichItemPtr != newItem )
    {
        *whichItemPtr = newItem;
        r = *menuRectPtr;
        r.top += ( (*whichItemPtr-1) * (MARGIN +
maxV) );
        r.bottom = r.top + maxV + MARGIN;
        InvertRect( &r );
    }
}
```

If the cursor is outside the menu rectangle and an item is currently selected, the program needs to deselect the item and set the item pointed to by `*whichItemPtr` to 0. Once this has been done, the next time through, no item selection will be indicated.

```
else if ( *whichItemPtr > 0 )
{
    r = *menuRectPtr;
    r.top += ((*whichItemPtr-1) * (MARGIN + maxV));
    r.bottom = r.top + maxV + MARGIN;
    InvertRect( &r );
    *whichItemPtr = 0;
}
break;
```

When the program receives the `mSizeMsg` message, it calls `GetNumPicts()` to retrieve the first `PICT` ID and the number of `PICT`s. It then calls `CalcMaxHV()` to calculate the height and width of each menu item. Next, the program sets the `menuWidth` and `menuHeight` field of the menu data structure to the desired size for the menu rectangle. This message is received before the draw message.

```
    case mSizeMsg:
        GetNumPicts( theMenu, &PICTResID, &numPicts );
        CalcMaxHV( PICTResID, numPicts, &maxH, &maxV );
        (**theMenu).menuWidth = maxH + 2 * MARGIN;
        (**theMenu).menuHeight = (maxV + MARGIN) *
                                        numPicts;
        break;
    }
}
```

`CenterPict()` is identical to the routine used in ShowPICT in Volume I.

```
/*************************** CenterPict *********/

CenterPict( thePicture, myRectPtr )
PicHandle   thePicture;
Rect        *myRectPtr;
{
```

```
    Rect    windRect, pictureRect;

    windRect = *myRectPtr;
    pictureRect = (**( thePicture )).picFrame;
    myRectPtr->top = (windRect.bottom - windRect.top -
                    (pictureRect.bottom - pictureRect.top))
        / 2 + windRect.top;
    myRectPtr->bottom = myRectPtr->top + (pictureRect.bottom -
                                        pictureRect.top);
    myRectPtr->left = (windRect.right - windRect.left -
                    (pictureRect.right - pictureRect.left))
        / 2 + windRect.left;
    myRectPtr->right = myRectPtr->left + (pictureRect.right -
                                        pictureRect.left);
}
```

CalcMaxHV() looks at the width and height of each PICT and returns the height of the tallest PICT and the width of the widest PICT.

```
/*************************************************************
*   CalcMaxHV  ***/

CalcMaxHV( PICTResID, numPicts, hPtr, vPtr )
short      PICTResID, numPicts, *hPtr, *vPtr;
{
    short      i;
    Rect       r;
    PicHandle  myPicture;

    *hPtr = 0;
    *vPtr = 0;
    for ( i=0; i<numPicts; i++ )
    {
        myPicture = GetPicture( PICTResID + i );
        r = (**myPicture).picFrame;

        if ( r.bottom - r.top > *vPtr )
            *vPtr = r.bottom - r.top;
        if ( r.right - r.left > *hPtr )
            *hPtr = r.right - r.left;
    }
}
```

GetNumPicts() returns the first two bytes of the enableFlags field as the base PICT resource ID and the second two bytes of the enableFlags field as the number of PICT resources.

```
/****************************************************
*   GetNumPicts  ***/

GetNumPicts( theMenu, baseIDPtr, numPictsPtr )
MenuHandle theMenu;
short       *baseIDPtr, *numPictsPtr;
{
    *baseIDPtr = HiWord((**theMenu).enableFlags);
    *numPictsPtr = LoWord((**theMenu).enableFlags);
}
```

Here's a tip for you pop-up menu programmers. *Macintosh Programming Primer, Volume I,* Chapter 5 showed you how to add pop-up menus to your own programs. When Apple added pop-up menus to the Toolbox, the company also added a new message to the list of standard MDEF messages. The message mPopUpMsg asks your MDEF to calculate the menu rectangle of your pop-up. Note the difference between mPopUpMsg and mSizeMsg, which asks your MDEF to calculate the height and width of your menu. Read about the mPopUpMsg in *Inside Macintosh, Volume 5,* page 248.

If you are going to write your own MDEF, you'll want to add scrolling capabilities. This MDEF won't work properly if there are more PICTs than will fit on the Macintosh screen. Adding pop-up and scrolling features to your MDEF can get pretty complex. The listing of MDEF.c found in Appendix B handles both pop-ups and scrolling. If you're going to develop your own MDEF, start with the listing in Appendix B.

Dialog Filter Procedures

The final topic addressed in this chapter is that of filter procedures, specifically those for dialog boxes. What exactly is a filter procedure (affectionately known as a **filter proc**)? A filter proc is a procedure or function you write, called repeatedly by the Toolbox to filter events that are normally not accessible to you.

For example, consider the two dialogs shown in Figure 3.33. Both dialogs allow the user to enter a password. The dialog on the left does not make use of a filter proc. As the user types his or her password, the characters appear normally.

The dialog on the right uses a filter proc. Before `ModalDialog()` processes an event, it calls the filter proc, passing the event to the filter proc as a parameter. If the event was a `keyDown`, the filter proc saves the character typed in a global string variable, then substitutes the • character for the typed character in the `EventRecord`. When the filter proc returns to `ModalDialog()`, the event looks like a `keyDown` with a character of •. `ModalDialog()` processes the event as usual, and the • appears instead of the typed character.

The final program for this chapter is a simple filter proc that works with the dialog box pictured in Figure 3.34. In this dialog loop, before the filter proc calls `ModalDialog()`, it checks the contents of the editable text field. If the field is empty, the filter proc dims the OK button. If the field isn't empty, the filter proc enables the OK button.

Figure 3.33 Dialogs with echoed and filtered password fields.

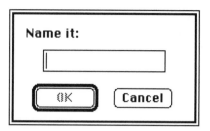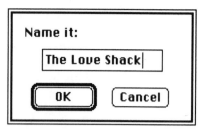

Figure 3.34   The Name it dialog box, with the OK button disabled and enabled.

ModalDialog() calls this filter proc before it processes an event. Each time it gets called, the filter proc checks to see if either the Enter key or the Carriage Return was pressed. If one of these keys was pressed and the text field is empty, the filter proc tells ModalDialog() to ignore the event. To the user, this means that his or her keyDown was ignored. This makes sense, because the OK button was dimmed when the key was pressed.

If the field wasn't empty when the user pressed Enter or Carriage Return, the filter proc tells ModalDialog() that the OK button was pressed. ModalDialog() returns to the filter proc, telling it that the OK button was pressed (otherwise ignoring the event).

> Why go to the bother of writing a filter proc, when you could just enable and disable the button inside the dialog loop? Good question. The trouble is, ModalDialog() doesn't check the state of the OK button when it receives a Carriage Return or Enter keyDown. Even if the OK button is disabled when an Enter or Carriage Return is pressed, ModalDialog() will tell the filter proc that the OK button (actually, item #1) was pressed. Try it for yourself.

Creating the DLOG Resources

Create a new folder in your development folder called **DLOG ƒ**. Using ResEdit, create a new file in the DLOG ƒ folder called **DLOG.π.rsrc**. You'll create two resources in **DLOG.π.rsrc**, a DLOG and a DITL.

Create a DLOG with a resource ID of 400 according to the specifications in Figure 3.35.

Next, create a DITL with a resource ID of 400. The DITL will have four items. Build them according to the specifications in Figures 3.36, 3.37, 3.38, and 3.39.

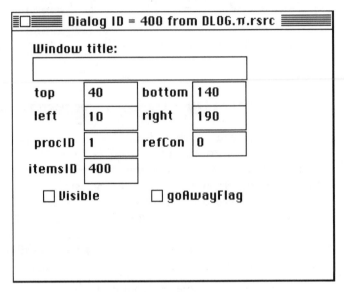

Figure 3.35 Specifications for DLOG 400.

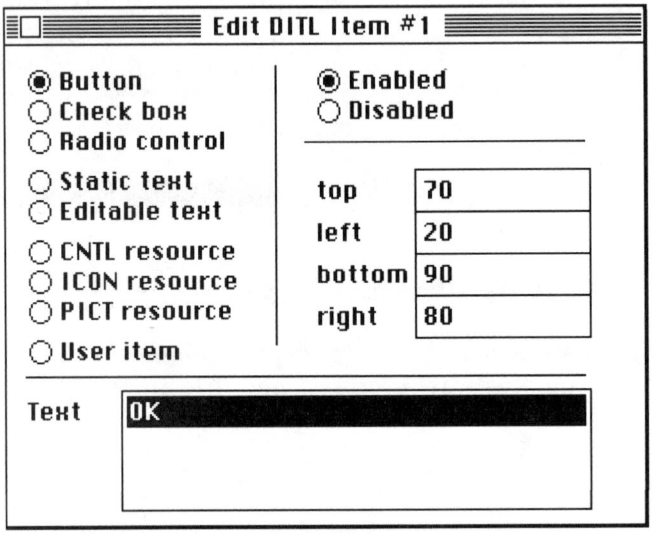

Figure 3.36 DITL Item #1.

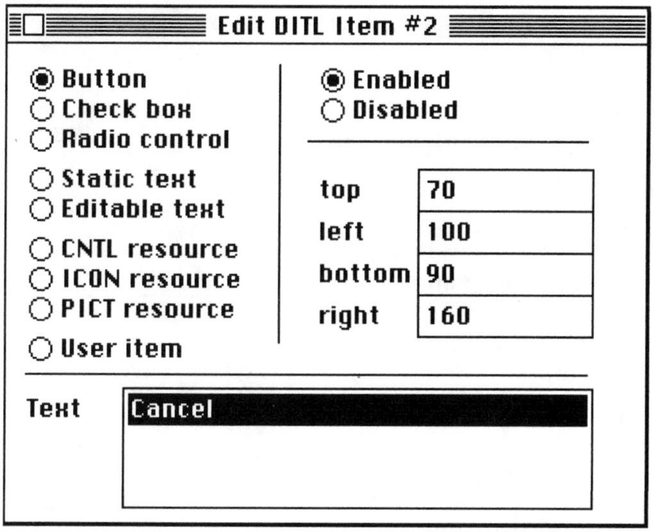

Edit DITL Item #2

- ⦿ Button
- ◯ Check box
- ◯ Radio control
- ◯ Static text
- ◯ Editable text
- ◯ CNTL resource
- ◯ ICON resource
- ◯ PICT resource
- ◯ User item

- ⦿ Enabled
- ◯ Disabled

top	70
left	100
bottom	90
right	160

Text Cancel

Figure 3.37 DITL Item #2.

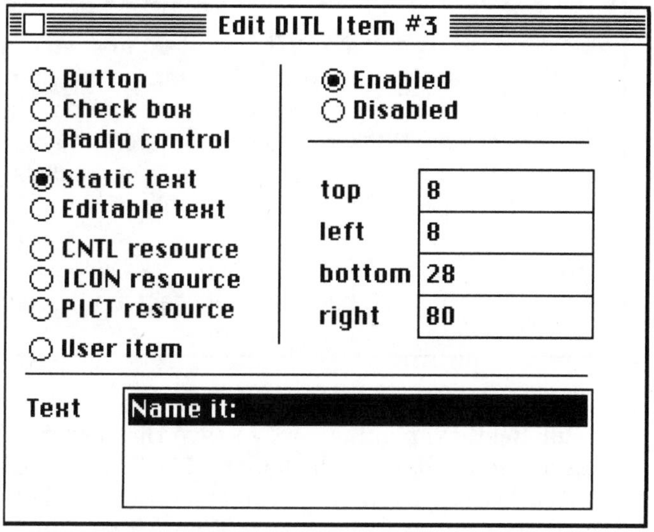

Edit DITL Item #3

- ◯ Button
- ◯ Check box
- ◯ Radio control
- ⦿ Static text
- ◯ Editable text
- ◯ CNTL resource
- ◯ ICON resource
- ◯ PICT resource
- ◯ User item

- ⦿ Enabled
- ◯ Disabled

top	8
left	8
bottom	28
right	80

Text Name it:

Figure 3.38 DITL Item #3.

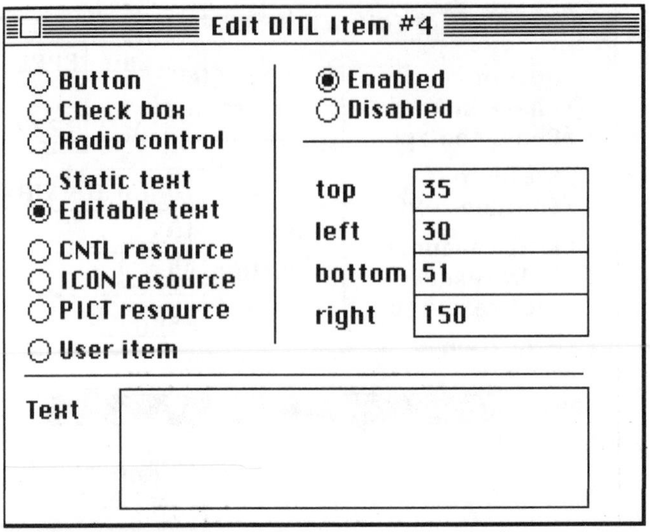

Figure 3.39   D I T L Item #4.

Both the DLOG and the DITL should be marked as purgeable (click on the purgeable check box in the Get Info window of each). When a dialog and its items are loaded, the Dialog Manager makes a copy of each. If the two resources aren't marked as purgeable, they'll hang around until the program exits (unless you release the resource first with ReleaseResource()).

Note that DisposDialog() disposes the Dialog Manager's copy of the DLOG and DITL and does not affect the resource itself.

Quit ResEdit, making sure to save the resources you just created. Create a new project in the folder DLOG ƒ called **DLOG.π**. Select Set Project Type... from the Project menu and set the project type according to the specifications in Figure 3.40.

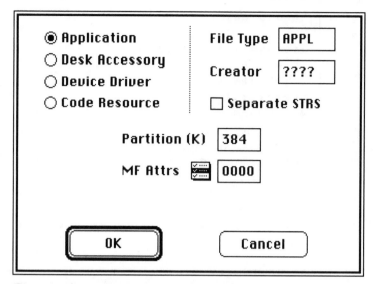

Figure 3.40 Set Project Type... dialog box.

Add MacTraps to the project. Next, select New from the File menu to create a new source code window. Save the window as **DLOG.c** and add it to the project. Enter the following source code:

```
#define BASE_RES_ID            400
#define NIL_POINTER            0L
#define MOVE_TO_FRONT          -1L
#define REMOVE_ALL_EVENTS      0

#define OK_ITEM                1
#define CANCEL_ITEM            2
#define TEXT_ITEM              4

#define TE_ENTER_KEY           3
#define TE_TAB_CHAR            9
#define TE_CARRIAGE_RETURN     13

pascal  Boolean DLOGFilter();

main()
{
```

```
    DialogPtr    theDialog;
    Boolean      done;
    int          itemHit, itemType;
    Handle       OKHandle, textHandle;
    Rect         itemRect;
    Str255       theText;

    ToolBoxInit();

    theDialog = GetNewDialog( BASE_RES_ID, NIL_POINTER,
                              MOVE_TO_FRONT );
    GetDItem( theDialog, OK_ITEM, &itemType, &OKHandle,
            &itemRect );
    GetDItem( theDialog, TEXT_ITEM, &itemType, &textHandle,
            &itemRect );

    CenterDialog( theDialog );
    ShowWindow( theDialog );
    SetPort( theDialog );
    DrawOKButton( theDialog );

    done = FALSE;
    while ( ! done )
    {
        GetIText( textHandle, &theText );
        if ( theText[ 0 ] == 0 )
            HiliteControl( OKHandle, 255 );
        else
            HiliteControl( OKHandle, 0 );
        ModalDialog( DLOGFilter, &itemHit );
        done = ( (itemHit == OK_ITEM) || (itemHit ==
                CANCEL_ITEM) );
    }
}


/********************************** ToolBoxInit */

ToolBoxInit()
{
    InitGraf( &thePort );
    InitFonts();
    FlushEvents( everyEvent, REMOVE_ALL_EVENTS );
```

```
    InitWindows();
    InitMenus();
    TEInit();
    InitDialogs( NIL_POINTER );
    InitCursor();
}


/****************************************** DLOGFilter  *****/

pascal Boolean DLOGFilter( theDialog, e, iPtr )
DialogPtr   theDialog;
EventRecord*e;
int         *iPtr;
{
    int         itemType;
    Rect        itemRect;
    Handle      item;
    Str255      tempStr;
    char        theChar;

    GetDItem( theDialog, TEXT_ITEM, &itemType, &item,
            &itemRect );
    GetIText( item, &tempStr );

    if (e->what == keyDown)
    {
        theChar = (e->message & charCodeMask);
        if ( (theChar == TE_CARRIAGE_RETURN) || (theChar ==
            TE_ENTER_KEY) )
        {
            if ( tempStr[ 0 ] != 0 )
            {
                *iPtr = OK_ITEM;
                GetDItem( theDialog, OK_ITEM, &itemType, &item,
                        &itemRect );
                HiliteControl( item, 1 );
                return( TRUE );
            }
            else
            {
```

```
                    *iPtr = TEXT_ITEM;
                    return( TRUE );
                }
            }
        }
    return( FALSE );
}


/*************************************** DrawOKButton *****/

DrawOKButton( theDialog )
DialogPtr  theDialog;
{
    int         itemType;
    Rect        itemRect;
    Handle      item;
    GrafPtr     oldPort;

    GetDItem(theDialog, OK_ITEM, &itemType, &item, &itemRect);
    GetPort( &oldPort );
    SetPort( theDialog );

    PenSize( 3, 3 );
    InsetRect( &itemRect, -4, -4 );
    FrameRoundRect( &itemRect, 16, 16 );
    PenNormal();

    SetPort( oldPort );
}


/*************************************** CenterDialog *****/

CenterDialog( theDialog )
DialogPtr  theDialog;
{
    Rect        r;
    int         width, height, sWidth, sHeight, h, v;

    r = theDialog->portRect;
```

```
width = r.right - r.left;
height = r.bottom - r.top;

sWidth = screenBits.bounds.right - screenBits.bounds.left;
sHeight = screenBits.bounds.bottom - screenBits.
          bounds.top;

h = (sWidth - width) / 2;
v = (sHeight - height) / 2;

MoveWindow( theDialog, h, v, FALSE );
}
```

When you have entered and saved the code, select Run from the Project menu. Once you get the source to compile, you should see something similar to Figure 3.34. Type some text in the text field. The OK button should light up. Select all the text in the text field and delete it by pressing the Delete or Backspace key. The OK button should dim. While the OK button is dimmed, press the Carriage Return. Nothing should happen. Type in some text, enabling the OK button. Press the Carriage Return. The dialog box should exit with the OK button selected.

Walking Through the DLOG Source Code

This section takes a look at the source code. DLOG.c starts with some pretty standard #defines. This program won't need many of the standard #defines because it does not include things like an event loop and a menu bar.

```
#define BASE_RES_ID          400
#define NIL_POINTER          0L
#define MOVE_TO_FRONT        -1L
#define REMOVE_ALL_EVENTS    0
```

OK_ITEM, CANCEL_ITEM, and TEXT_ITEM represent the DITL item numbers of the two buttons and the text field.

```
#define OK_ITEM              1
#define CANCEL_ITEM          2
#define TEXT_ITEM            4
```

TE_ENTER_KEY, TE_TAB_CHAR, and TE_CARRIAGE_
RETURN represent the character codes for the Enter key, the Tab key,
and the Carriage Return key.

```
#define TE_ENTER_KEY            3
#define TE_TAB_CHAR             9
#define TE_CARRIAGE_RETURN     13
```

The Toolbox routine ModalDialog() is described on page 415, of
Inside Macintosh, Volume I. Take a minute to look at the description
of the filterProc parameter. Basically, the filter proc is a
FUNCTION that returns a BOOLEAN. Following the rules established
in this book, this filter proc must be declared as type pascal
because it will be called by the Toolbox. It must be declared as type
Boolean because the FUNCTION returns a BOOLEAN.

```
pascal      Boolean       DLOGFilter();

main()
{
    DialogPtr    theDialog;
    Boolean      done;
    int          itemHit, itemType;
    Handle       OKHandle, textHandle;
    Rect         itemRect;
    Str255       theText;

    ToolBoxInit();
```

After initializing the Toolbox, the filter proc loads the DLOG from
the resource file. Next, it uses GetDItem() to get a handle to the
OK button and a handle to the editable text item.

```
    theDialog = GetNewDialog( BASE_RES_ID,
                NIL_POINTER, MOVE_TO_FRONT );
    GetDItem( theDialog, OK_ITEM, &itemType,
            &OKHandle, &itemRect );
    GetDItem( theDialog, TEXT_ITEM, &itemType,
            &textHandle, &itemRect );
```

CenterDialog() takes a DialogPtr as a parameter and
centers it on the main screen. After the dialog window is centered,
visible, and the current port, a ring is drawn around the OK button
with DrawOKButton().

```
CenterDialog( theDialog );
ShowWindow( theDialog );
SetPort( theDialog );
DrawOKButton( theDialog );
```

Now that the dialog is all set up, it's time to enter the dialog loop. If the text field is empty, the filter proc dims the button; otherwise, it enables the button.

```
done = FALSE;
while ( ! done )
{
        GetIText( textHandle, &theText );
        if ( theText[ 0 ] == 0 )
                HiliteControl( OKHandle, 255 );
        else
                HiliteControl( OKHandle, 0 );
```

When the filter proc calls `ModalDialog()`, it passes it a pointer to the filter proc. The filter proc drops out of the loop if either the OK or the Cancel button was pressed.

```
        ModalDialog( DLOGFilter, &itemHit );
        done = ( (itemHit == OK_ITEM) ||
                (itemHit == CANCEL_ITEM) );
    }
}
```

There's nothing new about `ToolBoxInit()`.

```
/********************************* ToolBoxInit
*/

ToolBoxInit()
{
    InitGraf( &thePort );
    InitFonts();
    FlushEvents( everyEvent, REMOVE_ALL_EVENTS );
    InitWindows();
    InitMenus();
    TEInit();
    InitDialogs( NIL_POINTER );
    InitCursor();
}
```

Filter procs take three parameters. The first is a `DialogPtr`, pointing to the dialog being filtered. Second is a pointer to the `EventRecord` being processed. This parameter is used here to decide whether an Enter or Carriage Return `keyDown` has occurred. The third parameter is a pointer to the item in which the event occurred. This parameter will be changed only if an Enter or Carriage Return `keyDown` is received.

```
/****************************DLOGFilter  ****/

pascal      Boolean      DLOGFilter( theDialog, e, iPtr )
DialogPtr   theDialog;
EventRecord*e;
int         *iPtr;

        int         itemType;
        Rect        itemRect;
        Handle      item;
        Str255      tempStr;
        char        theChar;
```

First, the filter proc gets a handle to the text field, and then it retrieves the text in `tempStr`.

```
GetDItem( theDialog, TEXT_ITEM, &itemType, &item, &itemRect );
GetIText( item, &tempStr );
```

If the event was a `keyDown`, check for either a Carriage Return or an Enter key.

```
if (e->what == keyDown)
{
    theChar = (e->message & charCodeMask);
    if ( (theChar == TE_CARRIAGE_RETURN) ||
         (theChar == TE_ENTER_KEY) )
    {
```

If a Carriage Return or an Enter key was pressed, check the length of the text field. If the text field is not empty, the filter proc sets the item pointer to the OK button's item number and then highlights (inverts) the OK button (just for effect). If `TRUE` is returned, the filter proc tells `ModalDialog()` to ignore the event and just pass the item number back to the application.

```
                  if ( tempStr[ 0 ] != 0 )
                  {
                          *iPtr = OK_ITEM;
                          GetDItem( theDialog, OK_ITEM, &itemType,
                                  &item, &itemRect );
                          HiliteControl( item, 1 );
                          return( TRUE );
                  }
                  else
```

If the text field was empty, the filter proc sets the item number to the text field (anything other than the Cancel or OK button numbers would do); then it tells `ModalDialog()` to ignore the event by returning `TRUE`.

```
                          {
                                  *iPtr = TEXT_ITEM;
                                  return( TRUE );
                          }
                  }
          }
```

If the event wasn't a Carriage Return or Enter `keyDown`, the filter proc returns `FALSE`, telling `ModalDialog()` to handle the event normally.

```
          return( FALSE );
  }
```

`DrawOKButton()` gets the OK button's `Rect`, sets the `PenSize`, makes the `Rect` 3 pixels larger, and then frames a rounded rectangle around the OK button. Finally, the pen and port are returned to their old values.

```
/*********************************** DrawOKButton *****/

DrawOKButton( theDialog )
DialogPtr   theDialog;
{
        int        itemType;
        Rect       itemRect;
        Handle     item;
        GrafPtr    oldPort;
```

```
        GetDItem( theDialog, OK_ITEM, &itemType, &item, &itemRect
);
        GetPort( &oldPort );
        SetPort( theDialog );

        PenSize( 3, 3 );
        InsetRect( &itemRect, -4, -4 );
        FrameRoundRect( &itemRect, 16, 16 );
        PenNormal();

        SetPort( oldPort );
}
```

CenterDialog() uses MoveWindow() to move the given dialog
so that it is centered with respect to the main screen. The QuickDraw
global screenBits.bounds describes the Rect surrounding the
main display.

```
/********************************** CenterDialog *****/

CenterDialog( theDialog )
DialogPtr    theDialog;
{
        Rect            r;
        int             width, height, sWidth, sHeight, h, v;

        r = theDialog->portRect;

        width =  r.right - r.left;
        height = r.bottom - r.top;

        sWidth = screenBits.bounds.right - screenBits.bounds.
                left;
        sHeight = screenBits.bounds.bottom - screenBits.bounds.
                top;

        h = (sWidth - width) / 2;
        v = (sHeight - height) / 2;

        MoveWindow( theDialog, h, v, FALSE );
}
```

In Review

You've covered a lot in this chapter. You learned how to create various code resources, including one, a `PROC`, that you loaded and ran from inside another program. We also illustrated the proper technique for declaring the main code routines, based on the calling sequence described in *Inside Macintosh*.

The next topic is Color QuickDraw. Chapter 4 shows you how you can add color to your applications while maintaining compatibility with the black-and-white world. It also covers the changes introduced by 32-bit QuickDraw.

4

Color
QuickDraw

*The next topic is Color QuickDraw.
This chapter shows you how to add
color to your applications while
maintaining compatibility with the
black-and-white world. It also covers
the changes introduced by 32-Bit
QuickDraw.*

When the Macintosh was first introduced (way back in 1984) life was simple. Ronald Reagan was in the White House, and Classic QuickDraw was king.

The Evolution of QuickDraw

Classic QuickDraw (also known as plain old QuickDraw) consists of a well-defined set of drawing routines operating on `GrafPort` data structures, using a palette of eight colors (black, white, red, green, blue, cyan, magenta, and yellow). Classic QuickDraw proved more than adequate for the small, black-and-white screens of the early Macintoshes.

In early 1987, things got more complicated. Apple introduced the Macintosh II and, with it, **Color QuickDraw**. Classic QuickDraw's Toolbox is largely black and white. Although you can specify one of the eight Classic QuickDraw colors while drawing, the resulting screen image appears in black and white.

> If your application draws in color using Classic QuickDraw, nonwhite colors will appear black on any machine that doesn't support Color QuickDraw. However, Classic QuickDraw colors will appear in color on both a Color QuickDraw machine and a color printer.

Color QuickDraw allows you to colorize all aspects of the user interface. You can add color to windows, controls, menus, and even the menu bar itself. Every drawing operation supported by Classic QuickDraw can be performed in color by Color QuickDraw.

Classic QuickDraw allows only a single display device. The memory that drives the display (called the **screen buffer**) is part of main memory. Color QuickDraw supports multiple display devices, each driven by its own video card. Color QuickDraw is currently supported by the entire Macintosh II family as well as the SE/30.

Color QuickDraw and Indexed Devices

The images that appear on your monitor are made up of pixels. The Mac Plus screen is 512 pixels wide and 342 pixels tall. Some Macintosh models (such as the Mac Plus and SE) dedicate a portion of their main memory (or RAM) to the 1s and 0s that define each pixel. Other Macs (such as the Mac II and IIcx) store this information in RAM mounted on a separate **video card**. The Mac IIci supports both methods.

Most video cards store pixel information as indices into a color table and thus, are called **indexed devices**. On an indexed device, each index is made up of either 8, 4, 2, or 1 bits. This index size is also known as the device's **depth**. If the video card supports multiple depths, the current depth is determined by the user via the Monitors cdev, found in the Control Panel.

The color table on a video card typically contains 24 bits per entry (8 bits red + 8 bits green + 8 bits blue). This approach lets you choose some small number (256, 16, 4, or 2) of colors out of a large set of possible colors for display at any one time. This cuts the amount of video RAM you need (thus lowering costs), as well as reducing the amount of data you need to send to the card to make changes (thus improving performance).

Color QuickDraw maintains its own structures, separate from the video cards, which contain color information specified by your application. Color QuickDraw's color tables use 48 bits to specify each color (16 bits red + 16 bits green + 16 bits blue):

```
typedef struct RGBColor
{
    unsigned short red;
    unsigned short green;
    unsigned short blue;
} RGBColor;
```

The RGBColor() is tied together with an index to form a ColorSpec:

```
typedef struct ColorSpec
{
    short value;        /*index or other value*/
    RGBColor rgb;
} ColorSpec;
```

126

Finally, a sequential list of `ColorSpec`s (along with some header information) makes up a `ColorTable`:

```
typedef struct ColorTable
{
   long ctSeed;              /*unique identifier for
                               table*/
   short ctFlags;
   short ctSize;             /*number of entries in
                               CTTable*/
   CSpecArray ctTable;       /*array [0..0] of
                               ColorSpec*/
} ColorTable;
```

These three data structures may seem complex, but don't panic. You'll probably never need to work with anything but the `red`, `green`, and `blue` fields of the `RGBColor` data structure.

Each `RGBColor` is 6 bytes (or 48 bits) long. By varying the intensities of red, green, and blue, you can describe 2^{48} possible colors. That's an awful lot of colors. Each of the fields `red`, `green`, and `blue` are **unsigned short**s and can take on values from 0 to 65535.

Figure 4.1 shows a sample color table, starting with 8 bytes of header information, followed by a `CSpecArray` consisting of a list of `value`s and associated `RGBColor`s. When it comes time to paint a particular pixel, Color QuickDraw looks up the pixel's value in the device's color table, retrieving an `RGBColor`. The processor paints the pixel with the `RGBColor` and moves on to the next pixel.

value	red	green	blue
ctSeed		**ctFlags**	**ctSize**

value	red	green	blue
200	0-65535	0-65535	0-65535
125	0-65535	0-65535	0-65535
113	0-65535	0-65535	0-65535
⋮			
36	0-65535	0-65535	0-65535

(CSpecArray)

Figure 4.1 A table of `RGBColor`s.

The CGrafPort and the CWindowPtr

In Classic QuickDraw, you create a new window using
`NewWindow()` or `GetNewWindow()`, both of which return a
`WindowPtr`. In Color QuickDraw, you'll create your color window
using `NewCWindow()` or `GetNewCWindow()`. These routines also
return a `WindowPtr`, which points to a window structure that
contains a `CGrafPort` data structure instead of a `GrafPort` data
structure. Note that a `CGrafPort` and a `GrafPort` are the same
size and that a window created by `NewWindow()` can be used
interchangeably with one created by `NewCWindow()`. This is true as
long as you are not using calls that are specific to Color QuickDraw,
which may not work correctly in a window created by
`NewWindow()`.

Remember, the routines `NewCWindow()` and `GetNewC
Window()` will work only on machines that support Color
QuickDraw. How does your application tell whether the machine it is
currently running on supports Color QuickDraw? That will be
covered in a minute. First, let's talk about drawing in a color window.

Ignoring the Palette Manager for now, the simplest way to draw in
a color window is by using the routines `RGBForeColor()` and
`RGBBackColor()`. Both of these routines take an `RGBColor` as a
parameter, changing the foreground or background color of the
current port to the specified color. The next drawing operation performed on that port will be performed using the new background or
foreground color. Here's a code fragment that will create a new color
window (based on a `WIND` resource) and paint a blue box right in the
middle of it:

```
BlueWindow()
{
    WindowPtr    window;
    RGBColor     myBlueColor;

    window = GetNewCWindow( 400, NIL_POINTER,
                            MOVE_TO_FRONT );
    SetPort( window );
    ShowWindow( window );

    myBlueColor.blue = 65535;
    myBlueColor.red = 0;
    myBlueColor.green = 0;
    RGBForeColor( &myBlueColor );
```

```
        SetRect( &r, 50, 50, 100, 100 );
        PaintRect( &r );
}
```

As you can see, things haven't changed much. The only thing added is a call to `RGBForeColor()` to change the drawing color. Notice that the foreground color was never changed back to its customary black (red=green=blue=0). That was actually pretty impolite. The next drawing operation performed will come out in bright blue. Keep track of your foreground and background colors. You might want always to return the foreground color to black and the background color to white (red=green=blue=65535) before you return from a drawing routine. Either way, be careful with that paintbrush!

What Machine Is the Program Running On?

As was mentioned earlier, you can't always count on Color QuickDraw being available. Fortunately, Apple provides a Toolbox utility that tells your programs whether Color QuickDraw is available. You'll want to add the following routine to your repertoire:

```
Boolean IsColor()
{
    SysEnvRec   mySE;

    SysEnvirons( 2, &mySE );
    return( mySE.hasColorQD );
}
```

`IsColor()` returns `TRUE` if Color QuickDraw is available and returns `FALSE` otherwise. At the heart of `IsColor()` is the call to `SysEnvirons()`. `SysEnvirons()` is described in *Inside Macintosh, Volume V*, Chapter 1. It takes a version number as an input parameter (as of this writing, version number 2 is the latest) and returns a filled-out `SysEnvRec` in return. Here's the declaration of a `SysEnvRec`:

```
typedef struct SysEnvRec
{
        short                   environsVersion;
        short                   machineType;
        short                   systemVersion;
        short                   processor;
        Boolean                 hasFPU;
        Boolean                 hasColorQD;
        short                   keyBoardType;
        short                   atDrvrVersNum;
        short                   sysVRefNum;
} SysEnvRec;
```

The SysEnvRec fields are described on pages 6–8 of *Inside Macintosh, Volume V.*

Having routines like SysEnvirons() and IsColor() doesn't solve all of your problems, though. Suppose you're writing a super-duper graphics application and you want it to run on both a Mac Plus and a Mac II. Your application will have to adopt different techniques for each platform. For example, you won't be able to draw in color on the Mac Plus. On the Mac II, you may not want to draw in color if the Monitors cdev is set to two colors (if the pixel depth is 1).

Although there is no strategy that will work for all applications, here are some tips that might help. First of all, you'll want to divide your approach between color and black and white. You'll have to decide if your application will be responsive to changes in the color environment. For example, a color drawing package had better be aware if the user used the Monitors cdev to turn off color. At the beginning of your program, set a Boolean global to TRUE or FALSE, depending on whether Color QuickDraw is installed. You might want to keep another global around that contains the pixel depth (bits per pixel). Because the user can change the pixel depth on the fly, this last global should be updated whenever there is an updateEvt. Finally, every time your program wants to make a QuickDraw call, check these globals, making one set of calls in a color world and another in a monochrome world. Never, ever call a Color QuickDraw routine if Color QuickDraw is not installed!

Keeping Track of Graphic Devices

The system maintains a separate data structure for each of its graphic devices (typically, one for each monitor). The data structure is called a `GDevice`:

```
typedef struct GDevice
{
        short                   gdRefNum;
        short                   gdID;
        short                   gdType;
        ITabHandle              gdITable;
        short                   gdResPref;
        SProcHndl               gdSearchProc;
        CProcHndl               gdCompProc;
        short                   gdFlags;
        PixMapHandle            gdPMap;
        long                    gdRefCon;
        struct GDevice          **gdNextGD;
        Rect                    gdRect;
        long                    gdMode;
        short                   gdCCBytes;
        short                   gdCCDepth;
        Handle                  gdCCXData;
        Handle                  gdCCXMask;
        long                    gdReserved;
} GDevice, *GDPtr, **GDHandle;
```

The fields of a `GDevice` are described on pages 120–121 of *Inside Macintosh, Volume V.* For the most part, you won't need to access a `GDevice` directly. Color QuickDraw provides several layers on top of the device layer that give you most of what your programs will need to do even the most sophisticated color graphics. Just so you know, however, here's how to access the `GDevices` that describe the graphics devices connected to your Mac.

The function `GetDeviceList()` returns a handle to the first device in Color QuickDraw's device list. `GetNextDevice()` takes a handle to the current device as an argument and returns a handle to the next device. When you get back a `NIL` handle, you've reached the end of the list. `GetMainDevice()` returns a handle to the main device (the device that the menu bar is drawn on). `GetMax Device()` takes a global `Rect` as an argument and returns a

131

handle to the deepest device (the device with the highest number of bits per pixel) that intersects that `Rect` or a NIL handle if the intersection is empty.

The Pixel Image

Classic QuickDraw supports BitMaps; Color QuickDraw supports PixMaps:

```
typedef struct PixMap
{
      Ptr                 baseAddr;
      short               rowBytes;
      Rect                bounds;
      short               pmVersion;
      short               packType;
      long                packSize;
      Fixed               hRes;
      Fixed               vRes;
      short               pixelType;
      short               pixelSize;
      short               cmpCount;
      short               cmpSize;
      long                planeBytes;
      CTabHandle          pmTable;
      long                pmReserved;
} PixMap, *PixMapPtr, **PixMapHandle;
```

A `PixMap`'s `baseAddr` field points to a contiguous block of bytes that define a color image. Each `GDevice` contains a handle to a `PixMap` in the `gdPMap` field. If the `GDevice` is a screen device, the `baseAddr` field of its `PixMap` points to the video RAM containing the pixels for the screen. Although you should not access a device's pixels directly, you can use other fields in the `GDevice`'s `PixMap` to find out a little more about the device. For example, the `pixelSize` field tells you the depth of each pixel in bits. The first program in this chapter, ColorInfo, makes use of this feature. The fields of a `PixMap` are described in detail in *Inside Macintosh, Volume V*, pages 53-54.

By the way, this brings up the point that a device's existence in the device list does not necessarily mean that it is a screen device. It is definitely abnormal to find a nonscreen device in the list, but it is a good idea for you to check this bit using `TestDeviceAttribute()` (*Inside Macintosh, Volume V*, p. 124.):

```
activeScreen = FALSE;

if ( TestDeviceAttribute( myDevice, screenDevice ) )
    if ( TestDeviceAttribute( myDevice, screenActive ) )
        activeScreen = TRUE;

if ( activeScreen )
{
}
```

The First Program: ColorInfo

Let's take a break from the theoretical and have a little fun. The first Color QuickDraw program in this chapter is called **ColorInfo**. ColorInfo starts by checking whether Color QuickDraw is installed. If it is, ColorInfo will step through every installed graphics device, displaying the color table for each device (at that device's current pixel depth) centered on the device's screen.

ColorInfo Resources

Create a folder in your development folder called **ColorInfo ƒ**. Launch ResEdit and create a new file inside the ColorInfo ƒ folder. Call the file **ColorInfo.π.rsrc**. You'll need only two resources for this program — an `ALRT` and a `DITL` for the `ALRT`. The program will use the `ALRT` to display messages to the user.

First, create a new `DITL` with a resource ID of 400. Select New from the File menu to create a new `DITL` item according to the specifications in Figure 4.2.

Next, create another new item according to the specifications in Figure 4.3.

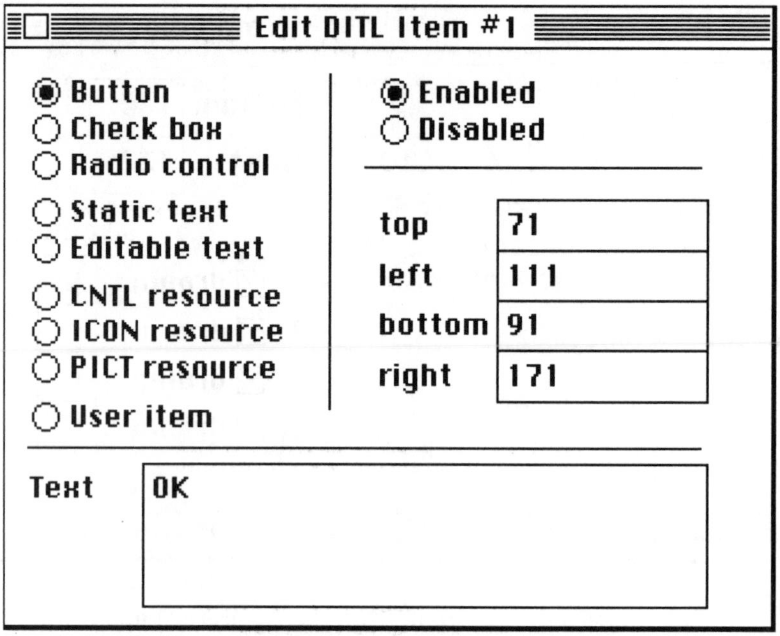

Figure 4.2 Specifications for item 1 of DITL 400.

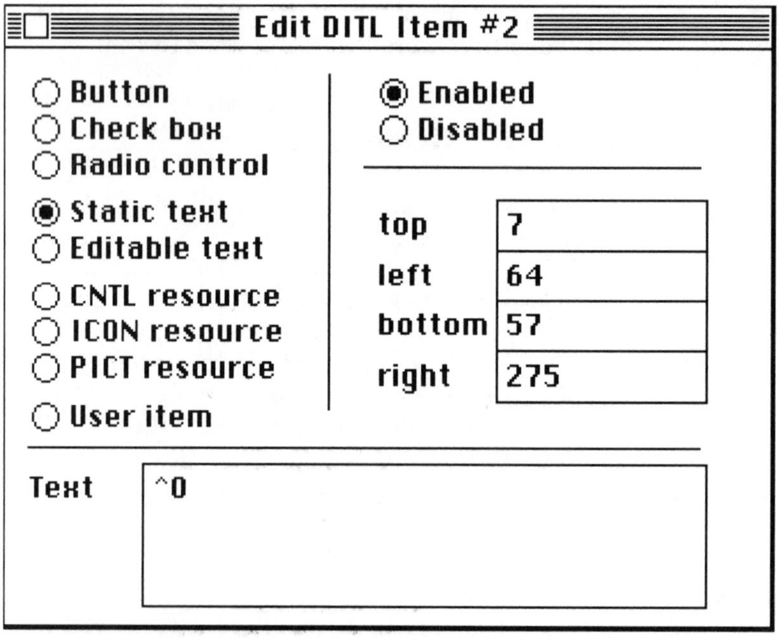

Figure 4.3 Specifications for item 2 of DITL 400.

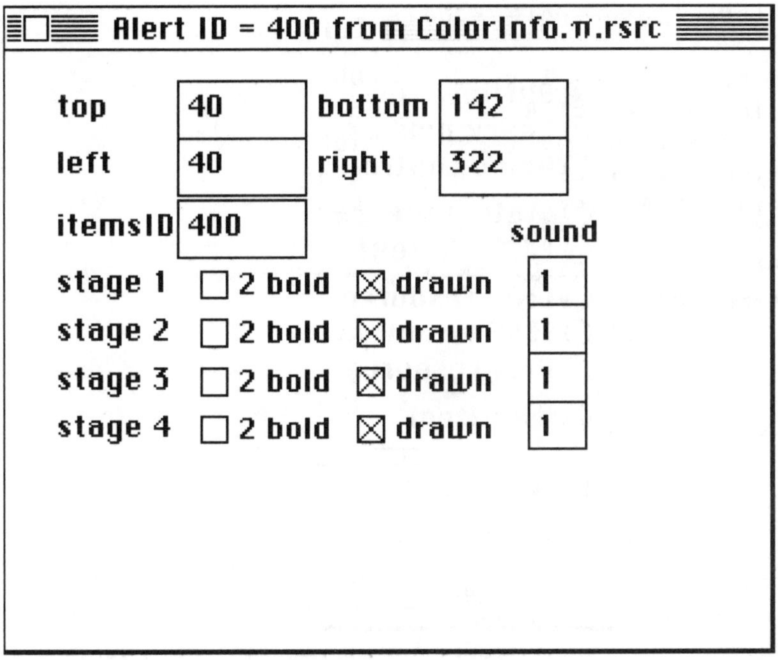

Figure 4.4 Specifications for ALRT 400.

Finally, create an ALRT resource according to the specifications in Figure 4.4. Set the ALRT's resource ID to 400. Excellent! The file ColorInfo.π.rsrc should now contain two resources — an ALRT and a DITL, both with resource IDs of 400. Save your changes and quit ResEdit.

Setting Up the Project

Inside the ColorInfo *f* folder, create a new project called **ColorInfo.π**. Then add MacTraps to the project. Create a new source code file and save it as **ColorInfo.c**. Add ColorInfo.c to the project. Type the following source code into ColorInfo.c:

```
#include "ColorToolbox.h"

#define BASE_RES_ID         400
#define NIL_POINTER         0L
#define NIL_STRING          "\p"
#define INVISIBLE           FALSE
#define NO_GOAWAY           FALSE
#define MOVE_TO_FRONT       (WindowPtr)-1L
#define REMOVE_ALL_EVENTS   0
#define INDEX_DEVICE        TRUE
#define DIRECT_DEVICE       FALSE


Boolean IsColor();


main()
{
    int         pixDepth;
    GDHandle    curDev;
    Rect        bounds;

    ToolBoxInit();

    if ( IsColor() )
    {
        curDev = GetDeviceList();

        while( curDev != NIL_POINTER )
        {
            bounds = (**curDev).gdRect;

            pixDepth = GetPixelDepth( curDev );
            switch( pixDepth )
            {
                case 1:
                    DisplayColors( &bounds, 1, 2, 128,
                                INDEX_DEVICE );
                    break;
                case 2:
                    DisplayColors( &bounds, 2, 2, 128,
                                INDEX_DEVICE );
```

```
                    break;
            case 4:
                DisplayColors( &bounds, 4, 4, 64,
                               INDEX_DEVICE );
                    break;
            case 8:
                DisplayColors( &bounds, 16, 16, 24,
                               INDEX_DEVICE );
                    break;
            default:
                DisplayColors( &bounds, 48, 48, 8,
                               DIRECT_DEVICE );
                    break;
          }
          curDev = GetNextDevice( curDev );
       }
       while( ! Button() ) ;
   }
   else
       DoAlert
         ( "\pThis machine does not support Color QuickDraw!" );
}


/******************************** ToolBoxInit */

ToolBoxInit()
{
    InitGraf( &thePort );
    InitFonts();
    FlushEvents( everyEvent, REMOVE_ALL_EVENTS );
    InitWindows();
    InitMenus();
    TEInit();
    InitDialogs( NIL_POINTER );
    InitCursor();
}
```

```
/****************************** GetPixelDepth ********/

int GetPixelDepth( theDevice )
GDHandle    theDevice;
{
    PixMapHandle    screenPMapH;
    int             pixelDepth;

    screenPMapH = (**theDevice).gdPMap;
    pixelDepth = (**screenPMapH).pixelSize;
    return( pixelDepth );
}


/****************************** IsColor ********/

Boolean IsColor()
{
    SysEnvRec   mySE;

    SysEnvirons( 2, &mySE );
    return( mySE.hasColorQD );
}


/****************************** DisplayColors */

DisplayColors( boundsPtr, width, height, pixPerBox, isIndex )
Rect    *boundsPtr;
int     width, height, pixPerBox;
Boolean isIndex;
{
    Rect        r;
    int         row, col;
    WindowPtr   cWindow;
    RGBColor    curColor;
    HSVColor    hsvColor;
    long        colorNum;

    hsvColor.value = hsvColor.saturation = 65535;

    r.top = 0;
    r.left = 0;
    r.right = width * pixPerBox;
    r.bottom = height * pixPerBox;
```

```
        cWindow = NewCWindow( NIL_POINTER, &r, "\pDevice Colors",
                INVISIBLE, noGrowDocProc, MOVE_TO_FRONT,
                NO_GOAWAY, NIL_POINTER );

        CenterWindow( cWindow, boundsPtr );
        ShowWindow( cWindow );
        SetPort( cWindow );

        for ( row=0; row<height; row++ )
        {
            for ( col=0; col<width; col++ )
            {
                r.top = row * pixPerBox;
                r.left = col * pixPerBox;
                r.bottom = r.top + pixPerBox;
                r.right = r.left + pixPerBox;

                if ( isIndex )
                    Index2Color( (long)(row*width + col), &curColor );
                else
                {
                    colorNum = (long)(row*width + col);
                    hsvColor.hue = 65535 * colorNum / (width * height );
                    HSV2RGB( &hsvColor, &curColor );
                }
                RGBForeColor( &curColor );
                PaintRect( &r );
            }
        }
    }


/********************************* CenterWindow */

CenterWindow( w, boundsPtr )
Rect        *boundsPtr;
WindowPtr   w;
{
    Rect        r;
    int         width, height, sWidth, sHeight, h, v;

    r = w->portRect;
```

```
    width = r.right - r.left;
    height = r.bottom - r.top;

    sWidth = boundsPtr->right - boundsPtr->left;
    sHeight = boundsPtr->bottom - boundsPtr->top;

    h = boundsPtr->left + ((sWidth - width) / 2);
    v = boundsPtr->top + ((sHeight - height) / 2);

    MoveWindow( w, h, v, FALSE );
}


/********************************** DoAlert */

DoAlert( s )
Str255      s;
{
    ParamText( s, NIL_STRING, NIL_STRING, NIL_STRING );
    NoteAlert( BASE_RES_ID, NIL_POINTER );
}
```

Running ColorInfo

OK. Let's run this sucker. Save your changes and select Run from the
Project menu. If the compiler points out any typos or other errors, fix
them.

   If you try to run ColorInfo on a machine that doesn't support Color
QuickDraw (such as a Mac Plus or an SE), the dialog pictured in
Figure 4.5 will appear and the program will exit.

Figure 4.5   The "I don't support Color QuickDraw" Alert.

Figure 4.6   ColorInfo on a 1-bit monitor.

If your machine does support Color QuickDraw, a window will appear centered on each monitor attached to the Macintosh, displaying the colors available on that monitor at the current settings. Figure 4.6 shows the window that appears on a monitor that is set to two colors.

Walking Through the ColorInfo Source Code

The source code starts off by including the file **ColorToolbox.h**. ColorToolbox.h contains some of the basic definitions necessary to call Color QuickDraw.

> Because you'll probably be including this file in lots of your code from now on, you might want to recompile MacHeaders to include ColorToolbox.h. automatically. See the THINK C *User's Guide* for more information.

```
#include "ColorToolbox.h"
```

Most of the program's #defines should be old hat to you by now. The last two, `INDEX_DEVICE` and `DIRECT_DEVICE,` relate to **32-Bit QuickDraw**, an extension to Color QuickDraw that Apple released in 1989. Whereas Color QuickDraw supports only index devices, 32-Bit QuickDraw additionally supports **direct devices**. A direct device holds the actual `RGB color` value in the pixel itself (instead of an index into a color table). This approach lets you choose almost any of the possible colors for display all at one time (the number of possible colors is realistically limited by the number of pixels available). This increases the amount of required video RAM (which makes the system more expensive — but memory prices drop!), as well as increasing the amount of data you need to send to the card to make changes (which makes this method slower than the indexed method). The 32-Bit QuickDraw INIT is available from APDA or comes with System 6.0.5 (or later systems). It is built into the Mac IIci and IIfx (and later machines that use Color QuickDraw).

For the most part, you won't care whether a direct or an indexed device is used. Color QuickDraw hides all that from you. Because this program is trying to draw each color available on a video card (as opposed to a particular `RGBColor`), it needs more information than you ordinarily would. You'll see how the program gets that information in the routine `DisplayColors()`, described a little later.

```
#define BASE_RES_ID         400
#define NIL_POINTER         0L
#define NIL_STRING          "\p"
#define INVISIBLE           FALSE
#define NO_GOAWAY           FALSE
#define MOVE_TO_FRONT       (WindowPtr)-1L
#define REMOVE_ALL_EVENTS   0
#define INDEX_DEVICE        TRUE
#define DIRECT_DEVICE       FALSE
```

Because the routine `IsColor()` returns a `Boolean`, as opposed to an `int`, ColorInfo must declare the routine before it can call it.

```
Boolean IsColor();
```

The program starts, as usual, with a call to `ToolBoxInit()`. Next, it checks to see whether Color QuickDraw is installed.

```
main()
{
    int         pixDepth;
    GDHandle    curDev;
    Rect        bounds;

    ToolBoxInit();
```

If Color QuickDraw is installed, ColorInfo uses `GetDevice List()` to fetch the first device in Color QuickDraw's device list. The "while list" steps through each device in the list.

```
if ( IsColor() )
{
        curDev = GetDeviceList();

        while( curDev != NIL_POINTER )
        {
```

The device's `gdRect` field contains the device's bounding `Rect`, in global coordinates. You can count on the fact that devices won't overlap.

```
                bounds = (**curDev).gdRect;
```

Next, ColorInfo fetches the device's pixel depth and calls `DisplayColors()` with arguments based on this depth. The second, third, and fourth arguments to `DisplayColors()` define the arrangements of color squares that appear on the device. For example, an 8-bit device supports 2^8 or 256 different colors. In this case, `DisplayColors()` will create a window big enough to hold 256 squares arranged in `<2nd argument>` columns and `<3rd argument>` rows, with each square being `<4th argument>` pixels on a side. The program arranges its 8-bit window as a 16-by-16 array of 64 pixel squares. The last argument tells `Display Colors()` whether it's drawing on an index device.

```
pixDepth = GetPixelDepth( curDev );
switch( pixDepth )
{
    case 1:
        DisplayColors( &bounds, 1, 2, 128,
                    INDEX_DEVICE );
```

```
                    break;
                case 2:
                    DisplayColors( &bounds, 2, 2, 128,
                                    INDEX_DEVICE );
                    break;
                case 4:
                    DisplayColors( &bounds, 4, 4, 64,
                                    INDEX_DEVICE );
                    break;
                case 8:
                    DisplayColors( &bounds, 16, 16, 24,
                                    INDEX_DEVICE );
                    break;
                default:
                    DisplayColors( &bounds, 48, 48, 8,
                                    DIRECT_DEVICE );
                    break;
            }
            curDev = GetNextDevice( curDev );
        }
```

Once ColorInfo has drawn a window on each device, it waits for a mouse click before it drops out of main().

```
            while( ! Button() ) ;
        }
```

If Color QuickDraw isn't installed, ColorInfo puts up an alert and drops out of main().

```
    else
        DoAlert( "\pThis machine does not support Color QuickDraw!" );
}
```

No changes here:

```
/******************************** ToolBoxInit */

ToolBoxInit()
{
    InitGraf( &thePort );
    InitFonts();
    FlushEvents( everyEvent, REMOVE_ALL_EVENTS );
```

```
        InitWindows();
        InitMenus();
        TEInit();
        InitDialogs( NIL_POINTER );
        InitCursor();
}
```

GetPixelDepth() returns the pixelSize field from the current device's PixMap.

```
/********************* GetPixelDepth *********/

int GetPixelDepth( theDevice )
GDHandle  theDevice;
{
    PixMapHandle      screenPMapH;
    int               pixelDepth;

    screenPMapH = (**theDevice).gdPMap;
    pixelDepth = (**screenPMapH).pixelSize;
    return( pixelDepth );
}
```

As was described earlier, IsColor() calls SysEnvirons() and returns the hasColorQD field.

```
/*********************** IsColor *********/

Boolean IsColor()
{
    SysEnvRec  mySE;

    SysEnvirons( 2, &mySE );
    return( mySE.hasColorQD );
}
```

The parameters to DisplayColors() were mentioned in the description of main(), above.

```
/****************************** DisplayColors */

DisplayColors( boundsPtr, width, height,
                  pixPerBox, isIndex )
```

```
Rect              *boundsPtr;
int               width, height, pixPerBox;
Boolean           isIndex;
{
    Rect          r;
    int           row, col;
    WindowPtr     cWindow;
    RGBColor      curColor;
    HSVColor      hsvColor;
    long          colorNum;
```

> RGBColor, the basic currency of Color QuickDraw, was described
> earlier. Every RGBColor is based on values of red, green, and
> blue that range from 0 to 65535. Actually many other color models
> describe the exact same colors. One of these, the HSVColor
> model, describes colors in terms of brightness, hue, and saturation.
> By setting brightness and saturation to 65535, you can vary the
> hue and produce a spectrum of only very bright, brilliant colors.
> This approach is illustrated throughout the chapter.
>
> The point of this note is this: Experiment with the different color
> models, building up a set of techniques for the production of
> particular families of colors. A routine exists for translating each
> model's colors to the identical RGBColor.

```
hsvColor.value = hsvColor.saturation = 65535;
```

ColorInfo defines a Rect that's the appropriate size for the
current parameters and then creates a new color window with
NewCWindow(). Notice that cWindow is declared as a WindowPtr.

```
r.top = 0;
r.left = 0;
r.right = width * pixPerBox;
r.bottom = height * pixPerBox;

cWindow = NewCWindow( NIL_POINTER, &r,
                "\pDevice Colors",
```

```
INVISIBLE, noGrowDocProc, MOVE_TO_FRONT,
NO_GOAWAY, NIL_POINTER );
```

Once the window is created, the program centers it in the device's `Rect` with `CenterWindow()`, makes it visible with `ShowWindow()`, and makes it the current port with `SetPort()`.

```
CenterWindow( cWindow, boundsPtr );
ShowWindow( cWindow );
SetPort( cWindow );
```

Next, ColorInfo starts the drawing process. It draws one row at a time, drawing each square in the row before moving on to the next row. The program sets up the `Rect` `r` to define the current square.

```
for ( row=0; row<height; row++ )
{
    for ( col=0; col<width; col++ )
    {
        r.top = row * pixPerBox;
        r.left = col * pixPerBox;
        r.bottom = r.top + pixPerBox;
        r.right = r.left + pixPerBox;
```

If the device is an index device, ColorInfo can fetch the current `RGBColor` by passing an index into `Index2Color()`. On an 8-bit device, the program can pass in an index from 0 to 255.

```
if ( isIndex )
    Index2Color( (long)(row*width
                + col), &curColor );
```

If the device is a direct device, ColorInfo can display virtually any color it wants. This example uses the index to select a bright color. Because the `hue` of an `HSVColor` can range from 0 to 65535, the program divides the range by the total number of color squares requested. It then translates the `hsvColor` to an `RGBColor` via a call to `HSV2RGB()`.

```
        else
        {
            colorNum = (long)(row*width + col);
            hsvColor.hue = 65535 * colorNum / (width * height );
            HSV2RGB( &hsvColor, &curColor );
        }
```

Once an `RGBColor` for the current square has been selected, the program sets the foreground color to that color and draws the `Rect` with `PaintRect()`.

```
                RGBForeColor( &curColor );
                PaintRect( &r );
            }
        }
    }
```

`CenterWindow()` uses `MoveWindow()` to center the specified window in the specified `Rect`. Notice that `MoveWindow()` only moves the window and doesn't change the window's size.

```
/******************************** CenterWindow */

CenterWindow( w, boundsPtr )
Rect        *boundsPtr;
WindowPtr   w;
{
    Rect        r;
    int         width, height, sWidth, sHeight, h, v;

    r = w->portRect;

    width = r.right - r.left;
    height = r.bottom - r.top;

    sWidth = boundsPtr->right - boundsPtr->left;
    sHeight = boundsPtr->bottom - boundsPtr->top;

    h = boundsPtr->left + ((sWidth - width) / 2);
    v = boundsPtr->top + ((sHeight - height) / 2);

    MoveWindow( w, h, v, FALSE );
}
```

DoAlert() displays the specified Pascal string in the program's ALRT, by first passing it as an argument to ParamText(). This routine is used throughout the chapter.

```
/******************************* DoAlert */

DoAlert( s )
Str255      s;
{
    ParamText( s, NIL_STRING, NIL_STRING, NIL_STRING );
    NoteAlert( BASE_RES_ID, NIL_POINTER );
}
```

The Palette Manager

The next program introduces an important companion of Color QuickDraw, the **Palette Manager**. The Palette Manager allows you to build a list of custom colors and attach that list to a specific window. When that window is in the front, the Palette Manager will do everything possible to ensure that those colors are available to the window.

For example, suppose you are using a Mac IIcx with an 8-bit video card and a color monitor. The video card is set at 8 bits, thus supporting 256 different colors (starring the two permanent colors, white, as color 0, and black, as color 255). Now suppose you wanted to display two different windows, one with 200 shades of red and one with 200 shades of green. Your first problem is with the video card's default color table. Odds are, the video card isn't set up with your 200 shades of red. You know it isn't set up with 200 shades of red and 200 shades of green because there's room for only 254 custom colors (not counting black and white).

By using the Palette Manager, you can set up a palette of 200 red colors and a separate palette of 200 green colors. You can then assign the red palette to one window and the green palette to another. When your red window is in front, the Palette Manager makes sure that your 200 shades of red are placed somewhere in the video card's color table. Note that this may mean the deletion of some nonpalette colors from the video card's color table. To access the palette colors, pass the palette color number to either PmForeColor() or PmBack Color() and then make your regular Color QuickDraw calls.

The great thing about the Palette Manager is that you can create 20 different palettes, assign each to a different window, and then sit back and let the Palette Manager do all the hard work of optimizing the device's color table so your frontmost window is drawn with colors as close as possible to your original request.

Using the Palette Manager

Create a new palette by calling either `NewPalette()` or `GetNewPalette()`. `NewPalette()` takes four arguments. The first specifies the number of entries in your palette. The second is a handle to a `ColorTable`, used to initialize your palette. In the example program, `NIL_POINTER` is passed as the second argument. This tells the Palette Manager to set all colors to black. This is a fine approach, as you can step through every entry in a palette, setting the colors individually.

If you are interested in setting up your own color table, the data structure is described in Volume V of *Inside Macintosh*, on the bottom of page 48. Before you try creating a color table, stop and ask yourself, "Could I have used a palette instead?"

Probably the best way to create a color table is by creating a `clut` resource and then loading it with `GetCTable()`. You can create a palette from a color table by calling `CTab2Palette()`. You can also create a color table from a palette by calling `Palette 2CTab()`.

The third argument to `NewPalette()` is `srcUsage`, an `int` that describes how these colors should be used. There are four legal color usage settings. By far, the most useful of these is `pmTolerant`. You will almost always create palettes of tolerant colors.

If the frontmost window requests a tolerant color, the Palette Manager will try to find a color in the color table that matches, within that tolerance (see the tech block below for the tolerance formula). If the Palette Manager can't find a match, it throws the unmatched color into the `ColorTable` and continues. When it finishes, the `ColorTable` will have colors within tolerance for all the front window's colors. The back windows will match as best they can with whatever is there.

Here's something for you math hounds. The Palette Manager computes the difference between two colors as the maximum of these three:

- abs(color1.red - color2.red)

- abs(color1.green - color2.green)

- abs(color1.blue - color2.blue)

A tolerance of 0x5000 will yield a reasonably close color match. Use a tolerance value of 0x0000 for the closest possible color match. All tolerance values greater than 0 and less than 0x1000 are reserved by Apple and shouldn't be used.

You specify the color tolerance via the fourth argument to `NewPalette()`, `srcTolerance`. The three other color usages are `pmCourteous`, `pmAnimated`, and `pmExplicit`. `pmCourteous` colors are there for reference only. You can draw using a `pmCourteous` palette color, but it will never cause the Palette Manager to adjust the color environment.

`pmAnimated` colors are a novelty. If you draw in a particular `pmAnimated` color, you can animate that color using calls to `AnimatePalette()` and `AnimateEntry()`. Animating a particular palette entry will affect every pixel drawn in that color. If you animate a red palette entry to blue, all the pixels drawn in that particular red will instantly (during the next screen refresh) be repainted in the animated color.

`pmExplicit` colors are used to access the video card color table. Colors specified in a `pmExplicit` palette are ignored. The index provided to `PmForeColor()` will cause the forecolor to be set to the corresponding index into the video card's color table. A palette of `pmExplicit` colors along with calls to `PmForeColor()` could have been used in the last program to draw each device's color table.

If you create a palette with `NewPalette()`, each entry in the palette is set to the usage specified in `srcUsage` and the tolerance specified in `srcTolerance`. You can set and get an entry's usage with `SetEntryUsage()` and `GetEntryUsage()`. You can set and get an entry's color with `SetEntryColor()` and `GetEntryColor()`. You can attach a palette to a window with `SetPalette()`. Finally, you can dispose of a palette with `DisposePalette()`.

Palette

The next program, **Palette**, demonstrates the Palette Manager in action. Palette creates three color windows, each with its own palette. Palette demonstrates what happens when multiple palettes vie for a limited number of colors. Each palette consists of 100 colors, for a total of 300 requested colors. In 8-bit mode, only 254 colors available to the Palette Manager (you can't change black and white). This program shows how well the Palette Manager handles both the front window, which should get all its colors, and the back windows, which won't.

Palette Resources

Palette uses the exact same resources as the last program, ColorInfo. Create a folder in your development folder called **Palette ƒ**. Copy the file ColorInfo.π.rsrc into the Palette ƒ folder. Change the name of the resource file to **Palette.π.rsrc**.

Setting Up the Project

Inside the Palette ƒ folder, create a new project called **Palette.π**. Next, add MacTraps to the project. Create a new source code file and save it as **Palette.c**. Add Palette.c to the project. Type the following source code into Palette.c:

```
#include "ColorToolbox.h"

#define BASE_RES_ID         400
#define NIL_POINTER         0L
#define NIL_STRING          "\p"
#define VISIBLE             TRUE
#define HAS_GOAWAY          TRUE
#define MOVE_TO_FRONT       -1L
#define REMOVE_ALL_EVENTS   0
#define MIN_SLEEP           0L
#define NIL_MOUSE_REGION    0L

#define PRECISE_TOLERANCE 0x0000
#define NUM_SQUARES     150


Boolean         IsColor();
WindowPtr       CreateColorWindow();
PaletteHandle   MakeRedPalette(), MakeBrightPalette(),
                MakeGrayPalette();


main()
{
    Point           corner;
    WindowPtr       window;
    PaletteHandle   pal;

    ToolBoxInit();

    if ( ! IsColor() )
        DoAlert( "\pThis machine does not support Color QuickDraw!" );
    else
    {
        corner.h = 10;
        corner.v = 40;
        window = CreateColorWindow( corner, "\pRed Palette" );
        pal = MakeRedPalette();
        SetPalette( window, pal, TRUE );
```

```
            corner.h = 170;
            corner.v = 177;
            window = CreateColorWindow( corner, "\pBright Palette" );
            pal = MakeBrightPalette();
            SetPalette( window, pal, TRUE );

            corner.h = 330;
            corner.v = 40;
            window = CreateColorWindow( corner, "\pGray Palette" );
            pal = MakeGrayPalette();
            SetPalette( window, pal, TRUE );

            DoEventLoop();
    }
}


/********************************* ToolBoxInit */

ToolBoxInit()
{
    InitGraf( &thePort );
    InitFonts();
    FlushEvents( everyEvent, REMOVE_ALL_EVENTS );
    InitWindows();
    InitMenus();
    TEInit();
    InitDialogs( NIL_POINTER );
    InitCursor();
}


/********************************* DoEventLoop */

DoEventLoop()
{
    Boolean         done;
    EventRecord     e;
    short           part;
    WindowPtr       window;

    done = FALSE;
    while ( ! done )
    {
```

```
            WaitNextEvent( everyEvent, &e, MIN_SLEEP, NIL_MOUSE_REGION );

            switch( e.what )
            {
                case mouseDown:
                    part = FindWindow( e.where, &window );
                    if ( part == inGoAway )
                        done = TRUE;
                    else if ( part == inDrag )
                        DragWindow( window, e.where,
                                    &screenBits.bounds );
                    else if ( part == inContent )
                    {
                        if ( window != FrontWindow() )
                            SelectWindow( window );
                    }
                    break;
                case updateEvt:
                    BeginUpdate( (WindowPtr)e.message );
                    SetPort( (WindowPtr)e.message );
                    DrawBullseye();
                    EndUpdate( (WindowPtr)e.message );
                    break;
            }
        }
}


/********************************* DrawBullseye */

DrawBullseye()
{
    int i, center;
    Rect    r;

    center = NUM_SQUARES;

    for ( i=1; i<=NUM_SQUARES; i++ )
    {
```

```
            PmForeColor( i - 1 );
            r.top = center - i;
            r.left = center - i;
            r.bottom = center + i;
            r.right = center + i;

            FrameRect( &r );
    }
}


/***************************** IsColor *********/

Boolean IsColor()
{
    SysEnvRec   mySE;

    SysEnvirons( 2, &mySE );
    return( mySE.hasColorQD );
}


/***************************** MakeRedPalette *********/

PaletteHandle  MakeRedPalette()
{
    RGBColor        c;
    long            i;
    PaletteHandle   redPalette;

    redPalette = NewPalette( NUM_SQUARES, NIL_POINTER,
                        pmTolerant, PRECISE_TOLERANCE );

    c.green = 0;
    c.blue =  0;

    for ( i=0; i<NUM_SQUARES; i++ )
    {
        c.red = (i * 65535) / NUM_SQUARES;
        SetEntryColor( redPalette, i, &c );
    }

    return( redPalette );
}
```

```
/****************************** MakeBrightPalette ********/

PaletteHandle  MakeBrightPalette()
{
    PaletteHandle  brightPalette;
    long           i;
    RGBColor       rgbColor;
    HSVColor       hsvColor;

    brightPalette = NewPalette( NUM_SQUARES, NIL_POINTER,
                              pmTolerant, PRECISE_TOLERANCE );

    hsvColor.value = 65535;
    hsvColor.saturation = 65535;

    for ( i=0; i<NUM_SQUARES; i++ )
    {
        hsvColor.hue = (i * 65535) / NUM_SQUARES;
        HSV2RGB( &hsvColor, &rgbColor );
        SetEntryColor( brightPalette, i, &rgbColor );
    }

    return( brightPalette );
}


/****************************** MakeGrayPalette ********/

PaletteHandle  MakeGrayPalette()
{
    PaletteHandle  grayPalette;
    long           i;
    RGBColor       rgbColor;

    grayPalette = NewPalette( NUM_SQUARES, NIL_POINTER,
                            pmTolerant, PRECISE_TOLERANCE );

    for ( i=0; i<NUM_SQUARES; i++ )
    {
```

```
            rgbColor.red = (i * 65535) / NUM_SQUARES;
            rgbColor.green = rgbColor.red;
            rgbColor.blue = rgbColor.red;
            SetEntryColor( grayPalette, i, &rgbColor );
    }

    return( grayPalette );
}


/******************************** CreateColorWindow */

WindowPtr   CreateColorWindow( corner, title )
Point       corner;
Str255      title;
{
    WindowPtr   cWindow;
    Rect        r;

    SetRect( &r, corner.h, corner.v, corner.h + (2 *
             NUM_SQUARES),
                          corner.v + (2 * NUM_SQUARES) );

    cWindow = NewCWindow( NIL_POINTER, &r, title,
              VISIBLE, noGrowDocProc, MOVE_TO_FRONT,
              HAS_GOAWAY, NIL_POINTER );

    return( cWindow );
}


/******************************** DoAlert */

DoAlert( s )
Str255 s;
{
    ParamText( s, NIL_STRING, NIL_STRING, NIL_STRING );
    NoteAlert( BASE_RES_ID, NIL_POINTER );
}
```

Running Palette

Now it's time to see how it turned out. Save your changes and select Run from the Project menu. If the compiler points out any typos or other errors, track them down and make them right.

Once again, if you try to run Palette on a machine that doesn't support Color QuickDraw (such as a Mac Plus or an SE), the dialog pictured in Figure 4.5 will appear and the program will exit.

Once the program runs, three windows should appear. All three should feature a series of concentric squares, each window painted using a different palette. One window will use a red palette, one a gray palette, and one a palette made up of a range of bright colors.

Click on each window in turn. When a window moves to the front, it should be redrawn using its requested colors. When a window moves towards the back, it also receives an update event and is redrawn. Notice that a window doesn't look quite as nice when it is in back as it does when it is in front. The Palette Manager is doing the best job it can to keep your reds red and your brights bright.

Click on any window's close box to exit Palette. The next section takes a look at the source code.

Walking Through the Palette Source Code

Just as in ColorInfo, the file **ColorToolbox.h** is included in Palette. You should recognize most of the #defines.

```
#include "ColorToolbox.h"

#define  BASE_RES_ID            400
#define  NIL_POINTER            0L
#define  NIL_STRING             "\p"
#define  VISIBLE                TRUE
#define  HAS_GOAWAY             TRUE
#define  MOVE_TO_FRONT          -1L
#define  REMOVE_ALL_EVENTS      0
#define  MIN_SLEEP              0L
#define  NIL_MOUSE_REGION       0L
```

The program creates its palettes with a very precise tolerance requirement. Once you've played with Palette for a while, try changing `PRECISE_TOLERANCE` to `0x1000` and then to `0x5000`.

This should give you a real feeling for palette tolerances. NUM_SQUARES specifies both the number of concentric squares drawn in each window and the size of each window.

```
#define PRECISE_TOLERANCE      0x0000
#define NUM_SQUARES            150
```

```
Boolean         IsColor();
WindowPtr       CreateColorWindow();
PaletteHandle   MakeRedPalette(), MakeBrightPalette(),
                MakeGrayPalette();
```

main() starts by checking for the presence of Color QuickDraw. If it's there, the program continues.

```
main()
{
    Point           corner;
    WindowPtr       window;
    PaletteHandle   pal;

    ToolBoxInit();

    if ( ! IsColor() )
        DoAlert( "\pThis machine does not support Color QuickDraw!" );
```

Palette creates a color window with an upper left corner at corner. It then creates a red palette and attaches the palette to the window.

```
    else
    {
        corner.h = 10;
        corner.v = 40;
        window = CreateColorWindow( corner,
                "\pRed Palette" );
        pal = MakeRedPalette();
        SetPalette( window, pal, TRUE );
```

Next, the program creates a second color window. It creates a palette of bright colors and attaches it to this second window.

```
          corner.h = 170;
          corner.v = 177;
          window = CreateColorWindow( corner,
                   "\pBright Palette" );
          pal = MakeBrightPalette();
          SetPalette( window, pal, TRUE );
```

Finally, Palette creates a third window. It creates a palette of grays and attaches the palette to this third window. The program then drops into its event loop.

```
          corner.h = 330;
          corner.v = 40;
          window = CreateColorWindow( corner,
                   "\pGray Palette" );
          pal = MakeGrayPalette();
          SetPalette( window, pal, TRUE );

          DoEventLoop();
     }
}
```

The next section is the same as it ever was.

```
/****************************** ToolBoxInit */

ToolBoxInit()
{
    InitGraf( &thePort );
    InitFonts();
    FlushEvents( everyEvent, REMOVE_ALL_EVENTS );
    InitWindows();
    InitMenus();
    TEInit();
    InitDialogs( NIL_POINTER );
    InitCursor();
}
```

The program's simple event loop handles only two events.

```
/********************************* DoEventLoop */

DoEventLoop()
{
    Boolean        done;
    EventRecord    e;
    short          part;
    WindowPtr      window;

    done = FALSE;
    while ( ! done )
    {
        WaitNextEvent( everyEvent, &e, MIN_SLEEP, NIL_MOUSE_REGION );

        switch( e.what )
        {
```

A mouseDown in any window's close box exits the program. A mouseDown in a window's drag region lets you drag the window around the screen. A mouseDown in a window's content region brings that window to the front.

```
            case mouseDown:
                part = FindWindow( e.where, &window );
                if ( part == inGoAway )
                    done = TRUE;
                else if ( part == inDrag )
                    DragWindow( window, e.where,
                            &screenBits.bounds );
                else if ( part == inContent )
                {
                    if ( window != FrontWindow() )
                        SelectWindow( window );
                }
                break;
```

When the program receives an updateEvt for a window, it simply redraws the window's contents.

```
case updateEvt:
   BeginUpdate( (WindowPtr)e.message );
   SetPort( (WindowPtr)e.message );
   DrawBullseye();
   EndUpdate( (WindowPtr)e.message );
   break;
   }
   }
}
```

DrawBullseye() draws a series of NUM_SQUARES concentric squares in the current port. The first square is drawn with the first palette entry as the foreground color, the second square is drawn using the second palette entry, etc. Note that this works because each palette was created with NUM_SQUARES entries. Note also that the program changed the foreground color with PmForeColor().

```
/***************************** DrawBullseye */

DrawBullseye()
{
    int   i, center;
    Rect  r;

    center = NUM_SQUARES;

    for ( i=1; i<=NUM_SQUARES; i++ )
    {
        PmForeColor( i - 1 );
        r.top = center - i;
        r.left = center - i;
        r.bottom = center + i;
        r.right = center + i;

        FrameRect( &r );
    }
}
```

IsColor() is the same as its counterpart in ColorInfo.

```
/*************************** IsColor *********/

Boolean IsColor()
{
    SysEnvRec   mySE;

    SysEnvirons( 2, &mySE );
    return( mySE.hasColorQD );
}
```

The next three routines are almost identical. MakeRed
Palette() creates a new palette with a call to NewPalette().
Each entry is a tolerant color with a tolerance of PRECISE_
TOLERANCE. Each color in the palette has a green and a blue value
of 0. The red values range from 0 in the first entry to just below
65535 on the final entry.

```
/****************************** MakeRedPalette *********/

PaletteHandle  MakeRedPalette()
{
    RGBColor        c;
    long            i;
    PaletteHandle   redPalette;

    redPalette = NewPalette( NUM_SQUARES, NIL_POINTER,
                        pmTolerant, PRECISE_TOLERANCE );

    c.green = 0;
    c.blue = 0;

    for ( i=0; i<NUM_SQUARES; i++ )
    {
        c.red = (i * 65535) / NUM_SQUARES;
        SetEntryColor( redPalette, i, &c );
    }

    return( redPalette );
}
```

The bright palette was created using the HSV color model described in ColorInfo. Instead of ranging the red colors, the program sets the value and saturation to 65535 and ranges the hues, producing only bright, saturated colors.

```
/***************************** MakeBrightPalette ********/

PaletteHandle  MakeBrightPalette()
{
    PaletteHandle   brightPalette;
    long            i;
    RGBColor        rgbColor;
    HSVColor        hsvColor;

    brightPalette = NewPalette( NUM_SQUARES, NIL_POINTER,
                          pmTolerant, PRECISE_TOLERANCE );

    hsvColor.value = 65535;
    hsvColor.saturation = 65535;

    for ( i=0; i<NUM_SQUARES; i++ )
    {
        hsvColor.hue = (i * 65535) / NUM_SQUARES;
        HSV2RGB( &hsvColor, &rgbColor );
        SetEntryColor( brightPalette, i, &rgbColor );
    }

    return( brightPalette );
}
```

The gray palette was created by ranging the red, green, and blue colors together, always keeping them equal. As in the previous two functions, the PaletteHandle is returned as the function value.

```
/****************************** MakeGrayPalette ********/

PaletteHandle  MakeGrayPalette()
{
    PaletteHandle   grayPalette;
    long            i;
    RGBColor        rgbColor;
```

```
    grayPalette = NewPalette( NUM_SQUARES, NIL_POINTER,
                        pmTolerant, PRECISE_TOLERANCE );

    for ( i=0; i<NUM_SQUARES; i++ )
    {
        rgbColor.red = (i * 65535) / NUM_SQUARES;
        rgbColor.green = rgbColor.red;
        rgbColor.blue = rgbColor.red;
        SetEntryColor( grayPalette, i, &rgbColor );
    }

    return( grayPalette );
}
```

CreateColorWindow() uses NewCWindow() to create a color window. The window is positioned with an upper left corner at corner. The width and height are both equal to 2 * NUM_SQUARES. As in ColorInfo, the WindowPtr is returned as the function value.

```
/********************************** CreateColorWindow */

WindowPtr    CreateColorWindow( corner, title )
Point        corner;
Str255       title;
{
    WindowPtr  cWindow;
    Rect       r;

    SetRect( &r, corner.h, corner.v, corner.h + (2 * NUM_SQUARES),
            corner.v + (2 * NUM_SQUARES) );

    cWindow = NewCWindow( NIL_POINTER, &r, title,
            VISIBLE, noGrowDocProc, MOVE_TO_FRONT,
            HAS_GOAWAY, NIL_POINTER );

    return( cWindow );
}
```

DoAlert() is the same as its counterpart in ColorInfo.

```
/******************************** DoAlert */

DoAlert( s )
Str255 s;
{
    ParamText( s, NIL_STRING, NIL_STRING, NIL_STRING );
    NoteAlert( BASE_RES_ID, NIL_POINTER );
}
```

Using the Arithmetic Color Modes

Classic QuickDraw supports eight transfer modes: Copy, Or, Xor, Bic, notCopy, notOr, notXor, and notBic. These transfer modes apply to all of the QuickDraw calls, most notably to the routine for copying BitMaps, CopyBits() and to the routines PenMode() and TextMode(). Color QuickDraw has introduced eight new transfer modes: blend, addPin, addOver, subPin, transparent, adMax, subOver, and adMin. These modes don't replace the Classic QuickDraw transfer modes, but rather supplement them. Each of these new modes is described in *Inside Macintosh, Volume V*, pages 59-60.

Another change brought on by the introduction of Color QuickDraw is the ability of CopyBits to copy PixMaps as well as BitMaps. Because color windows store their pixels in a PixMap, you can use CopyBits() to copy rectangular areas from a color window to a plain window and vice versa.

The next program, **ColorTutor**, demonstrates the use of CopyBits() with both the old and the new transfer modes.

ColorTutor: Hands-on Color

To truly understand the QuickDraw transfer modes, you have to see them in action. ColorTutor, demonstrates all sixteen transfer modes in conjunction with CopyBits(). Figure 4.7 shows a black-and-white rendering of the ColorTutor window.

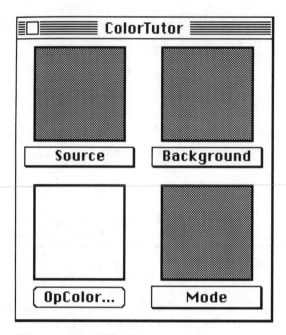

Figure 4.7   ColorTutor in action.

ColorTutor builds a window divided into four areas. In the upper left corner is the **source pane**, with the Source pop-up menu underneath it. In the upper right is the **background pane**, with the Background pop-up menu underneath it. In the lower left corner is the **opColor pane**, with the OpColor... pushbutton menu underneath it. In the lower right corner is the **destination** pane, with the Mode pop-up menu underneath it.

ColorTutor uses `CopyBits()` to copy the background pane onto the destination pane, using the `srcCopy` transfer mode. Next, ColorTutor uses `CopyBits()` to copy the source pane onto the destination pane, using the mode selected from the Mode pop-up menu. This process is repeated any time an `updateEvt` occurs, or any time a change is made to any of the settings.

Three of the transfer modes (`blend`, `addPin`, and `subPin`) require an `RGBColor` called the `opColor`, which you set by pressing the OpColor... pushbutton. Pressing this button brings up the Macintosh Color Picker, a piece of the Toolbox that allows you to specify any `RGBColor`. The Color Picker is documented in *Inside Macintosh, Volume V*, Chapter 8.

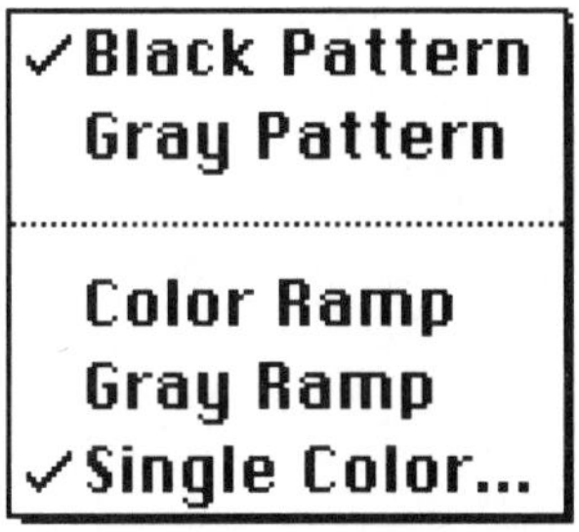

Figure 4.8 The Source and Background pop-up menu.

You can change both the source and the background panes in several ways by selecting from the Source or Background pop-up menu shown in Figure 4.8.

Selecting Black Pattern or Gray Pattern will draw the source or background after first setting the pen pattern to black or gray. Selecting Color Ramp draws a range of bright colors instead of just a single color. Selecting Gray Ramp draws a range of grays instead of just a single color. Selecting Single Color... brings up the Macintosh Color Picker and draws the selected RGBColor.

ColorTutor Resources

ColorTutor uses the same resources as the previous program, as well as a few others. Create a folder in your development folder called **ColorTutor ƒ**. Copy the file Palette.π.rsrc into the ColorTutor ƒ folder. Change the name of the resource file to **ColorTutor.π.rsrc**. Open ColorTutor.π.rsrc using ResEdit.

You'll need to create two MENUs to add to your resource file. MENU 400 has the items in Figure 4.8. Don't forget to give the line its own item. Set MenuID to 400, ProcID to 0, and the Enable Flags to $FFFFFFF7. You won't need a Title. Don't use any mark characters or command key equivalents. Set all the Styles to $00.

The second MENU has a resource ID of 401 and has the items in Figure 4.9. Again, don't forget to give the line its own item. Set the MenuID to 401, ProcID to 0, and the Enable Flags to $FFFFFDFF. You won't need a Title. Don't use any mark characters or command key equivalents. Set all the Styles to $00.

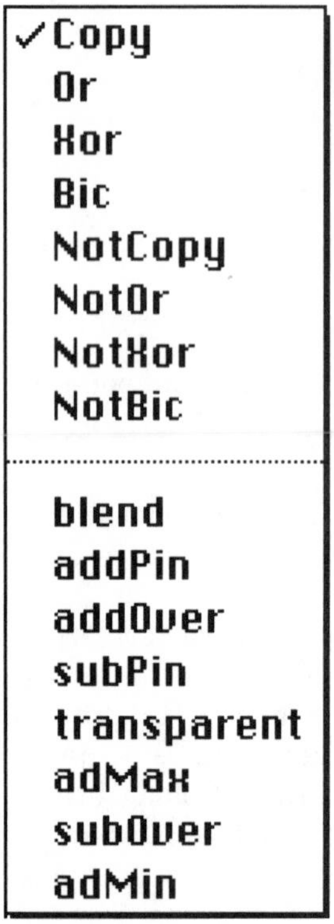

```
✓Copy
  Or
  Xor
  Bic
  NotCopy
  NotOr
  NotXor
  NotBic
..........................
  blend
  addPin
  addOver
  subPin
  transparent
  adMax
  subOver
  adMin
```

Figure 4.9   Items for MENU 401.

That's it. Save your changes and quit ResEdit. Next, you'll set up the project and type in the source code.

Setting Up the Project

Inside the ColorTutor ƒ folder, create a new project called **ColorTutor.π**. Next, add MacTraps to the project. Create a new source code file and save it as **ColorTutor.c**. Add ColorTutor.c to the project. Type the following source code into ColorTutor.c:

```
#include "ColorToolbox.h"

#define BASE_RES_ID          400
#define NIL_POINTER          OL
#define NIL_STRING           "\p"
#define VISIBLE              TRUE
#define HAS_GOAWAY           TRUE
#define MOVE_TO_FRONT        -1L
#define REMOVE_ALL_EVENTS    0
#define MIN_SLEEP            OL
#define NIL_MOUSE_REGION     OL
#define NOT_A_NORMAL_MENU    -1


#define PRECISE_TOLERANCE    0x0000

#define BLACK_PATTERN        1
#define GRAY_PATTERN         2
#define COLOR_RAMP           4
#define GRAY_RAMP            5
#define SINGLE_COLOR         6


#define SRC_AND_BACK_MENU    400
#define MODE_MENU            401


Boolean     IsColor(), PickColor();

Rect        gSrcRect, gBackRect, gDestRect,
            gSrcMenuRect, gBackMenuRect, gModeMenuRect,
            gOpColorRect;
int         gSrcPattern, gBackPattern, gCopyMode,
            gSrcType, gBackType;
RGBColor    gSrcColor, gBackColor, gOpColor;
MenuHandle  gSrcMenu, gBackMenu, gModeMenu;
WindowPtr   gColorWindow;
```

```
main()
{
    Point          corner;
    PaletteHandle  pal;

    ToolBoxInit();

    if ( ! IsColor() )
        DoAlert( "\pThis machine does not support Color QuickDraw!" );
    else
    {
        SetUpWindow();
        SetUpGlobals();

        DoEventLoop();
    }
}



/********************************** ToolBoxInit */

ToolBoxInit()
{
    InitGraf( &thePort );
    InitFonts();
    FlushEvents( everyEvent, REMOVE_ALL_EVENTS );
    InitWindows();
    InitMenus();
    TEInit();
    InitDialogs( NIL_POINTER );
    InitCursor();
}



/********************************** SetUpWindow */

SetUpWindow()
{
    Rect          r;

    SetRect( &r, 5, 40, 225, 275 );
```

```
    gColorWindow = NewCWindow( NIL_POINTER, &r, "\pColorTutor",
            VISIBLE, noGrowDocProc, MOVE_TO_FRONT,
            HAS_GOAWAY, NIL_POINTER );

    SetRect( &r, 15, 207, 95, 225 );
    NewControl( gColorWindow, &r, "\pOpColor...",
            VISIBLE, 0, 0, 1, pushButProc, NIL_POINTER );

    SetPort( gColorWindow );
    TextFont( systemFont );
}


/********************************** SetUpGlobals */

SetUpGlobals()
{
    SetRect( &gSrcRect, 15, 6, 95, 86 );
    SetRect( &gBackRect, 125, 6, 205, 86 );
    SetRect( &gDestRect, 125, 122, 205, 202 );
    SetRect( &gOpColorRect, 15, 122, 95, 202 );

    SetRect( &gSrcMenuRect, 7, 90, 103, 108 );
    SetRect( &gBackMenuRect, 117, 90, 213, 108 );
    SetRect( &gModeMenuRect, 117, 206, 213, 226 );

    gSrcPattern = BLACK_PATTERN;
    gBackPattern = BLACK_PATTERN;

    gCopyMode = srcCopy;

    gSrcColor.red = 65535;
    gSrcColor.green = gSrcColor.blue = 0;
    gSrcType = SINGLE_COLOR;

    gBackColor.blue = 0xFFFF;
    gBackColor.red = gBackColor.green = 0;
    gBackType = SINGLE_COLOR;

    gOpColor.green = 32767;
    gOpColor.red = 32767;
    gOpColor.blue = 32767;
    OpColor( &gOpColor );
```

```
        gSrcMenu = GetMenu( SRC_AND_BACK_MENU );
        InsertMenu( gSrcMenu, NOT_A_NORMAL_MENU );

        gBackMenu = GetMenu( SRC_AND_BACK_MENU );
        InsertMenu( gBackMenu, NOT_A_NORMAL_MENU );

        gModeMenu = GetMenu( MODE_MENU );
        InsertMenu( gModeMenu, NOT_A_NORMAL_MENU );
}


/********************************* DoEventLoop */

DoEventLoop()
{
    Boolean       done;
    EventRecord   e;
    short         part;
    WindowPtr     window;
    Point         p;

    done = FALSE;
    while ( ! done )
    {
        WaitNextEvent( everyEvent, &e, MIN_SLEEP, NIL_MOUSE_REGION );

        switch( e.what )
        {
            case mouseDown:
                part = FindWindow( e.where, &window );
                if ( part == inGoAway )
                    done = TRUE;
                else if ( part == inDrag )
                    DragWindow( window, e.where, &screenBits.bounds );
                else if ( part == inContent )
                {
                    p = e.where;
                    GlobalToLocal( &p );
                    DoContent( p );
                }
                break;
            case updateEvt:
                BeginUpdate( (WindowPtr)e.message );
```

```
                    SetPort( (WindowPtr)e.message );
                    DrawWindow();
                    DrawControls( (WindowPtr)e.message );
                    EndUpdate( (WindowPtr)e.message );
                    break;
        }
    }
}


/********************************** DoContent */

DoContent( p )
Point   p;
{
    int             choice;
    ControlHandle   control;
    RGBColor        rgbColor;

    if ( FindControl( p, gColorWindow, &control ) )
    {
        if ( TrackControl( control, p, NIL_POINTER ) )
        {
            rgbColor = gOpColor;
            if ( PickColor( &rgbColor ) )
            {
                gOpColor = rgbColor;
                InvalRect( &gOpColorRect );
                InvalRect( &gDestRect );
                OpColor( &gOpColor );
            }
        }
    }
    else if ( PtInRect( p, &gSrcMenuRect ) )
    {
        UpdateSrcMenu();
        choice = DoPopup( gSrcMenu, &gSrcMenuRect );
        if ( choice > 0 )
        {
            DoSrcChoice( choice );
            InvalRect( &gSrcRect );
            InvalRect( &gDestRect );
        }
    }
```

```
        else if ( PtInRect( p, &gBackMenuRect ) )
        {
            UpdateBackMenu();
            choice = DoPopup( gBackMenu, &gBackMenuRect );
            if ( choice > 0 )
            {
                DoBackChoice( choice );
                InvalRect( &gBackRect );
                InvalRect( &gDestRect );
            }
        }
        else if ( PtInRect( p, &gModeMenuRect ) )
        {
            UpdateModeMenu();
            choice = DoPopup( gModeMenu, &gModeMenuRect );
            if ( choice > 0 )
            {
                DoModeChoice( choice );
                InvalRect( &gDestRect );
            }
        }
    }
}


/********************************* DrawWindow */

DrawWindow()
{
    RGBColor    rgbBlack;
    Rect        source, dest;

    rgbBlack.red = rgbBlack.green = rgbBlack.blue = 0;

    if ( gSrcPattern == BLACK_PATTERN )
        PenPat( black );
    else
        PenPat( gray );

    if ( gSrcType == COLOR_RAMP )
        DrawColorRamp( &gSrcRect );
    else if ( gSrcType == GRAY_RAMP )
        DrawGrayRamp( &gSrcRect );
    else
    {
```

```
        RGBForeColor( &gSrcColor );
        PaintRect( &gSrcRect );
}

if ( gBackPattern == BLACK_PATTERN )
    PenPat( black );
else
    PenPat( gray );

if ( gBackType == COLOR_RAMP )
    DrawColorRamp( &gBackRect );
else if ( gBackType == GRAY_RAMP )
    DrawGrayRamp( &gBackRect );
else
{
    RGBForeColor( &gBackColor );
    PaintRect( &gBackRect );
}
PenPat( black );

RGBForeColor( &gOpColor );
PaintRect( &gOpColorRect );

RGBForeColor( &rgbBlack );
DrawLabel( &gSrcMenuRect, "\pSource" );
DrawLabel( &gBackMenuRect, "\pBackground" );
DrawLabel( &gModeMenuRect, "\pMode" );

PenSize( 2, 2 );
FrameRect( &gSrcRect );
FrameRect( &gBackRect );
FrameRect( &gDestRect );
FrameRect( &gOpColorRect );

PenNormal();

source = gBackRect;
InsetRect( &source, 2, 2 );

dest = gDestRect;
InsetRect( &dest, 2, 2 );
```

```
    CopyBits( &((CGrafPtr)gColorWindow)->portPixMap,
             &((CGrafPtr)gColorWindow)->portPixMap,
             &source, &dest, srcCopy, NIL_POINTER );

    source = gSrcRect;
    InsetRect( &source, 2, 2 );

    CopyBits( &((CGrafPtr)gColorWindow)->portPixMap,
             &((CGrafPtr)gColorWindow)->portPixMap,
             &source, &dest, gCopyMode, NIL_POINTER );
}



/******************************* DrawColorRamp */

DrawColorRamp( rPtr )
Rect    *rPtr;
{
    long        numColors, i;
    HSVColor    hsvColor;
    RGBColor    rgbColor;
    Rect        r;

    r = *rPtr;
    InsetRect( &r, 2, 2 );
    numColors = (rPtr->right - rPtr->left - 2) / 2;
    hsvColor.value = hsvColor.saturation = 65535;

    for ( i=0; i<numColors; i++ )
    {
        hsvColor.hue = i * 65535 / numColors;
        HSV2RGB( &hsvColor, &rgbColor );
        RGBForeColor( &rgbColor );
        FrameRect( &r );
        InsetRect( &r, 1, 1 );
    }
}



/******************************* DrawGrayRamp */

DrawGrayRamp( rPtr )
Rect    *rPtr;
{
```

```
    long        numColors, i;
    RGBColor    rgbColor;
    Rect        r;

    r = *rPtr;
    InsetRect( &r, 2, 2 );
    numColors = (rPtr->right - rPtr->left - 2) / 2;

    for ( i=0; i<numColors; i++ )
    {
        rgbColor.red = i * 65535 / numColors;
        rgbColor.green = rgbColor.red;
        rgbColor.blue = rgbColor.red;
        RGBForeColor( &rgbColor );
        FrameRect( &r );
        InsetRect( &r, 1, 1 );
    }
}


/********************************* DrawLabel */

DrawLabel( rPtr, s )
Rect        *rPtr;
Str255      s;
{
    Rect    tempRect;
    int     size;

    tempRect = *rPtr;
    tempRect.bottom -= 1;
    tempRect.right -= 1;
    FrameRect( &tempRect );

    MoveTo( tempRect.left + 1, tempRect.bottom );
    LineTo( tempRect.right, tempRect.bottom );
    LineTo( tempRect.right, tempRect.top + 1 );

    size = rPtr->right - rPtr->left - StringWidth( s );
    MoveTo( rPtr->left + size/2, rPtr->bottom - 6 );
    DrawString( s );
}
```

```
/******************************* UpdateSrcMenu */

UpdateSrcMenu()
{
    int     i;

    for ( i=1; i<=6; i++ )
        CheckItem( gSrcMenu, i, FALSE );

    if ( gSrcPattern == BLACK_PATTERN )
        CheckItem( gSrcMenu, BLACK_PATTERN, TRUE );
    else
        CheckItem( gSrcMenu, GRAY_PATTERN, TRUE );

    if ( gSrcType == COLOR_RAMP )
        CheckItem( gSrcMenu, COLOR_RAMP, TRUE );
    else if ( gSrcType == GRAY_RAMP )
        CheckItem( gSrcMenu, GRAY_RAMP, TRUE );
    else if ( gSrcType == SINGLE_COLOR )
        CheckItem( gSrcMenu, SINGLE_COLOR, TRUE );
}


/******************************* UpdateBackMenu */

UpdateBackMenu()
{
    int i;

    for ( i=1; i<=6; i++ )
        CheckItem( gBackMenu, i, FALSE );

    if ( gBackPattern == BLACK_PATTERN )
        CheckItem( gBackMenu, BLACK_PATTERN, TRUE );
    else
        CheckItem( gBackMenu, GRAY_PATTERN, TRUE );

    if ( gBackType == COLOR_RAMP )
        CheckItem( gBackMenu, COLOR_RAMP, TRUE );
    else if ( gBackType == GRAY_RAMP )
        CheckItem( gBackMenu, GRAY_RAMP, TRUE );
    else if ( gBackType == SINGLE_COLOR )
        CheckItem( gBackMenu, SINGLE_COLOR, TRUE );
}
```

```
/********************************* UpdateModeMenu */

UpdateModeMenu()
{
    int     i;

    for ( i=1; i<=17; i++ )
        CheckItem( gModeMenu, i, FALSE );

    if ( ( gCopyMode >=0 ) && ( gCopyMode <= 7 ) )
        CheckItem( gModeMenu, gCopyMode + 1, TRUE );
    else
        CheckItem( gModeMenu, gCopyMode - 22, TRUE );
}



/********************************* DoSrcChoice */

DoSrcChoice( item )
int         item;
{
    RGBColor        rgbColor;

    switch( item )
    {
        case BLACK_PATTERN:
            gSrcPattern = BLACK_PATTERN;
            break;
        case GRAY_PATTERN:
            gSrcPattern = GRAY_PATTERN;
            break;
        case COLOR_RAMP:
            gSrcType = COLOR_RAMP;
            break;
        case GRAY_RAMP:
            gSrcType = GRAY_RAMP;
            break;
        case SINGLE_COLOR:
            gSrcType = SINGLE_COLOR;
            rgbColor = gSrcColor;
            if ( PickColor( &rgbColor ) )
                gSrcColor = rgbColor;
            break;
    }
}
```

```c
/******************************** DoBackChoice */

DoBackChoice( item )
int        item;
{
    RGBColor        rgbColor;

    switch( item )
    {
        case BLACK_PATTERN:
            gBackPattern = BLACK_PATTERN;
            break;
        case GRAY_PATTERN:
            gBackPattern = GRAY_PATTERN;
            break;
        case COLOR_RAMP:
            gBackType = COLOR_RAMP;
            break;
        case GRAY_RAMP:
            gBackType = GRAY_RAMP;
            break;
        case SINGLE_COLOR:
            gBackType = SINGLE_COLOR;
            rgbColor = gBackColor;
            if ( PickColor( &rgbColor ) )
                gBackColor = rgbColor;
            break;
    }
}


/******************************** DoModeChoice */

DoModeChoice( item )
int        item;
{
    if ( ( item >= 1 ) && ( item <= 8 ) )
        gCopyMode = item - 1;
    else
        gCopyMode = item + 22;
}
```

```
/***************************** DoPopup ******/

int        DoPopup( menu, rPtr )
MenuHandle menu;
Rect       *rPtr;
{
    Point   corner;
    long    theChoice = 0L;

    corner.h = rPtr->left;
    corner.v = rPtr->bottom;

    LocalToGlobal( &corner );

    InvertRect( rPtr );
    theChoice = PopUpMenuSelect( menu, corner.v - 1, corner.h
                                  + 1, 0 );
    InvertRect( rPtr );

    return( LoWord( theChoice ) );
}



/****************************** PickColor *********/

Boolean PickColor( colorPtr )
RGBColor    *colorPtr;
{
    Point where;

    where.h = -1;
    where.v = -1;

    return( GetColor( where, "\pChoose a color...", colorPtr,
            colorPtr ) );
}
```

```
/******************************* IsColor *********/

Boolean IsColor()
{
    SysEnvRec   mySE;

    SysEnvirons( 2, &mySE );
    return( mySE.hasColorQD );
}


/********************************** DoAlert */

DoAlert( s )
Str255          s;
{
    ParamText( s, NIL_STRING, NIL_STRING, NIL_STRING );
    NoteAlert( BASE_RES_ID, NIL_POINTER );
}
```

Running ColorTutor

Say, that was pretty good. You typed that program much faster than everyone else. Save your changes and select Run from the Project menu. If the compiler points out any typos or other errors, fix the problems.

As always, if you try to run ColorTutor on a machine that doesn't support Color QuickDraw (such as a Mac Plus or an SE), the dialog pictured in Figure 4.5 will appear and the program will exit.

Once the program runs, the ColorTutor window pictured in Figure 4.7 will appear. Because the default transfer mode is Copy, the destination pane should look exactly like the source pane. Play with all sixteen modes, reading about each mode in *Inside Macintosh, Volume V*, pages 58–60. As we mentioned before, the opColor affects the addPin, subPin, and blend modes. You can change the opColor by pressing the OpColor... pushbutton. When you're finished, click the close box and ColorTutor will exit.

ColorTutor is an ideal environment for learning about the color transfer modes. You may want to build ColorTutor as an application so that you can experiment with color without having to run THINK C.

Walking Through the ColorTutor Source Code

Like Palette, ColorTutor includes the file ColorToolbox.h. Most of the
#defines should be self-explanatory.

```
#include "ColorToolbox.h"

#define BASE_RES_ID            400
#define NIL_POINTER            0L
#define NIL_STRING             "\p"
#define VISIBLE                TRUE
#define HAS_GOAWAY             TRUE
#define MOVE_TO_FRONT          -1L
#define REMOVE_ALL_EVENTS      0
#define MIN_SLEEP              0L
#define NIL_MOUSE_REGION       0L
#define NOT_A_NORMAL_MENU      -1

#define PRECISE_TOLERANCE      0x0000

#define BLACK_PATTERN          1
#define GRAY_PATTERN           2
#define COLOR_RAMP             4
#define GRAY_RAMP              5
#define SINGLE_COLOR           6

#define SRC_AND_BACK_MENU      400
#define MODE_MENU              401


Boolean   IsColor(), PickColor();
```

   gSrcRect defines the source pane in local coordinates.
gBackRect, gDestRect, gSrcMenuRect, gBackMenuRect,
gModeMenuRect, gOpColorRect do the same thing for the
background pane, the destination pane, the Source popup, the
Background pop-up menu, the Mode pop-up menu, and the opColor
pane.
   gSrcPattern and gBackPattern store the current pattern
(gray versus black) of the source and background panes.
gCopyMode stores the current Mode pop-up setting. gSrcType and
gBackType store the type of color (COLOR_RAMP versus

GRAY_RAMP versus SINGLE_COLOR) in the source and background panes.

gSrcColor, gBackColor, and gOpColor store the current source, background, and opColor RGBColors.

gSrcMenu, gBackMenu, and gModeMenu are handles to their respective menus.

gColorWindow is the ColorTutor color window.

```
Rect              gSrcRect, gBackRect, gDestRect,
                  gSrcMenuRect, gBackMenuRect,
                  gModeMenuRect, gOpColorRect;
int               gSrcPattern, gBackPattern, gCopyMode,
                  gSrcType, gBackType;
RGBColor          gSrcColor, gBackColor, gOpColor;
MenuHandle        gSrcMenu, gBackMenu, gModeMenu;
WindowPtr         gColorWindow;
```

As usual, the program initializes the Toolbox and checks to see if Color QuickDraw is installed. If so, the program creates the ColorTutor window, initializes all the globals, and drops into the event loop.

```
main()
{
    Point            corner;
    PaletteHandle    pal;

    ToolBoxInit();

    if ( ! IsColor() )
        DoAlert( "\pThis machine does not support Color QuickDraw!" );
    else
    {
        SetUpWindow();
        SetUpGlobals();

        DoEventLoop();
    }
}
```

```
/******************************** ToolBoxInit */

ToolBoxInit()
{
    InitGraf( &thePort );
    InitFonts();
    FlushEvents( everyEvent, REMOVE_ALL_EVENTS );
    InitWindows();
    InitMenus();
    TEInit();
    InitDialogs( NIL_POINTER );
    InitCursor();
}
```

SetUpWindow() creates the color window and then creates the OpColor... pushbutton control. The program changes the window's font to systemFont so that the pop-up labels will be drawn in Chicago.

```
/******************************** SetUpWindow */

SetUpWindow()
{
    Rect        r;

    SetRect( &r, 5, 40, 225, 275 );

    gColorWindow = NewCWindow( NIL_POINTER, &r, "\pColorTutor",
            VISIBLE, noGrowDocProc, MOVE_TO_FRONT,
            HAS_GOAWAY, NIL_POINTER );

    SetRect( &r, 15, 207, 95, 225 );
    NewControl( gColorWindow, &r, "\pOpColor...",
            VISIBLE, 0, 0, 1, pushButProc, NIL_POINTER );

    SetPort( gColorWindow );
    TextFont( systemFont );
}
```

SetUpGlobals() initializes all the globals and loads the menus from the resource fork. Note that gSrcMenu and gBackMenu are both initialized from the same MENU resource.

```
/****************************** SetUpGlobals */

SetUpGlobals()
{
    SetRect( &gSrcRect, 15, 6, 95, 86 );
    SetRect( &gBackRect, 125, 6, 205, 86 );
    SetRect( &gDestRect, 125, 122, 205, 202 );
    SetRect( &gOpColorRect, 15, 122, 95, 202 );

    SetRect( &gSrcMenuRect, 7, 90, 103, 108 );
    SetRect( &gBackMenuRect, 117, 90, 213, 108 );
    SetRect( &gModeMenuRect, 117, 206, 213, 226
);

    gSrcPattern = BLACK_PATTERN;
    gBackPattern = BLACK_PATTERN;

    gCopyMode = srcCopy;

    gSrcColor.red = 65535;
    gSrcColor.green = gSrcColor.blue = 0;
    gSrcType = SINGLE_COLOR;

    gBackColor.blue = 0xFFFF;
    gBackColor.red = gBackColor.green = 0;
    gBackType = SINGLE_COLOR;

    gOpColor.green = 32767;
    gOpColor.red =  32767;
    gOpColor.blue = 32767;
    OpColor( &gOpColor );

    gSrcMenu = GetMenu( SRC_AND_BACK_MENU );
    InsertMenu( gSrcMenu, NOT_A_NORMAL_MENU );

    gBackMenu = GetMenu( SRC_AND_BACK_MENU );
    InsertMenu( gBackMenu, NOT_A_NORMAL_MENU );

    gModeMenu = GetMenu( MODE_MENU );
    InsertMenu( gModeMenu, NOT_A_NORMAL_MENU );
}
```

DoEventLoop() is remarkably similar to its Palette counterpart. The difference lies in the handling of the updateEvt.

```
/******************************** DoEventLoop */

DoEventLoop()
{
    Boolean     done;
    EventRecorde;
    short       part;
    WindowPtr   window;
    Point       p;

    done = FALSE;
    while ( ! done )
    {
        WaitNextEvent( everyEvent, &e, MIN_SLEEP, NIL_MOUSE_REGION );

        switch( e.what )
        {
            case mouseDown:
                part = FindWindow( e.where, &window );
                if ( part == inGoAway )
                    done = TRUE;
                else if ( part == inDrag )
                    DragWindow( window, e.where, &screenBits.bounds );
```

If the program detects a mouseDown in the content region, it converts the mouse location to local coordinates and then passes the point on to DoContent().

```
                else if ( part == inContent )
                {
                    p = e.where;
                    GlobalToLocal( &p );
                    DoContent( p );
                }
                break;
```

When the program gets an updateEvt, it redraws the ColorTutor window and then redraws the OpColor... pushbutton menu with a call to DrawControls().

```
                      case updateEvt:
                          BeginUpdate( (WindowPtr)e.message );
                          SetPort( (WindowPtr)e.message );
                          DrawWindow();
                          DrawControls( (WindowPtr)e.message );
                          EndUpdate( (WindowPtr)e.message );
                          break;
                  }
              }
          }
```

When the program gets a mouse click in the content region, it needs to find out if the click was in the OpColor... pushbutton menu or possibly in one of the three pop-up menus.

```
/********************************* DoContent */

DoContent( p )
Point p;
{
    int                 choice;
    ControlHandle       control;
    RGBColor            rgbColor;
```

If the click was in the pushbutton menu, the program calls `TrackControl()` to track the mouse until the mouse button is released. If the button was released with the mouse still in the control, `PickColor()` is called to put up the Color Picker. If the user pressed the Picker's OK button, the program updates `gOpColor`, forces an `updateEvt`, and calls `OpColor()` to let Color QuickDraw know about the new opColor.

```
if ( FindControl( p, gColorWindow, &control ) )
{
    if ( TrackControl( control, p, NIL_POINTER ) )
    {
        rgbColor = gOpColor;
        if ( PickColor( &rgbColor ) )
        {
            gOpColor = rgbColor;
            InvalRect( &gOpColorRect );
            InvalRect( &gDestRect );
            OpColor( &gOpColor );
        }
    }
}
```

If the click was in one of the three pop-up menus, the program calls `UpdateSrcMenu()`, `UpdateBackMenu()`, or `UpdateMode Menu()` to update the appropriate menu's check marks and then calls `DoPopup()`. If `choice` is nonzero (if an item was chosen), the program calls the appropriate handling routine and then forces an `updateEvt` with `InvalRect()`.

```
else if ( PtInRect( p, &gSrcMenuRect ) )
{
    UpdateSrcMenu();
    choice = DoPopup( gSrcMenu, &gSrcMenuRect );
    if ( choice > 0 )
    {
        DoSrcChoice( choice );
        InvalRect( &gSrcRect );
        InvalRect( &gDestRect );
    }
}
else if ( PtInRect( p, &gBackMenuRect ) )
{
    UpdateBackMenu();
    choice = DoPopup( gBackMenu, &gBackMenuRect );
    if ( choice > 0 )
    {
        DoBackChoice( choice );
        InvalRect( &gBackRect );
        InvalRect( &gDestRect );
    }
}
else if ( PtInRect( p, &gModeMenuRect ) )
{
    UpdateModeMenu();
    choice = DoPopup( gModeMenu, &gModeMenuRect );
    if ( choice > 0 )
    {
        DoModeChoice( choice );
        InvalRect( &gDestRect );
    }
}
}
}
```

`DrawWindow()` performs all of ColorTutor's drawing operations. It starts by creating its own black `RGBColor`.

```
/******************************** DrawWindow */

DrawWindow()
{
    RGBColor    rgbBlack;
    Rect        source, dest;

    rgbBlack.red = rgbBlack.green = rgbBlack.blue = 0;
```

Before drawing the source pane, the program has to set the pattern to the currently selected pattern.

```
if ( gSrcPattern == BLACK_PATTERN )
        PenPat( black );
else
        PenPat( gray );
```

Next, the program draws a color ramp, a gray ramp, or a solid color, depending on the setting of gSrcType.

```
if ( gSrcType == COLOR_RAMP )
        DrawColorRamp( &gSrcRect );
else if ( gSrcType == GRAY_RAMP )
        DrawGrayRamp( &gSrcRect );
else
{
        RGBForeColor( &gSrcColor );
        PaintRect( &gSrcRect );
}
```

This procedure is repeated for the background pane. When this has been done, the pen pattern is returned to black, so that the remainder of the routine will draw correctly.

```
if ( gBackPattern == BLACK_PATTERN )
        PenPat( black );
else
        PenPat( gray );

if ( gBackType == COLOR_RAMP )
        DrawColorRamp( &gBackRect );
else if ( gBackType == GRAY_RAMP )
        DrawGrayRamp( &gBackRect );
```

```
else
{
    RGBForeColor( &gBackColor );
    PaintRect( &gBackRect );
}
PenPat( black );
```

Next, the program paints the opColor pane using the `RGBColor`, `gOpColor`.

```
RGBForeColor( &gOpColor );
PaintRect( &gOpColorRect );
```

Now the program draws the Source, Background, and Mode pop-up labels.

```
RGBForeColor( &rgbBlack );
DrawLabel( &gSrcMenuRect, "\pSource" );
DrawLabel( &gBackMenuRect, "\pBackground" );
DrawLabel( &gModeMenuRect, "\pMode" );
```

The program draws a 2-pixel border around all four panes and then returns the pen to its normal 1-pixel-by-1-pixel state.

```
PenSize( 2, 2 );
FrameRect( &gSrcRect );
FrameRect( &gBackRect );
FrameRect( &gDestRect );
FrameRect( &gOpColorRect );

PenNormal();
```

Next, the program sets up source and destination `Rects`. It insets each by 2 pixels all around so that it doesn't `CopyBits()` the frame. This is both for speed and aesthetics.

```
source = gBackRect;
InsetRect( &source, 2, 2 );

dest = gDestRect;
InsetRect( &dest, 2, 2 );
```

This first call of `CopyBits()` copies the background pane onto the destination pane using plain old `srcCopy`.

```
CopyBits( &((CGrafPtr)gColorWindow)->portPixMap,
        &((CGrafPtr)gColorWindow)->portPixMap,
        &source, &dest, srcCopy, NIL_POINTER );
```

Next, the program sets the source `Rect` so that copying is done from the source pane. Once again, the program insets the `Rect` so that the frame is not copied.

```
source = gSrcRect;
InsetRect( &source, 2, 2 );
```

This call to `CopyBits()` is where all the action is. As before, the program is copying from the color window's `PixMap` back to itself, but this time it is using the currently selected transfer mode. See! `CopyBits()` is easy!

```
CopyBits( &((CGrafPtr)gColorWindow)->portPixMap,
        &((CGrafPtr)gColorWindow)->portPixMap,
        &source, &dest, gCopyMode, NIL_POINTER
);
}
```

The program draws the color ramp using the HSV bright colors, as was done in the other programs.

```
/********************************** DrawColorRamp */

DrawColorRamp( rPtr )
Rect *rPtr;
{
    long        numColors, i;
    HSVColor    hsvColor;
    RGBColor    rgbColor;
    Rect        r;

    r = *rPtr;
    InsetRect( &r, 2, 2 );
    numColors = (rPtr->right - rPtr->left - 2) / 2;
    hsvColor.value = hsvColor.saturation = 65535;

    for ( i=0; i<numColors; i++ )
    {
```

```
            hsvColor.hue = i * 65535 / numColors;
            HSV2RGB( &hsvColor, &rgbColor );
            RGBForeColor( &rgbColor );
            FrameRect( &r );
            InsetRect( &r, 1, 1 );
        }
    }
```

The program draws the gray ramp as it did before, by keeping the red, green, and blue components of the RGBColor equal, varying their value from 0 to 65535.

```
/********************************* DrawGrayRamp */

DrawGrayRamp( rPtr )
Rect *rPtr;
{
    long        numColors, i;
    RGBColor    rgbColor;
    Rect        r;

    r = *rPtr;
    InsetRect( &r, 2, 2 );
    numColors = (rPtr->right - rPtr->left - 2) / 2;

    for ( i=0; i<numColors; i++ )
    {
        rgbColor.red = i * 65535 / numColors;
        rgbColor.green = rgbColor.red;
        rgbColor.blue = rgbColor.red;
        RGBForeColor( &rgbColor );
        FrameRect( &r );
        InsetRect( &r, 1, 1 );
    }
}
```

DrawLabel() draws a pop-up menu frame around the Rect pointed to by rPtr. It then uses StringWidth() to calculate the proper centering for the string s and then draws the string.

```
/******************************* DrawLabel */

DrawLabel( rPtr, s )
Rect        *rPtr;
Str255      s;
{
    Rect    tempRect;
    int     size;

    tempRect = *rPtr;
    tempRect.bottom -= 1;
    tempRect.right -= 1;
    FrameRect( &tempRect );

    MoveTo( tempRect.left + 1, tempRect.bottom );
    LineTo( tempRect.right, tempRect.bottom );
    LineTo( tempRect.right, tempRect.top + 1 );

    size = rPtr->right - rPtr->left - StringWidth( s );
    MoveTo( rPtr->left + size/2, rPtr->bottom - 6 );
    DrawString( s );
}
```

UpdateSrcMenu() starts off by removing all the check marks from the Source pop-up menu. It then adds a check mark to either the BLACK_PATTERN or the GRAY_PATTERN item, depending on the value of gSrcPattern. Next, it adds a check mark to the COLOR_RAMP, the GRAY_RAMP, or the SINGLE_COLOR item, depending on the value of gSrcType.

```
/******************************** UpdateSrcMenu */

UpdateSrcMenu()
{
    int i;

    for ( i=1; i<=6; i++ )
        CheckItem( gSrcMenu, i, FALSE );

    if ( gSrcPattern == BLACK_PATTERN )
        CheckItem( gSrcMenu, BLACK_PATTERN, TRUE );
    else
        CheckItem( gSrcMenu, GRAY_PATTERN, TRUE );
```

```
    if ( gSrcType == COLOR_RAMP )
        CheckItem( gSrcMenu, COLOR_RAMP, TRUE );
    else if ( gSrcType == GRAY_RAMP )
        CheckItem( gSrcMenu, GRAY_RAMP, TRUE );
    else if ( gSrcType == SINGLE_COLOR )
        CheckItem( gSrcMenu, SINGLE_COLOR, TRUE );
}
```

UpdateBackMenu() works the same way as UpdateSrcMenu(), using the values of gBackPattern and gBackType to determine the position of the check marks.

```
/********************************** UpdateBackMenu */

UpdateBackMenu()
{
    int i;

    for ( i=1; i<=6; i++ )
        CheckItem( gBackMenu, i, FALSE );

    if ( gBackPattern == BLACK_PATTERN )
        CheckItem( gBackMenu, BLACK_PATTERN, TRUE );
    else
        CheckItem( gBackMenu, GRAY_PATTERN, TRUE );

    if ( gBackType == COLOR_RAMP )
        CheckItem( gBackMenu, COLOR_RAMP, TRUE );
    else if ( gBackType == GRAY_RAMP )
        CheckItem( gBackMenu, GRAY_RAMP, TRUE );
    else if ( gBackType == SINGLE_COLOR )
        CheckItem( gBackMenu, SINGLE_COLOR, TRUE );
}
```

UpdateModeMenu() starts by unchecking all of gModeMenu's items. Next, if gCopyMode is one of the first eight modes, it places the check mark using this formula: item = mode + 1. If gCopyMode is one of the arithmetic modes, it sets the check mark using this formula: item = mode - 22. This method takes advantage of the declaration of the modes in the include file and the fact that each block of modes consists of eight consecutive values.

```
/******************************** UpdateModeMenu */

UpdateModeMenu()
{
    int i;

    for ( i=1; i<=17; i++ )
        CheckItem( gModeMenu, i, FALSE );

    if ( ( gCopyMode >=0 ) && ( gCopyMode <= 7 ) )
        CheckItem( gModeMenu, gCopyMode + 1, TRUE );
    else
        CheckItem( gModeMenu, gCopyMode - 22, TRUE );
}
```

Once a selection is made from the Source pop-up menu, it gets passed on to `DoSrcChoice()`. `DoSrcChoice()` updates the appropriate global, depending on the item selected.

```
/******************************** DoSrcChoice */

DoSrcChoice( item )
int      item;
{
    RGBColor          rgbColor;

    switch( item )
    {
        case BLACK_PATTERN:
            gSrcPattern = BLACK_PATTERN;
            break;
        case GRAY_PATTERN:
            gSrcPattern = GRAY_PATTERN;
            break;
        case COLOR_RAMP:
            gSrcType = COLOR_RAMP;
            break;
        case GRAY_RAMP:
            gSrcType = GRAY_RAMP;
            break;
```

If `SINGLE_COLOR` was selected, the program brings up the Color Picker. If the OK button was clicked, the program updates the source pane's `RGBColor`.

```
            case SINGLE_COLOR:
                gSrcType = SINGLE_COLOR;
                rgbColor = gSrcColor;
                if ( PickColor( &rgbColor ) )
                    gSrcColor = rgbColor;
                break;
        }
}
```

DoBackChoice() works in the same way as DoSrcChoice(). It should, because both pop-up menus use the same MENU resource.

```
/***************************** DoBackChoice */

DoBackChoice( item )
int     item;
{
    RGBColor        rgbColor;

    switch( item )
    {
        case BLACK_PATTERN:
            gBackPattern = BLACK_PATTERN;
            break;
        case GRAY_PATTERN:
            gBackPattern = GRAY_PATTERN;
            break;
        case COLOR_RAMP:
            gBackType = COLOR_RAMP;
            break;
        case GRAY_RAMP:
            gBackType = GRAY_RAMP;
            break;
        case SINGLE_COLOR:
            gBackType = SINGLE_COLOR;
            rgbColor = gBackColor;
            if ( PickColor( &rgbColor ) )
                gBackColor = rgbColor;
            break;
    }
}
```

DoModeChoice() converts the item number into a mode constant and updates gCopyMode.

```
/******************************* DoModeChoice */

DoModeChoice( item )
int         item;
{
    if ( ( item >= 1 ) && ( item <= 8 ) )
        gCopyMode = item - 1;
    else
        gCopyMode = item + 22;
}
```

DoPopup() inverts the label, brings up the specified pop-up menu, uninverts the label, and returns the selected item number. PopUpMenuSelect() (and thus, DoPopup()) returns 0 if no item is selected.

```
/***************************** DoPopup *******/

int         DoPopup( menu, rPtr )
MenuHandle  menu;
Rect        *rPtr;
{
    Point corner;
    long  theChoice = 0L;

    corner.h = rPtr->left;
    corner.v = rPtr->bottom;

    LocalToGlobal( &corner );

    InvertRect( rPtr );
    theChoice = PopUpMenuSelect( menu, corner.v - 1, corner.h
                            + 1, 0 );
    InvertRect( rPtr );

    return( LoWord( theChoice ) );
}
```

PickColor() calls GetColor(), which brings up the Color Picker at the point, where. If where is set to (0, 0), the Color Picker will appear centered on the main display (the display with the menu bar). If `where` is set to (-1, -1), the Color Picker will appear centered on the deepest display (the display with the highest number of bits per pixel).

   `GetColor()` returns `TRUE` if the user exited by clicking the OK button; it returns `FALSE` otherwise.

```
/****************************** PickColor *********/

Boolean PickColor( colorPtr )
RGBColor    *colorPtr;
{
    Point where;

    where.h = -1;
    where.v = -1;

    return( GetColor( where, "\pChoose a color...", colorPtr,
            colorPtr ) );
}
```

   You've seen the routines `IsColor()` and `DoAlert()` before.

```
/****************************** IsColor *********/

Boolean IsColor()
{
    SysEnvRec   mySE;

    SysEnvirons( 2, &mySE );
    return( mySE.hasColorQD );
}



/******************************** DoAlert */

DoAlert( s )
Str255      s;
{
    ParamText( s, NIL_STRING, NIL_STRING, NIL_STRING );
    NoteAlert( BASE_RES_ID, NIL_POINTER );
}
```

Working with Off-screen Drawing Environments

In addition to support for direct video devices, 32-Bit QuickDraw introduced a set of routines that make it easy for you to create and manipulate off-screen drawing environments. Why would you want to use an off-screen drawing environment? There are several reasons.

One of the primary uses for off-screen environments is in the production of flicker-free animation. If you were writing a game, for example, and you wanted X-wing fighters to zip across the screen, you'd first create an off-screen environment of the graphic background, leaving the X-wing out of the picture. Then you'd create an off-screen environment depicting the X-wing, making it as detailed as you like. When it comes time for the fighters to fly across the screen, you'd call `CopyBits()` to copy the image of the X-wing from the X-wing off-screen environment onto the game window. You'd then enter a loop, using `CopyBits()` to overdraw the X-wing image from the background off-screen environment and then copy the X-wing from its off-screen environment to its new location in the game window.

Producing flicker-free animation is actually a bit more complex than this, but you get the basic idea. The next program, **GWorld**, demonstrates the new 32-Bit QuickDraw off-screen graphic world routines. You create an offscreen graphics world (gworld) by calling `NewGWorld()`. When you're ready to draw in your gworld, save the old drawing environment by calling `GetGWorld()` and then make your gworld the current world by passing it to `SetGWorld()`. Because gworlds are relocatable, you'll have to lock the pixels down with `LockPixels()` before you do any drawing. Make sure you unlock the pixels with a call to `UnlockPixels()` when you're done drawing.

32-Bit QuickDraw is described in detail in the *32-Bit QuickDraw Developer Note* available from APDA. This section is intended to introduce you to 32-Bit QuickDraw's off-screen graphics capabilities. Get the note. You'll be glad you did.

GWorld

GWorld, takes a look at off-screen graphic worlds in action. It creates an off-screen graphics world, filling it with both a gray and a color ramp. GWorld then uses `CopyBits()` to copy the off-screen graphics world to a color window using four different magnifications.

GWorld Resources

GWorld uses the exact same resources as the first program, ColorInfo. Create a folder in your development folder called **GWorld ƒ**. Copy the file ColorInfo.π.rsrc into the GWorld ƒ folder. Change the name of the resource file to **GWorld.π.rsrc**.

Setting Up the Project

Inside the GWorld ƒ folder, create a new project called **GWorld.π**. Next, add MacTraps to the project. Create a new source code file and save it as **QuickDraw32Bit.h**. Do *not* add this file to the project. It is an include file that will give GWorld access to the 32-Bit QuickDraw routines. The source code for QuickDraw32Bit.h can be found in Appendix B. Type in the file (or copy it into GWorld ƒ if you already have a copy) and save it.

Create another new source code file and save it as **GWorld.c**. Add GWorld.c to the project. Type the following source code into GWorld.c:

```
#include "ColorToolbox.h"
#include "QuickDraw32Bit.h"

#define BASE_RES_ID        400
#define NIL_POINTER        0L
#define NIL_STRING         "\p"
#define VISIBLE            TRUE
#define NO_GOAWAY          FALSE
#define MOVE_TO_FRONT      -1L
#define REMOVE_ALL_EVENTS  0
```

```
#define MAX_PIXEL_DEPTH    32
#define WORLD_WIDTH        100
#define WORLD_HEIGHT       100
#define NO_FLAGS           0L

#define QD32TRAP           0xAB03
#define UNIMPL_TRAP        0xA89F


Boolean         Is32Bit();
GWorldPtr       MakeGWorld();
WindowPtr       CreateColorWindow();


main()
{
    WindowPtr       window;
    GWorldPtr       world;
    Rect            worldBounds, windowRect, destRect;

    ToolBoxInit();

    if ( ! Is32Bit() )
        DoAlert( "\pThis machine does not support 32-Bit QuickDraw!" );
    else
    {
        SetRect( &worldBounds, 0, 0, WORLD_HEIGHT, WORLD_WIDTH );
        world = MakeGWorld( &worldBounds );
        window = CreateColorWindow();

        SetRect( &destRect, 0, 0, 4 * WORLD_WIDTH, 4 *
                WORLD_HEIGHT );
        CopyWorldBits( world, window, &destRect );

        SetRect( &destRect, 0, 0, 2 * WORLD_WIDTH, 2 *
                WORLD_HEIGHT );
        CopyWorldBits( world, window, &destRect );

        SetRect( &destRect, 0, 0, WORLD_WIDTH, WORLD_HEIGHT );
        CopyWorldBits( world, window, &destRect );
```

```
        SetRect( &destRect, 0, 0, WORLD_WIDTH / 2, WORLD_HEIGHT
                / 2 );
        CopyWorldBits( world, window, &destRect );

        SetRect( &destRect, 0, 0, WORLD_WIDTH / 4, WORLD_HEIGHT
                / 4 );
        CopyWorldBits( world, window, &destRect );

        while ( ! Button() ) ;
    }
}




/******************************** ToolBoxInit */

ToolBoxInit()
{
    InitGraf( &thePort );
    InitFonts();
    FlushEvents( everyEvent, REMOVE_ALL_EVENTS );
    InitWindows();
    InitMenus();
    TEInit();
    InitDialogs( NIL_POINTER );
    InitCursor();
}




/******************************** CreateColorWindow */

WindowPtr   CreateColorWindow()
{
    WindowPtr   cWindow;
    Rect        r;

    SetRect( &r, 10, 40, 10 + (4 * WORLD_WIDTH),
            40 + (4 * WORLD_HEIGHT) );

    cWindow = NewCWindow( NIL_POINTER, &r, "\pColor Test",
            VISIBLE, noGrowDocProc, MOVE_TO_FRONT,
            NO_GOAWAY, NIL_POINTER );

    SetPort( cWindow );

    return( cWindow );
}
```

```
/********************************** MakeGWorld */

GWorldPtr MakeGWorld( boundsPtr )
Rect     *boundsPtr;
{
    GDHandle    oldGD;
    GWorldPtr   oldGW, newWorld;
    HSVColor    hsvColor;
    RGBColor    rgbColor;
    long        i;
    Rect        r;
    QDErr       errorCode;

    GetGWorld( &oldGW, &oldGD );

    errorCode = NewGWorld( &newWorld, MAX_PIXEL_DEPTH,
                        boundsPtr, NIL_POINTER,
                        NIL_POINTER, NO_FLAGS );
    if ( errorCode != noErr )
    {
        DoAlert( "\pMy call to NewGWorld died!  Bye..." );
        ExitToShell();
    }

    LockPixels( newWorld->portPixMap );
    SetGWorld( newWorld, NIL_POINTER );

    hsvColor.value = 65535;
    hsvColor.saturation = 65535;

    for( i=boundsPtr->left; i<=boundsPtr->right; i++ )
    {
        hsvColor.hue = i * 65535 / ( boundsPtr->right - 1 );
        HSV2RGB( &hsvColor, &rgbColor );
        RGBForeColor( &rgbColor );
        MoveTo( i, boundsPtr->bottom / 2 );
        LineTo( i, boundsPtr->bottom );

        rgbColor.red = i * 65535 / ( boundsPtr->right - 1 );
        rgbColor.green = rgbColor.red;
        rgbColor.blue = rgbColor.red;
```

```
        RGBForeColor( &rgbColor );
        MoveTo( i, 0 );
        LineTo( i, boundsPtr->bottom / 2 );
    }

    SetGWorld(oldGW,oldGD);
    UnlockPixels( newWorld->portPixMap );

    return( newWorld );
}


/******************************** CopyWorldBits */

CopyWorldBits( world, window, destRectPtr )
GWorldPtr   world;
WindowPtr   window;
Rect        *destRectPtr;
{
    RGBColor    rgbBlack;

    rgbBlack.red = rgbBlack.green = rgbBlack.blue = 0;
    RGBForeColor( &rgbBlack );

    LockPixels( world->portPixMap );
    CopyBits( &world->portPixMap, &thePort->portBits,
        &world->portRect, destRectPtr, ditherCopy, 0 );
    UnlockPixels( world->portPixMap );
}


/****************************** Is32Bit ********/

Boolean Is32Bit()
{
    SysEnvRec   mySE;

    SysEnvirons( 2, &mySE );

    if ( ! mySE.hasColorQD )
        return( FALSE );

    return( NGetTrapAddress( QD32TRAP, ToolTrap ) !=
        NGetTrapAddress( UNIMPL_TRAP, ToolTrap ) );
}
```

```
/******************************** DoAlert */

DoAlert( s )
Str255          s;
{
    ParamText( s, NIL_STRING, NIL_STRING, NIL_STRING );
    NoteAlert( BASE_RES_ID, NIL_POINTER );
}
```

Running GWorld

Now you're ready to save your changes and select Run from the Project menu. If the compiler points out any typos or other errors, get rid of them.

If you try to run GWorld without 32-Bit QuickDraw installed, an error alert will appear and the program will exit. If 32-Bit QuickDraw is present, a color window will appear. The off-screen graphic will be drawn five times. The first time it will be drawn so that it fills the window. Each successive time it will be drawn at half the previous size, always pinned to the upper left corner.

Each of the five drawings is a CopyBits() copy of the original off-screen graphic. The only difference between the calls to CopyBits() is the size of the destination Rect.

Walking Through the GWorld Source Code

GWorld includes the file ColorToolbox.h as well as the new include file **QuickDraw32Bit.h**.

```
#include "ColorToolbox.h"
#include "QuickDraw32Bit.h"

#define BASE_RES_ID         400
#define NIL_POINTER         0L
#define NIL_STRING          "\p"
#define VISIBLE             TRUE
#define NO_GOAWAY           FALSE
#define MOVE_TO_FRONT       -1L
#define REMOVE_ALL_EVENTS   0
```

MAX_PIXEL_DEPTH determines the maximum depth device the program supports. The higher the number, the more memory the off-screen graphic will take up. The off-screen world for this program will be WORLD_WIDTH pixels wide and WORLD_HEIGHT pixels tall. The program uses no unusual flag settings when it creates the off-screen world. This is done by passing NO_FLAGS as the last argument to NewGWorld(). The flags are described in detail in the *32-Bit QuickDraw Developer Note*.

```
#define MAX_PIXEL_DEPTH        32
#define WORLD_WIDTH            100
#define WORLD_HEIGHT           100
#define NO_FLAGS               0L
```

The #defines QD32TRAP and UNIMPL_TRAP are used to determine whether 32-Bit QuickDraw is installed.

```
#define QD32TRAP               0xAB03
#define UNIMPL_TRAP            0xA89F
```

```
Boolean        Is32Bit();
GWorldPtr      MakeGWorld();
WindowPtr      CreateColorWindow();
```

main() starts off with a call to Is32Bit() to determine whether 32-Bit QuickDraw is installed. If not, an alert is displayed and the program exits.

```
main()
{
    WindowPtr        window;
    GWorldPtr        world;
    Rect             worldBounds, windowRect, destRect;

    ToolBoxInit();

    if ( ! Is32Bit() )
        DoAlert( "\pThis machine does not support 32-Bit QuickDraw!" );
```

If 32-Bit QuickDraw is installed, the program defines the boundary of the off-screen world and then creates it by calling MakeGWorld(). Next, it creates a color window by calling CreateColorWindow().

```
else
{
    SetRect( &worldBounds, 0, 0, WORLD_HEIGHT, WORLD_WIDTH );
    world = MakeGWorld( &worldBounds );
    window = CreateColorWindow();
```

Next, the off-screen world is put to work. Each call to `SetRect()` sets up the destination `Rect` within the color window. The calls to `CopyWorldBits()` do the actual copying of the off-screen world to the specified `Rect` in the specified window.

```
    SetRect( &destRect, 0, 0, 4 * WORLD_WIDTH, 4 *
            WORLD_HEIGHT );
    CopyWorldBits( world, window, &destRect );

    SetRect( &destRect, 0, 0, 2 * WORLD_WIDTH, 2 *
            WORLD_HEIGHT );
    CopyWorldBits( world, window, &destRect );

    SetRect( &destRect, 0, 0, WORLD_WIDTH, WORLD_HEIGHT );
    CopyWorldBits( world, window, &destRect );

    SetRect( &destRect, 0, 0, WORLD_WIDTH / 2, WORLD_HEIGHT
            / 2 );
    CopyWorldBits( world, window, &destRect );

    SetRect( &destRect, 0, 0, WORLD_WIDTH / 4, WORLD_HEIGHT
            / 4 );
    CopyWorldBits( world, window, &destRect );
```

Once the copies are made, the program waits for a mouse click.

```
    while ( ! Button() ) ;
}
}
```

Next is yet another copy of `ToolBoxInit()`.

```
/********************************* ToolBoxInit */

ToolBoxInit()
{
    InitGraf( &thePort );
    InitFonts();
    FlushEvents( everyEvent, REMOVE_ALL_EVENTS );
    InitWindows();
    InitMenus();
    TEInit();
    InitDialogs( NIL_POINTER );
    InitCursor();
}
```

CreateColorWindow() creates a color window big enough to accommodate a bitmap four times wider and four times taller than the off-screen graphic.

```
/********************************* CreateColorWindow */

WindowPtr   CreateColorWindow()
{
    WindowPtr   cWindow;
    Rect        r;

    SetRect( &r, 10, 40, 10 + (4 * WORLD_WIDTH),
            40 + (4 * WORLD_HEIGHT) );

    cWindow = NewCWindow( NIL_POINTER, &r, "\pColor Test",
            VISIBLE, noGrowDocProc, MOVE_TO_FRONT,
            NO_GOAWAY, NIL_POINTER );

    SetPort( cWindow );

    return( cWindow );
}
```

MakeGWorld() creates an off-screen graphics world using the specified Rect as a bounding rectangle.

```
/******************************* MakeGWorld */

GWorldPtr MakeGWorld( boundsPtr )
Rect      *boundsPtr;
{
    GDHandle  oldGD;
    GWorldPtr oldGW, newWorld;
    HSVColor  hsvColor;
    RGBColor  rgbColor;
    long      i;
    Rect      r;
    QDErr errorCode;
```

The program calls GetGWorld() to save the current graphics world for later restoration.

```
    GetGWorld( &oldGW, &oldGD );
```

NewGWorld() returns an error code, describing any problems encountered in creating the off-screen graphics world. The most typical error occurs when 32-Bit QuickDraw can't allocate enough memory to create the off-screen graphics world. If an error occurs, the program puts up an error message and bails out.

```
errorCode = NewGWorld( &newWorld, MAX_PIXEL_DEPTH,
                  boundsPtr, NIL_POINTER,
                  NIL_POINTER, NO_FLAGS );
if ( errorCode != noErr )
{
    DoAlert( "\pMy call to NewGWorld died! Bye..." );
    ExitToShell();
}
```

LockPixels() locks the pixels down so that the program can draw on them. SetGWorld() makes the newly created world the current world.

```
    LockPixels( newWorld->portPixMap );
    SetGWorld( newWorld, NIL_POINTER );
```

The program uses the HSVColor model to create a bright color ramp across the bottom half of the off-screen graphics world. It uses the RGBColor model to create a gray ramp across the top of the off-screen world.

```
hsvColor.value = 65535;
hsvColor.saturation = 65535;

for( i=boundsPtr->left; i<=boundsPtr->right; i++ )
{
    hsvColor.hue = i * 65535 / ( boundsPtr->right - 1 );
    HSV2RGB( &hsvColor, &rgbColor );
    RGBForeColor( &rgbColor );
    MoveTo( i, boundsPtr->bottom / 2 );
    LineTo( i, boundsPtr->bottom );

    rgbColor.red = i * 65535 / ( boundsPtr->right - 1 );
    rgbColor.green = rgbColor.red;
    rgbColor.blue = rgbColor.red;

    RGBForeColor( &rgbColor );
    MoveTo( i, 0 );
    LineTo( i, boundsPtr->bottom / 2 );
}
```

When done, the program restores the graphics world to its original
state, unlocks the pixels, and returns `newWorld`.

```
    SetGWorld(oldGW,oldGD);
    UnlockPixels( newWorld->portPixMap );

    return( newWorld );
}
```

Inside Macintosh recommends that you set the background color to
white and the foreground color to black before you call `CopyBits()`,
because `CopyBits()` applies the foreground and background colors
to an image during the call.

```
/***************************** CopyWorldBits */

CopyWorldBits( world, window, destRectPtr )
GWorldPtr       world;
WindowPtr       window;
Rect            *destRectPtr;
{
    RGBColor    rgbBlack;
```

```
rgbBlack.red = rgbBlack.green = rgbBlack.blue = 0;
RGBForeColor( &rgbBlack );
```

The call to `CopyBits()` illustrates the use of a newly defined mode, `ditherCopy`. `ditherCopy` was defined in the new include file QuickDraw32Bit.h. Try running the program using `srcCopy` instead of `ditherCopy`. `ditherCopy` uses a dithering technique to smooth the transitions between colors that are pretty different. Because the dithering algorithm is complex, `ditherCopy` tends to slow things down a bit. As always, the program locks the pixels before it accesses them and unlocks them when it's done.

```
    LockPixels( world->portPixMap );
    CopyBits( &world->portPixMap, &thePort->portBits,
        &world->portRect, destRectPtr, ditherCopy, 0 );
    UnlockPixels( world->portPixMap );
}
```

`Is32Bit()` first checks to see whether Color QuickDraw is available. If not, it returns `FALSE`, because 32-Bit QuickDraw can't exist without Color QuickDraw. If Color QuickDraw is present, `Is32Bit()` checks for the existence of the 32-Bit QuickDraw trap, returning `TRUE` if the trap exists.

```
/******************************** Is32Bit *********/

Boolean Is32Bit()
{
    SysEnvRec   mySE;

    SysEnvirons( 2, &mySE );

    if ( ! mySE.hasColorQD )
        return( FALSE );

    return( NGetTrapAddress( QD32TRAP, ToolTrap ) !=
        NGetTrapAddress( UNIMPL_TRAP, ToolTrap ) );
}
```

`DoAlert()` has survived intact.

```
/********************************* DoAlert */

DoAlert( s )
Str255      s;
{
    ParamText( s, NIL_STRING, NIL_STRING, NIL_STRING );
    NoteAlert( BASE_RES_ID, NIL_POINTER );
}
```

In Review

This chapter has made every effort to cover Color QuickDraw from all angles. However, there's no substitute for a thorough reading of *Inside Macintosh, Volume V*. You'll find lots of important information, probably even one or two morsels that were overlooked here. If you can, get a copy of the official Apple Color disk, the one that includes 32-Bit QuickDraw. The disk also includes the include file QuickDraw32Bit.h. Also highly recommended is Apple's excellent technical publication, *develop,* which debuted in January, 1990. The premier issue contains several articles that focus on Color QuickDraw. The magazine also comes with a CD containing all the programs in the magazine, as well as the text and graphics of the magazine itself. How recursive!

The next chapter deals with TextEdit, the powerful text editor built into every single Macintosh.

Text Edit

*This chapter explains the use of
TextEdit within your programs. First,
the chapter discusses the Toolbox
routines that make up TextEdit. Next,
it presents a program that makes
extensive use of TextEdit and that can
be used as a basis for your own
applications. The text also touches on
the changes that have occurred since
TextEdit was first introduced.*

It's hard to imagine a Mac scenario that doesn't include some form of TextEdit. When you rename an icon in the Finder, you make use of TextEdit. When you edit the file name in a Standard File dialog box, you also use TextEdit. The next section takes a look at some examples of TextEdit in action.

Exploring TextEdit

Take a look at the dialog box in Figure 5.1. This is a classic example of the use of TextEdit in an application. When your application calls `ModalDialog()` to bring up a dialog box containing an editable text field, the Dialog Manager uses TextEdit to allow editing in that field. If a `keyDown` event occurs while the dialog is still up, the dialog manager first checks to see if the key pressed was either the Return or the Enter key. If neither, the Dialog Manager passes the character code of the key on to TextEdit. TextEdit is in charge of adding (or deleting) the new character to the text field and drawing (or erasing) the new character.

If the mouse is clicked in the text field, the Dialog Manager passes the location of the mouse on to TextEdit, and TextEdit takes care of the detailed work, such as moving the insertion point and selecting text as the mouse is dragged over it.

Here's another example. Figure 5.2 shows a THINK C source code window. Note that the window has both a horizontal and a vertical scroll bar. When the mouse is clicked in a scroll bar, THINK C first works with the Control Manager to determine how far and in which

Figure 5.1 TextEdit field in dialog box.

direction the text should be scrolled. Next, THINK C calls TextEdit to actually scroll the text.

When the cursor is moved over an area of editable text, THINK C changes the cursor to an I-Beam cursor. TextEdit never changes the cursor. That's the job of the application.

> Dear Apple,
>
> Why doesn't the Dialog Manager change the cursor to the I-Beam cursor when the cursor is moved over an editable text field in a dialog box? Just wondering. . . .
>
>   Dave

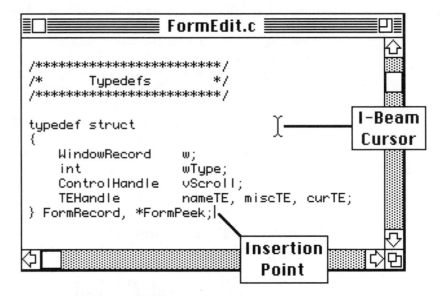

Figure 5.2   TextEdit source code editor.

Figure 5.3 TextEdit selection range.

Text is entered at the blinking insertion point. The insertion point always occurs between two character positions, and it doesn't occupy a character position itself. The selection range is also aligned between character positions. In Figure 5.3, the selection range goes from position 9 to position 13. If the insertion point occurred at position 0, new characters typed would appear at the beginning of the text. Likewise, if the insertion point were at position 16, new characters would appear at the end of the text.

Using TextEdit

As is the case with the rest of the Toolbox, to use TextEdit you need to know about two things: TextEdit data structures and the TextEdit routines.

TextEdit Record

All TextEdit revolves around a single data structure, the `TERec`. You'll need a separate `TERec` for each piece of text you want to edit. For example, if you were writing a small text editor, you'd want one `TERec` for each open document. The first program in this chapter, FormEdit, displays a two-part form in a window. FormEdit allows more than one window to be open at a time. This means that FormEdit will require two `TERec`s for every open window. (FormEdit is discussed later in the chapter.) Here's the THINK C declaration for a `TERec`:

```
typedef  struct
{
    Rect        destRect;
    Rect        viewRect;
    Rect        selRect;
```

```
     int          lineHeight;
     int          fontAscent;
     Point        selPoint;
     int          selStart;
     int          selEnd;
     int          active;
     ProcPtr      wordBreak;
     ProcPtr      clikLoop;
     long         clickTime;
     int          clickLoc;
     long         caretTime;
     int          caretState;
     int          just;
     int          teLength;
     Handle       hText;
     int          recalBack;
     int          recalLines;
     int          clikStuff;
     int          crOnly;
     int          txFont;
     char         txFace;
     int          txMode;
     int          txSize;
     GrafPtr      inPort;
     ProcPtr      highHook;
     ProcPtr      caretHook;
     int          nLines;
     int          lineStarts[];
} TERec, *TEPtr, **TEHandle;
```

Most of the fields in the TERec either are internal to TextEdit or are accessed via TextEdit routines. The first field, destRect, defines in local coordinates a Rect that is used to hold all the text, even text that's currently scrolled out of view. The destRect determines where the text is word-wrapped. Figure 5.4 shows some text word-wrapped to a destRect.

The second field, viewRect, also defines a Rect in local coordinates. This Rect determines what portion of the destRect is visible. Figure 5.4 shows a viewRect laid on top of a destRect. Figure 5.5 shows the text as it would appear on the screen.

The actual text is stored off of the handle hText. The text in a TERec is limited to 32K characters. This should prove more than adequate for most applications. The remaining TERec fields will be discussed as they are encountered.

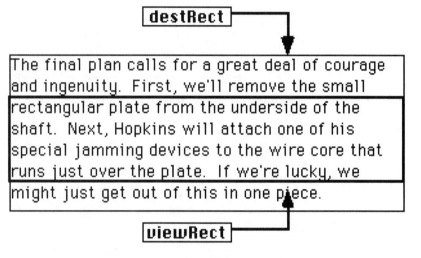

Figure 5.4 Sample viewRect and destRect.

```
rectangular plate from the underside of the
shaft. Next, Hopkins will attach one of his
special jamming devices to the wire core that
runs just over the plate. If we're lucky, we
```

Figure 5.5 Text showing through the viewRect.

Inside Macintosh, Volume V introduces a new version of TextEdit, now available for Mac Pluses on up, running system 4.1 or higher. What's the major difference between old and new TextEdit? Well, old TextEdit limited a `TERec` to a single style, determined by the fields `txFont`, `txFace`, `txMode`, and `txSize`. New TextEdit allows your application to associate a specific style with the current selection. This means that the user of your application can select some text, choose Bold from your application's Style menu, and have the selected text appear in bold-face. They can then choose other text within the same TextEdit record, select Underline from the Style menu, and have that text appear underlined. New TextEdit means that 12-point Geneva Bold can live in the same TextEdit record as 24-point Times Shadow.

Before working on the sample application, let's take a look at the toolbox routines that make up TextEdit.

TextEdit Routines

Before you can use any other TextEdit routine, you must initialize TextEdit via a call to `TEInit()`. Once that's done, you'll want to allocate a `TERec` using `TENew()`. You provide the viewRect and the destRect as parameters to `TENew()`. `TENew()` returns a `TEHandle`, which is a handle to a `TERec`. One of the nice things about TextEdit is that you never have to allocate memory for dynamically changing blocks of text. TextEdit takes care of this for you!

If you want to take advantage of new TextEdit, use the function `TEStylNew()` to allocate your `TERec`. Before you do, though, you'd better read *Inside Macintosh, Volume V*, Chapter 14. You might want to get your feet wet with old (classic?) TextEdit before you dive into new TextEdit. New TextEdit is more of a supplement than a replacement.

Once you're done with the `TERec`, dispose of it (free up any memory allocated for it) by passing its `TEHandle` to `TEDispose()`. You can get at the text of a `TERec` directly by accessing its `hText` field. A cleaner way is to use the handle returned by `TEGetText()`.

Both methods give you a handle to the actual text. `TEGetText()` does not make a copy of the data!

There are several ways to change the text of a `TERec`. You can use `TESetText( length, text, myTEHandle )` to copy `length` bytes of the text pointed to by `text` into the `TERec` handled by `myTEHandle`. This approach doesn't free up any text that might have been in the `TERec` before the call to `TESetText()`, however, so make sure you do some housekeeping before you call `TESetText()`.

Use `TEActivate()` to tell TextEdit which `TERec` is currently active. The currently active `TERec` will have its selection highlighted or, if there is no current selection, will have a blinking caret at the insertion point. `TEDeactivate()` tells TextEdit to unhighlight any selection or, if there is no selection, not to draw a caret at the insertion point.

Typical applications will call `TEActivate()` when they receive an activate event for a window, passing a handle to the `TERec` associated with that window. They'll call `TEDeactivate()` when they receive a deactivate event.

If your application has more than one `TERec` associated with each window (as does FormEdit, the sample application presented later in this chapter), you'll have to decide on a `TEActivate()` strategy. FormEdit calls `TEDeactivate()` when it gets a deactivate event, when the mouse is clicked in a `TERec` other than the current one, or when a Tab character is typed. Each `TEDeactivate()` not associated with a deactivate event is coupled with a `TEActivate()`.

`TEIdle()` takes a handle to the currently active `TERec` and, if the minimal blink interval has passed, it blinks the caret at the insertion point. `TEIdle()` should be called as frequently as possible. `TEIdle()` won't blink the caret until the blink interval has passed, no matter how frequently you call it. If you don't call it frequently enough, however, the caret will stutter.

The blink interval is tied to a byte in memory that gets loaded from Parameter-RAM. You can access the value via the system global `SPClikCaret`, found at 0x209 in memory. Four bits of the byte determine the blink interval; the other four determine the maximum time between clicks in a double-click. Just thought you'd like to know . . . .

When your application gets a mouseDown event inside the `viewRect` of a `TERec`, pass the click on to TextEdit by calling `TEClick()`. `TEClick()` takes a `Point`, a `Boolean`, and a `TEHandle` as parameters. Convert the mouse location (passed in `theEvent.where`) to local coordinates and pass it as the `Point` parameter. Determine whether the Shift key was down:

```
shiftDown = ( gTheEvent.modifiers & shiftKey) != 0;
```

and pass the result in the `Boolean` parameter. Finally, as the third parameter, pass the `TEHandle` in which the mouse was clicked.

In exchange for these three parameters, `TEClick()` will do the right thing. If the Shift key was down, `TEClick()` will extend the current selection. If the Shift key wasn't down, `TEClick()` will unhighlight the current selection and move the insertion point as close as it can to where the mouse click occurred. While the mouse button remains pressed, `TEClick()` will track the movement of the mouse, changing the selection to match. If the mouse movement started with a double-click, `TEClick()` will extend the selection a word at a time (I'll bet even you didn't know that!).

You can set the selection yourself by calling `TESetSelect()`. To select all the text in the `TERec`, use this line:

```
TESetSelect( 0, 32767, myTEHandle );
```

The first parameter is the character position of the start of the selection (see Figure 5.3). The second parameter is the character position of the end of the selection.

When a `keyDown` event occurs, first check for a command-key equivalent such as ⌘Q. You should also check for special keys, such as Return, Enter, or Tab, if they hold special meaning for your application. If the `keyDown` makes it through this, pass it on to TextEdit via a call to `TEKey()`. If there is a current selection,

TEKey() replaces the selected text with the character passed in the first parameter. If there is no selection, TEKey() inserts the character at the insertion point. If you pass the delete character, TEKey() will delete the selection, if there is one, or the character to the left of the insertion point, if there is no selection.

TESetJust() sets the justification of the TERec's text to teJustLeft, teJustCenter, or teJustRight. The default setting is teJustLeft.

When your application gets an updateEvt for a window associated with a TERec, first call EraseRect() to erase the TERec's viewRect (sometimes TextEdit is messy and leaves a caret around after a TEDeactivate()) and then call TEUpdate(). TEUpdate() will redraw the TERec's text in the viewRect. Remember to call BeginUpdate() and EndUpdate().

Scrolling Text in TextEdit

When a mouseDown occurs in a scroll bar associated with a TERec, first calculate how far you need to scroll. You'll probably need to access the TERec field lineHeight to figure out exactly how many pixels you'll need to scroll (figure lineHeight pixels for every click in a scroll bar arrow). Now pass the horizontal and vertical deltas (in pixels) to TEScroll(). TEScroll() effectively slides the viewRect up and down and side to side on the destRect (sounds perverse, doesn't it?). What the user sees is exactly what you want them to see: the text scrolling up and down and side to side in response to their clicking the mouse in the scroll bar.

TEAutoView() turns on and off the automatic scrolling of text. Automatic scrolling occurs when the user clicks the mouse in the viewRect and drags the mouse outside the viewRect. For example, if the user clicked on the text in Figure 5.6 and dragged down below the bottom of the viewRect, the text would automatically scroll up. This is great if you don't have a scroll bar associated with your TERec. If there is a scroll bar associated with your TERec, you have no way of telling TextEdit to scroll the scroll bar in tandem with the automatic scrolling of text. In other words, TEAutoView() knows about your TERec but doesn't know about your scroll bars. Although your text may scroll automatically, your scroll bar will sit there as dumb as a disabled radio button.

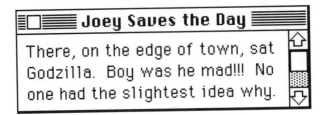

Figure 5.6 AutoScroll() example.

As you might have guessed, there is an alternative for those times when you need automatic scrolling and have to maintain a scroll bar as well. The `clikLoop` field in a `TERec` points to a routine to be called continuously, as long as the mouse is held down in the `viewRect`. By default, `clikLoop` points to a routine that works well with `TEAutoView()` but doesn't know about things like scroll bars. You can write your own routine (the sample application shows you how) to replace the default `clikLoop`. You install the new `clikLoop` by calling `SetClikLoop()`, passing a pointer to your new `clikLoop` as a parameter.

A similar mechanism is available for installing a custom word-break routine in a `TERec`. The default word-break routine takes a text pointer and a character position as input and returns `TRUE` if the character at that position is a legal word-break character (in this case, any value less than or equal to 0x20 causes a return value of `TRUE`). Install your routine by passing a pointer to the routine to `SetWordBreak()`.

Resizing the `DestRect`

If your application supports resizable windows, you'll need a strategy for dealing with changing `destRects`. Figure 5.7 shows a window with a single, vertical scroll bar. The text in the window is associated with a `TERec`. The `destRect` of this window is just big enough to fit around the top and two sides of the text. The bottom of the `destRect` goes down several inches below the bottom of the window. The `viewRect` is just big enough to fit around the text on all four sides.

When the window is resized, you have a decision to make. Figure 5.8 shows one approach. In this window, `viewRect.right` was made smaller to coincide with the left side of the scroll bar. The `destRect` was left unchanged. This has the effect of clipping the text, leaving its word-wrap the same.

Figure 5.9 shows a different approach. In this window, both the `viewRect` and the `destRect` were made skinnier. The `viewRect` changed as before, but this time the `destRect` changed as well. This had the effect of changing the word-wrap of the text to coincide with the size of the window.

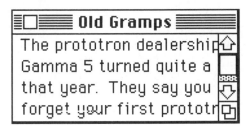

Figure 5.7. Textwindow with grow box.

Figure 5.8. Resized text window, no change to `destRect`.

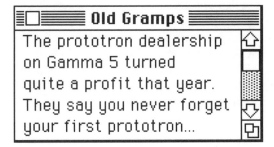

Figure 5.9. Resized text window, `destRect` changed.

The approach in Figure 5.8 is good for applications such as source code editing, in which you don't want the word-wrap to change when you resize the window. In this case, you may want to add a horizontal scroll bar on the bottom of the window so you can still reach the text clipped on the right.

The approach in Figure 5.9 is good when you want to minimize the clipping of text. This is especially true when you care about the contents of the text but not the format. An example of this might be a note pad application, or a dictionary. This approach allows you to make the most efficient use of your desk space.

TextEdit's Private Scrap

If you aren't familiar with the Scrap Manager, now is a good time to go back and review it. TextEdit maintains its own, private scrap and has a set of routines to access that scrap. `TECut()` and `TECopy()` cut and copy the selection range to the TextEdit scrap. `TEPaste()` pastes the text in the TextEdit scrap, either replacing the selection or, if there is no selection, inserting the text before the insertion point. `TEDelete()` is analogous to the Clear item under the Edit menu. It deletes the selection, if there is one, but doesn't copy it to the scrap. If there is no selection, `TEDelete()` does nothing.

`TEInsert()` inserts a copy of the specified text immediately before the selection, if there is one. Note that `TEInsert()` has no effect on the selection. If there is no selection, `TEInsert()` inserts the text immediately before the insertion point.

`TEFromScrap()` and `TEToScrap()` copy the TextEdit scrap from and to the desk scrap, respectively.

FormEdit

Now that you've seen the routines that make up TextEdit, you're ready to take a look at them in action. The sample program for this chapter is called FormEdit. FormEdit creates a menu bar with three menus: ✦, File, and Edit. The File menu will allow you to create and close a form window, as shown in Figure 5.10.

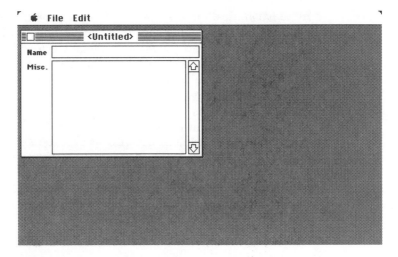

Figure 5.10   FormEdit.

As you can see, the form has two fields, **Name** and **Misc**. When more text is typed in the Misc field than can be seen at once, the scroll bar to the right of the field is activated, allowing you to scroll through the text. When you type in the Name field, the title of the window is changed to reflect the text in the field. Anytime there is no text in the Name field, the window's title is changed back to <Untitled>.

The File menu's New option allows you to create an unlimited number of windows. The Close option lets you close the windows and is dimmed when no open windows belonging to your application are left on the screen.

The Edit menu items Cut, Copy, Paste, and Clear are fully supported. The Undo item is present but remains dimmed throughout the application.

Although the Undo command is an important part of any Macintosh application, it does not represent a programming problem specific to the Toolbox. As you design your application, you must decide what form of Undo you will support. Will you support Undos of an Undo? Will your Undos be limited to text operations involving TextEdit? Once you resolve these design issues, you can design your program's data structures specifically to support this Undo approach. The point is, there is no universal Undo strategy.

To keep the programs in this book as focused as possible, no specific Undo strategy is presented. If you are interested in a chapter on Undo strategies, please let me know.

In addition, desk accessories are fully supported. In the programs presented in *Macintosh Programming Primer, Volume I* the Edit menu items Cut, Copy, Paste, and Clear were not fully supported. You can use FormEdit as a model for your own applications.

Now that you know what to expect, it's time to create the resources FormEdit will use.

> Before you go any further, you should be familiar with the techniques of creating resources for your programs. If you need a refresher, you might want to step through Chapter 8 of the *Macintosh Programming Primer, Volume I.*

FormEdit Resources

Create a folder called **FormEdit** in your source code folder. Then use ResEdit to create a new file inside the new folder called **WindowMaker.π.rsrc**.

Create a WIND resource according to the specifications in Figure 5.11. Set the WIND's resource ID to 400.

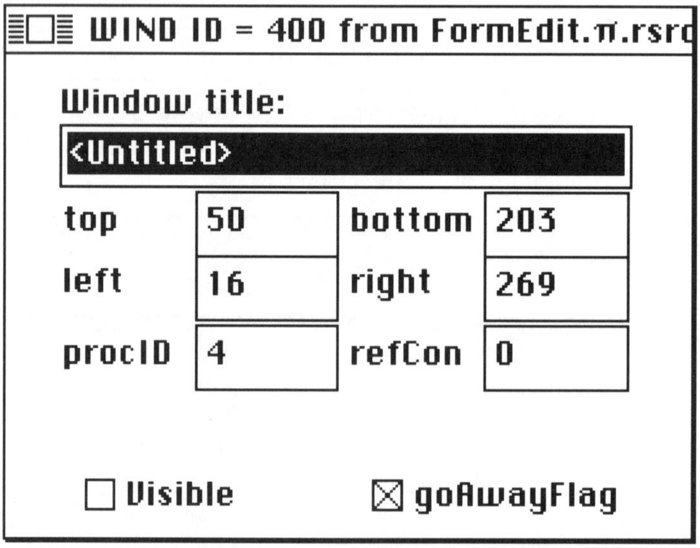

Figure 5.11   Specification for WIND 400.

Next, build the 'STR' resources used by ErrorHandler() as error messages. Remember to include the space after the three letters 'STR'. Create three 'STR' resources (numbered 400, 401, and 402) according to the specifications in Figure 5.12.

Next, build an MBAR resource as shown in Figure 5.13. Change the MBAR resource ID to 400.

Next, build the three MENU resources. First, build the MENU according to the specification in Figure 5.14. Remember to type the Apple Character () in the Title field. You can do this by typing Control-t (if you don't have a Control key on your key board, use ResEdit to copy an from another application's MENU). Because ResEdit doesn't display the Title field using the Chicago font, a rectangle will appear instead of the . Don't worry; the will appear when you run the program. Make sure you change the resource ID of the MENU to 400.

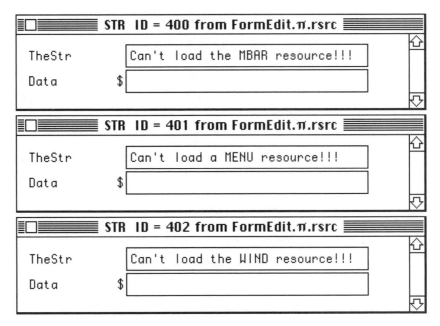

Figure 5.12 Specification for the three 'STR' resources.

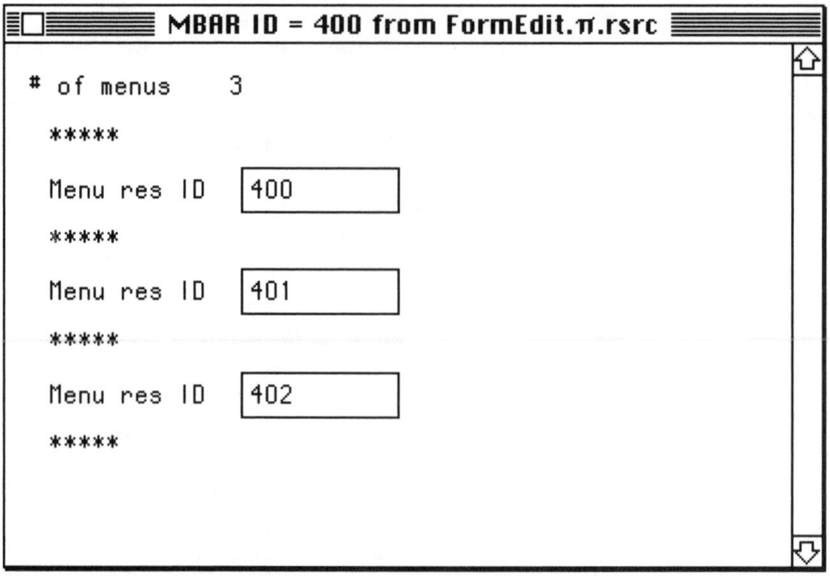

Figure 5.13   Specification for MBAR 400.

Build the File MENU resource according to Figure 5.15. Change the resource ID of the File MENU to 401.

Build the Edit MENU resource according to Figure 5.16. Change the resource ID of the Edit MENU to 402.

Next, you'll create the DITL resources for your error and About ALRTs. First, create the About DITL. Create a new DITL with two items that match the specifications in Figures 5.17 and 5.18. Change the About DITL's resource ID to 400.

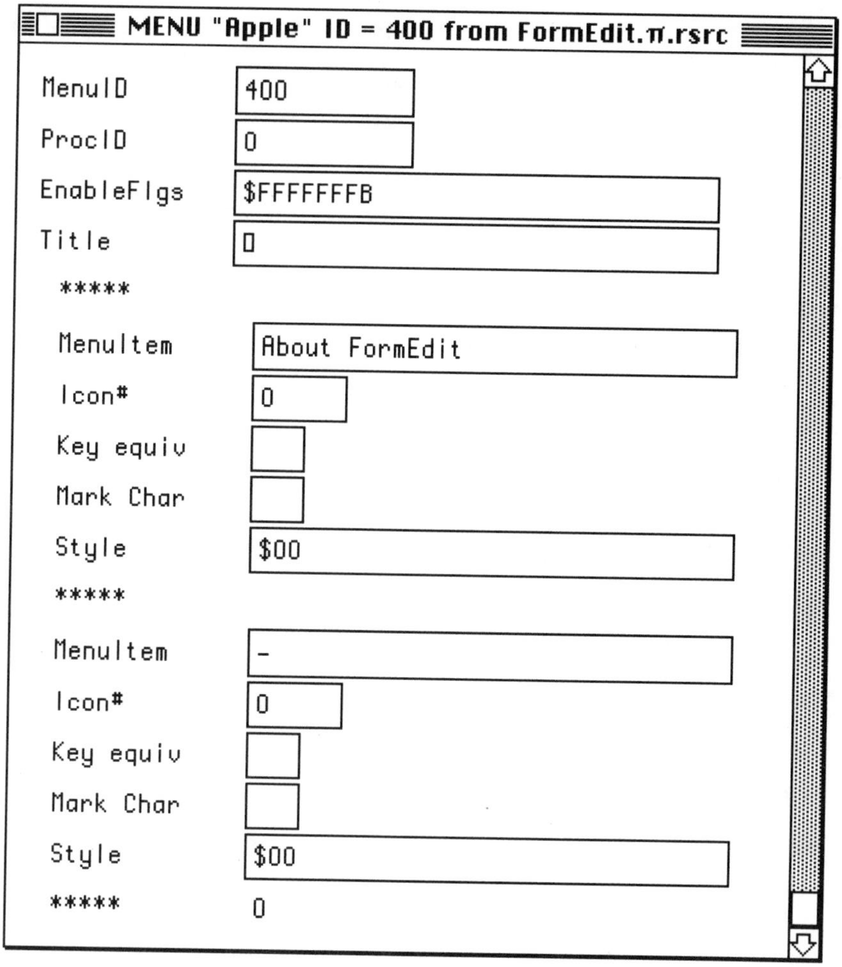

```
┌─────────────────────────────────────────────────────────────┐
│ ▤▢▤  MENU "Apple" ID = 400 from FormEdit.π.rsrc ▤           ⬆ │
│                                                               │
│  MenuID        ┌──────────────┐                               │
│                │ 400          │                               │
│  ProcID        ┌──────────────┐                               │
│                │ 0            │                               │
│  EnableFlgs    ┌──────────────────────────────────┐          │
│                │ $FFFFFFFB    │                               │
│  Title         ┌──────────────────────────────────┐          │
│                │ ☐            │                               │
│     *****                                                     │
│                                                               │
│    MenuItem    ┌──────────────────────────────────┐          │
│                │ About FormEdit                   │          │
│    Icon#       ┌──────────────┐                               │
│                │ 0            │                               │
│    Key equiv   ┌────┐                                         │
│                │    │                                         │
│    Mark Char   ┌────┐                                         │
│                │    │                                         │
│    Style       ┌──────────────────────────────────┐          │
│                │ $00          │                               │
│     *****                                                     │
│                                                               │
│    MenuItem    ┌──────────────────────────────────┐          │
│                │ –                                │          │
│    Icon#       ┌──────────────┐                               │
│                │ 0            │                               │
│    Key equiv   ┌────┐                                         │
│                │    │                                         │
│    Mark Char   ┌────┐                                         │
│                │    │                                         │
│    Style       ┌──────────────────────────────────┐          │
│                │ $00          │                               │
│     *****        0                                          ⬇ │
└─────────────────────────────────────────────────────────────┘
```

Figure 5.14   Specification for MENU 400.

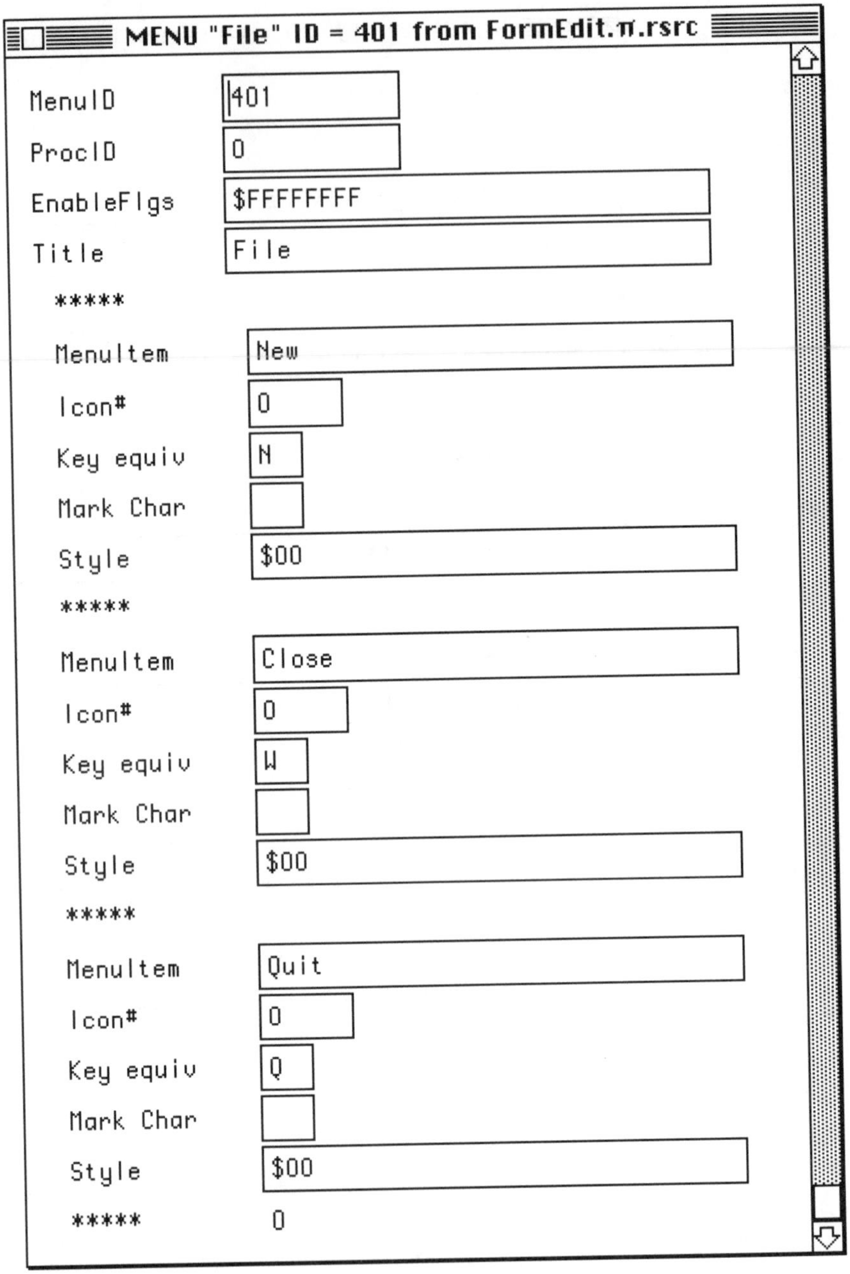

```
┌─────────────────────────────────────────────────────────────┐
│ ▤ ▢ ▤▤▤   MENU "File" ID = 401 from FormEdit.π.rsrc ▤▤▤      ⇧│
│                                                               ▒│
│  MenuID          │401          │                             ▒│
│  ProcID          │0            │                             ▒│
│  EnableFlgs      │$FFFFFFFF              │                    ▒│
│  Title           │File                  │                    ▒│
│     *****                                                     ▒│
│  MenuItem        │New                              │          ▒│
│  Icon#           │0        │                                  ▒│
│  Key equiv       │N   │                                       ▒│
│  Mark Char       │    │                                       ▒│
│  Style           │$00                      │                  ▒│
│     *****                                                     ▒│
│  MenuItem        │Close                            │          ▒│
│  Icon#           │0        │                                  ▒│
│  Key equiv       │W   │                                       ▒│
│  Mark Char       │    │                                       ▒│
│  Style           │$00                      │                  ▒│
│     *****                                                     ▒│
│  MenuItem        │Quit                             │          ▒│
│  Icon#           │0        │                                  ▒│
│  Key equiv       │Q   │                                       ▒│
│  Mark Char       │    │                                       ▒│
│  Style           │$00                      │                  ▒│
│     *****            0                                        ▒│
│                                                              ⇩│
└─────────────────────────────────────────────────────────────┘
```

Figure 5.15   Specification for MENU 401.

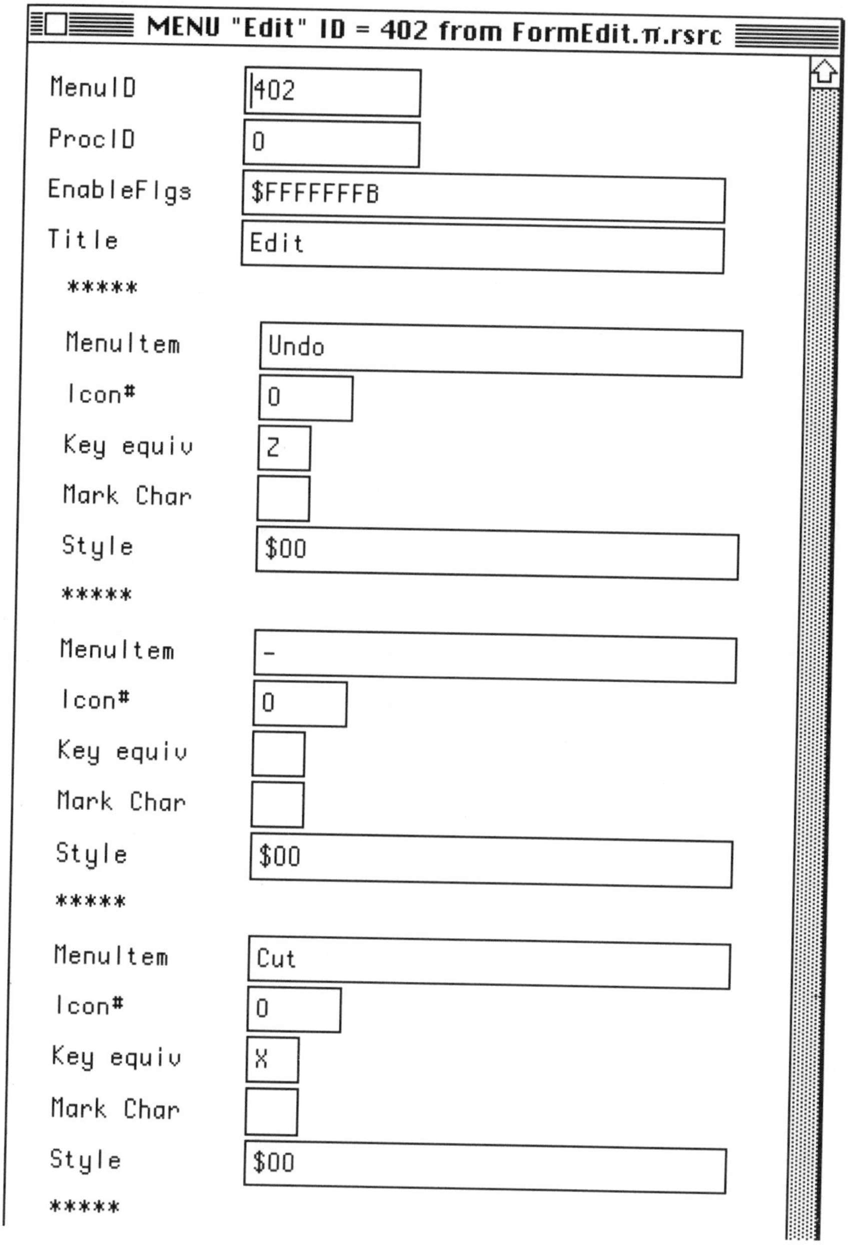

```
┌──────────────────────────────────────────────────────────────┐
│ ▤□▦▬▬   MENU "Edit" ID = 402 from FormEdit.π.rsrc  ▬▬         │
├──────────────────────────────────────────────────────────────┤
│  MenuID         ┌────────────┐                              ⇧ │
│                 │402         │                                │
│  ProcID         ┌────────────┐                                │
│                 │0           │                                │
│  EnableFlgs     ┌──────────────────────────────────┐          │
│                 │$FFFFFFFB                          │          │
│  Title          ┌──────────────────────────────────┐          │
│                 │Edit                               │          │
│     *****                                                      │
│     MenuItem    ┌──────────────────────────────────┐          │
│                 │Undo                               │          │
│     Icon#       ┌────────────┐                                 │
│                 │0           │                                 │
│     Key equiv   ┌──────┐                                       │
│                 │Z     │                                       │
│     Mark Char   ┌──────┐                                       │
│                 │      │                                       │
│     Style       ┌──────────────────────────────────┐          │
│                 │$00                                │          │
│     *****                                                      │
│     MenuItem    ┌──────────────────────────────────┐          │
│                 │-                                  │          │
│     Icon#       ┌────────────┐                                 │
│                 │0           │                                 │
│     Key equiv   ┌──────┐                                       │
│                 │      │                                       │
│     Mark Char   ┌──────┐                                       │
│                 │      │                                       │
│     Style       ┌──────────────────────────────────┐          │
│                 │$00                                │          │
│     *****                                                      │
│     MenuItem    ┌──────────────────────────────────┐          │
│                 │Cut                                │          │
│     Icon#       ┌────────────┐                                 │
│                 │0           │                                 │
│     Key equiv   ┌──────┐                                       │
│                 │X     │                                       │
│     Mark Char   ┌──────┐                                       │
│                 │      │                                       │
│     Style       ┌──────────────────────────────────┐          │
│                 │$00                                │          │
│     *****                                                      │
└──────────────────────────────────────────────────────────────┘
```

Figure 5.16   Specification for MENU 402.

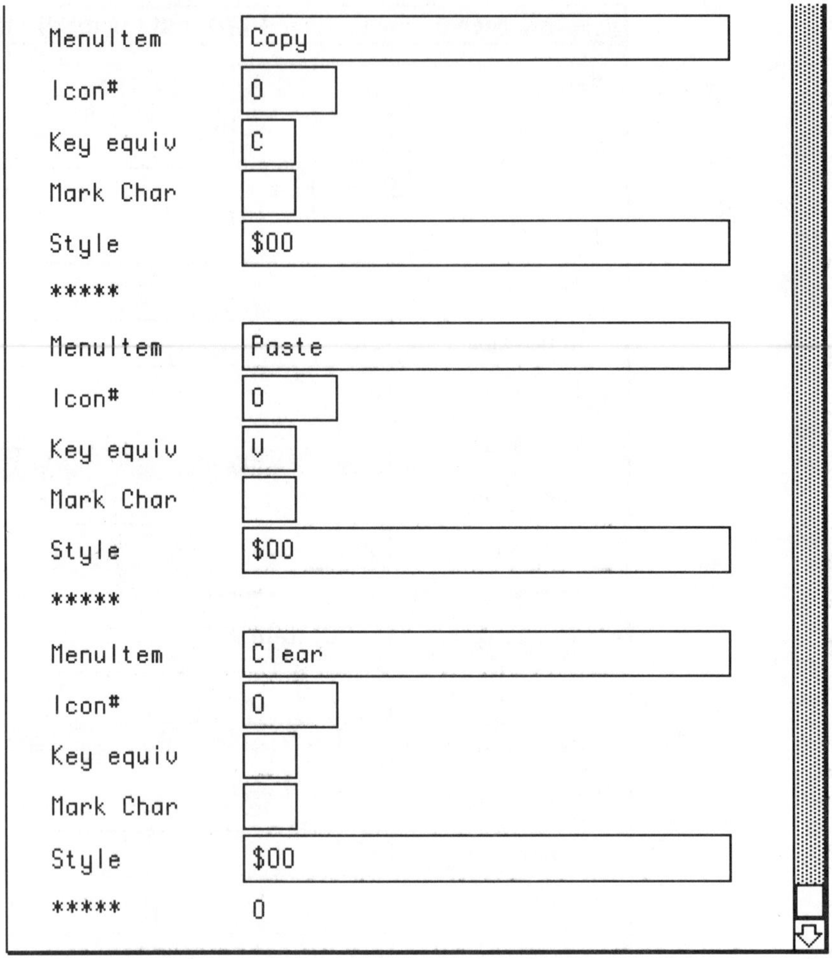

Figure 5.16 *(continued)*

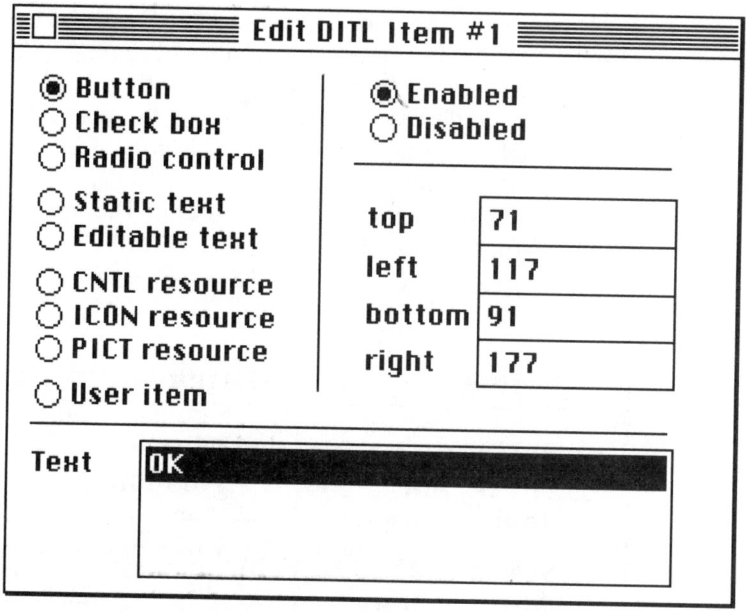

Figure 5.17 DITL 400, Item #1.

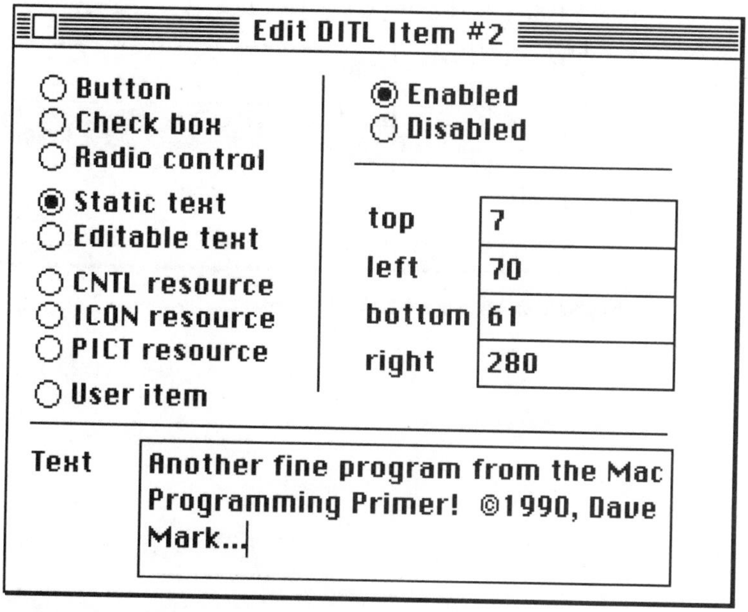

Figure 5.18 DITL 400, Item #2.

Now create the Fatal Error DITL. Create a new DITL with two items that match the specifications in Figures 5.19 and 5.20. Change the Fatal Error DITL's resource ID to 401.

Finally, you'll create the two ALRT resources. Create a new ALRT that matches the specifications in Figure 5.21. Change this ALRT's resource ID to 400.

Create a second ALRT that matches the specifications in Figure 5.22. Change this ALRT's resource ID to 401.

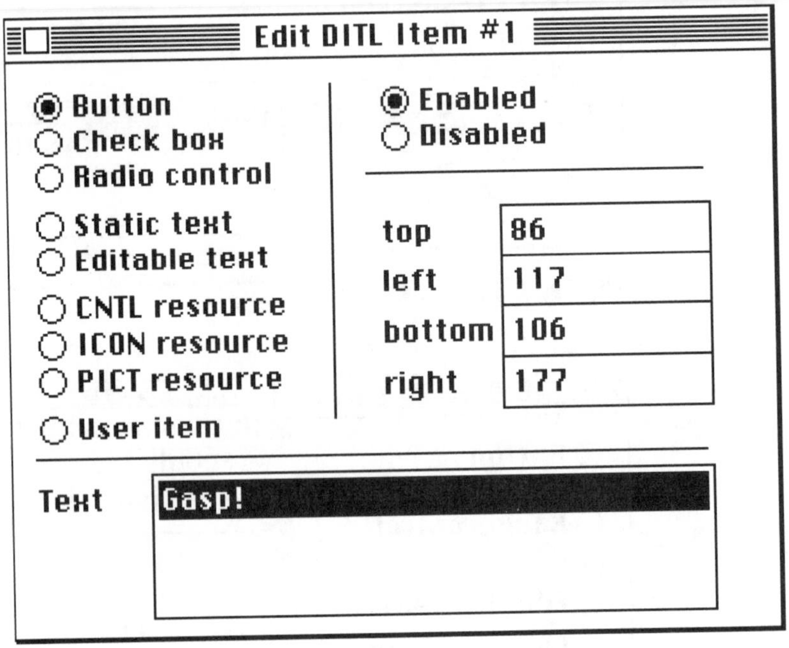

Figure 5.19   DITL 401, Item #1.

```
┌──────────────────────────────────────────────────┐
│▤□▤▤▤▤▤▤▤▤▤  Edit DITL Item #2  ▤▤▤▤▤▤▤▤▤▤│
├──────────────────────────────────────────────────┤
│  ○ Button              ◉ Enabled                   │
│  ○ Check box           ○ Disabled                  │
│  ○ Radio control    ─────────────────              │
│  ◉ Static text                                     │
│  ○ Editable text       top    │ 5   │              │
│                        left   │ 67  │              │
│  ○ CNTL resource       bottom │ 71  │              │
│  ○ ICON resource                                   │
│  ○ PICT resource       right  │ 283 │              │
│                                                    │
│  ○ User item                                       │
│ ─────────────────────────────────────             │
│  Text   │ An incredibly fatal error has just │     │
│         │ occurred:  ^0                      │     │
│         │                                    │     │
└──────────────────────────────────────────────────┘
```

Figure 5.20   DITL 401, Item #2.

```
┌──────────────────────────────────────────────────┐
│▤□▤ Alert "About" ID = 400 from FormEd              │
├──────────────────────────────────────────────────┤
│     top    │ 40 │   bottom │ 142 │                 │
│     left   │ 40 │   right  │ 332 │                 │
│     itemsID│ 400 │                 sound           │
│     stage 1  □ 2 bold  ⊠ drawn  │ 1 │              │
│     stage 2  □ 2 bold  ⊠ drawn  │ 1 │              │
│     stage 3  □ 2 bold  ⊠ drawn  │ 1 │              │
│     stage 4  □ 2 bold  ⊠ drawn  │ 1 │              │
└──────────────────────────────────────────────────┘
```

Figure 5.21   ALRT 400, viewed as text.

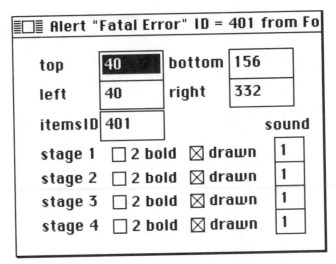

Figure 5.22   ALRT 401, viewed as text.

That's it for resources! Now comes the fun part — typing in the code (see the coupon on back page for a time-saving offer). This is a pretty long program (probably the longest in the book), so you might want to get your CD player cranked up and put on your typing slippers.

The Code

Start up THINK C and create a project (in the same folder as your resource file) called **FormEdit.π**. Add the MacTraps library to the project. Create a new source code window and save it as **FormEdit.c**. Add this window to your project. Now you're ready to type in the code. Here goes:

```
/*******************/
/*      MENUs      */
/*******************/

#define APPLE_MENU_ID         400
#define A_ABOUT_ITEM          1

#define FILE_MENU_ID          401
#define F_NEW_ITEM            1
#define F_CLOSE_ITEM          2
#define F_QUIT_ITEM           3

#define EDIT_MENU_ID          402
#define E_UNDO_ITEM           1
#define E_CUT_ITEM            3
#define E_COPY_ITEM           4
#define E_PASTE_ITEM          5
#define E_CLEAR_ITEM          6


/*******************/
/*  Window Types   */
/*******************/

#define NIL_WINDOW            0
#define UNKNOWN_WINDOW        1
#define DA_WINDOW             2
#define FORM_WINDOW           3


/*******************/
/*      ALRTs      */
/*******************/

#define ABOUT_ALERT           400
#define ERROR_ALERT_ID        401


/*******************/
/*   Error STRs    */
/*******************/

#define NO_MBAR                         BASE_RES_ID
#define NO_MENU                         BASE_RES_ID+1
#define NO_WIND                         BASE_RES_ID+2
```

```
/*******************/
/*     TextEdit     */
/*******************/

#define TE_NAME_AREA           0
#define TE_MISC_AREA           1

#define TE_ENTER_KEY           3
#define TE_DELETE_CHAR         8
#define TE_TAB_CHAR            9
#define TE_CARRIAGE_RETURN     13


/***********************/
/*  General Defines       */
/***********************/

#define BASE_RES_ID            400
#define NIL_POINTER            0L
#define MOVE_TO_FRONT          -1L
#define REMOVE_ALL_EVENTS      0

#define DRAG_THRESHOLD         30

#define WINDOW_HOME_LEFT5
#define WINDOW_HOME_TOP        45
#define NEW_WINDOW_OFFSET      20

#define MIN_SLEEP              60L
#define NIL_MOUSE_REGION0L

#define LEAVE_WHERE_IT_IS      FALSE

#define WNE_TRAP_NUM           0x60
#define UNIMPL_TRAP_NUM        0x9F
#define SUSPEND_RESUME_BIT     0x0001
#define RESUMING               1

#define NIL_STRING             "\p"
#define UNTITLED_STRING        "\p<Untitled>"
#define VISIBLE                      TRUE
#define HOPELESSLY_FATAL_ERROR "\pGame over, man!"
```

```
/************************/
/*    Useful Macros        */
/************************/


#define TopLeft( myRect )    (* (Point *) &(myRect.top) )
#define BotRight( myRect )  (* (Point *) &(myRect.bottom) )


/************************/
/*      Typedefs       */
/************************/

typedef struct
{
    WindowRecord    w;
    int             wType;
    ControlHandle   vScroll;
    TEHandle        nameTE, miscTE, curTE;
} FormRecord, *FormPeek;


/************************/
/*      Globals        */
/************************/

Boolean          gDone, gWNEImplemented, gInBackground;
EventRecord      gTheEvent;
MenuHandle       gAppleMenu,
                 gFileMenu,
                 gEditMenu;
int              gNewWindowLeft = WINDOW_HOME_LEFT,
                 gNewWindowTop = WINDOW_HOME_TOP;
Rect             gNameRect = { 3, 43, 19, 250 },
                 gMiscRect = { 22, 43, 150, 231 },
                 gScrollBarRect = { 22, 234, 150, 250 };
```

```
/***********************/
/*       Routines      */
/***********************/

void           AdjustCursor( Point mouse, RgnHandle region );
void           AdjustMenus( void );
void           AdjustScrollBar( FormPeek form );
void           CommonAction( ControlHandle  control, short
                            *amount );
void           CreateWindow( void );
void           DoActivate( WindowPtr window, Boolean
                            becomingActive );
void           DoCloseWindow( WindowPtr window );
void           DoContentClick( WindowPtr window, Point mouse );
void           DoIdle( void );
void           DoTEKey( char c );
void           DoUpdate( WindowPtr window );
void           DrawForm( WindowPtr window );
void           ErrorHandler( int stringNum );
void           HandleAppleChoice( int theItem );
void           HandleEditChoice( int theItem );
void           HandleEvent( void );
void           HandleFileChoice( int theItem );
void           HandleMenuChoice( long int menuChoice );
void           HandleMouseDown( void );
void           MainLoop( void );
void           MenuBarInit( void );
pascal Boolean NewClikLoop( void );
void           StartTextEdit( FormPeek form );
void           SwitchToNewArea( FormPeek form, int newArea );
void           ToolBoxInit( void );
void           TurnOffTextArea( FormPeek form, int whichArea );
void           TurnOnTextArea( FormPeek form, int whichArea );
pascal void    VActionProc( ControlHandle control, int part );
int            WindowType( WindowPtr window );
```

```
/****************************** main ********/

main()
{
    ToolBoxInit();
    MenuBarInit();

    MainLoop();
}


/******************************** ToolBoxInit */

void    ToolBoxInit()
{
    InitGraf( &thePort );
    InitFonts();
    FlushEvents( everyEvent, REMOVE_ALL_EVENTS );
    InitWindows();
    InitMenus();
    TEInit();
    InitDialogs( NIL_POINTER );
    InitCursor();
}


/******************************** MenuBarInit*/

void    MenuBarInit()
{
    Handle      myMenuBar;

    if ( ( myMenuBar = GetNewMBar( BASE_RES_ID ) ) ==
                                    NIL_POINTER )
        ErrorHandler( NO_MBAR );
    SetMenuBar( myMenuBar );

    if ( ( gAppleMenu = GetMHandle( APPLE_MENU_ID ) ) ==
                                    NIL_POINTER )
        ErrorHandler( NO_MENU );
    AddResMenu( gAppleMenu, 'DRVR' );
```

```
    if ( ( gFileMenu = GetMHandle( FILE_MENU_ID ) ) ==
                                    NIL_POINTER )
        ErrorHandler( NO_MENU );

    if ( ( gEditMenu = GetMHandle( EDIT_MENU_ID ) ) ==
                                    NIL_POINTER )
        ErrorHandler( NO_MENU );

    DrawMenuBar();
}



/****************************** MainLoop ********/

void    MainLoop()
{
    RgnHandle   cursorRgn;
    Boolean     gotEvent;

    gDone = FALSE;
    gInBackground = FALSE;

    cursorRgn = NewRgn();

    gWNEImplemented = ( NGetTrapAddress( WNE_TRAP_NUM,
                    ToolTrap ) !=
                    NGetTrapAddress( UNIMPL_TRAP_NUM,
                    ToolTrap ) );
    while ( gDone == FALSE )
    {
        if ( gWNEImplemented )
            gotEvent = WaitNextEvent( everyEvent, &gTheEvent,
                                    MIN_SLEEP, cursorRgn );
        else
        {
            SystemTask();
            gotEvent = GetNextEvent( everyEvent, &gTheEvent );
        }

        AdjustCursor( gTheEvent.where, cursorRgn );
```

```
                 if ( gotEvent )
                     HandleEvent();
                 else
                     DoIdle();
         }
}


/********************************** HandleEvent   */

void    HandleEvent()
{
     char        c;

     switch ( gTheEvent.what )
     {
         case nullEvent:
             DoIdle();
             break;
         case mouseDown:
             HandleMouseDown();
             break;
         case keyDown:
         case autoKey:
             c = gTheEvent.message & charCodeMask;
             if (( gTheEvent.modifiers & cmdKey ) != 0)
             {
                 AdjustMenus();
                 HandleMenuChoice( MenuKey( c ) );
             }
             else
                 DoTEKey( c );
             break;
         case activateEvt:
             DoActivate( (WindowPtr)gTheEvent.message,
                         (gTheEvent.modifiers & activeFlag) != 0 );
             break;
         case updateEvt:
             DoUpdate( (WindowPtr)gTheEvent.message );
             break;
         case app4Evt:
             if ( ( gTheEvent.message & SUSPEND_RESUME_BIT ) ==
                     RESUMING )
             {
```

```
                    gInBackground = (gTheEvent.message & 0x01) == 0;
                    DoActivate(FrontWindow(), !gInBackground);
                }
                else
                    DoIdle();
                break;
        }
    }


/*********************************** DoTEKey    */

void    DoTEKey( c )
char    c;
{
    WindowPtr       window;
    FormPeek        form;
    int             wType, length, i;
    CharsHandle     text;
    Str255          tempStr;

    window = FrontWindow();
    wType = WindowType( window );

    if ( wType == FORM_WINDOW )
    {
        form = (FormPeek)window;

        if ( c == TE_TAB_CHAR )
        {
            if ( form->curTE == form->nameTE )
                SwitchToNewArea( form, TE_MISC_AREA );
            else
            {
                SwitchToNewArea( form, TE_NAME_AREA );
                TESetSelect( 0, 32767, form->curTE );
            }
        }
        else
        {
            TEKey( c, form->curTE );
            if ( form->curTE == form->nameTE )
            {
```

```
                    length = (*form->nameTE)->teLength;
                    if ( length == 0 )
                        SetWTitle( window, UNTITLED_STRING );
                    else
                    {
                        text = TEGetText( form->nameTE );
                        tempStr[ 0 ] = length;
                        for ( i=0; ( (i<length) && (i<256) ); i++ )
                        {
                            tempStr[ i+1 ] = (*text)[ i ];
                        }
                        SetWTitle( window, tempStr );
                    }
                }
                else
                    AdjustScrollBar( form );
            }
        }
    }


/*********************************** DoIdle     */

void    DoIdle()
{
    WindowPtr    window;
    int          wType;

    window = FrontWindow();
    wType = WindowType( window );

    if ( wType == FORM_WINDOW )
        TEIdle( ((FormPeek)window)->curTE );
}


/*********************************** HandleMouseDown */

void    HandleMouseDown()
{
    WindowPtr    window;
    short int    thePart;
    long int     menuChoice, windSize;
```

```
        thePart = FindWindow( gTheEvent.where, &window );
        switch ( thePart )
        {
            case inMenuBar:
                AdjustMenus();
                menuChoice = MenuSelect( gTheEvent.where );
                HandleMenuChoice( menuChoice );
                break;
            case inSysWindow:
                SystemClick( &gTheEvent, window );
                break;
            case inContent:
                if ( window != FrontWindow() )
                {
                    SelectWindow(window);
                }
                else
                    DoContentClick( window, gTheEvent.where );
                break;
            case inDrag:
                DragWindow( window, gTheEvent.where,
                        &(screenBits.bounds) );
                break;
            case inGoAway:
                if ( TrackGoAway(window, gTheEvent.where) )
                    DoCloseWindow( window );
                break;
        }
}


/********************************* DoCloseWindow */

void    DoCloseWindow( window )
WindowPtr   window;
{
    HideWindow( window );
    DisposeControl( ((FormPeek)window)->vScroll );
    TEDispose( ((FormPeek)window)->nameTE );
    TEDispose( ((FormPeek)window)->miscTE );
    CloseWindow( window );
    DisposPtr( window );
}
```

```
/********************************** AdjustMenus */

void    AdjustMenus()
{
    WindowPtr   window;
    int         wType;
    int         offset;
    TEHandle    te;

    window = FrontWindow();
    wType = WindowType( window );

    if ( window == NIL_POINTER )
    {
        DisableItem( gFileMenu, F_CLOSE_ITEM );

        DisableItem( gEditMenu, E_UNDO_ITEM );
        DisableItem( gEditMenu, E_CUT_ITEM );
        DisableItem( gEditMenu, E_COPY_ITEM );
        DisableItem( gEditMenu, E_PASTE_ITEM );
        DisableItem( gEditMenu, E_CLEAR_ITEM );
    }
    else if ( wType == DA_WINDOW )
    {
        DisableItem( gFileMenu, F_CLOSE_ITEM );

        EnableItem( gEditMenu, E_UNDO_ITEM );
        EnableItem( gEditMenu, E_CUT_ITEM );
        EnableItem( gEditMenu, E_COPY_ITEM );
        EnableItem( gEditMenu, E_PASTE_ITEM );
        EnableItem( gEditMenu, E_CLEAR_ITEM );
    }
    else if ( wType == FORM_WINDOW )
    {
        EnableItem( gFileMenu, F_CLOSE_ITEM );

        DisableItem( gEditMenu, E_UNDO_ITEM );
        DisableItem( gEditMenu, E_CUT_ITEM );
        DisableItem( gEditMenu, E_COPY_ITEM );
        DisableItem( gEditMenu, E_PASTE_ITEM );
        DisableItem( gEditMenu, E_CLEAR_ITEM );

        te = ((FormPeek)window)->curTE;
        if ( (*te)->selStart < (*te)->selEnd )
        {
```

```
                    EnableItem( gEditMenu, E_CUT_ITEM );
                    EnableItem( gEditMenu, E_COPY_ITEM );
                    EnableItem( gEditMenu, E_CLEAR_ITEM );
                }
            if ( GetScrap( NIL_POINTER, 'TEXT', &offset)  > 0 )
                EnableItem( gEditMenu, E_PASTE_ITEM );
        }
}


/*********************************** WindowType */

int WindowType( window )
WindowPtr   window;
{
    if ( window == NIL_POINTER )
        return( NIL_WINDOW );

    if ( ((WindowPeek)window)->windowKind < 0 )
        return( DA_WINDOW );

    if ( ((FormPeek)window)->wType == FORM_WINDOW )
        return( FORM_WINDOW );

    return( UNKNOWN_WINDOW );
}


/*********************************** HandleMenuChoice */

void    HandleMenuChoice( menuChoice )
long int    menuChoice;
{
    int theMenu;
    int theItem;

    if ( menuChoice != 0 )
    {
        theMenu = HiWord( menuChoice );
        theItem = LoWord( menuChoice );
        switch ( theMenu )
        {
            case APPLE_MENU_ID :
                HandleAppleChoice( theItem );
                break;
```

```
                case FILE_MENU_ID :
                    HandleFileChoice( theItem );
                    break;
                case EDIT_MENU_ID :
                    HandleEditChoice( theItem );
            }
            HiliteMenu( O );
        }
}


/****************************** HandleAppleChoice ******/

void    HandleAppleChoice( theItem )
int theItem;
{
    Str255      accName;
    int         accNumber;

    switch ( theItem )
    {
        case A_ABOUT_ITEM :
            NoteAlert( ABOUT_ALERT, NIL_POINTER );
            break;
        default :
            GetItem( gAppleMenu, theItem, accName );
            accNumber = OpenDeskAcc( accName );
            break;
    }
}


/****************************** HandleFileChoice ******/

void    HandleFileChoice( theItem )
int theItem;
{
    WindowPtr  window;
    switch ( theItem )
    {
        case F_NEW_ITEM :
            CreateWindow();
            break;
```

```
            case F_CLOSE_ITEM :
                if ( ( window = FrontWindow() ) != NIL_POINTER )
                    DoCloseWindow( window );
                break;
            case F_QUIT_ITEM :
                gDone = TRUE;
                break;
        }
    }


/****************************** HandleEditChoice   *******/

void    HandleEditChoice( theItem )
int theItem;
{
    TEHandle    te;
    WindowPtr   window;
    int         wType, length, i;
    CharsHandle text;
    Str255      tempStr;
    FormPeek    form;

    if ( ! SystemEdit( theItem - 1 ) )
    {
        window = FrontWindow();
        wType = WindowType( window );

        if ( wType == FORM_WINDOW )
        {
            form = (FormPeek)window;
            te = form->curTE;
            switch ( theItem )
            {
                case E_UNDO_ITEM:
                    break;
                case E_CUT_ITEM:
                    if ( ZeroScrap() == noErr )
                    {
                        TECut(te);
                        AdjustScrollBar( form );
                        if ( TEToScrap() != noErr )
                            ZeroScrap();
                    }
```

```
            break;
        case E_COPY_ITEM:
            if ( ZeroScrap() == noErr )
            {
                TECopy(te);
                if ( TEToScrap() != noErr )
                    ZeroScrap();
            }
            break;
        case E_PASTE_ITEM:
            if ( TEFromScrap() == noErr )
            {
                TEPaste(te);
                AdjustScrollBar( form );
            }
            break;
        case E_CLEAR_ITEM:
            TEDelete(te);
            AdjustScrollBar( form );
            break;
    }

    if ( te == form->nameTE )
    {
        length = (*form->nameTE)->teLength;
        if ( length == 0 )
            SetWTitle( window, UNTITLED_STRING );
        else
        {
            text = TEGetText( form->nameTE );
            tempStr[ 0 ] = length;
            for ( i=0; ( (i<length) && (i<256) ); i++ )
            {
                tempStr[ i+1 ] = (*text)[ i ];
            }
            SetWTitle( window, tempStr );
        }
    }

    }
  }
}
```

```
/*****************************DoContentClick *******/

void    DoContentClick( window, mouse )
WindowPtr    window;
Point        mouse;
{
    int             wType, value;
    int             thePart;
    Boolean         shiftDown;
    Point           locMouse;
    ControlHandle   control;
    FormPeek        form;

    wType = WindowType( window );

    if ( wType == FORM_WINDOW )
    {
        form = (FormPeek)window;
        locMouse = mouse;
        GlobalToLocal( &locMouse );

        if ( ( thePart = FindControl( locMouse, window,
                                    &control ) ) != 0 )
        {
            switch( thePart )
            {
                case inUpButton:
                case inDownButton:
                case inPageUp:
                case inPageDown:
                    value = TrackControl( control, locMouse,
                                        (ProcPtr) VActionProc );
                    break;
                case inThumb:
                    value = GetCtlValue( control );
                    thePart = TrackControl( control, locMouse,
                                        NIL_POINTER );
                    if ( thePart != 0 )
                    {
                        value -= GetCtlValue( control );
                        if ( value != 0 )
                            TEScroll(0, value * (*form->curTE)-
                                    >lineHeight, form->miscTE );
                    }
            }
```

```
                        break;
                }
        }
        else if ( PtInRect( locMouse, &gNameRect ) )
        {
            if ( form->curTE == form->nameTE )
            {
                shiftDown = ( gTheEvent.modifiers & shiftKey) != 0;
                TEClick( locMouse, shiftDown, form->nameTE );
            }
            else
            {
                SwitchToNewArea( form, TE_NAME_AREA );
                TEClick( locMouse, FALSE, form->nameTE );
            }
        }
        else if ( PtInRect( locMouse, &gMiscRect ) )
        {
            if ( form->curTE == form->miscTE )
            {
                shiftDown = ( gTheEvent.modifiers & shiftKey) != 0;
                TEClick( locMouse, shiftDown, form->miscTE );
            }
            else
            {
                SwitchToNewArea( form, TE_MISC_AREA );
                TEClick( locMouse, FALSE, form->miscTE );
            }
        }
    }
}


/*********************************** VActionProc */

pascal voidVActionProc(control, part)
ControlHandle   control;
int             part;
{
    short       amount;
    WindowPtr   window;
    TEPtr       te;
```

```
    if ( part != 0 )
    {
        window = (*control)->contrlOwner;
        te = *((FormPeek)window)->miscTE;
        switch ( part ) {
            case inUpButton:
            case inDownButton:      /* one line */
                amount = 1;
                break;
            case inPageUp:          /* one page */
            case inPageDown:
                amount = (te->viewRect.bottom - te-
                        >viewRect.top) / te->lineHeight;
                break;
        }
        if ( (part == inDownButton) || (part == inPageDown) )
            amount = -amount;
        CommonAction(control, &amount);
        if ( amount != 0 )
            TEScroll( 0, amount * te->lineHeight,
                    ((FormPeek)window)->miscTE );
    }
}


/*********************************** CommonAction */

void    CommonAction( control, amount )
ControlHandle   control;
short           *amount;
{
    short       value, max;

    value = GetCtlValue( control );   /* get current value */
    max = GetCtlMax( control );        /* and maximum value */
    *amount = value - *amount;
    if ( *amount < 0 )
        *amount = 0;
    else if ( *amount > max )
        *amount = max;
    SetCtlValue( control, *amount );
    *amount = value - *amount;         /* calculate the real change */
}
```

```
/********************************** DoActivate   */

void    DoActivate( window, becomingActive )
WindowPtr   window;
Boolean     becomingActive;
{
    FormPeek    form;
    int         wType;

    wType = WindowType( window );

    if ( wType == FORM_WINDOW )
    {
        form = (FormPeek)window;
        if ( becomingActive )
        {
            SetPort( window );
            if ( form->curTE == form->miscTE )
                TurnOnTextArea( form, TE_MISC_AREA );
            else
                TurnOnTextArea( form, TE_NAME_AREA );
            HiliteControl( form->vScroll, 0 );
        }
        else
        {
            if ( form->curTE == form->miscTE )
                TurnOffTextArea( form, TE_MISC_AREA );
            else
                TurnOffTextArea( form, TE_NAME_AREA );
            HiliteControl( form->vScroll, 255 );
        }
    }
}



/********************************** AdjustCursor *********/

void    AdjustCursor( mouse, region )
Point       mouse;
RgnHandle   region;
{
```

```
WindowPtr        window;
RgnHandle        arrowRgn, iBeamRgn, tempRgn;
Rect             tempRect;
int              wType;
GrafPtr          oldPort;

window = FrontWindow();
wType = WindowType( window );

if ( gInBackground || ( wType != FORM_WINDOW ) )
{
    SetCursor( &arrow );
    return;
}

GetPort( &oldPort );
SetPort( window );

arrowRgn = NewRgn();
iBeamRgn = NewRgn();
tempRgn = NewRgn();

SetRectRgn( arrowRgn, -32700, -32700, 32700, 32700 );

tempRect = gNameRect;
LocalToGlobal( &TopLeft(tempRect) );
LocalToGlobal( &BotRight(tempRect) );
RectRgn( tempRgn, &tempRect );
UnionRgn( iBeamRgn, tempRgn, iBeamRgn );

tempRect = gMiscRect;
LocalToGlobal( &TopLeft(tempRect) );
LocalToGlobal( &BotRight(tempRect) );
RectRgn( tempRgn, &tempRect );
UnionRgn( iBeamRgn, tempRgn, iBeamRgn );

DiffRgn( arrowRgn, iBeamRgn, arrowRgn );

if ( PtInRgn( mouse, iBeamRgn ) )
{
    SetCursor( *GetCursor( iBeamCursor ) );
    CopyRgn( iBeamRgn, region );
}
```

```
    else
    {
        SetCursor( &arrow );
        CopyRgn( arrowRgn, region );
    }
    DisposeRgn( arrowRgn );
    DisposeRgn( iBeamRgn );
    DisposeRgn( tempRgn );

    SetPort( oldPort );
}


/********************************** DoUpdate  */

void    DoUpdate( window )
WindowPtr   window;
{
    FormPeek    form;
    int         wType;
    GrafPtr     oldPort;

    GetPort( &oldPort );
    SetPort( window );

    wType = WindowType( window );

    if ( wType == FORM_WINDOW )
    {
        BeginUpdate( window );
        EraseRect( &window->portRect );
        DrawForm( window );
        EndUpdate( window );
    }

    SetPort( oldPort );
}
```

```
/********************************* DrawForm   */

void    DrawForm( window )
WindowPtr   window;
{
    FrameRect( &gNameRect );
    FrameRect( &gMiscRect );
    DrawControls( window );

    TextFont( geneva );
    TextFace( bold );

    MoveTo( gNameRect.left - 34, gNameRect.top + 12 );
    DrawString( "\pName" );
    MoveTo( gMiscRect.left - 34, gMiscRect.top + 12 );
    DrawString( "\pMisc." );

    TextFont( monaco );
    TextFace( 0 );

    TEUpdate( &window->portRect, ((FormPeek)window)->nameTE );
    TEUpdate( &window->portRect, ((FormPeek)window)->miscTE );
}


/********************************* CreateWindow   */

void    CreateWindow()
{
    WindowPtr   theNewestWindow;
    Ptr         wStorage;
    FormPeek    form;

    wStorage = NewPtr( sizeof(FormRecord) );

    if ( ( theNewestWindow = GetNewWindow( BASE_RES_ID,
        wStorage, MOVE_TO_FRONT ) ) == NIL_POINTER )
        ErrorHandler( NO_WIND );
    if ( ( (screenBits.bounds.right - gNewWindowLeft) <
        DRAG_THRESHOLD ) ||
        ( ( screenBits.bounds.bottom - gNewWindowTop) <
        DRAG_THRESHOLD ) )
```

```
    {
        gNewWindowLeft = WINDOW_HOME_LEFT;
        gNewWindowTop = WINDOW_HOME_TOP;
    }

    MoveWindow( theNewestWindow, gNewWindowLeft,
            gNewWindowTop, LEAVE_WHERE_IT_IS );
    gNewWindowLeft += NEW_WINDOW_OFFSET;
    gNewWindowTop += NEW_WINDOW_OFFSET;

    form = (FormPeek)theNewestWindow;
    form->wType = FORM_WINDOW;

    form->vScroll = NewControl( theNewestWindow,
                                &gScrollBarRect, NIL_STRING,
            VISIBLE, 0, 0, 0, scrollBarProc, OL);

    ShowWindow( theNewestWindow );
    SetPort( theNewestWindow );
    TextFont( monaco );
    TextFace( 0 );
    TextSize( 9 );
    StartTextEdit( form );
}


/******************************* StartTextEdit ********/

void        StartTextEdit( form )
FormPeek    form;
{
    Rect    r;

    r = gNameRect;
    InsetRect( &r, 2, 2 );
    form->nameTE = TENew( &r, &r );

    r = gMiscRect;
    InsetRect( &r, 2, 2 );
    form->miscTE = TENew( &r, &r );
    SetClikLoop( NewClikLoop, form->miscTE );

    TEAutoView( TRUE, form->miscTE );

    form->curTE = form->nameTE;
}
```

```
/****************************** NewClikLoop *********/

pascal Boolean NewClikLoop()
{
    WindowPtr   window;
    FormPeek    form;
    TEHandle    te;
    Rect        tempRect;
    Point       mouse;
    GrafPtr     oldPort;
    int         amount;
    RgnHandle   oldClip;

    window = FrontWindow();
    if ( WindowType( window ) != FORM_WINDOW )
        return( FALSE );

    form = (FormPeek)window;
    te = form->curTE;

    GetPort( &oldPort );
    SetPort( window );
    oldClip = NewRgn();
    GetClip( oldClip );

    SetRect( &tempRect, -32767, -32767, 32767, 32767 );
    ClipRect( &tempRect );

    GetMouse( &mouse );

    if ( mouse.v < gMiscRect.top )
    {
        amount = 1;
        CommonAction( form->vScroll, &amount );
        if ( amount != 0 )
            TEScroll( 0, amount * ((*te)->lineHeight), te );
    }
    else if ( mouse.v > gMiscRect.bottom )
    {
        amount = -1;
        CommonAction( form->vScroll, &amount );
        if ( amount != 0 )
            TEScroll( 0, amount * ((*te)->lineHeight), te );
    }
```

```
        SetClip( oldClip );
        DisposeRgn( oldClip );
        SetPort( oldPort );
        return( TRUE );
}


/**************************** SwitchToNewArea ********/

void        SwitchToNewArea( form, newArea )
FormPeek    form;
int         newArea;
{
    if ( form->curTE == form->nameTE )
    {
        TurnOffTextArea( form, TE_NAME_AREA );
        TurnOnTextArea( form, TE_MISC_AREA );
    }
    else
    {
        TurnOffTextArea( form, TE_MISC_AREA );
        TurnOnTextArea( form, TE_NAME_AREA );
    }
}


/***************************** TurnOnTextArea ********/

void        TurnOnTextArea( form, whichArea )
FormPeek    form;
int         whichArea;
{
    TEPtr   te;

    if ( whichArea == TE_MISC_AREA )
    {
        te = *form->miscTE;
        te->viewRect.bottom = ((((te->viewRect.bottom - te-
>viewRect.top) / te->lineHeight)
                        * te->lineHeight) + te-
>viewRect.top;
        te->destRect.bottom = te->viewRect.bottom;
        AdjustScrollBar( form );
        form->curTE = form->miscTE;
    }
```

```
    else
        form->curTE = form->nameTE;

    TEActivate( form->curTE );
}



/****************************** TurnOffTextArea ********/

void        TurnOffTextArea( form, whichArea )
FormPeek    form;
int         whichArea;
{
    if ( whichArea == TE_MISC_AREA )
        TEDeactivate( form->miscTE );
    else
        TEDeactivate( form->nameTE );
}



/****************************** AdjustScrollBar ********/

void        AdjustScrollBar( form )
FormPeek    form;
{
    short   value, lines, max;
    short   oldValue, oldMax;
    TEPtr   te;

    oldValue = GetCtlValue( form->vScroll );
    oldMax = GetCtlMax( form->vScroll );
    te = *(form->miscTE);

    lines = te->nLines;
    if ( *(*te->hText + te->teLength - 1) ==
TE_CARRIAGE_RETURN )
        lines += 1;
    max = lines - ((te->viewRect.bottom - te->viewRect.top) /
        te->lineHeight);

    if ( max < 0 ) max = 0;
    SetCtlMax( form->vScroll, max);
```

```
        te = *(form->miscTE);
        value = (te->viewRect.top - te->destRect.top) / te-
                >lineHeight;

        if ( value < 0 ) value = 0;
        else if ( value >  max ) value = max;

        SetCtlValue( form->vScroll, value);

        TEScroll( 0, (te->viewRect.top - te->destRect.top) -
                (GetCtlValue( form->vScroll ) * te-
                >lineHeight), form->miscTE );
}


/******************************* ErrorHandler ********/

void    ErrorHandler( stringNum )
int stringNum;
{
    StringHandle   errorStringH;

    if ( ( errorStringH = GetString( stringNum ) ) ==
NIL_POINTER )
        ParamText( HOPELESSLY_FATAL_ERROR, NIL_STRING,
NIL_STRING, NIL_STRING );
    else
    {
        HLock( errorStringH );
        ParamText( *errorStringH, NIL_STRING, NIL_STRING,
NIL_STRING );
        HUnlock( errorStringH );
    }
    StopAlert( ERROR_ALERT_ID, NIL_POINTER );
    ExitToShell();
}
```

Running FormEdit

Whew! That was a long one. Now you're ready to see if it runs. Select Run from the Project menu. When asked to "Bring the project up to date?", click the Yes button. THINK C will try to compile FormEdit.c. If you run into problems, check for typos and missing code. Once FormEdit.c compiles, THINK C will try to load MacTraps (did you remember to add MacTraps to the project?). If you haven't saved your source code, THINK C will give you a chance to save just before it runs the program. Always save before you run. Wouldn't you just hate to lose all that typing because your program crashed and you had forgotten to save? Do it.

Once FormEdit starts running, the , File, and Edit menus should appear on the menu bar. If your program crashes at this point, THINK C may not have been able to locate your resource file. Select **About FormEdit** from the  menu. The About Alert should appear. Click the OK button. Now select New from the File menu. A form window should appear, much like the one in Figure 5.10.

Notice that the cursor changes to an I-Beam cursor when you move it over either of the two TextEdit fields. The cursor should change back to the arrow cursor when it is not over either the Name or the Misc field.

Type your name in the Name field. The title of the window should change to agree with the text in the Name field. Type enough text in the Misc field to cause the scroll bar to appear. Select some text in the Misc field. You should see something like Figure 5.23.

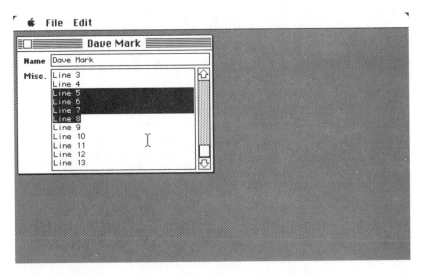

Figure 5.23   Some text selected in the scrolling field.

Try selecting some text in the Misc field, dragging the cursor both above and below the boundaries of the Misc field. The text should scroll automatically up and down to the end of the field. Test the scroll bar. Click in the up and down arrows as well as the page areas and the thumb of the scroll bar.

Select some text, select Copy from the Edit menu, click somewhere else, and select Paste from the Edit menu. Press the Tab key a few times. TextEdit will switch between the two fields. When TextEdit switches into the Name field, the entire name field is selected. When TextEdit switches into the Misc field, the selection remains as it was the last time you were in the Misc field.

Finally, create some extra windows by selecting New from the File menu. Experiment with activate and update events by selecting different windows and by covering one window with another.

Walking Through the Form Edit Source Code

If you've read the first volume of the *Macintosh Programming Primer,* much of FormEdit's code will seem familiar. The descriptions that follow don't spend a lot of time going over old concepts; instead, they focus on the new stuff.

As usual, the program starts off with the #defines. Notice the naming convention used for menu items.

```
/*******************/
/*       MENUs      */
/*******************/

#define  APPLE_MENU_ID       400
#define  A_ABOUT_ITEM        1

#define  FILE_MENU_ID        401
#define  F_NEW_ITEM          1
#define  F_CLOSE_ITEM        2
#define  F_QUIT_ITEM         3

#define  EDIT_MENU_ID        402
#define  E_UNDO_ITEM         1
#define  E_CUT_ITEM          3
#define  E_COPY_ITEM         4
#define  E_PASTE_ITEM        5
#define  E_CLEAR_ITEM        6
```

These four window types are the legal returns by the function
`WindowType()`.

```
/*******************/
/*   Window Types   */
/*******************/

#define NIL_WINDOW        0
#define UNKNOWN_WINDOW    1
#define DA_WINDOW         2
#define FORM_WINDOW       3
```

These are the resource IDs for the `ALRT` and `'STR'` resources.

```
/*******************/
/*      ALRTs       */
/*******************/

#define ABOUT_ALERT           400
#define ERROR_ALERT_ID        401


/*******************/
/*   Error STRs    */
/*******************/

#define NO_MBAR               BASE_RES_ID
#define NO_MENU               BASE_RES_ID+1
#define NO_WIND               BASE_RES_ID+2
```

`TE_NAME_AREA` and `TE_MISC_AREA` are used to refer to the two
fields in a form window. Following these are defines for some
standard TextEdit keys.

```
/*******************/
/*    TextEdit      */
/*******************/

#define TE_NAME_AREA          0
#define TE_MISC_AREA          1

#define TE_ENTER_KEY          3
#define TE_DELETE_CHAR        8
#define TE_TAB_CHAR           9
#define TE_CARRIAGE_RETURN   13
```

These general defines should be familiar to you. If not, go back to Volume I of this book.

```
/***********************/
/*  General Defines        */
/***********************/

#define BASE_RES_ID          400
#define NIL_POINTER          0L
#define MOVE_TO_FRONT        -1L
#define REMOVE_ALL_EVENTS    0

#define DRAG_THRESHOLD 30

#define WINDOW_HOME_LEFT     5
#define WINDOW_HOME_TOP      45
#define NEW_WINDOW_OFFSET    20

#define MIN_SLEEP            60L
#define NIL_MOUSE_REGION     0L

#define LEAVE_WHERE_IT_IS    FALSE

#define WNE_TRAP_NUM         0x60
#define UNIMPL_TRAP_NUM      0x9F
#define SUSPEND_RESUME_BIT   0x0001
#define RESUMING             1

#define NIL_STRING              "\p"
#define UNTITLED_STRING         "\p<Untitled>"
#define VISIBLE                 TRUE
#define HOPELESSLY_FATAL_ERROR  "\pGame over, man!"
```

The macros `TopLeft()` and `BotRight()` take a `Rect` as a parameter and convert it to a `Point`. They both rely on the relationship between the `Rect` and `Point` data structures, counting on the fact that the first two fields of the `Rect` struct are exactly identical to the `Point` struct.

Many Macintosh programs use these macros. It's probably all right to use them in your programs, too, but be aware; you are counting on Apple's never changing the relationship between `Point`s and `Rect`s. If they ever do, your program will break. Don't worry, Apple won't change this relationship. But your "Danger, Will Robinson" alarm should go off every time you use a technique like this. For more comments on this topic, see the notes on being 32-bit clean in Chapter 2.

```
/***********************/
/*     Useful Macros       */
/***********************/

#define TopLeft( myRect )      (* (Point *) &(myRect.top) )
#define BotRight( myRect )     (* (Point *) &(myRect.bottom) )
```

Remember the discussion on the window piggybacking technique in Chapter 2? This is exactly the basis behind `FormRecords` and `FormPeeks`. By casting a `FormPeek` as a `WindowPtr`, you can give routines like `SetPort()` access to your form as a window, yet by passing the `FormPeek` directly, you can access the scroll bar and the `TEHandle`s.

`vScroll` is a handle for the scroll bar adjacent to the Misc field.

`nameTE` is a handle to the Name field's TextEdit data and `miscTE` is a handle to the Misc field's TextEdit data. We use `curTE` as a temporary variable. It will be set to either `nameTE` or `miscTE`.

```
/***********************/
/*      Typedefs         */
/***********************/

typedef    struct
{
    WindowRecord       w;
    int                wType;
    ControlHandle      vScroll;
    TEHandle           nameTE, miscTE, curTE;
} FormRecord,          *FormPeek;
```

Most of these globals should be familiar to you from *Macintosh Programming, Volume I* of this book. The new globals, gNameRect, gMiscRect, and gScrollRect, hold the local coordinates for the rectangles defining the Name field, the Misc field, and the scroll bar.

```
/*********************/
/*        Globals        */
/*********************/

Boolean        gDone, gWNEImplemented, gInBackground;
EventRecord    gTheEvent;
MenuHandle     gAppleMenu,
               gFileMenu,
               gEditMenu;
int            gNewWindowLeft = WINDOW_HOME_LEFT,
               gNewWindowTop = WINDOW_HOME_TOP;
Rect           gNameRect = { 3, 43, 19, 250 },
               gMiscRect = { 22, 43, 150, 231 },
               gScrollBarRect = { 22, 234, 150, 250 };
```

The use of routine and parameter prototypes was discussed in Chapter 2. For quick programs, these prototypes probably aren't necessary. Once your programs get to any size and complexity, however, prototypes will really save the day.

```
/*********************/
/*      Routines       */
/*********************/

void           AdjustCursor( Point mouse, RgnHandle region );
void           AdjustMenus( void );
void           AdjustScrollBar( FormPeek form );
void           CommonAction( ControlHandle   control, short
                       *amount );
void           CreateWindow( void );
void           DoActivate( WindowPtr window, Boolean
                       becomingActive );
void           DoCloseWindow( WindowPtr window );
void           DoContentClick( WindowPtr window, Point mouse );
void           DoIdle( void );
void           DoTEKey( char c );
void           DoUpdate( WindowPtr window );
void           DrawForm( WindowPtr window );
```

```
void            ErrorHandler( int stringNum );
void            HandleAppleChoice( int theItem );
void            HandleEditChoice( int theItem );
void            HandleEvent( void );
void            HandleFileChoice( int theItem );
void            HandleMenuChoice( long int menuChoice );
void            HandleMouseDown( void );
void            MainLoop( void );
void            MenuBarInit( void );
pascal Boolean  NewClikLoop( void );
void            StartTextEdit( FormPeek form );
void            SwitchToNewArea( FormPeek form, int newArea );
void            ToolBoxInit( void );
void            TurnOffTextArea( FormPeek form, int whichArea );
void            TurnOnTextArea( FormPeek form, int whichArea );
pascal void     VActionProc( ControlHandle control, int part );
int             WindowType( WindowPtr window );
```

main() initializes the toolbox, loads the menu bar, and starts the main event loop.

```
/****************************** main ********/

main()
{
    ToolBoxInit();
    MenuBarInit();

    MainLoop();
}
```

There's nothing new in ToolBoxInit().

```
/********************************* ToolBoxInit */

void    ToolBoxInit()
{
    InitGraf( &thePort );
    InitFonts();
    FlushEvents( everyEvent, REMOVE_ALL_EVENTS );
    InitWindows();
    InitMenus();
    TEInit();
    InitDialogs( NIL_POINTER );
    InitCursor();
}
```

MenuBarInit() is pretty much the same as always. You'll need gAppleMenu for desk accessory management, gFileMenu to disable the Close item when there are no open windows, and gEditMenu to disable and enable the Cut, Copy, Paste, and Clear items as appropriate.

```
/********************************** MenuBarInit */

void    MenuBarInit()
{
    Handle      myMenuBar;

    if ( ( myMenuBar = GetNewMBar( BASE_RES_ID ) ) ==
        NIL_POINTER )
        ErrorHandler( NO_MBAR );
    SetMenuBar( myMenuBar );

    if ( ( gAppleMenu = GetMHandle( APPLE_MENU_ID ) ) ==
        NIL_POINTER )
        ErrorHandler( NO_MENU );
    AddResMenu( gAppleMenu, 'DRVR' );

    if ( ( gFileMenu = GetMHandle( FILE_MENU_ID ) ) ==
        NIL_POINTER )
        ErrorHandler( NO_MENU );

    if ( ( gEditMenu = GetMHandle( EDIT_MENU_ID ) ) ==
        NIL_POINTER )
        ErrorHandler( NO_MENU );

    DrawMenuBar();
}
```

Now things start to get interesting. The variable cursorRgn defines the region appropriate to the current cursor. FormEdit makes use of two basic regions. The first is the union of gNameRect and gMiscRect. When the cursor is inside this region, it is set to the I-Beam cursor normally used for TextEdit fields. The second region consists of the biggest Rect that can be defined with holes punched in it, leaving out gNameRect and gMiscRect. When the cursor is in this region, it is set to the standard arrow cursor.

```
/************************** MainLoop *********/

void    MainLoop()
{
    RgnHandle   cursorRgn;
    Boolean             gotEvent;

    gDone = FALSE;
    gInBackground = FALSE;
```

Before the call to NewRgn(), cursorRgn is an uninitialized variable. After the call, cursorRgn is a handle to a nil region. The difference is that after the call, cursorRgn can be passed to region operations such as SetRectRgn() and UnionRgn().

```
    cursorRgn = NewRgn();
```

As usual, the program finds out if WaitNextEvent() is available. If it is, the program calls it. Notice that cursorRgn is passed as a parameter to WaitNextEvent().

One of the events discussed in *Macintosh Programming Primer, Volume I* was the app4Evt. The Event Manager uses the app4Evt to pass several new event types to your program. The first two are the suspend and resume events you should already be familiar with (check out EventTutor from Volume I if you're not). The suspend/resume events are indicated by a high-byte value of 0x01 in the event.message field of an app4Evt. Bit 0 of the event.message field indicates either a suspend (0) or a resume (1) event. Bit 1 of the event.message field indicates whether (1) or not (0) scrap-conversion should be performed by your application on a resume event.

A high-byte value of 0xFA in the event.message field of an app4Evt indicates a mouse-moved event. The mouse-moved event tells your application that the cursor has been moved out of the last cursorRgn passed to WaitNextEvent(). As long as the cursor stays within the bounds of the current cursorRgn, no mouse-moved event will be generated.

The techniques used in this program were distilled from several applications distributed by Apple to developers, as well as from the *Programmer's Guide to MultiFinder* (available from APDA). Although FormEdit doesn't make full use of the scrap-conversion bit or the mouse-moved events, both of these features are supported within the program. Feel free to use FormEdit's approach to cursor support and scrap conversion or to develop your own method designed more specifically around the mouse-moved event and the scrap-conversion bit.

```
gWNEImplemented = ( NGetTrapAddress( WNE_TRAP_NUM,
                    ToolTrap ) != NGetTrapAddress
                    ( UNIMPL_TRAP_NUM, ToolTrap ) );
while ( gDone == FALSE )
{
    if ( gWNEImplemented )
        gotEvent = WaitNextEvent( everyEvent, &gTheEvent,
                                  MIN_SLEEP, cursorRgn );
    else
    {
        SystemTask();
        gotEvent = GetNextEvent( everyEvent, &gTheEvent );
    }
```

Once the appropriate event routine has been called, the program makes its periodic call to `AdjustCursor()` to make sure the correct cursor is in place.

```
        AdjustCursor( gTheEvent.where, cursorRgn );
```

If this call received an event, the program handles it. If not, it calls `DoIdle()` to take care of any housekeeping chores, such as blinking the caret at the text insertion point.

```
        if ( gotEvent )
            HandleEvent();
        else
            DoIdle();
    }
}
```

The basic structure of `HandleEvent()` remains the same. On a `nullEvent`, the program takes care of housekeeping chores with `DoIdle()`. It handles `mouseDowns` via a call to to `HandleMouseDown()`.

```
/*************************** HandleEvent */

void        HandleEvent()
{
    char        c;

    switch ( gTheEvent.what )
    {
        case nullEvent:
            DoIdle();
            break;
        case mouseDown:
            HandleMouseDown();
            break;
```

On `keyDown` and `autoKey` events, if the ⌘ key was held down the program calls `AdjustMenus()` to disable and enable the appropriate menus. Then it calls `MenuKey()` and `HandleMenuChoice()` to handle the command key equivalents. If the ⌘ key was not held down, the program passes the key on to TextEdit, which will use the key to edit the currently activated TEHandle.

```
        case keyDown:
        case autoKey:
            c = gTheEvent.message &
charCodeMask;
            if (( gTheEvent.modifiers & cmdKey
) != 0)
            {
                AdjustMenus();
                HandleMenuChoice( MenuKey( c
) );
            }
            else
                DoTEKey( c );
            break;
```

On an `activateEvt`, the program calls `DoActivate()`, passing as the second parameter a `BOOLEAN` set to `TRUE` if the window is becoming active, `FALSE` otherwise. On an `updateEvt`, the program passes the `WindowPtr` to `DoUpdate()`. Finally, the program handles the `app4Evt`s. If the event is a suspend/resume event, the global `gInBackground` is set to `TRUE` if the application is running in the foreground and `FALSE` otherwise. If the event wasn't an `app4Evt`, the program treats it like a `nullEvt` and uses the time to do its periodic housekeeping chores.

```
case activateEvt:
    DoActivate( (WindowPtr)gTheEvent.message,
                (gTheEvent.modifiers & activeFlag) != 0 );
    break;
case updateEvt:
    DoUpdate( (WindowPtr)gTheEvent.message );
    break;
case app4Evt:
    if ( ( gTheEvent.message & SUSPEND_RESUME_BIT ) ==
        RESUMING )
    {
        gInBackground = (gTheEvent.message & 0x01) == 0;
        DoActivate(FrontWindow(), !gInBackground);
    }
    else
        DoIdle();
    break;
    }
}
```

`DoTEKey()` starts out with a call to `WindowType()` to make sure that the window receiving the keystroke is of type `FORM_WINDOW`. If the program didn't check this, it would be taking a real risk when it casts the `WindowPtr` to a `FormPeek` to access the `FormRecord` fields.

```
/************************************ DoTEKey
*/

void        DoTEKey( c )
char        c;
{
    WindowPtr           window;
    FormPeek            form;
    int                 wType, length, i;
    CharsHandle         text;
    Str255              tempStr;

    window = FrontWindow();
    wType = WindowType( window );

    if ( wType == FORM_WINDOW )
    {
        form = (FormPeek)window;
```

Once the program knows it is looking at a `FORM_WINDOW`, the next step is to process the character. If the character is a Tab, the user wants to switch TextEdit fields. If the cursor is in the name field, the program calls `SwitchToNewArea()` to switch to the misc field.

If the cursor is in the misc field, the program switches to the name field, but this time it highlights all the characters in the name field with a call to `TESetSelect()`. Because a TextEdit field is limited to 32K characters, passing 0 as the start of the selection and 32767 as the end of the selection guarantees that all available text will be selected.

The same technique could be used to select the entire Misc field when the program switches to it, but this approach leaves the selection as it was the last time the user was in the Misc field. Experiment.

```
if ( c == TE_TAB_CHAR )
{
    if ( form->curTE == form->nameT.E )
        SwitchToNewArea( form, TE_MISC_AREA );
    else
    {
        SwitchToNewArea( form, TE_NAME_AREA );
        TESetSelect( 0, 32767, form->curTE );
    }
}
```

If the character is not a tab key, the program passes the key to TextEdit, letting TextEdit do its thing. If the key was pressed in the Name field, the program adjusts the window's title to reflect the contents of the name field. If the field is empty (perhaps as the result of a Delete key press), the program sets the tile of the window to whatever was #defined in `UNTITLED_STRING`. If the field is not empty, the program converts the number of bytes designated by the `TEHandle`'s `teLength` field into a Pascal string and passes the result to `SetWTitle()`.

> Remember, Pascal strings consist of a length byte followed by up to 255 consecutive bytes of characters. The `TEHandle` can't use Pascal strings, as it must handle up to 32K characters. The `teLength` field determines how many bytes are handled by the `hText` field. The routine `TEGetText()` returns a handle that is functionally equivalent to the `hText` field. In other words, `TEGetText()` returns, not a copy of the text, but a handle to the actual text.

```
else
{
    TEKey( c, form->curTE );
    if ( form->curTE == form->nameTE )
    {
        length = (*form->nameTE)->teLength;
        if ( length == 0 )
            SetWTitle( window, UNTITLED_STRING );
        else
        {
            text = TEGetText( form->nameTE );
            tempStr[ 0 ] = length;
            for ( i=0; ( (i<length) && (i<256) ); i++ )
            {
                tempStr[ i+1 ] = (*text)[ i ];
            }
            SetWTitle( window, tempStr );
        }
    }
}
```

If the key is destined for the Misc field, the only thing the program needs to do is adjust the value in the scroll bar in case the number of lines in the text field has changed. Note that the number of lines can be changed through the addition of a single character, as well as through the deletion of a character (or many selected characters).

```
        else
            AdjustScrollBar( form );
    }
  }
}
```

`DoIdle()` calls `TEIdle()` if the `FrontWindow()` is a `FORM_WINDOW`. `TEIdle()` blinks the caret at the insertion point of the currently active TextEdit record if a certain amount of time has passed since the last blink. The program always keeps the `curTE` field set to the currently active TextEdit record. This means the value of `curTE` will always be equal to either `nameTE` or `miscTE`.

> By the way, the blinking time is determined by the four bytes starting at 0x2F4 in low memory. You can access this value using the low-memory global `CaretTime`.

```
/********************************  DoIdle  */

void        DoIdle()
{
    WindowPtr    window;
    int          wType;

    window = FrontWindow();
    wType = WindowType( window );

    if ( wType == FORM_WINDOW )
        TEIdle( ((FormPeek)window)->curTE );
}
```

`HandleMouseDown()` should be pretty familiar to you. There are a few changes, however. When a `mouseDown` occurs in the menu bar, the program calls `AdjustMenus()` before it pulls down the menu with `MenuSelect()`. As was mentioned before, `AdjustMenus()` enables and disables the appropriate menus before every menu selection.

```
/**************************************
HandleMouseDown */

void      HandleMouseDown()
{
    WindowPtr   window;
    short int   thePart;
    long int    menuChoice, windSize;

    thePart = FindWindow( gTheEvent.where, &window );
    switch ( thePart )
    {
        case inMenuBar:
            AdjustMenus();
            menuChoice = MenuSelect(
                        gTheEvent.where );
            HandleMenuChoice( menuChoice );
            break;
        case inSysWindow:
            SystemClick( &gTheEvent, window );
            break;
```

If the `inContent` event occurs in a window that isn't the frontmost window, the program brings the window to the front with `SelectWindow()`. If the window is already in front, the program passes the `WindowPtr` and the mouse location to `DoContentClick()`.

```
        case inContent:
            if ( window != FrontWindow() )
            {
                SelectWindow(window);
            }
            else
                DoContentClick( window,
                            gTheEvent.where );
            break;
```

```
case inDrag:
    DragWindow( window, gTheEvent.where,
            &(screenBits.bounds) );
    break;
```

Finally, if the mouse is clicked in a window's close box (also known as the goAway box), the program calls `TrackGoAway()` to animate the close box and, if the mouse is released in the close box, it calls `DoCloseWindow()`.

```
case inGoAway:
    if ( TrackGoAway(window,
        gTheEvent.where) )
        DoCloseWindow( window );
    break;
    }
}
```

When the program closes a window, it must properly dispose of the elements that make up the window (such as controls, TextEdit records, etc.). First, the program hides the window so the user doesn't see things disappear one by one as they are freed.

For example, when the program calls `DisposeControl()`, the memory occupied by the scroll bar we allocated with `NewControl()` is freed. If the window weren't hidden when this was done, the scroll bar would disappear while the window were still up. If a lot of housekeeping needed to be done before the window were finally closed, the window contents would disappear, one at a time, giving the process a jerky feel. Not good!

`TEDispose()` frees up the text handled by the `TERecord` and the `TERecord` itself. `CloseWindow()` frees up the window-related data structures (closing the window, if necessary) and adjusts the application's window list to reflect the loss of a window. `CloseWindow()` does not free up the memory that was allocated (or that will be allocated) within the call to `CreateWindow()`. If the program had allocated the window normally, it could just call `DisposeWindow()` to free up the window. Because it used `NewPtr()` to allocate the window's memory (to take advantage of the window piggybacking technique described in Chapter 2), the program must free up the window's memory itself using `DisposPtr()`.

```
/**************************** DoCloseWindow */

void      DoCloseWindow( window )
WindowPtr window;
{
    HideWindow( window );
    DisposeControl( ((FormPeek)window)->vScroll );
    TEDispose( ((FormPeek)window)->nameTE );
    TEDispose( ((FormPeek)window)->miscTE );
    CloseWindow( window );
    DisposPtr( window );
}
```

AdjustMenus() is responsible for disabling and enabling the appropriate menu items in the menu bar. For starters, if there is no front window, the program disables the File menu's Close item (because there's no window to close). In addition, it disables all the items in the Edit menu (because there's no active TextEdit record, so there is nothing to cut, copy, paste, or clear).

```
/***************************** AdjustMenus */

void    AdjustMenus()
{
    WindowPtr    window;
    int          wType;
    int          offset;
    TEHandle     te;

    window = FrontWindow();
    wType = WindowType( window );

    if ( window == NIL_POINTER )
    {
        DisableItem( gFileMenu, F_CLOSE_ITEM );

        DisableItem( gEditMenu, E_UNDO_ITEM );
        DisableItem( gEditMenu, E_CUT_ITEM );
        DisableItem( gEditMenu, E_COPY_ITEM );
        DisableItem( gEditMenu, E_PASTE_ITEM );
        DisableItem( gEditMenu, E_CLEAR_ITEM );
    }
```

If there is a front window and the window belongs to a desk accessory, the program disables the File menu's Close item. If the program left the Close item enabled, some code would have to be added to `HandleFileChoice()` to handle the closing of a desk accessories. The program also enables all of the Edit menu items, making them available to the DA.

```
else if ( wType == DA_WINDOW )
{
    DisableItem( gFileMenu, F_CLOSE_ITEM );

    EnableItem( gEditMenu, E_UNDO_ITEM );
    EnableItem( gEditMenu, E_CUT_ITEM );
    EnableItem( gEditMenu, E_COPY_ITEM );
    EnableItem( gEditMenu, E_PASTE_ITEM );
    EnableItem( gEditMenu, E_CLEAR_ITEM );
}
```

If the front window belongs to this application (if its type is `FORM_WINDOW`), the program enables the File menu's Close item. Next, it (temporarily) disables all the Edit items. If at least one character is selected, the program enables the Cut, Copy, and Clear items. If the scrap isn't empty, the program enables the Paste item.

```
else if ( wType == FORM_WINDOW )
{
    EnableItem( gFileMenu, F_CLOSE_ITEM );

    DisableItem( gEditMenu, E_UNDO_ITEM );
    DisableItem( gEditMenu, E_CUT_ITEM );
    DisableItem( gEditMenu, E_COPY_ITEM );
    DisableItem( gEditMenu, E_PASTE_ITEM );
    DisableItem( gEditMenu, E_CLEAR_ITEM );

    te = ((FormPeek)window)->curTE;
    if ( (*te)->selStart < (*te)->selEnd )
    {
        EnableItem( gEditMenu, E_CUT_ITEM );
        EnableItem( gEditMenu, E_COPY_ITEM );
        EnableItem( gEditMenu, E_CLEAR_ITEM );
    }
    if ( GetScrap( NIL_POINTER, 'TEXT',
        &offset) > 0 )
        EnableItem( gEditMenu, E_PASTE_ITEM );
}
}
```

WindowType() returns one of the four window type constants: NIL_WINDOW, DA_WINDOW, FORM_WINDOW, or, if it doesn't match one of these, UNKNOWN_WINDOW. All desk accessories have a negative value in the windowKind field of the WindowRecord. When the program creates a new window, it declares it as a FormRecord and sets the windowType field to FORM_WINDOW (check out CreateWindow() below).

Why does the program cast the window to WindowPeek to get at the windowKind field? Good question! When programmers work with windows, they normally work with WindowPtrs. If you turn to *Inside Macintosh, Volume I,* page 275, you'll see that WindowPtrs are really just GrafPtrs, which are pointers to GrafPorts, not WindowRecords. Most of the fields that are associated with windows are really part of the GrafPort declared at the top of every WindowRecord.

Remember the window piggybacking technique from Chapter 2? Well, WindowRecords piggyback their window data on top of a GrafPort. WindowPeeks are pointers to WindowRecords and thus give you access to extra fields like windowKind.

```
/*********************************** WindowType */

int WindowType( window )
WindowPtr   window;
{
    if ( window == NIL_POINTER )
        return( NIL_WINDOW );

    if ( ((WindowPeek)window)->windowKind < 0 )
        return( DA_WINDOW );

    if ( ((FormPeek)window)->wType == FORM_WINDOW )
        return( FORM_WINDOW );

    return( UNKNOWN_WINDOW );
}
```

`HandleMenuChoice()` dispatches menu selections to one of the three menu-handling routines.

```
/********************************** HandleMenuChoice */

void    HandleMenuChoice( menuChoice )
long int    menuChoice;
{
    int theMenu;
    int theItem;

    if ( menuChoice != 0 )
    {
        theMenu = HiWord( menuChoice );
        theItem = LoWord( menuChoice );
        switch ( theMenu )
        {
            case APPLE_MENU_ID :
                HandleAppleChoice( theItem );
                break;
            case FILE_MENU_ID :
                HandleFileChoice( theItem );
                break;
            case EDIT_MENU_ID :
                HandleEditChoice( theItem );
        }
        HiliteMenu( 0 );
    }
}
```

You should recognize `HandleAppleChoice()` from *Macintosh Programming, Volume I.*

```
/************************** HandleAppleChoice ******/

void    HandleAppleChoice( theItem )
int theItem;
{
    Str255      accName;
    int         accNumber;
```

```
    switch ( theItem )
    {
        case A_ABOUT_ITEM :
            NoteAlert( ABOUT_ALERT, NIL_POINTER );
            break;
        default :
            GetItem( gAppleMenu, theItem, accName );
            accNumber = OpenDeskAcc( accName );
            break;
    }
}
```

HandleFileChoice() calls CreateWindow() when the File
menu's New item is selected. If the Close item is selected,
HandleFileChoice() calls DoCloseWindow(). If the Quit item
is selected, the global gDone is set to TRUE, allowing FormEdit to
exit gracefully.

```
/***************************         HandleFileChoice    *******/

void    HandleFileChoice( theItem )
int theItem;
{
    WindowPtr    window;
    switch ( theItem )
    {
        case F_NEW_ITEM :
            CreateWindow();
            break;
        case F_CLOSE_ITEM :
            if ( ( window = FrontWindow() ) != NIL_POINTER )
                DoCloseWindow( window );
            break;
        case F_QUIT_ITEM :
            gDone = TRUE;
            break;
    }
}
```

HandleEditChoice() starts off with a call to SystemEdit().
The parameter represents one of these Edit menu commands: Undo,
Cut, Copy, Paste, or Clear. If the frontmost window belongs to a desk
accessory (DA), SystemEdit() passes the Edit command to the DA

and returns `TRUE`. In this case, the program is done, as the Edit command wasn't meant for this application.

If the frontmost window doesn't belong to a DA (or doesn't exist), `SystemEdit()` will return `FALSE`. In this case, the menu selection was intended for this application and the program must handle it.

```
/*****************************  HandleEditChoice  *******/

void    HandleEditChoice( theItem )
int theItem;
{
    TEHandle        te;
    WindowPtr       window;
    int                 wType, length, i;
    CharsHandle     text;
    Str255          tempStr;
    FormPeek        form;

    if ( ! SystemEdit( theItem - 1 ) )
    {
        window = FrontWindow();
        wType = WindowType( window );

        if ( wType == FORM_WINDOW )
        {
            form = (FormPeek)window;
            te = form->curTE;
            switch ( theItem )
            {
```

The sample program shown here doesn't support an Undo strategy, but your programs should. You'll have to decide on an Undo strategy that makes sense, given the specifics of your application. Are you using TextEdit? If so, you may want to keep the last set of keystrokes since the last delete in a buffer, in preparation for an Undo command. If your application focuses on graphics, you might want to build a table of undoable graphics commands, keeping the most recent in a global variable or struct.

Whatever you decide, lay out your Undo strategy early on in your development cycle. This is important, even if you don't plan on supporting Undo in Version 1.0. Trying to retrofit an Undo strategy can be extremely difficult.

```
                case E_UNDO_ITEM:
                    break;
```

You should also settle on a clipboard strategy early in your development strategy. Because TextEdit maintains its own scrap, the sample program's strategy is quite simple. Whenever it does a Cut or Copy, it calls the appropriate TextEdit routine (either `TECut()` or `TECopy()`) and then exports TextEdit's private scrap to the Mac's main scrap, making the selection available to other programs.

If you need some review on the Scrap Manager, go back to *Macintosh Programming Primer, Volume I,* Chapter 7. `ZeroScrap()` clears the Mac's main scrap. If the program had no problem clearing the scrap, it calls either `TECopy()` or `TECut()` (in which case it also calls `AdjustScrollBar()`, because the number of lines in the TextEdit record could be changed). Then, the program calls `TEToScrap()` to keep the main scrap current with TextEdit's scrap. If the program had a problem exporting the TextEdit scrap, it cleans up as best as it can by calling `ZeroScrap()` again.

```
case E_CUT_ITEM:
    if ( ZeroScrap() == noErr )
    {
        TECut(te);
        AdjustScrollBar( form );
        if ( TEToScrap() != noErr )
            ZeroScrap();
    }
    break;
case E_COPY_ITEM:
    if ( ZeroScrap() == noErr )
    {
        TECopy(te);
        if ( TEToScrap() != noErr )
            ZeroScrap();
    }
    break;
```

On a Paste, the program imports the main scrap to TextEdit's scrap, does a `TEPaste()`, and then adjusts the scroll bar.

```
case E_PASTE_ITEM:
    if ( TEFromScrap() == noErr )
    {
        TEPaste(te);
        AdjustScrollBar( form );
    }
    break;
```

On a Clear, the program deletes the current selection with
`TEDelete()` and then adjusts the scroll bar to compensate for any
lost lines of text.

```
case E_CLEAR_ITEM:
    TEDelete(te);
    AdjustScrollBar( form );
    break;
}
```

You may have noticed when you ran FormEdit that the title of
each window is changed so that it always reflects the contents of its
name field. If the Name field is empty, the program changes the title
to <Untitled>. This next bit of code (in conjunction with `DoTEKey()`)
handles this situation.

If the current length of the `nameTE` TextEdit record is 0, change
the window title to <Untitled>. If not, call `TEGetText()` to get a
handle to the text, copy it into a Pascal string (making sure to create
a Pascal string length byte first), then set the window's title.

```
if ( te == form->nameTE )
{
    length = (*form->nameTE)->teLength;
    if ( length == 0 )
        SetWTitle( window, UNTITLED_STRING );
    else
    {
        text = TEGetText( form->nameTE );
        tempStr[ 0 ] = length;
        for ( i=0; ( (i<length) && (i<256) ); i++ )
        {
            tempStr[ i+1 ] = (*text)[ i ];
        }
        SetWTitle( window, tempStr );
    }
}

        }
    }
}
```

`DoContentClick()` handles a mouse click in the content region
of a `FORM_WINDOW`. For a refresher course in window structure,
check out *Macintosh Programming Primer, Volume I,* Chapter 3.

```
/****************************** DoContentClick    ******/

void    DoContentClick( window, mouse )
WindowPtr   window;
Point       mouse;
{
    int             wType, value;
    int             thePart;
    Boolean         shiftDown;
    Point           locMouse;
    ControlHandle   control;
    FormPeek        form;

    wType = WindowType( window );

    if ( wType == FORM_WINDOW )
    {
```

The program is interested in three different categories of content region mouse clicks: a click in the scroll bar, a click in the name field, and a click in the misc field. First, the program gets the mouse location and converts it to this window's local coordinate system.

```
        form = (FormPeek)window;
        locMouse = mouse;
        GlobalToLocal( &locMouse );
```

Because only one control exists in this program's window, `FindControl()` will return `TRUE` only if the mouse click was in the scroll bar. If the click was in the scroll bar, `FindControl()` will return a part code, indicating whether the click was in the up arrow, down arrow, page up gray region, page down gray region, or in the thumb of the scroll bar.

If the click was in the up arrow, down arrow, page up, or page down region, the program needs to scroll the contents of the misc field continuously, as long as the mouse button is held down. It is not good enough just to scroll once and then wait for the next `mouseDown`. This would force the user to constantly click-click-click the mouse to scroll using the up arrow.

Passing a procedure pointer to `TrackControl()` causes this procedure to be called again and again, as long as the mouse button is held down in the tracked control part. If the user presses and holds the mouse button in the up arrow, for example, this procedure

(VActionProc()) will be called again and again until the user either releases the mouse button or moves the cursor out of the up arrow. In this case, VActionProc() will scroll the text up one line every time it is called.

```
if ( ( thePart = FindControl( locMouse, window,
    &control ) ) != 0 )
{
    switch( thePart )
    {
        case inUpButton:
        case inDownButton:
        case inPageUp:
        case inPageDown:
            value = TrackControl( control, locMouse,
                                  (ProcPtr) VActionProc );
            break;
```

If the mouse click was in the thumb of the scroll bar, there's no need to scroll continuously, so the program passes a NIL_POINTER for an action procedure, asking TrackControl() not to call an action procedure. Instead, the program gets the current value of the scroll bar, tracks the movement of the scroll bar thumb, and then, if the mouse button was released in the thumb, gets the new value of the control. If the thumb has moved, the program calls TEScroll(), telling it the line to which the Misc field should be scrolled. Notice that the program doesn't call TEScroll() if the scroll bar doesn't change value. You should also note that the program allows the Misc field to scroll, even if the Name field is the current field.

This last point is not intended to be a demonstration of proper text etiquette. TextEdit gives you the freedom to design your programs any way you like. FormEdit could have been designed to deactivate the scroll bar when the Misc field wasn't the current TextEdit record. It seems better this way, though.

```
        case inThumb:
            value = GetCtlValue( control );
            thePart = TrackControl( control, locMouse,
                                    NIL_POINTER );
```

```
                    if ( thePart != 0 )
                    {
                        value -= GetCtlValue( control );
                        if ( value != 0 )
                            TEScroll(0, value * (*form->curTE)-
                            >lineHeight, form->miscTE );
                    }
                    break;
            }
    }
```

If the mouse was clicked in the Name field and the Name field is the current field, the program checks to see whether the Shift key was held down. That information is then passed to TEClick(). TEClick() handles the mouse click, extending the selection and moving the insertion point as appropriate.

If the Name field isn't the current field, the program makes it the current field (via a call to SwitchToNewArea()) and then passes the mouse click to TEClick().

```
else if ( PtInRect( locMouse, &gNameRect ) )
{
    if ( form->curTE == form->nameTE )
    {
        shiftDown = ( gTheEvent.modifiers & shiftKey) != 0;
        TEClick( locMouse, shiftDown, form->nameTE );
    }
    else
    {
        SwitchToNewArea( form, TE_NAME_AREA );
        TEClick( locMouse, FALSE, form->nameTE );
    }
}
```

A mouse click in the Misc field is handled in exactly the same way as a click in the Name field.

```
else if ( PtInRect( locMouse, &gMiscRect ) )
{
    if ( form->curTE == form->miscTE )
    {
        shiftDown = ( gTheEvent.modifiers & shiftKey) != 0;
        TEClick( locMouse, shiftDown, form->miscTE );
    }
```

```
        else
        {
            SwitchToNewArea( form, TE_MISC_AREA );
            TEClick( locMouse, FALSE, form->miscTE );
        }
    }
  }
}
```

As was described in the section about `DoContentClick()`, `VActionProc()` scrolls the `Misc` field once in one direction, depending on the part code.

```
/****************************** VActionProc */

pascal void       VActionProc(control, part)
ControlHandle     control;
int               part;
{
    short amount;
    WindowPtr window;
    TEPtr     te;

    if ( part != 0 )
    {
```

Every window contains a list of controls. Conversely, every control has an owning window. This fact conveniently allows the program to conjure up a misc `TEHandle` given a handle to the Misc scroll bar.

The program sets `amount` to 1 for a click in the up or down arrow, or to the number of lines on a page if the click was in the page up or page down area.

```
window = (*control)->contrlOwner;
te = *((FormPeek)window)->miscTE;
switch ( part ) {
    case inUpButton:
    case inDownButton:        /* one line */
        amount = 1;
        break;
    case inPageUp:            /* one page */
    case inPageDown:
```

```
                    amount = (te->viewRect.bottom - te-
                            >viewRect.top) / te->lineHeight;
                    break;
          }
```

If the click was in a down arrow or page area, the program multiplies ***amount*** by -1 so that the scroll happens in the opposite direction.

```
    if ( (part == inDownButton) || (part == inPageDown) )
        amount = -amount;
```

CommonAction() checks whether the scroll bar can indeed be scrolled by amount without exceeding its limits in either the minimum or maximum settings. CommonAction() sets ***amount*** to allow as much of the requested change as possible. Finally, amount is converted from lines to pixels, and the result is passed to TEScroll().

```
    CommonAction(control, &amount);
    if ( amount != 0 )
        TEScroll( 0, amount * te->lineHeight,
                ((FormPeek)window)->miscTE );
    }
}


/********************************** CommonAction */

void    CommonAction( control, amount )
ControlHandle    control;
short            *amount;
{
    short        value, max;

    value = GetCtlValue( control );    /* get current value */
    max = GetCtlMax( control );        /* and maximum value */
    *amount = value - *amount;
    if ( *amount < 0 )
        *amount = 0;
    else if ( *amount > max )
        *amount = max;
    SetCtlValue( control, *amount );
    *amount = value - *amount;         /* calculate the real
                                          change */
}
```

`DoActivate()` is called on both an activate event (with `becomingActive` set to `TRUE`) and a deactivate event (with `becomingActive` set to `FALSE`). On an activate event, the current TextEdit area is turned on and the scroll bar is activated. On a deactivate event, the current TextEdit area is turned off and the scroll bar is deactivated.

```
/********************************** DoActivate   */

void        DoActivate( window, becomingActive )
WindowPtr   window;
Boolean     becomingActive;
{
    FormPeek    form;
    int         wType;

    wType = WindowType( window );

    if ( wType == FORM_WINDOW )
    {
        form = (FormPeek)window;
        if ( becomingActive )
        {
            SetPort( window );
            if ( form->curTE == form->miscTE )
                TurnOnTextArea( form, TE_MISC_AREA );
            else
                TurnOnTextArea( form, TE_NAME_AREA );
            HiliteControl( form->vScroll, 0 );
        }
        else
        {
            if ( form->curTE == form->miscTE )
                TurnOffTextArea( form, TE_MISC_AREA );
            else
                TurnOffTextArea( form, TE_NAME_AREA );
            HiliteControl( form->vScroll, 255 );
        }
    }
}
```

`AdjustCursor()` sets the cursor to an I-beam cursor if the cursor is in either `gMiscRect` or `gNameRect` and to an arrow cursor otherwise.

```
/***************************** AdjustCursor ********/

void        AdjustCursor( mouse, region )
Point       mouse;
RgnHandle   region;
{
    WindowPtr        window;
    RgnHandle        arrowRgn, iBeamRgn, tempRgn;
    Rect             tempRect;
    int              wType;
    GrafPtr          oldPort;

    window = FrontWindow();
    wType = WindowType( window );
```

If FormEdit is in the background (under MultiFinder) or if the frontmost window is not a `FORM_WINDOW`, the program just sets the cursor to an arrow and returns.

```
        if ( gInBackground || ( wType != FORM_WINDOW ) )
        {
                SetCursor( &arrow );
                return;
        }
```

Just to be safe, the program does a `SetPort()` to the frontmost window. Then, it allocates three new regions. The program sets the `arrowRgn` to the largest possible `Rect`.

```
        GetPort( &oldPort );
        SetPort( window );

        arrowRgn = NewRgn();
        iBeamRgn = NewRgn();
        tempRgn = NewRgn();

        SetRectRgn( arrowRgn, -32700, -32700, 32700,
                    32700 );
```

Next, the program creates a `tempRgn` the size of `gNameRect`, copies it into `iBeamRgn`, creates a `tempRgn` the size of `gMiscRect`, and unions it into `iBeamRgn`. Now, `iBeamRgn` is a noncontiguous region the shape of the Misc field plus the Name field. Next, the program calls `DiffRgn()` to punch a hole in `arrowRgn` using `iBeamRgn`.

```
tempRect = gNameRect;
LocalToGlobal( &TopLeft(tempRect) );
LocalToGlobal( &BotRight(tempRect) );
RectRgn( tempRgn, &tempRect );
UnionRgn( iBeamRgn, tempRgn, iBeamRgn );

tempRect = gMiscRect;
LocalToGlobal( &TopLeft(tempRect) );
LocalToGlobal( &BotRight(tempRect) );
RectRgn( tempRgn, &tempRect );
UnionRgn( iBeamRgn, tempRgn, iBeamRgn );

DiffRgn( arrowRgn, iBeamRgn, arrowRgn );
```

If the mouse is in the `iBeamRgn`, the program sets the cursor to the `iBeamCursor`. If not, it sets the cursor to the `arrow`. The program also sets the return parameter `region` to the appropriate region to pass to the next call to `WaitNextEvent()`. Finally, it frees up the three allocated regions and sets the port back to the saved value.

```
if ( PtInRgn( mouse, iBeamRgn ) )
{
    SetCursor( *GetCursor( iBeamCursor ) );
    CopyRgn( iBeamRgn, region );
}
else
{
    SetCursor( &arrow );
    CopyRgn( arrowRgn, region );
}
DisposeRgn( arrowRgn );
DisposeRgn( iBeamRgn );
DisposeRgn( tempRgn );

SetPort( oldPort );
}
```

On an `updateEvt`, the program calls `BeginUpdate()`, erases the window, draws the window contents, and calls `EndUpdate()`.

```
/********************************** DoUpdate */

void    DoUpdate( window )
WindowPtr  window;
{
    FormPeek     form;
    int          wType;
    GrafPtr      oldPort;

    GetPort( &oldPort );
    SetPort( window );

    wType = WindowType( window );

    if ( wType == FORM_WINDOW )
    {
        BeginUpdate( window );
        EraseRect( &window->portRect );
        DrawForm( window );
        EndUpdate( window );
    }

    SetPort( oldPort );
}
```

DrawForm() starts by framing the outline of the Name and Misc TextEdit fields and then drawing the scroll bar.

```
/********************************** DrawForm */

void    DrawForm( window )
WindowPtr  window;
{
    FrameRect( &gNameRect );
    FrameRect( &gMiscRect );
    DrawControls( window );
```

Because the words "Name" and "Misc" will appear in bold Geneva, the program first calls TextFont() and TextFace(), then draws the two strings, and then resets the font and style to plain Monaco.

```
        TextFont( geneva );
        TextFace( bold );

        MoveTo( gNameRect.left - 34, gNameRect.top + 12 );
        DrawString( "\pName" );
        MoveTo( gMiscRect.left - 34, gMiscRect.top + 12 );
        DrawString( "\pMisc." );

        TextFont( monaco );
        TextFace( 0 );
```

Finally, the program asks TextEdit to redraw the contents of the Misc. and Name fields with calls to `TEUpdate()`.

```
        TEUpdate( &window->portRect, ((FormPeek)
                window)->nameTE );
        TEUpdate( &window->portRect, ((FormPeek)
                window)->miscTE );
}
```

The program creates a new `FORM_WINDOW` using the piggyback method described in Chapter 2. It starts off by allocating a `FormRecord` using `NewPtr()`. It then passes this storage as a parameter to `GetNewWindow()`. Remember, because the program allocated the storage itself, it is responsible for deallocating the memory later with `DisposePtr()`.

The use of the globals `gNewWindowLeft` and `gNewWindowTop` should be familiar to you (if not, see WindowMaker in *Macintosh Programming Primer, Volume I,* Chapter 7).

```
/*********************************** CreateWindow  */

void    CreateWindow()
{
    WindowPtr   theNewestWindow;
    Ptr         wStorage;
    FormPeek    form;

    wStorage = NewPtr( sizeof(FormRecord) );

    if ( ( theNewestWindow = GetNewWindow( BASE_RES_ID,
        wStorage, MOVE_TO_FRONT ) ) == NIL_POINTER )
        ErrorHandler( NO_WIND );
```

```
if ( ( (screenBits.bounds.right - gNewWindowLeft) <
    DRAG_THRESHOLD ) ||
    ( ( screenBits.bounds.bottom - gNewWindowTop) <
    DRAG_THRESHOLD ) )
{
    gNewWindowLeft = WINDOW_HOME_LEFT;
    gNewWindowTop = WINDOW_HOME_TOP;
}

MoveWindow( theNewestWindow, gNewWindowLeft,
        gNewWindowTop, LEAVE_WHERE_IT_IS );
gNewWindowLeft += NEW_WINDOW_OFFSET;
gNewWindowTop += NEW_WINDOW_OFFSET;
```

Next, the program sets the `wType` field of the `FormRecord` to `FORM_WINDOW`. After that, it creates a scroll bar for the Misc field using `NewControl()`.

```
form = (FormPeek)theNewestWindow;
form->wType = FORM_WINDOW;

form->vScroll = NewControl( theNewestWindow,
        &gScrollBarRect, NIL_STRING,
        VISIBLE, 0, 0, 0, scrollBarProc, 0L);
```

Finally, the program makes the window visible, makes it the current port, sets the default font for the port (which will be used automatically by TextEdit), and starts up TextEdit for this window.

```
        ShowWindow( theNewestWindow );
        SetPort( theNewestWindow );
        TextFont( monaco );
        TextFace( 0 );
        TextSize( 9 );
        StartTextEdit( form );
    }
```

`StartTextEdit()` calls `TENew()` to create two new TextEdit records, one for the Name field and one for the Misc field.

`SetClikLoop()` gives TextEdit the address of a routine to call continuously, as long as the mouse is held down in the associated TextEdit field (in this case, the Misc field). The program passes a pointer to the routine `NewClikLoop()`. `NewClikLoop()`

automatically will scroll both the text and the scroll bar if the mouse is scrolled either above or below the boundary of the Misc field while the mouse button is still down.

TEAutoView() ensures that the TextEdit field scrolls when a new line is created that appears below the lower boundary of the Misc field. Try commenting the call to TEAutoView() and type enough text to enable the scroll bar.

```
/***************************** StartTextEdit ********/

void    StartTextEdit( form )
FormPeek    form;
{
    Rect    r;

    r = gNameRect;
    InsetRect( &r, 2, 2 );
    form->nameTE = TENew( &r, &r );

    r = gMiscRect;
    InsetRect( &r, 2, 2 );
    form->miscTE = TENew( &r, &r );
    SetClikLoop( NewClikLoop, form->miscTE );

    TEAutoView( TRUE, form->miscTE );

    form->curTE = form->nameTE;
}
```

NewClikLoop() sets the ClipRect of the current window to ensure that when the value of the scroll bar is changed, the scroll bar can be redrawn appropriately.

```
/***************************** NewClikLoop ********/

pascal Boolean NewClikLoop()
{
    WindowPtr    window;
    FormPeek     form;
    TEHandle     te;
    Rect         tempRect;
    Point        mouse;
    GrafPtr      oldPort;
    int          amount;
    RgnHandle    oldClip;
```

```
window = FrontWindow();
if ( WindowType( window ) != FORM_WINDOW ) return( FALSE );

form = (FormPeek)window;
te = form->curTE;

GetPort( &oldPort );
SetPort( window );
oldClip = NewRgn();
GetClip( oldClip );

SetRect( &tempRect, -32767, -32767, 32767, 32767 );
ClipRect( &tempRect );
```

Next, the program gets the mouse location and compares it to the top and bottom of the Misc TextEdit field. If the mouse is above that field, the program scrolls the text down one line. If the mouse is below that field, the program scrolls the text up one line.

```
GetMouse( &mouse );

if ( mouse.v < gMiscRect.top )
{
    amount = 1;
    CommonAction( form->vScroll, &amount );
    if ( amount != 0 )
        TEScroll( 0, amount * ((*te)->lineHeight), te );
}
else if ( mouse.v > gMiscRect.bottom )
{
    amount = -1;
    CommonAction( form->vScroll, &amount );
    if ( amount != 0 )
        TEScroll( 0, amount * ((*te)->lineHeight), te );
}
```

After restoring the `ClipRect`, disposing of the temporary clipping region, and setting the port to its saved value, `NewClikLoop()` returns `TRUE`, telling TextEdit that it handled the scrolling with no problems. If the program returned `FALSE`, TextEdit would stop calling it, as if the user had released the mouse button.

```
            SetClip( oldClip );
            DisposeRgn( oldClip );
            SetPort( oldPort );
            return( TRUE );
    }
```

SwitchToNewArea() turns off the current area and turns on the other area, alternating between the Name and Misc TextEdit fields.

```
/****************************** SwitchToNewArea *********/

void      SwitchToNewArea( form, newArea )
FormPeek      form;
int           newArea;
{
    if ( form->curTE == form->nameTE )
    {
        TurnOffTextArea( form, TE_NAME_AREA );
        TurnOnTextArea( form, TE_MISC_AREA );
    }
    else
    {
        TurnOffTextArea( form, TE_MISC_AREA );
        TurnOnTextArea( form, TE_NAME_AREA );
    }
}
```

If the text area to be turned on is the Misc field, TurnOnTextArea() starts by adjusting the bottom of miscTE's viewRect and destRect so that the bottom of the Rects ends just below a complete line of text. This will prevent a partially obscured line of text from appearing at the bottom of the misc field. Next, the scroll bar is adjusted, and curTE is set to the misc field.

If the text area to be turned on is the name field, the program just sets curTE to the name field. In both cases, TEActivate() is called to activate the current TextEdit field.

```
/****************************** TurnOnTextArea *********/

void      TurnOnTextArea( form, whichArea )
FormPeek      form;
int           whichArea;
{
```

```
    TEPtr      te;

            if ( whichArea == TE_MISC_AREA )
    {
        te = *form->miscTE;
        te->viewRect.bottom = (((te->viewRect.bottom - te-
                            >viewRect.top) / te->lineHeight)
                        * te->lineHeight) + te-
>viewRect.top;
        te->destRect.bottom = te->viewRect.bottom;
        AdjustScrollBar( form );
        form->curTE = form->miscTE;
    }
    else
        form->curTE = form->nameTE;

    TEActivate( form->curTE );
}
```

> TurnOffTextArea() deactivates the current TextEdit area with a call to TEDeactivate().

```
/****************************** TurnOffTextArea ********/

void    TurnOffTextArea( form, whichArea )
FormPeek    form;
int         whichArea;
{
    if ( whichArea == TE_MISC_AREA )
        TEDeactivate( form->miscTE );
    else
        TEDeactivate( form->nameTE );
}
```

> AdjustScrollBar() starts by saving the current value and maximum value of the misc scroll bar. Next, it calculates the number of lines in the Misc field and sets max to the number of lines not currently in view. This should be the max setting of the scroll bar.

```
/***************************** AdjustScrollBar *********/

void    AdjustScrollBar( form )
FormPeek    form;
{
    short       value, lines, max;
    short       oldValue, oldMax;
    TEPtr       te;

    oldValue = GetCtlValue( form->vScroll );
    oldMax = GetCtlMax( form->vScroll );
    te = *(form->miscTE);

    lines = te->nLines;
    if ( *(*te->hText + te->teLength - 1) ==
        TE_CARRIAGE_RETURN )
        lines += 1;
    max = lines - ((te->viewRect.bottom - te->viewRect.top) /
                te->lineHeight);

    if ( max < 0 ) max = 0;
    SetCtlMax( form->vScroll, max);
```

Using a similar calculation, the program comes up with a current value for the scroll bar. Once the max and value for the scroll bar have been set, the program makes sure the Misc field is scrolled to the setting indicated by the scroll bar by calling TEScroll().

```
    te = *(form->miscTE);
    value = (te->viewRect.top - te->destRect.top) / te-
            >lineHeight;

    if ( value < 0 ) value = 0;
    else if ( value >  max ) value = max;

    SetCtlValue( form->vScroll, value);

    TEScroll( 0, (te->viewRect.top - te->destRect.top) -
            (GetCtlValue( form->vScroll ) * te-
>lineHeight), form->miscTE );
}
```

ErrorHandler() remains the same as the routine presented in *Macintosh Programming Primer, Volume I.*

```
/******************************** ErrorHandler *********/

void    ErrorHandler( stringNum )
int stringNum;
{
    StringHandle    errorStringH;

    if ( ( errorStringH = GetString( stringNum ) ) ==
        NIL_POINTER )
        ParamText( HOPELESSLY_FATAL_ERROR, NIL_STRING,
                NIL_STRING, NIL_STRING );
    else
    {
        HLock( errorStringH );
        ParamText( *errorStringH, NIL_STRING, NIL_STRING,
                NIL_STRING );
        HUnlock( errorStringH );
    }
    StopAlert( ERROR_ALERT_ID, NIL_POINTER );
    ExitToShell();
}
```

In Review

Congratulations. That was a long one! You can use FormEdit as the basis for your own TextEdit-based applications. You should definitely read up on the Styled TextEdit described in *Inside Macintosh, Volume V.* If you understand the basics of FormEdit, you should have no trouble mastering the few extra routines involved in supporting multiple styles within a single TextEdit field.

The next chapter introduces you to the world of object-oriented programming, also known as OOP.

Object Programming

Object programming is definitely the future of Macintosh development. Apple is making a big investment in the technology, and is asking its developers to do the same. This chapter presents the concepts you'll need to get started with THINK's object environment.

For the last year or so, object-oriented programming has been an extremely hot topic in the Macintosh development community. Apple has made no secret of the fact that it expects developers to move in this direction. The company encourages the use of MacApp, Apple's object-oriented development environment that runs with the Macintosh Programmer's Workshop (MPW). If Apple has its way, someday all Macintosh development will be object-oriented.

This doesn't mean you should junk your college programming texts and burn your back issues of *MacTutor*. Instead, take a gradual approach. Sharpen your Macintosh programming techniques. Even in an object-oriented world, knowledge of the Macintosh Toolbox is essential. Fortunately, THINK C will let you program both ways. As you'll see in this chapter, the **THINK Class Library** (TCL) extends the THINK C environment you're used to, allowing you to program using both object-oriented and procedural techniques.

About Object Programming

Throughout this chapter, you may notice the use of the term **object programming**, as opposed to **object-oriented programming**. Object programming is the term preferred by Apple; it refers to programming using a specific set of objects, like those found in the THINK Class Library or in MacApp. Object-oriented programming has traditionally referred to programming in an object-oriented language such as C++, without the benefit of prebuilt object classes.

This chapter focuses on object programming, making use of the incredible benefits offered by the THINK Class Library. The THINK Class Library is a set of objects that implements the entire Macintosh interface. Without it, you'd have two problems to solve. First, you'd have to learn the techniques of object programming. Then, you'd have to develop your own set of objects to implement pull-down menus, event-handling, printing, MultiFinder friendliness, etc. A good class library is worth its weight in gold.

This chapter introduces the basics of object programming, using an imaginary application called Shaper. It will also walk you through the THINK Class Library, starting with the sample TCL applications found on your THINK C disks and ending with a new application built completely with TCL objects.

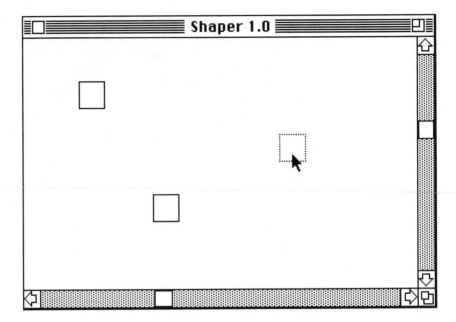

Figure 6.1   Dragging a shape in Shaper.

The Shaper Application

Imagine a Macintosh application called Shaper, made up of a single window, with scroll bars on the right and bottom sides of the window. Shaper allows you to create shapes by clicking the mouse in the content region of the window. When you click the mouse inside a shape, the shape is highlighted and follows the mouse around the window. If you drag a shape outside the window, the window will autoscroll (if it can) to follow the mouse. When you release the mouse, the shape stays where you left it.

Version 1.0 of Shaper supports only a single shape, the square. Figure 6.1 shows a Shaper window. The three squares in the Shaper window were created via mouse clicks. The highlighted square is being dragged inside the window.

An Object View of Shaper

How does this relate to object programming? Good question! The next few sections of this chapter concentrate on laying out the elements necessary to create the Shaper application using an object-oriented approach. The first step is designing the necessary **object classes**.

An object class can be thought of as a category of objects. Imagine the Shaper window filled with lots of different shapes—some squares, some circles, but all of them shapes. Each of the individual shapes can be thought of as an **object**, with its own individual properties, such as height or position. Every one of the objects, no matter how big or how small, belongs to the shape category. Each object is said to be a **member** of the shape **class**.

Some shapes might have a different set of properties than others. Circles have a radius; squares have a width. Both squares and circles have a position, however. These properties are implemented as the **instance variables** of a class. The circle class might have a `radius` instance variable, whereas the square class would have a `width` instance variable. Both the circle class and the square class would be **subclasses** of the shape object class.

An Example

The following example translates some of this theory into code. It starts simply, with the world defined by Shaper 1.0 (as seen in Figure 6.1). This example begins with a single object class, called `Shape`. Each of the squares shown in Figure 6.1 is an **instance** of the `Shape` class.

The following C code defines our `Shape` object class:

```
struct Shape : indirect
{
    Rect        bounds;

    void        IShape( Point corner, int width,
                    int height );
    void        Draw();
    void        DoClick( Point hitPt );
};
```

Object classes are declared to look remarkably like a normal `struct`. Don't be fooled! Object classes are *not* the same as `struct`s. Object class declarations always take this form:

```
struct class : superclass
{
    instance variables...

    method declarations...
};
```

In this case, the class declared is `Shape`. There is nothing special about the name `Shape`. You may give names to classes, instance variables, and methods just as you would any variable or procedure. Because `Shape` is not based on a previous class, it doesn't have a superclass.

Classes that don't have superclasses are called **root classes**. Root classes use the keywords `direct` or `indirect` in place of a superclass. Direct classes use pointers to implement their object data structures. Indirect classes use handles to implement their object data structures. If an object's superclass is defined as indirect, the object is defined as indirect. The same is true for direct object classes.

All the examples presented in this book use indirect classes. All of the classes defined in THINK's Class Library are defined as indirect. Don't use direct classes unless you have a specific reason to do so.

Instance Variables and Methods

Inside a class declaration, the first things you'll encounter are any instance variables that might be declared. An instance variable holds a value for a specific instance of an object. For example, the `Shape` object class has a single instance variable, the `Rect` called `bounds`, which defines the bounding rectangle of a `Shape`. Each of the squares in Figure 6.1's window are `Shapes`, and each one will have its own copy of `bounds`, defining its location in the window.

Following the declaration of any instance variables are the **method** declarations. The methods of an object allow access to that object by other objects. For example, each `Shape` object has a `Draw()` method. The `Draw()` method is nothing more than a routine for drawing a `Shape` object. If you had a list of `Shape` objects and you wanted to draw them all, you'd step through your list, calling each `Shape`'s `Draw()` method.

Calling an object's method is also known as passing or sending a message to that object. For example, calling a `Shape`'s `Draw()` method is exactly the same as sending a `Draw()` message to that `Shape`.

In general, most object classes support an initialization method. In `Shape`'s case, the initialization method is `IShape()`. By convention, the initialization method for an object class is always an uppercase I followed by the class name.

`IShape()` takes three parameters: `corner` is a `Point`, defining the upper left corner of the shape, defined in the window's local coordinate system; `width` and `height` are `int`s, defining the width and height of the shape; and `IShape()` uses these parameters to set the instance variable `bounds`. Because `bounds` is an instance variable, it can be accessed by any of the object's methods. Used this way, instance variables are like globals, limited to a single object.

The `Draw()` method gets called whenever the `Shape` needs to be redrawn (in response to an `updateEvt`, for example). As you might expect, `Draw()` draws the `Shape`. So far, it's been assumed that the `Shape` is a square. For the moment, that's a valid assumption, but, as you'll soon see, there are circles on the horizon. For now, the `Draw()` method draws its `Shape` with a call to `FrameRect()`.

The `DoClick()` method gets called whenever a `mouseDown` occurs within an object's `bounds` rectangle. The parameter is a `Point` that defines where the mouse click occurred.

The `IShape()` method is called by the object that creates the `Shape` object. The `Draw()` and `DoClick()` methods are called from within the application's main event loop. As you'll see (when the THINK Class Library is discussed), you can arrange your program so that these methods are called for you automatically.

Creating Some Shape Objects

The last section concentrated on designing the `Shape` object class. This section shows you how to create an instance of a `Shape` object from within your program.

Suppose for the moment that you had a routine (call it `CreateShape()`) that got called whenever a `mouseDown` occurred in the content region of the Shaper window. The routine would be passed a `Point` in the window's local coordinates, where the `mouseDown` occurred. The new `Shape` would use this `Point` as its upper left corner. Take a look at this code:

```
#define SQUARE_SIDE 15

struct Shape: indirect
{
    Rect        bounds;

    void        IShape( Point corner, int width,
                        int height );
    void        Draw();
    void        DoClick( Point hitPt );
};

void        CreateShape( corner, height, width )
Point       corner;
int         height;
int         width;
{
    Shape *newShape;

    newShape = new( Shape );
    newShape->IShape( corner, height, width );
}
```

The `Shape` object remains as declared above. The `#define` `SQUARE_SIDE` defines the default size of a square side, in pixels. To create a square (such as the ones shown in the Shaper window in Figure 6.1), you'd call `CreateShape()` with identical values for `height` and `width`, like this:

```
CreateShape( myPoint, SQUARE_SIDE, SQUARE_SIDE );
```

Object References

Things start to get interesting when you look at the local variable declared within the routine `CreateShape()`. The variable `newShape` looks like a regular pointer. When the compiler encounters a variable declared as if it were a pointer to an object, the compiler knows that the variable is actually an **object reference**. Object references are similar to struct pointers. Imagine a pointer to a `Rect`:

```
Rect            *rectPtr;
```

To access the fields of `rectPtr`'s `Rect`, you'd use something like this:

```
rectPtr->top = 20;
```

To access an object's instance variable, you'd use a line like:

```
newShape->bounds.top = 20;
```

To call an object's method, you'd use a similar technique:

```
newShape->IShape( corner, SQUARE_SIDE,
SQUARE_SIDE );
```

It's important to realize that although object references might look like (and even behave a bit like) pointers to structs, they are not the same. *Object references are not pointers.* This is especially true for indirect classes, which are based on handles, not pointers. The compiler is smart enough to translate:

```
newShape->bounds.top = 20;
```

into the appropriate level of indirection. This means that you'd use the same notation whether your class is declared as indirect or a direct (based on handles or based on pointers).

Return to the routine `CreateShape()`, declared above. A new `Shape` object is created by passing the class name `Shape` to the routine `new()`. `new()` is a function that returns an object reference and that can be used to create a new object of any class. To delete an object, call the routine `delete()`, like this:

```
delete( newShape );
```

Both of these functions can be found in the **oops** library. Just as you add MacTraps to your project to access the Toolbox, you'll need to add oops to your project to use these routines.

Once `CreateShape()` creates the new `Shape`, it calls the object's initialization method:

```
newShape->IShape( corner, width, height );
```

Shape's Methods

Let's take a look at Shape's initialization routine, IShape():

```
void IShape( corner, width, height )
Point     corner;
int       width;
int       height;
{
    SetRect( &bounds, corner.h, corner.v,
            corner.h + width, corner.v + height );

}
```

IShape() uses the upper left corner (specified by the corner parameter), along with the width and height parameters, to calculate the Shape's bounding rectangle. The result is stored in the Shape's instance variable, bounds. Because IShape() is one of Shape's methods, it automatically has access to all of Shape's instance variables.

THINK C automatically creates an object reference called this, making it available to all of an object's methods. Within a method, the object reference this is set automatically to reference the method's object. You can use this to access an object's instance variables and methods. IShape's call to SetRect() could have been written as:

```
    SetRect( &( this->bounds ), corner.h,
corner.v, corner.h + width, corner.v + height );
```

Both calls to SetRect() will work. Take a look at Shape's Draw() method:

```
void Draw()
{
    Rect          r;

    r = bounds;
    FrameRect( &r );
}
```

Notice that Draw() made a copy of the instance variable bounds and then passed the copy to FrameRect(). This has to do with the compiler's use of pointers to access instance variables. Treat an instance variable as you would a dereferenced handle. Don't pass the address of an instance variable to a routine that can move or purge memory. Because you can't use `HLock()` and `HUnlock()` to lock and unlock the instance variables (they're not handles), you'll have to make a copy of the variable and pass the copy.

Before the instance variable `bounds` was passed to `SetRect()`, `SetRect()` was checked against the routines in Appendix A of the *Inside Macintosh X-Ref*, the routines that may move or purge memory. Because `SetRect()` isn't on the list, it's fine to pass the address of `bounds` to it. Because `FrameRect()` is on the list, a copy of `bounds` had to be used.

Adding Subclasses to Shaper

Version 1.0 of Shaper supported a single object class, `Shape`. Now, two subclasses of `Shape` are created. Here's the declaration for a subclass called `Square`:

```
struct Square : Shape
{
    void        ISquare( Point corner,
                int width );
    void        Draw();
    void        DoClick( Point hitPt );
};
```

Subclasses **inherit** the instance variables of their **ancestors**. An ancestor of a class is any superclass of that class, any superclass of a superclass of that class, *ad infinitum*. Because `Square` was made a subclass of `Shape`, any `Square`s that are created automatically have their own `bounds` instance variable.

Subclasses also inherit their ancestor's methods. In part, this means that within `ISquare()`, `IShape()` can be called. Here's the code for `ISquare()`:

```
void ISquare( corner, width )
Point       corner;
int         width;
{
    IShape( corner, width, width );
}
```

Before the object class `Square` was defined, a new shape was created by calling `CreateShape()`. `CreateShape()` created a square by creating a `Shape` object and then passing `IShape()` the same value for the width and the height parameters. Now that the `Square` class has been defined, there's another way to create a shape:

```
void        CreateSquare( corner, width )
Point       corner;
int         width;
{
    Square       *newSquare;

    newSquare = new( Square );
    newSquare->ISquare( corner, width );
}
```

Before, a square was created by calling `CreateShape()`:

```
CreateShape( myPoint, SQUARE_SIDE, SQUARE_SIDE );
```

Now, a square can be created by calling `CreateSquare()`:

```
CreateSquare( myPoint, SQUARE_SIDE );
```

CreateSquare( ) versus CreateShape( )

There are some important differences between creating a square with `CreateSquare()` and creating a square with `CreateShape()`. The most obvious difference is in the number of parameters, and this is exactly as it should be. Because squares always have equal sides, it makes sense to specify the size of the square with a single parameter. In a sense, `Squares` are customized or specialized `Shapes`. On the flip side, `Shapes` are generalized `Squares`. You'll run into this specialization and generalization frequently when defining your own object classes.

Notice also that the code was able to call `IShape()` from within `ISquare()` as if it were a local routine. This is method inheritance at work.

A Second Shape Subclass

Here's the declaration of a second `Shape` subclass, called `Circle`:

```
struct Circle : Shape
{
    void        ICircle( Point center, int radius );
    void        Draw();
    void        DoClick( Point hitPt );
};
```

Circle defines a circle, based on a center and a radius. Like the Square class, Circle is a subclass of Shape. Here's the source code for ICircle():

```
void ICircle( center, radius )
Point      center;
int        radius;
{
    Point corner;

    corner.h = center.h - radius;
    corner.v = center.v - radius;

    IShape( corner, 2 * radius, 2 * radius );
}
```

ICircle() is pretty similar to ISquare(). Unlike ISquare(), ICircle() has to convert its two parameters to another form before passing them on to IShape(). The center is converted to a corner, and the radius is doubled to achieve the size of one side of the bounding rectangle.

Here's a routine for creating a Circle object:

```
void CreateCircle( center, radius )
Point      center;
int        radius;
{
    Circle      *newCircle;

    newCircle = new( Circle );
    newCircle->ICircle( center, radius );
}
```

If you wanted to maintain a list of Circles, you might have designed CreateCircle() as a function returning a Circle object reference:

```
Circle    *CreateCircle( center, radius );
```

This same logic holds true for `CreateShape()` and `CreateSquare()`. You'll make these decisions as you lay out your program's design.

Object Classes Exist on Levels

Why would you want to create three different object classes (`Shape`, `Square`, and `Circle`) when you could get away with only creating two (`Square` and `Circle`)? There's an important object programming lesson here. Object classes exist on different levels, sharing a hierarchical relationship. In the previous example, every object is represented by a `Shape`. If you maintained a list of every `Shape` created, you could redraw all the shapes by sending a `Draw()` message to every object on the list. By doing this, you'd be focused on drawing, without regard for the type of object you're drawing.

On the other hand, you might want to perform some function on a particular shape. For example, suppose you added a method to the `Circle` class that returned the area of the object (area of a circle = π * radius^2). By stepping through a list of `Circle`s and calling each `Circle`'s area method, you could calculate the average area of all the `Circle`s.

By maintaining general (`Shape`) and specific (`Circle`, `Square`) views of the same objects, you can take advantage of the view that makes sense for the current task. It's important to note that routines like `CreateSquare()` and `CreateCircle()` (which represent the programmer's interface) get the benefits of both levels in the object hierarchy even though they themselves only work at one level. The programmer calling `CreateSquare()` is intent only on creating a `Square` object. Because of the way the object methods were designed, that programmer gets the benefits of two object classes (`Square` and `Shape`) with the creation of a single object.

The benefit of object class typecasting should also be considered. For example, if you had a `Circle` and you wanted to add it to a list of `Shape`s, you could just typecast the `Circle` to look like a `Shape`:

```
ShapeList->AddShapeToList( (Shape *)myCircle );
```

In this example, a list object class called `ShapeList` supports a method called `AddShapeToList()`. `AddShapeToList()` takes a single parameter, a `Shape` object reference. By casting the `Circle` reference `myCircle` to look like a `Shape` reference, you can pass the typecast `Circle` to `AddShapeToList()`.

Another benefit of object programming is the openness and maintainability of the program architecture. Think about the process of adding rectangles or ovals to Shaper. Rather than rewriting the program, modifying the data structures that form the basis of the program architecture, you merely create a new class, providing the declarations and methods for the class. The routines that work on all objects within a class don't change at all!

For example, say that you create a new oval class as a subclass of `Shape`. As long as you provide a `Draw()` method with your new class, the routine that draws all `Shapes` will pass a `Draw()` message to each `Oval`, because each `Oval` is a subclass of `Shape`. Even more importantly, the routine that draws all `Shapes` did not have to be modified.

More about Methods

An interesting property of object methods is their inheritance mechanism. One example of this involves the `Draw()` methods described earlier. Shaper sends a `Draw()` message to the lowest objects in the `Shape` class hierarchy. As shown in Figure 6.2, the lowest objects in Shaper's object hierarchy are `Circles` and `Squares`.

When a message is sent to an object, the object's method matching that message is executed. If the object doesn't have a method that matches the message, the object's superclass is checked for a matching method. This process is repeated until either a match is

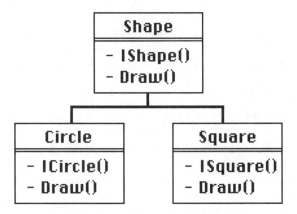

Figure 6.2 Shaper's object hierarchy.

found and a method is executed, or the last class checked was a root class. Of course, sending a message to an object that doesn't support a corresponding method is an error that will be detected at compile time.

If a `Draw()` message is sent to a `Circle`, the `Circle`'s `Draw()` method is executed. Suppose a new subclass, called `Oval`, is created under `Shape`. Suppose also that `Oval` does not support a `Draw()` method. The object hierarchy described is pictured in Figure 6.3.

If a `Draw()` message is sent to an `Oval`, no matching method will be found. When this happens, `Oval`'s superclass will be searched for a matching method. This means that `Shape`'s `Draw()` method will be executed. If you design `Shape`'s `Draw()` method to draw a square with a question mark in the middle of it when called, the result will look something like Figure 6.4.

If a new shape is added to Shaper and the new shape doesn't come with its own `Draw()` method, `Shape`'s draw method will be executed, and the square/question mark combination will be drawn.

Notice that no code had to be written to handle this case. Technically, a subclass with a method that matches a method in its superclass is said to override its superclass's method. The concepts of inheritance and method-overriding are a big part of what makes object programming such a valuable technique.

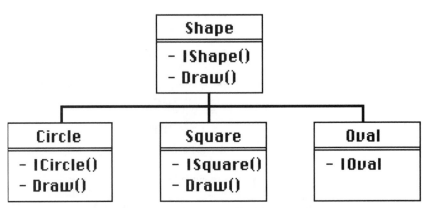

Figure 6.3 An `Oval` class with no `Draw()` method..

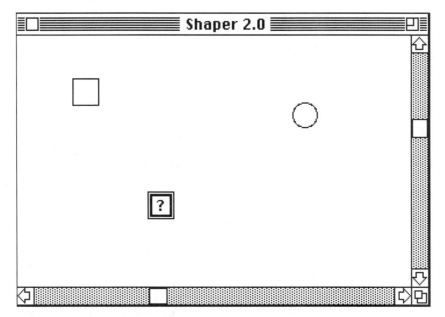

Figure 6.4 An `Oval` drawn with `Shape`'s `Draw()` method.

The THINK Class Library

Another valuable facet of object programming is the reusability of object classes. Once you build an object class and all its methods, it is easy to reuse the class in another program. A great example of this is the THINK Class Library, or TCL. The TCL is an extensive set of object classes, complete with methods, that implements a large part of the Macintosh interface.

The TCL has classes that take care of things like event handling, menu processing, clipboard management, printing, desk accessories, and even MultiFinder compatibility. Think about that for a second. By taking advantage of the TCL, your program will automatically have a complete, standard, Macintosh user interface. You won't have to worry about MultiFinder friendliness—it's already there. You won't have to deal with the clipboard unless you want to do so. TCL even supports TextEdit.

TCL Organization

The TCL is organized in three different ways. The **class hierarchy** represents all of the classes found in the TCL, organized as shown in Figure 6.5.

> Each of the TCL classes start with the letter **C**. To make things a little easier to read, the letter C was left off the class names in Figure 6.5. For example, the name of the highest level class is actually `CObject`, not `Object`.

The relationships shown in Figure 6.5 are strictly subclass- and superclass-oriented; they are inheritance relationships, like those described by a family tree. For example, the `CObject` class is a root class (it has no superclass). The `CDirector` class is a subclass of the `CBureaucrat` class and a superclass of the `CDocument` and `CClipboard` classes.

The Visual Hierarchy

Each TCL program has a **visual hierarchy**, which may change dynamically as the program runs. The visual hierarchy lays objects out in relationships based on visual events, such as `mouseDowns`, `activateEvts`, and `updateEvts`. Take a look at the sample application window shown in Figure 6.6. The top of the visual hierarchy in this picture is the gray area representing the Macintosh desktop. The Macintosh desktop is modeled by the `CDesktop` class. `mouseDowns`, `activateEvts`, and `updateEvts` that involve the Macintosh desktop are sent to a `CDesktop` object.

Next in the visual hierarchy is the window, modeled by the `CWindow` class. The window is said to be **enclosed** by the desktop. A `CWindow` object most likely would be enclosed by a `CDesktop` object.

The window is divided into areas called **panes**. At the top of the window is a pane that contains two subpanes, one for each of two pop-up menus. Each of these areas is modeled by the `CPane` class. The bottom half of the window is a scrolling pane—a pane with vertical and horizontal scroll bars that enable scrolling of a larger

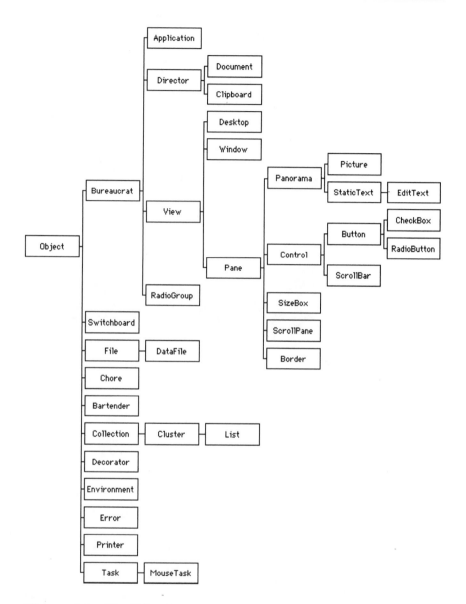

Figure 6.5 The TCL classes. Note the omission of the leading **C** in each class name.

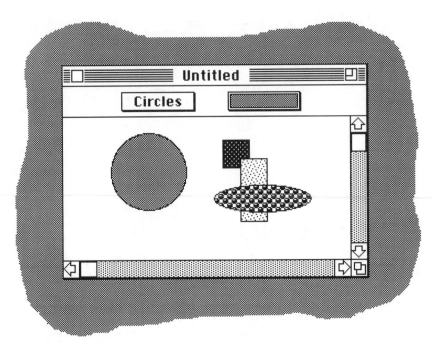

Figure 6.6   A sample application window.

pane, called a **panorama**. The scroll bars each are modeled by the CScrollBar class. Together with the scrolling pane, the scroll bars make up an object of the CScrollPane class. The larger pane (the pane in which all the shapes are drawn) is a CPanorama object. If a program draws directly in a CPanorama, scrolling is handled automatically. When a mouseDown occurs in a CScrollPane's scroll bar, the CPanorama associated with that CScrollPane is scrolled automatically. This means that any panes enclosed by the CPanorama (such as the circles, ovals, and rectangles shown in Figure 6.6) will be scrolled as well.

Figure 6.7 shows a portion of the sample application window's visual hierarchy. As is usually the case, a CDesktop object is the highest-level enclosure. Next comes the CWindow, followed by the CPane from the top half of the window and the two CPanes that implement the pop-up menus.

Just as the TCL classes handle mouseDown events, they also handle updateEvts and activateEvts. In the example shown in Figure 6.6, each of the pattern-filled shapes drawn in the window is

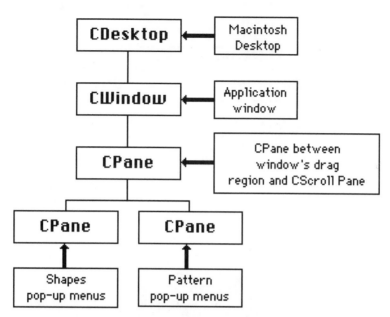

Figure 6.7 Part of the sample application window's visual hierarchy.

an individual CPane, enclosed by the CPanorama associated with the CScrollPane. When the CPanorama scrolls so that a piece of one of its enclosed CPanes is revealed, the TCL will receive an updateEvt and will automatically send a Draw() message to that CPane. You'll see an example of this when the sample object program is presented later in the chapter.

The Chain of Command

A TCL program is also organized as a **chain of command**. Just as the visual hierarchy is driven by visual messages, the chain of command is driven by **direct commands**. A direct command is a request that an object perform an action, usually as a result of a menu selection. The chain of command specifies which object handles which direct command.

Under the chain of command, objects are organized according to a hierarchy of **supervisors**. If a direct command is passed to an object

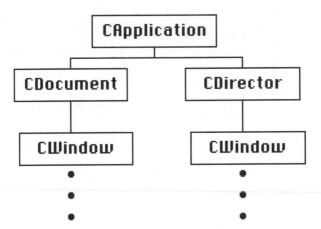

Figure 6.8   Typical chain of command.

and the object can't handle the command, it passes the command on to its supervisor. The CApplication is the highest object class in the chain of command and is the only class that doesn't have a supervisor.

Every object in the chain of command is a descendant of the CBureaucrat class and is thus called a bureaucrat. Every bureaucrat has a DoCommand() method that can be overridden by any of its subclasses. The default DoCommand() method sends a DoCommand() message to its supervisor. The various bureaucrats in your program will support DoCommand() methods that handle your program's commands. Many of the TCL classes come with built-in DoCommand() methods to handle parts of the Macintosh interface.

Figure 6.8 shows a chain of command organization for a typical Macintosh application. As always, a CApplication object is in charge. Every one of your application's windows will report to either a CDirector or to a CDocument. Windows reporting to a CDocument always have a file associated with them. Window reporting to a CDirector don't have a file associated with them. CDirector windows are typically status or palette windows. Below the CWindow in the chain of command you'd find objects such as CPanes and CPanoramas, as described earlier. Because these are all subclasses of CBureaucrat, they all support the DoCommand() method.

The object that will get the first chance to handle a command is called the **gopher**. Your application must set the global variable gGopher to reference the gopher object. If the gopher can't handle the command, it will pass the command to its supervisor. This completes the chain of command.

The Switchboard and the Bartender

The main event loop in a TCL application is implemented by an object called the **switchboard**. Naturally enough, the switchboard is an object in the CSwitchboard class. The switchboard calls WaitNextEvent() or GetNextEvent() and routes the retrieved event (in the form of a message) to the appropriate object. Every application has one (and only one) switchboard.

Some of these events get routed to an object called the **bartender** (of class CBartender). The bartender is in charge of the menu bar ("menu bar," "bartender" . . . get it?). This is a pretty far-reaching responsibility. When a command-key equivalent is typed, or when a mouseDown occurs in the menu bar, the bartender has to make sure that every menu and menu item is enabled or disabled properly before the user gets to use the menu bar. Whenever a menu selection is imminent, the bartender sends a message to the chain of command (starting at the gopher), asking the bureaucrats to update their menu items. The nice thing about this approach is that menu items that don't make sense at the moment are disabled. It's important that you program with this in mind.

Building an Application with the TCL

Although you can build a complete TCL application from scratch, there's really no need to do so. Version 4.0 of THINK C shipped with several sample applications that you can use as building blocks for your own applications. If you start off with an application that supports printing, you won't have to create your own print-handling objects. You'd be amazed at how much functionality can be reused in even the simplest of the THINK C sample programs. The next sections take a look at some of them.

Art Class

One of the most sophisticated of the THINK C TCL sample applications is called Art Class. Art Class, shown in Figure 6.9, is a MacPaint-like painting program. It features full paint support, full printing support, and tear-off tool and pattern palette menus. The Art Class project is so big, it had to be broken down into five separate segments. The first segment contains source code specific to the Art Class project. The last four segments contain source code from the THINK Class Library. These last are files such as **CApplication.c**, **CBartender.c**, etc. When you build your own projects, you'll add these same TCL source files.

If you look inside the Art Class Folder that comes with THINK C, you'll see one folder called **Art Class Sources** and another called **Art Class Headers**. Figure 6.10 shows a Finder listing of both of these folders. The Art Class Sources folder contains the sources from the first Art Class segment. The Art Class Headers folder contains one header file for every one of the source files. This one-to-one correspondence is pretty typical. Although you may not maintain

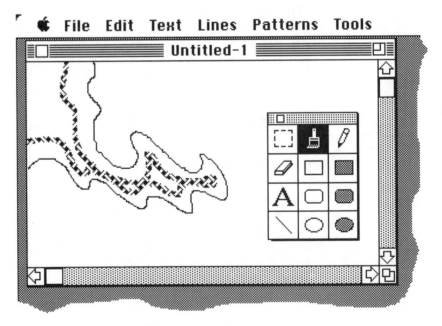

Figure 6.9   An Art Class screen shot.

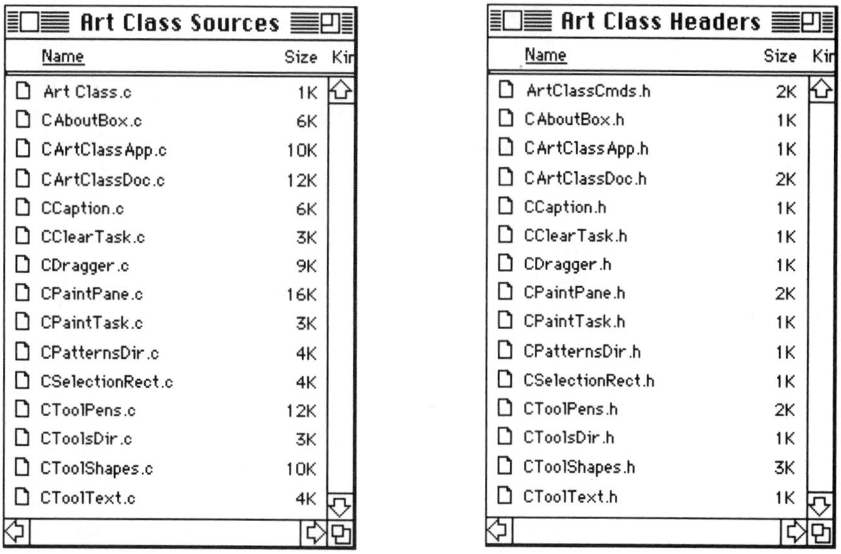

Figure 6.10 Art Class source and header files.

separate source and header folders, you'll probably end up with one header file for every source file you provide.

Notice that the majority of the source files in the Art Class project are not found in the Art Class Folder. Instead, both the sources and the include files for the TCL classes can be found inside the THINK Class Library folder, which is inside the THINK C Folder in your development folder. You'll use these same sources in your own projects.

TinyEdit

TinyEdit is actually a full-fledged text editor, based completely on TextEdit. Figure 6.11 shows a screen shot of TinyEdit in action. If you're going to write an object-based TextEdit application, TinyEdit is definitely the place to start.

Once again, the first segment of the TinyEdit project contains the TinyEdit-specific files. The other segments contain TCL-specific files.

The Starter Application

The Starter application that comes with THINK C is exactly what its name implies: a starting point for your own (non-TextEdit) applications. Figure 6.12 shows a Starter screen shot, with its three menus and an open window. Of all the TCL sample applications, Starter is the simplest; it is the best application to work with while you are learning object programming.

Before you go any further, now would be a good time to install the Starter project on your hard drive. If you're running without a hard drive, or with less than two megabytes of RAM, you might want to think about upgrading your system. Programming with objects is a memory- and disk-intensive proposition.

If you are running with THINK C version 4.0, you might want to check out AutoWeave, the THINK C upgrade program available on the Symantec BBS (and others as well).

Autoweave uses scripts to update selected parts of your THINK C environment. For instance, one AutoWeave script is designed to update the THINK C program, and a separate one is designed to update the TCL demo programs. Download the whole package and update as much as you can. The sample programs in this chapter are based on THINK C, version 4.02. Some of the source code may contain references to Autoweave in the form of comments. Your code should work whether or not you run Autoweave.

The Symantec BBS is a service of Symantec Corporation, 10201 Torre Avenue, Cupertino, CA 95014. It is provided primarily for customers of Symantec, although anyone may browse and make use of this BBS. There are no subscription or use charges. The phone number for the BBS is 1–408–973–9598. The BBS supports 300-, 1,200-, and 2,400-baud rates and the download protocols supported are XMODEM, YMODEM and KERMIT. The primary use of the bulletin board is to provide a quick and cheap way for users to obtain free upgrades to Symantec software.

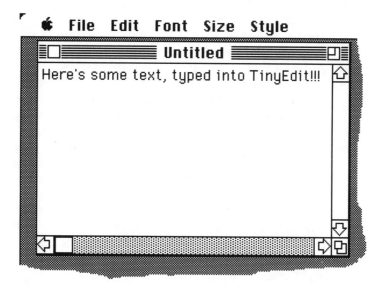

Figure 6.11   A TinyEdit screen shot.

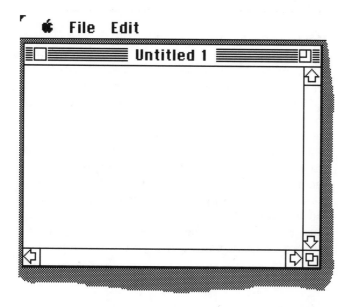

Figure 6.12   The TCL Starter application.

Once your Starter project is installed, launch THINK C and open Starter.π. Select Run from the Project menu and then go do the dishes while the project compiles. If you encounter any problems getting Starter to run, check your THINK C *User's Guide*. If you really run into a wall, try calling THINK C's technical support line.

Once you get Starter running, you should see something like Figure 6.12. The open window represents a `CDocument`, linking a `CWindow` and a `CFile`. Because the window hasn't been saved yet, the file hasn't been specified. Try saving to and opening up files. The mechanisms are in place for performing these operations, but no data is being saved or read. Starter is like a blank canvas. You'll customize Starter by adding your own objects to it. Some of these objects will define the file format and the data to be saved in Starter's files. Still other objects will refine the window, adding pop-up menus, tool palettes, or whatever helps to make your application unique.

Starter will form the basis for your first object program, called **MyStarter**.

MyStarter

MyStarter behaves much like Starter, the sample TCL application. MyStarter's windows, however, are much more interesting. First of all, MyStarter's windows are designed to scroll. The window is based on a `CPanorama` controlled by a `CScrollPane`.

When your mouse cursor is over a blank portion of the window, it changes into a three-dimensional plus sign (like the one shown in Figure 6.13).

If you click the three-dimensional plus sign cursor in the window, a random rectangle, filled with a random pattern, will appear. This rectangle is an instance of a `CDragPane` object. (The `CDragPane` class is defined a bit later in the chapter.) When your mouse cursor moves over a `CDragPane` it changes automatically into an arrow cursor. If you click the mouse in a `CDragPane`, an outline of the `CDragPane` appears, and you can drag the object around the

Figure 6.13 The 3D plus sign cursor.

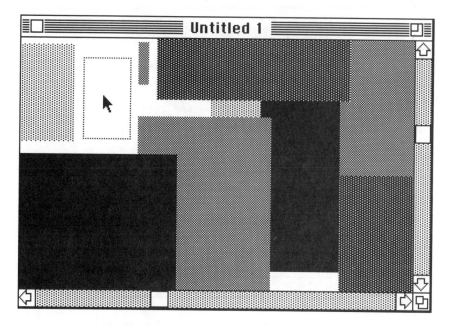

Figure 6.14   MyStarter in action.

window. If you drag the object beyond the window boundaries, the `CScrollPane` scrolls automatically until either you release the mouse button or the scroll bar hits its limit. The dragging operation is implemented by a `CMouse` object. Figure 6.14 shows MyStarter in action.

Creating a Folder for MyStarter

Make a copy of the Starter folder and place it in your development folder. Rename the folder to **MyStarter ƒ**. Figure 6.15 shows a Finder listing of the files in MyStarter ƒ. The files **CStarterApp.c** and **CStarterApp.h** define the Starter's `CApplication` object class, called `CStarterApp`. The files **CStarterDoc.c** and **CStarterDoc.h** define Starter's `CDocument` object class, called `CStarterDoc`. The files **CStarterPane.c** and **CStarterPane.h** define Starter's `CPane` object class, called `CStarterPane`. You'll make a slight change to the CStarterDoc files and completely replace the CStarterPane files. This is pretty much how you'll start most of your Starter-based development efforts.

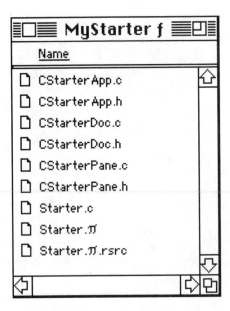

Figure 6.15   A copy of the Starter folder.

The file **Starter.c** contains a single routine, main(), which creates a new CStarterApp object and starts it running. The file **Starter.π** contains the Starter project. The file **Starter.π.rsrc** contains the project resources. You won't be making any changes to these three files.

You'll be adding two new .c files and two new include files to the project. The files **CDragPane.c** and **CDragPane.h** implement the CDragPane described previously. The files **CMouse.c** and **CMouse.h** implement the CMouse, also described previously.

Changing CStarterDoc.c

The file CStarterDoc.c contains the methods for the CStarterDoc object class. One of these methods, BuildWindow(), creates a new window and also creates the objects associated with that window. The BuildWindow() that comes with Starter doesn't know about the extensions planned for this example, so the routine will be replaced.

Launch THINK C by double-clicking on the file Starter.π in the MyStarter ƒ folder. Now open the file CStarterDoc.c. About two-

thirds of the way down in CStarterDoc.c, you'll find the routine
BuildWindow(). Replace the existing BuildWindow() with the
following code:

```
/***
 * BuildWindow
 *
 *    Replace the old BuildWindow with this one...
 *
 ***/

void CStarterDoc::BuildWindow (Handle theData)
{
      CScrollPane        *theScrollPane;
      CStarterPane       *thePanorama;
      Rect               panFrame;

      itsWindow = new( CWindow );
      itsWindow->IWindow( WINDStarter, FALSE, gDesktop, this );

      theScrollPane = new( CScrollPane );

      theScrollPane->IScrollPane( itsWindow, this,
                        0, 0, 0, 0,
                        sizELASTIC, sizELASTIC,
                        TRUE, TRUE, TRUE );

      theScrollPane->FitToEnclFrame( TRUE, TRUE );
      theScrollPane->SetSteps( 10, 10 );

      thePanorama = new( CStarterPane );
      thePanorama->IStarterPane( theScrollPane, this,
                        0, 0, 0, 0,
                        sizELASTIC, sizELASTIC );

      thePanorama->FitToEnclosure( TRUE, TRUE );
      theScrollPane->InstallPanorama( thePanorama );

      itsMainPane = thePanorama;
      itsGopher = thePanorama;
```

```
        itsWindow->Zoom(inZoomOut);
        thePanorama->GetFrame(&panFrame);
        thePanorama->SetBounds(&panFrame);

        gDecorator->PlaceNewWindow( itsWindow );

}
```

That's the only change you'll need to make to CStarterDoc.c. Close the file and save your changes.

Replacing CStarterPane.c

The next step is completely replacing the contents of the file CStarterPane.c. Open the file CStarterPane.c and delete all of its contents. One way to do this is to select Select All from the Edit menu and then press the Delete or Backspace key. Once you've deleted the contents of the file, type in the following replacement code:

```
#include "CStarterPane.h"
#include "CDragPane.h"
#include "CMouse.h"


/*********************************** IStarterPane   */

void CStarterPane::IStarterPane( anEnclosure,
                                 aSupervisor,
                                 aWidth, aHeight,
                                 aHEncl, aVEncl,
                                 aHSizing, aVSizing )
CView           *anEnclosure;
CBureaucrat     *aSupervisor;
short           aWidth, aHeight, aHEncl, aVEncl;
SizingOption    aHSizing, aVSizing;
{
        CPanorama::IPanorama( anEnclosure, aSupervisor,
                                       aWidth, aHeight,
                                       aHEncl, aVEncl,
                                       aHSizing, aVSizing );
```

```
        GetDateTime( &randSeed );

        SetWantsClicks( TRUE );
}


/***************************** DoClick ********/

void CStarterPane::DoClick( hitPt, modifierKeys, when )
Point   hitPt;
short   modifierKeys;
long    when;
{
        int          width, height, patNum;
        CDragPane    *myDragPane;

        width = Randomize( MAX_PANE_SIZE );
        height = Randomize( MAX_PANE_SIZE );
        patNum = Randomize( NUM_PATS );

        myDragPane = new( CDragPane );
        myDragPane->IDragPane( hitPt, height, width,
                               patNum, this, this );
}


/***************************** AdjustCursor ********/

void CStarterPane::AdjustCursor( where, mouseRgn )
Point       where;
RgnHandle   mouseRgn;
{
        SetCursor( *GetCursor( plusCursor ) );
}


/***************************** DoDrag ********/

void CStarterPane::DoDrag( objWidth, objHeight,
                hitPt, startLocation, endLocation )
int     objWidth, objHeight;
Point   hitPt;
Rect    startLocation, *endLocation;
```

```
{
    CMouse      *aMouseTask;
    Rect        boundsRect;
    Point p;

    gIsScrolling = TRUE;

    boundsRect = bounds;

    aMouseTask = new( CMouse );

    aMouseTask->IMouse( NO_UNDO_STRING, objWidth,
            objHeight, hitPt, startLocation, this );

    Prepare();

    GetMouse( &p );
    TrackMouse( aMouseTask, p, &boundsRect );

    gIsScrolling = FALSE;

    aMouseTask->GetLocation( endLocation );

    Refresh();
}


/***************************** Randomize *********/

Randomize( range )
int     range;
{
    long  rawResult;

    rawResult = Random();
    if ( rawResult < 0 ) rawResult *= -1;
    return( (rawResult * range) / 32768 );
}
```

Once the code is typed in, save the changes and close the file.

Replacing CStarterPane.h

Next, replace the contents of the include file CStarterPane.h. Open the file CStarterPane.h and, just as you did with CStarterPane.c, delete the contents. Once you've deleted the contents of the file, type in the following replacement code:

```
#define _H_CStarterPane
#include <CPanorama.h>

#define MAX_PANE_SIZE 200
#define NUM_PATS       4
#define NO_UNDO_STRING 0

struct CStarterPane : CPanorama
{
        void        IStarterPane( CView *anEnclosure,
                        CBureaucrat *aSupervisor,
                        short aWidth, short aHeight,
                        short aHEncl, short aVEncl,
                        SizingOption aHSizing,
                        SizingOption aVSizing);

        void        DoClick( Point hitPt,
                        short modifierKeys, long when );

        void        AdjustCursor( Point where,
                        RgnHandle mouseRgn );

        void        DoDrag( int objWidth, int objHeight,
                        Point hitPt, Rect frame,
                        Rect *endLocation );
};
```

Once the code is typed in, save the changes and close the file.

Creating CDragPane.c

The last four steps in this process involve the creation of four new source files. Create a new source code file by selecting New from the File menu. Save the file as **CDragPane.c** and add the file to the project. Make sure you add the file to the first code segment. You can do this by clicking on any file in the first code segment (such as Starter.c) and then adding the file CDragPane.c to the project. Once the file is added, type in the following code:

```
#include "CStarterPane.h"
#include "CDragPane.h"

Boolean           gIsScrolling = FALSE;



/****************************** IDragPane *********/

void CDragPane::IDragPane( corner, height, width,
                 patNum, anEnclosure, aSupervisor )
Point           corner;
int             height;
int             width;
int             patNum
CView           *anEnclosure;
CBureaucrat     *aSupervisor;
{
     Rect r;

     ((CPanorama *)anEnclosure)->GetBounds( &r );

     if ((corner.h + width) > r.right)
          corner.h -= corner.h + width - r.right;

     if ((corner.v + height) > r.bottom)
          corner.v -= corner.v + height - r.bottom;

     IPane( anEnclosure, aSupervisor,
             width, height,
             corner.h, corner.v,
             sizFIXEDSTICKY, sizFIXEDSTICKY );

     patNumber = patNum;

     SetWantsClicks( TRUE );
     Refresh();
}
```

```
/***************************** Draw *********/

void CDragPane::Draw( rPtr )
Rect  *rPtr;
{
      if ( ! gIsScrolling )
      {
            Prepare();

            switch( patNumber )
            {
                  case 0:
                        PenPat( ltGray );
                        break;
                  case 1:
                        PenPat( gray );
                        break;
                  case 2:
                        PenPat( dkGray );
                        break;
                  default:
                        PenPat( black );
                        break;
            }

            PaintRect( rPtr );
      }
}


/***************************** DoClick *********/

void CDragPane::DoClick( hitPt, modifierKeys, when )
Point   hitPt;
short   modifierKeys;
long    when;
{
      Rect  r;
      Rect  endLocation;

      r = frame;
      EraseRect( &r );
```

```
FrameToEnclR(&r);

((CStarterPane *)itsEnclosure)->DoDrag( width,
        height, hitPt, r, &endLocation );

Place( endLocation.left, endLocation.top, TRUE );
}
```

Save the changes and close the file.

Creating CDragPane.h

Select New from the File menu to create a new source code file. Save the file as **CDragPane.h**. Add the file to the project, making sure you add it to the first code segment. Type the following code into CDragPane.h:

```
#define _H_CDragPane

#include "CPane.h"

extern Boolean          gIsScrolling;

struct CDragPane : CPane
{
        int          patNumber;

        void         IDragPane( Point corner, int height,
                        int width, int patNum,
                        CView *anEnclosure,
                        CBureaucrat *aSupervisor );

        void         Draw( Rect *area );

        void         DoClick( Point hitPt,
                        short modifierKeys, long when );
};
```

Save the changes and close the file.

Creating CMouse.c

Select New from the File menu to create a new source code file. Save the file as **CMouse.c**. Add the file to the project, making sure you add it to the first code segment. Type the following code into CMouse.c:

```
#include "CMouse.h"


/******************************* IMouse ********/

void CMouse::IMouse( strID, objWidth, objHeight,
                     hitPt, theLoc, theRama )
int         strID;
int         objWidth;
int         objHeight;
Point       hitPt;
Rect        theLoc;
CPanorama   *theRama;
{
      Rect  r;

      IMouseTask( strID );

      thePanorama = theRama;
      theLocation = theLoc;

      thePanorama->GetBounds( &r );
      r.left += hitPt.h;
      r.top += hitPt.v;
      r.right -= ( objWidth - hitPt.h );
      r.bottom -= ( objHeight - hitPt.v );
      theBounds = r;
}



/******************************* BeginTracking ********/

void CMouse::BeginTracking( startPt )
Point *startPt;
{
```

```
        Rect   r;

        PenMode( patXor );
        PenPat( gray );

        r = theLocation;
        FrameRect( &r );
}



/****************************** KeepTracking ********/

void CMouse::KeepTracking( currPt, prevPt, startPt )
Point *currPt;
Point *prevPt;
Point *startPt;
{
        Rect        r, f;
        long        curTicks;
        Point       startPosit, newPosit, cp, pp;
        RgnHandle   clipRgn;

        thePanorama->GetPosition( &startPosit );

        clipRgn = NewRgn();

        if ( thePanorama->AutoScroll( *currPt )
                || ! EqualPt( *currPt, *prevPt ) )
        {
            thePanorama->GetPosition( &newPosit );

            GetClip( clipRgn );
            r = (**clipRgn).rgnBBox;
            OffsetRect( &r, startPosit.h - newPosit.h,
                        startPosit.v - newPosit.v );

            thePanorama->GetFrame(&f);
            PinInRect(&f, &(r.top));
            PinInRect(&f, &(r.bottom));

            ClipRect( &r );
```

```
            r = theLocation;

            curTicks = TickCount();
            while ( curTicks == TickCount() ) ;
            FrameRect( &r );

            cp = *currPt;
            pp = *prevPt;
            PinInRect(&theBounds, &cp);
            PinInRect(&theBounds, &pp);

            OffsetRect(&r, cp.h - pp.h, cp.v - pp.v);

            SetClip( clipRgn );

            curTicks = TickCount();
            while ( curTicks == TickCount() ) ;
            FrameRect( &r );

            theLocation = r;
        }

    DisposeRgn( clipRgn );
}


/***************************** EndTracking ********/

void CMouse::EndTracking( currPt, prevPt, startPt )
Point *currPt;
Point *prevPt;
Point *startPt;
{
    Rect  r;

    r = theLocation;
    FrameRect( &r );
    PenNormal();
}
```

```
/***************************** GetLocation ********/

void CMouse::GetLocation( theLoc )
Rect  *theLoc;
{
      *theLoc = theLocation;
}
```

Save the changes and close the file.

Creating CMouse.h

Select New from the File menu to create a new source code file. Save the file as **CMouse.h**. Add the file to the project, making sure you add it to the first code segment. Type the following code into CMouse.h:

```
#define _H_CMouse

#include "CMouseTask.h"
#include <CPanorama.h>

struct CMouse : CMouseTask
{
      CPanorama    *thePanorama;
      Rect         theLocation, theBounds;

      void         IMouse( int strID,
                        int objWidth, int objHeight,
                        Point hitPt, Rect theLoc,
                        CPanorama *theRama );

      void         BeginTracking( Point *startPt );

      void         KeepTracking( Point *currPt,
                        Point *prevPt, Point *startPt );

      void         EndTracking( Point *currPt,
                        Point *prevPt, Point *startPt );

      void         GetLocation(Rect*);
};
```

Save the changes and close the file.

Checking Your Work

That's it! Now that you've entered all the source code, you might want to check your project window against the project window in Figure 6.16. There should be a total of four segments in the project. All the new files you created should be in the first segment.

You should also compare your Finder listing of the folder MyStarter ƒ with the Finder listing in Figure 6.17. Make sure you're not missing any files.

OK. Ready to run? In THINK C, select Run from the Project menu. Fix any compilation errors that come up and save any changes before you run. You may want to run AutoWeave (described earlier in the chapter) to bring your copy of the TCL up to date).

Once the program runs, a blank window should appear, and the menus **&**, File, and Edit should appear on the menu bar. When you move your cursor over the content region of the window, the cursor should change to the three-dimensional plus sign shown earlier in Figure 6.13.

Starter.π	
Name	**obj size**
CDragPane.c	384
CMouse.c	636
CStarterApp.c	376
CStarterDoc.c	1118
CStarterPane.c	476
Starter.c	46
GlobalVars.c	0
Jumps	32
MacTraps	9458
oops	240
OSChecks.c	228
TBUtilities.c	1232
CBorder.c	614
CButton.c	420
CCheckBox.c	168
CControl.c	1534
CDesktop.c	2508
CEditText.c	2098
CPane.c	4348
CPanorama.c	2464
CPicture.c	926
CRadioButton.c	164
CScrollBar.c	812
CScrollPane.c	2138

CSizeBox.c	358
CStaticText.c	2760
CView.c	2276
CWindow.c	2712
CApplication.c	3358
CBartender.c	3492
CBureaucrat.c	422
CChore.c	24
CClipboard.c	1756
CCluster.c	1106
CCollection.c	96
CDataFile.c	794
CDecorator.c	532
CDirector.c	674
CDocument.c	2020
CEnvironment.c	26
CError.c	1146
CFile.c	558
CList.c	1724
CMouseTask.c	108
CObject.c	76
CPrinter.c	1184
CRadioGroup.c	572
CSwitchboard.c	1644
CTask.c	142

Figure 6.16 MyStarter's project file.

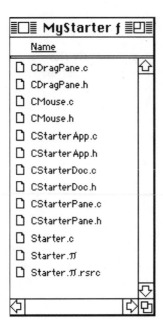

Figure 6.17 These files should be in the folder MyStarter ƒ.

Click the mouse in the window. A rectangle should appear, filled with one of the gray patterns (or black). As you move the mouse over the rectangle, the cursor should change back into an arrow. Click the mouse inside a rectangle. A gray outline should appear in place of the rectangle. The outline should follow the mouse. When you release the mouse button, the rectangle should reappear in the new position.

Try dragging a rectangle outside the window boundaries. If the window can scroll in that direction, it will. If it can't, the rectangle will be pinned to the edge of the rectangle.

Experiment. Try opening multiple windows. Fill a window with rectangles, then drag a piece of the window off screen, then on-screen again. All the rectangles should be redrawn. When you're ready, quit by selecting Quit from the File menu.

The next section takes a look at the source code.

Walking Through the MyStarter Source Code

Because of the complexity of the THINK Class Library, this section doesn't attempt to walk through all the source code involved in this program. That's one of the beauties of object programming: you don't necessarily have to understand the inner workings of the TCL to take full advantage of it.

The Routine BuildWindow( )

To start with, look at the routine `BuildWindow()` that was replaced in the file CStarterDoc.c. Notice the way it is declared. The two colons preceding a method name are a convention used throughout the TCL. You should definitely read through as much of the TCL source as you can. A good place to start is with the original version of CStarterDoc.c.

The routine `BuildWindow()` is called whenever the application wants to create a new window. The parameter `theData` is a handle to the data that will be associated with the window. Although `theData` is not used in this particular program, it is an important part of the `CDocument`'s `OpenFile()` method.

```
void CStarterDoc::BuildWindow (Handle theData)
{
    CScrollPane      *theScrollPane;
    CStarterPane     *thePanorama;
    Rect             panFrame;
```

First, a new `CWindow` object is created and initialized. `itsWindow` is a `CDirector` instance variable. `CDocument` is a subclass of `CDirector`, so it inherits the instance variable. While you are coming up to speed, it is a good idea to look up everything you can in the THINK C *User's Guide*. The major classes are described alphabetically in chapters 17–53. Each chapter lists a single class, along with the class's instance variables and methods.

```
    itsWindow = new( CWindow );
    itsWindow->IWindow( WINDStarter, FALSE,
                        gDesktop, this );
```

Once the `CWindow` is initialized, a `CScrollPane` is created and initialized. When you look up a class in the *User's Guide*, it's a good idea to look at the parameters of the class's initialization method. If you can't find a method or an instance variable referred to by a class, try looking in the documentation for the class's superclass.

```
theScrollPane = new( CScrollPane );

theScrollPane->IScrollPane( itsWindow, this,
                0, 0, 0, 0,
                sizELASTIC, sizELASTIC,
                TRUE, TRUE, TRUE );
```

FitToEnclFrame() makes the CScrollPane the same size as its enclosure, which, in this case, is the CWindow just created. SetSteps() sets the resolution of the CScrollPane's scroll bars.

```
theScrollPane->FitToEnclFrame( TRUE, TRUE );
theScrollPane->SetSteps( 10, 10 );
```

thePanorama is the CPanorama that slides around under the CScrollPane. thePanorama is actually declared as a CStarterPane, one of the new object classes you created yourself. The parameters to IStarterPane() will be used to call IPanorama() within IStarterPane(). Look up IPanorama() in the *User's Guide*.

```
thePanorama = new( CStarterPane );
thePanorama->IStarterPane( theScrollPane, this,
                0, 0, 0, 0,
                sizELASTIC, sizELASTIC );
```

Calling FitToEnclosure() is not the same as calling FitToEnclFrame(). FitToEnclosure() will make the visible part of the panorama coincide with the interior (not the frame) of the panorama's enclosure (theScrollPane). InstallPanorama() tells theScrollPane that thePanorama is its panorama.

```
thePanorama->FitToEnclosure( TRUE, TRUE );
theScrollPane->InstallPanorama( thePanorama );
```

itsMainPane is a CDocument instance variable. itsGopher is a CDirector instance variable.

```
itsMainPane = thePanorama;
itsGopher = thePanorama;
```

Zoom() will zoom the window so that it is the size of the main display. Next, the panorama's bounds are set to equal the size of the panorama's frame. The frame of the panorama is like a picture frame sliding around on top of the panorama. The bounds of the panorama define the outer boundaries of the panorama. The frame of the panorama (set earlier) is used to set the bounds of the panorama.

```
itsWindow->Zoom(inZoomOut);
thePanorama->GetFrame(&panFrame);
thePanorama->SetBounds(&panFrame);
```

Finally, the window is added to the desktop. For more information on how this was accomplished, read about the CDecorator class.

```
gDecorator->PlaceNewWindow( itsWindow );
```

```
}
```

The CStarterPane Object Class

The panorama created by BuildWindow() was actually a newly defined subclass of CPanorama called CStarterPane. CStarterPane.h defines three constants, as well as the four methods that make up CStarterPane. The #define of _H_CStarterPane at the beginning of the file sets a flag so that the compiler doesn't include this file more than once. The file **CPanorama.h** is included in this file to provide access to the CPanorama class definition. What if CPanorama.h included the file CStarterPane.h? Without the _H_CStarterPane flag, the compiler would enter an infinite loop, first including one file, then including the other. Every time you define a new class, you'll create a .c file and a corresponding .h file. At the beginning of the .h file, always #define something of the form _H_xxxx, where the xxxx is the class name.

```
#define _H_CStarterPane
#include <CPanorama.h>
```

Within the file CStarterPane.c, the methods for the CStarterPane class are defined. First, the .h files corresponding to the classes referenced by CStarterPane are included.

```
#include "CStarterPane.h"
#include "CDragPane.h"
#include "CMouse.h"
```

IStarterPane() initializes the panorama and then seeds the random number generator. SetWantsClicks(TRUE) tells the switchboard that the panorama wants its DoClick() method to be called when a mouseDown occurs inside itself.

```
/**************************************** IStarterPane */

void CStarterPane::IStarterPane( anEnclosure,
                                 aSupervisor,
                                 aWidth, aHeight,
                                 aHEncl, aVEncl,
                                 aHSizing, aVSizing )
CView          *anEnclosure;
CBureaucrat    *aSupervisor;
short          aWidth, aHeight, aHEncl, aVEncl;
SizingOption   aHSizing, aVSizing;
{
    CPanorama::IPanorama( anEnclosure, aSupervisor,
                          aWidth, aHeight,
                        • aHEncl, aVEncl,
                          aHSizing, aVSizing );

    GetDateTime( &randSeed );

    SetWantsClicks( TRUE );
}
```

The CStarterPane's DoClick() method creates a new CDragPane and initializes it with a call to IDragPane().

```
/****************************** DoClick ********/

void CStarterPane::DoClick( hitPt, modifierKeys, when )
Point   hitPt;
short   modifierKeys;
long    when;
{
    int          width, height, patNum;
    CDragPane    *myDragPane;
```

```
        width = Randomize( MAX_PANE_SIZE );
        height = Randomize( MAX_PANE_SIZE );
        patNum = Randomize( NUM_PATS );

        myDragPane = new( CDragPane );
        myDragPane->IDragPane( hitPt, height, width,
                               patNum, this, this );
}
```

The default `AdjustCursor()` method sets the cursor to an arrow. `CStarterPane`'s `AdjustCursor()` method sets the cursor to the three-dimensional plus sign shown earlier in Figure 6.13. Isn't cursor manipulation easy with object programming?

```
/****************************** AdjustCursor ********/

void CStarterPane::AdjustCursor( where, mouseRgn )
Point       where;
RgnHandle   mouseRgn;
{
        SetCursor( *GetCursor( plusCursor ) );
}
```

The `DoDrag()` method is called by a `CDragPane`'s `DoClick()` method. The global `gIsScrolling` is set to `TRUE` so that the `CDragPanes` won't try to redraw themselves. If they did, they might screw up the gray rectangle outline that's being dragged around the screen. Try setting the global to `FALSE` instead of `TRUE` and then cause the panorama to autoscroll by dragging a rectangle outside the panorama's bounds.

```
/****************************** DoDrag ********/

void CStarterPane::DoDrag( objWidth, objHeight,
                hitPt, startLocation, endLocation )
int     objWidth, objHeight;
Point   hitPt;
Rect    startLocation, *endLocation;
{
        CMouse      *aMouseTask;
        Rect        boundsRect;
        Point       p;
```

```
gIsScrolling = TRUE;

boundsRect = bounds;
```

The CMouseTask class implements mouse tracking. CMouse is a subclass of CMouseTask. DoDrag() creates a new CMouse and then initializes it. Read up on CMouseTask in the *User's Guide*.

```
aMouseTask = new( CMouse );

aMouseTask->IMouse( NO_UNDO_STRING, objWidth,
            objHeight, hitPt, startLocation, this );
```

The Prepare() method is similar to a SetPort(). Call it before you draw in a pane to make sure the drawing environment is set up properly for drawing in that pane.

```
        Prepare();
```

TrackMouse() starts the mouse task running. TrackMouse() is passed the mouse position returned by GetMouse().

```
        GetMouse( &p );
        TrackMouse( aMouseTask, p, &boundsRect );
```

Once the mouse task completes (that is, once the mouse button is released), gIsScrolling is set back to FALSE. The parameter endLocation is set to the last location of the dragged gray rectangle.

```
        gIsScrolling = FALSE;

        aMouseTask->GetLocation( endLocation );
```

The call to Refresh() is pretty powerful. It will cause a Draw() message to be sent to all the panes enclosed by the CStarterPane(). This call is made because use of the global gIsScrolling may have caused some drawing to be missed.

```
        Refresh();
}
```

Randomize() is exactly the same as the version in the first
volume of the *Macintosh Programming Primer*.

```
/******************************* Randomize *********/

Randomize( range )
int    range;
{
       long  rawResult;

       rawResult = Random();
       if ( rawResult < 0 ) rawResult *= -1;
       return( (rawResult * range) / 32768 );
}
```

The CDragPane Object Class

The file CDragPane.h defines the flag _H_CDragPane, includes its
superclass definition file **CPane.h**, and defines access to the global
gIsScrolling with an extern declaration. Any file that includes
this file will have access to that global.

Next, the file defines the instance variable patNumber, which
defines the fill pattern for this CDragPane. Finally, CDragPane.h
defines the interfaces for the three access methods IDragPane(),
Draw(), and DoClick().

The file CDragPane.c includes the CStarterPane and
CDragPane include files. The global gIsScrolling is defined and
autoinitialized here.

```
#include "CStarterPane.h"
#include "CDragPane.h"

Boolean            gIsScrolling = FALSE;
```

The method IDragPane() gets the bounds of its enclosure (the
CStarterPane) and puts them in the local variable r.

```
/***************************** IDragPane *********/

void CDragPane::IDragPane( corner, height, width,
                           patNum, anEnclosure, aSupervisor )
Point          corner;
int            height;
int            width;
int            patNum;
CView          *anEnclosure;
CBureaucrat    *aSupervisor;
{
       Rect r;

       ((CPanorama *)anEnclosure)->GetBounds( &r );
```

The two if statements make sure the CDragPane is created within the bounds of the enclosure.

```
       if ((corner.h + width) > r.right)
              corner.h -= corner.h + width - r.right;

       if ((corner.v + height) > r.bottom)
              corner.v -= corner.v + height - r.bottom;
```

Next, the pane is initialized with a call to IPane(). Read about IPane() in the *User's Guide*. You'll want to get comfortable with IPane()'s parameters and how they work.

```
       IPane( anEnclosure, aSupervisor,
              width, height,
              corner.h, corner.v,
              sizFIXEDSTICKY, sizFIXEDSTICKY );
```

The instance variable patNumber is initialized using the parameter patNum. The method SetWantsClicks() is called to enable clicks in the CDragPane. The Refresh() method is called to force the CDragPane to draw itself.

```
       patNumber = patNum;

       SetWantsClicks( TRUE );
       Refresh();
}
```

The `Draw()` method paints the `CDragPane` with the correct pattern only if the `gIsScrolling` flag is set to `FALSE`.

```
/***************************** Draw ********/

void CDragPane::Draw( rPtr )
Rect        *rPtr;
{
    if ( ! gIsScrolling )
    {
        Prepare();

        switch( patNumber )
        {
            case 0:
                PenPat( ltGray );
                break;
            case 1:
                PenPat( gray );
                break;
            case 2:
                PenPat( dkGray );
                break;
            default:
                PenPat( black );
                break;
        }

        PaintRect( rPtr );
    }
}
```

The `DoClick()` method erases the `CDragPane` and then converts the local variable r from local coordinates to the enclosure's coordinates. Then, r is passed to the enclosure's `DoDrag()` method. When `DoDrag()` returns the new `endLocation`, the pane is moved to the new position and redrawn.

```
/***************************** DoClick ********/

void CDragPane::DoClick( hitPt, modifierKeys, when )
Point       hitPt;
short       modifierKeys;
long        when;
```

```
{
        Rect  r;
        Rect  endLocation;

        r = frame;
        EraseRect( &r );

        FrameToEnclR(&r);

        ((CStarterPane *)itsEnclosure)->DoDrag( width,
                height, hitPt, r, &endLocation );

        Place( endLocation.left, endLocation.top, TRUE );
}
```

The CMouse Object Class

The file CMouse.h starts by defining `_H_CMouse` and including the `CMouseTask` and `CPanorama` object class include files. The instance variable `thePanorama` holds a reference to the panorama that started the mouse task. The instance variable `theLocation` marks the current location of the dragged rectangle. The instance variable `theBounds` defines the boundary used to constrain the dragging of the rectangle. CMouse.h then defines the calling sequences for the methods `IMouse()`, `BeginTracking()`, `KeepTracking()`, `EndTracking()`, and `GetLocation()`.

CMouse.c contains the methods for the object class `CMouse`. It includes the file CMouse.h.

```
#include "CMouse.h"
```

Read about the `CMouseTask` object class in the THINK C *User's Guide*. The `strID` passed to `IMouseTask()` is defined there. The undo string referenced by `strID` will be ignored in this program, but the description in the *User's Guide* tells you how to use the undo mechanism.

```
/****************************** IMouse ********/

void CMouse::IMouse( strID, objWidth, objHeight,
                    hitPt, theLoc, theRama )
```

```
int        strID;
int        objWidth;
int        objHeight;
Point      hitPt;
Rect       theLoc;
CPanorama  *theRama;
{
      Rect  r;

      IMouseTask( strID );
```

The instance variables thePanorama and theLocation are initialized from the parameters theRama and theLoc.

```
      thePanorama = theRama;
      theLocation = theLoc;
```

The next few lines adjust the instance variable theBounds to reflect the enclosing panorama's bounds, inset to account for the mouse's position within the CDragPane. To see the effect this has, try commenting out the four lines that set r's left, top, right, and bottom and dragging the CDragPane outside the bounds of the panorama.

```
      thePanorama->GetBounds( &r );
      r.left += hitPt.h;
      r.top += hitPt.v;
      r.right -= ( objWidth - hitPt.h );
      r.bottom -= ( objHeight - hitPt.v );
      theBounds = r;
}
```

BeginTracking() sets the current port up for drawing a gray, Xored rectangle. The initial gray rectangle is drawn.

```
/******************************* BeginTracking ********/

void CMouse::BeginTracking( startPt )
Point *startPt;
{
      Rect  r;
```

```
      PenMode( patXor );
      PenPat( gray );

      r = theLocation;
      FrameRect( &r );
}
```

KeepTracking() starts by calling GetPosition() to get the position of the scroll bars.

```
/****************************** KeepTracking ********/

void CMouse::KeepTracking( currPt, prevPt, startPt )
Point *currPt;
Point *prevPt;
Point *startPt;
{
      Rect          r, f;
      long          curTicks;
      Point start Posit, newPosit, cp, pp;
      RgnHandle     clipRgn;

      thePanorama->GetPosition( &startPosit );
```

The clipRgn is set to handle a brand new region. It will be used to hold the window's clipping rectangle.

```
      clipRgn = NewRgn();
```

If the mouse position is causing an autoscroll or if the mouse has moved, the gray rectangle will be drawn once in its old position (to erase it) and once in its new position (to create a new one).

```
      if ( thePanorama->AutoScroll( *currPt )
                  || ! EqualPt( *currPt, *prevPt ) )
      {
```

Next, GetPosition() is called to get the new position of the scroll bars. Subtracting the new position from the old position produces an offset. If the panorama was autoscrolled, the offset will indicate the difference (in number of pixels) between where the gray rectangle appears to be and where it actually is.

```
thePanorama->GetPosition( &newPosit );

GetClip( clipRgn );
r = (**clipRgn).rgnBBox;
OffsetRect( &r, startPosit.h - newPosit.h,
            startPosit.v - newPosit.v );
```

PinInRect() is a utility routine provided by THINK C that can be found in the file **TBUtilities.c**. It pins a point inside a rectangle. This call to PinInRect() pins the top left and the bottom right points of r inside the panorama's frame. Because r is going to be used as a clipping rectangle, it's important not to allow any drawing to occur outside the panorama's frame (on the scroll bar, for example). If you're not comfortable with this algorithm, try commenting out the call to ClipRect() and causing an autoscroll by dragging a CDragPane outside the window's boundary. The algorithm itself has little to do with object programming, so don't get distracted by its details.

```
thePanorama->GetFrame(&f);
PinInRect(&f, &(r.top));
PinInRect(&f, &(r.bottom));

ClipRect( &r );
```

Next, the gray rectangle is drawn at the old location to erase the old position.

```
r = theLocation;

curTicks = TickCount();
while ( curTicks == TickCount() ) ;
FrameRect( &r );
```

After that, the new position is pinned inside theBounds, the clipping region is restored, and the gray rectangle is drawn at the new position.

```
cp = *currPt;
pp = *prevPt;
PinInRect(&theBounds, &cp);
PinInRect(&theBounds, &pp);
```

```
        OffsetRect(&r, cp.h - pp.h, cp.v - pp.v);

        SetClip( clipRgn );

        curTicks = TickCount();
        while ( curTicks == TickCount() ) ;
        FrameRect( &r );
```

Finally, the program updates theLocation to the new position and disposes of clipRgn.

```
        theLocation = r;
    }

    DisposeRgn( clipRgn );
}
```

EndTracking() erases the gray rectangle and restores the pen to its normal settings.

```
/*********************** EndTracking ********/

void CMouse::EndTracking( currPt, prevPt, startPt )
Point *currPt;
Point *prevPt;
Point *startPt;
{
    Rect  r;

    r = theLocation;
    FrameRect( &r );
    PenNormal();
}
```

GetLocation() returns the value stored in the instance variable theLocation. This brings up an important point. A routine that has access to the GetLocation() method also has access to the instance variable theLocation. Whenever possible, provide a method if a nonrelated class needs to access an instance variable.

```
/*********************** GetLocation *********/

void CMouse::GetLocation( theLoc )
Rect        *theLoc;
{
    *theLoc = theLocation;
}
```

In Review

There's a lot more to learn about object programming. Hopefully, you've seen the value of a good class library. Spend some time curled up with your THINK C *User's Guide*—it will be time well spent. Don't let the sheer size of the TCL overwhelm you. Start with the sample program provided in this chapter and add some of your own features. Read about the CBartender class and add your own menus to the program. How about a menu that allows you to select the shape that gets plotted? You'll want to work out the program's chain of command and establish a methodology for setting the global variable gGopher. If you take things one step at a time, you can do it!

I hope you've enjoyed this volume of the *Macintosh Programming Primer*. If you have any suggestions for the third volume, please write. I'd love to hear from you. Ciao, for now...

Appendix A

Glossary

access path: A description of the route that the File Manager follows to access a file; created when a file is opened.

access path buffer: Memory used by the File Manager to transfer data between an application and a file.

action procedure: A procedure, used by the Control Manager function TrackControl, that defines an action to be performed repeatedly for as long as the mouse button is held down.

activate event: An event generated by the Window Manager when a window changes from active to inactive or vice versa.

active control: A control that will respond to the user's actions with the mouse.

active end: In a selection, the location to which the insertion point moves to complete the selection.

active window: The frontmost window on the desktop.

ADB device table: A structure in the system heap that lists all devices connected to the Apple DeskTop Bus.

address: A number used to identify a location in the computer's address space. Some locations are allocated to memory, others to I/O devices.

alert: A warning or report of an error, in the form of an alert box, sound from the Macintosh's speaker, or both.

alert box: A box that appears on the screen to give a warning or report an error during a Macintosh application.

alert template: A resource that contains information from which the Dialog Manager can create an alert.

Source: *Inside Macintosh X-Ref* © 1988 Apple Computer, Inc. Reprinted with permission of Addison-Wesley Publishing Company.

alert window: The window in which an alert box is displayed.

allocate: To reserve an area of memory for use.

application font: The font your application will use unless you specify otherwise—Geneva, by default.

application heap: The portion of the heap available to the running application program and the Toolbox.

application heap limit: The boundary between the space available for the application heap and the space available for the stack.

application heap zone: The heap zone initially provided by the Memory Manager for use by the application program and the Toolbox; initially equivalent to the application heap, but may be subdivided into two or more independent heap zones.

application list: A data structure, kept in the Desktop file, for launching applications from their documents in the hierarchical file system. For each application in the list, an entry is maintained that includes the name and signature of the application, as well as the directory ID of the folder containing it.

application parameters: Thirty-two bytes of memory, located above the application globals, reserved for system use. The first application parameter is the address of the first QuickDraw global variable.

application space: Memory that's available for dynamic allocation by applications.

application window: A window created as the result of something done by the application, either directly or indirectly (as through the Dialog Manager).

asynchronous execution: After calling a routine asynchronously, an application is free to perform other tasks until the routine is completed.

auto-key event: An event generated repeatedly when the user presses and holds down a character key on the keyboard or keypad.

auto-key rate: The rate at which a character key repeats after it's begun to do so.

auto-key threshold: The length of time a character key must be held down before it begins to repeat.

auxiliary control record: A Control Manager data structure containing the information needed for drawing controls in color.

auxiliary window record: A Window Manager data structure that stores the color information needed for each color window.

background activity: A program or process that runs while the user is engaged with another application.

bit image: A collection of bits in memory that have a rectilinear representation. The screen is a visible bit image.

bit map: A set of bits that represent the position and state of a corresponding set of items; in QuickDraw, a pointer to a bit image, the row width of that image, and its boundary rectangle.

block: A group regarded as a unit; usually refers to data or memory in which data is stored. See **allocation block** and **memory block**.

block contents: The area that's available for use in a memory block.

boundary rectangle: A rectangle, defined as part of a QuickDraw bit map, that encloses the active area of the bit image and imposes a coordinate system on it. Its top left corner is always aligned around the first bit in the bit image.

bundle: A resource that maps local IDs of resources to their actual resource IDs; used to provide mappings for file references and icon lists needed by the Finder.

button: A standard Macintosh control that causes some immediate or continuous action when clicked or pressed with the mouse. See also **radio button**.

caret-blink time: The interval between blinks of the caret that marks an insertion point.

caret: A generic term meaning a symbol that indicates where something should be inserted in text. The specific symbol used is a vertical bar (|).

catalog tree file: A file that maintains the relationships between the files and directories on a hierarchical directory volume. It corresponds to the file directory on a flat directory volume.

cdev: A resource file containing device information, used by the Control Panel.

cGrafPort: The drawing environment in Color QuickDraw, including elements such as a pixel map, pixel patterns, transfer modes, and arithmetic drawing modes.

channel: A queue that's used by an application to send commands to the Sound Manager.

character code: An integer representing the character that a key or combination of keys on the keyboard or keypad stands for.

character key: A key that generates a keyboard event when pressed; any key except Shift, Caps Lock, Command, or Option.

character style: A set of stylistic variations, such as bold, italic, and underline. The empty set indicates plain text (no stylistic variations).

character width: The distance to move the pen from one character's origin to the next character's origin.

check box: A standard Macintosh control that displays a setting, either checked (on) or unchecked (off). Clicking inside a check box reverses its setting.

Chooser: A desk accessory that provides a standard interface for device drivers to solicit and accept specific choices from the user.

chunky: A pixel image in which all of a pixel's bits are stored consecutively in memory, all of a row's pixels are stored consecutively, and rowBytes indicates the offset from one row to the next.

clipping: Limiting drawing to within the bounds of a particular area.

clipping region: Same as clipRgn.

clipRgn: The region to which an application limits drawing in a grafPort.

closed file: A file without an access path. Closed files cannot be read from or written to.

Color Look-Up Table (CLUT): A data structure that maps color indices, specified using QuickDraw, into actual color values. Color Look-Up Tables are internal to certain types of video cards.

Color Look-Up Table device: This kind of video device contains hardware that converts an arbitrary pixel value stored in the frame buffer to some actual RGB video value, which is changeable.

Color Manager: The part of the Toolbox that supplies color-selection support for Color QuickDraw on the Macintosh II.

Color QuickDraw: The part of the Toolbox that performs color graphics operations on the Macintosh II.

color table animation: Color table animation involves changing the index entries in the video device's color table to achieve a change in color, as opposed to changing the pixel values themselves. All pixel values corresponding to the altered index entries suddenly appear on the display device in the new color.

color table: A set of colors is grouped into a QuickDraw data structure called a color table. Applications can pass a handle to this color table in order to use color entries.

compaction: The process of moving allocated blocks within a heap zone in order to collect the free space into a single block.

completion routine: Any application-defined code to be executed when an asynchronous call to a routine is completed.

content region: The area of a window that the application draws in.

control: An object in a window on the Macintosh screen with which the user, using the mouse, can cause instant action with visible results or change settings to modify a future action.

Control Manager: The part of the Toolbox that provides routines for creating and manipulating controls (such as buttons, check boxes, and scroll bars).

control definition function: A function called by the Control Manager when it needs to perform type-dependent operations on a particular type of control, such as drawing the control.

control definition ID: A number passed to control-creation routines to indicate the type of control. It consists of the control definition function's resource ID and a variation code.

control list: A list of all the controls associated with a given window.

control record: The internal representation of a control, where the Control Manager stores all the information it needs for its operations on that control.

control template: A resource that contains information from which the Control Manager can create a control.

coordinate plane: A two-dimensional grid. In QuickDraw, the grid coordinates are integers ranging from −32767 to 32767, and all grid lines are infinitely thin.

current heap zone: The heap zone currently under attention, to which most Memory Manager operations implicitly apply.

current resource file: The last resource file opened, unless you specify otherwise with a Resource Manager routine.

cursor: A 16-by-16 bit image that appears on the screen and is controlled by the mouse; called the "pointer" in Macintosh user manuals.

cursor level: A value, initialized by InitCursor, that keeps track of the number of times the cursor has been hidden.

data fork: The part of a file that contains data accessed via the File Manager.

data mark: In a sector, information that primarily contains data from an application.

date/time record: An alternate representation of the date and time (which is stored on the clock chip in seconds since midnight, January 1, 1904).

default button: In an alert box or modal dialog, the button whose effect will occur if the user presses Return or Enter. In an alert box, it's boldly outlined; in a modal dialog, it's boldly outlined or the OK button.

default directory: A directory that will be used in File Manager routines whenever no other directory is specified. It may be the root directory, in which case the default directory is equivalent to the default volume.

default volume: A volume that will receive I/O during a File Manager routine call, whenever no other volume is specified.

dereference: To refer to a block by its master pointer instead of its handle.

Desk Manager: The part of the Toolbox that supports the use of desk accessories from an application.

desk accessory: A "mini-application," implemented as a device driver, that can be run at the same time as a Macintosh application.

desk scrap: The place where data is stored when it's cut (or copied) and pasted among applications and desk accessories.

desktop: The screen as a surface for doing work on the Macintosh.

Desktop file: A resource file in which the Finder stores the version data, bundle, icons, and file references for each application on the volume.

destination rectangle: In TextEdit, the rectangle in which the text is drawn.

device driver event: An event generated by one of the Macintosh's device drivers.

device driver: A program that controls the exchange of information between an application and a device.

dial: A control with a moving indicator that displays a quantitative setting or value. Depending on the type of dial, the user may be able to change the setting by dragging the indicator with the mouse.

dialog: Same as **dialog box.**

dialog box: A box that a Macintosh application displays to request information it needs to complete a command, or to report that it's waiting for a process to complete.

Dialog Manager: The part of the Toolbox that provides routines for implementing dialogs and alerts.

dialog record: The internal representation of a dialog, where the Dialog Manager stores all the information it needs for its operations on that dialog.

dialog template: A resource that contains information from which the Dialog Manager can create a dialog.

dialog window: The window in which a dialog box is displayed.

dimmed: Drawn in gray rather than black.

direct device: A video device that has a direct correlation between the value placed in the video card and the color you see on the screen.

directory ID: A unique number assigned to a directory, which the File Manager uses to distinguish it from other directories on the volume. (It's functionally equivalent to the file number assigned to a file; in fact, both directory IDs and file numbers are assigned from the same set of numbers.)

directory: A subdivision of a volume that can contain files as well as other directories; equivalent to a folder.

disabled: A disabled menu item or menu is one that cannot be chosen; the menu item or menu title appears dimmed. A disabled item in a dialog or alert box has no effect when clicked.

Disk Initialization Package: A Macintosh package for initializing and naming new disks; called by the Standard File Package.

disk-inserted event: An event generated when the user inserts a disk in a disk drive or takes any other action that requires a volume to be mounted.

display rectangle: A rectangle that determines where an item is displayed within a dialog or alert box.

dithering: A technique for mixing existing colors together to create the illusion of a third color that may be unavailable on a particular device.

document window: The standard Macintosh window for presenting a document.

double-click time: The greatest interval between a mouse-up and mouse-down event that would qualify two mouse clicks as a double-click.

draft printing: Printing a document immediately as it's drawn in the printing grafPort.

drag delay: A length of time that allows a user to drag diagonally across a main menu, moving from a submenu title into the submenu itself without the submenu disappearing.

drag region: A region in a window frame. Dragging inside this region moves the window to a new location and makes it the active window unless the Command key was down.

drive number: A number used to identify a disk drive. The internal drive is number 1, the external drive is number 2, and any additional drives will have larger numbers.

edit record: A complete editing environment in TextEdit, which includes the text to be edited, the grafPort and rectangle in which to display the text, the arrangement of the text within the rectangle, and other editing and display information.

empty handle: A handle that points to a NIL master pointer, signifying that the underlying relocatable block has been purged.

end-of-file: See **logical end-of-file** or **physical end-of-file**.

entity name: An identifier for an entity, of the form object:type@zone.

event: A notification to an application of some occurrence that the application may want to respond to.

event code: An integer representing a particular type of event.

Event Manager: See **Toolbox Event Manager** or **Operating System Event Manager.**

event mask: A parameter passed to an Event Manager routine to specify which types of events the routine should apply to.

event message: A field of an event record containing information specific to the particular type of event.

event queue: The Operating System Event Manager's list of pending events.

event record: The internal representation of an event, through which your program learns all pertinent information about that event.

exception: An error or abnormal condition detected by the processor in the course of program execution; includes interrupts and traps.

external reference: A reference to a routine or variable defined in a separate compilation or assembly.

file: A named, ordered sequence of bytes; a principal means by which data is stored and transmitted on the Macintosh.

file catalog: A hierarchical file directory.

file control block: A fixed-length data structure, contained in the file-control-block buffer, where information about an access path is stored.

file directory: The part of a volume that contains descriptions and locations of all the files and directories on the volume. There are two types of file directories: hierarchical file directories and flat file directories.

File Manager: The part of the Operating System that supports file I/O.

file name: A sequence of up to 255 printing characters, excluding colons (:), that identifies a file.

file number: A unique number assigned to a file, which the File Manager uses to distinguish it from other files on the volume. A file number specifies the file's entry in a file directory.

file reference: A resource that provides the Finder with file and icon information about an application.

file type: A four-character sequence, specified when a file is created, that identifies the type of file.

Finder information: Information that the Finder provides to an application upon starting it up, telling it which documents to open or print.

font: A complete set of characters of one typeface, which may be restricted to a particular size and style, or may comprise multiple sizes, or multiple sizes and styles, as in the context of menus.

Font Manager: The part of the Toolbox that supports the use of various character fonts for QuickDraw when it draws text.

font number: The number by which you identify a font to QuickDraw or the Font Manager.

font size: The size of a font in points; equivalent to the distance between the ascent line of one line of text and the ascent line of the next line of single-spaced text.

fork: One of the two parts of a file; see **data fork** and **resource fork.**

free block: A memory block containing space available for allocation.

full pathname: A pathname beginning from the root directory.

gamma table: A table that compensates for nonlinearities in a monitor's color response.

gDevice: A QuickDraw data structure that allows an application to access a given device. A gDevice is a logical device, which the software treats the same whether it is a video card, a display device, or an offscreen pixel map.

global coordinate system: The coordinate system based on the top left corner of the bit image being at (0,0).

go-away region: A region in a window frame. Clicking inside this region of the active window makes the window close or disappear.

grafPort: A complete drawing environment, including such elements as a bit map, a subset of it in which to draw, a character font, patterns for drawing and erasing, and other pen characteristics.

graphics device: A video card, a printer, a display device, or an offscreen pixel map. Any of these device types may be used with Color QuickDraw.

GrayRgn: The global variable that in the multiple screen desktop describes and defines the desktop, the area on which windows can be dragged.

grow image: The image pulled around when the user drags inside the grow region; whatever is appropriate to show that the window's size will change.

grow region: A window region, usually within the content region, where dragging changes the size of an active window.

grow zone function: A function supplied by the application program to help the Memory Manager create free space within a heap zone.

handle: A pointer to a master pointer, which designates a relocatable block in the heap by double indirection.

heap: The area of memory in which space is dynamically allocated and released on demand, using the Memory Manager.

heap zone: An area of memory initialized by the Memory Manager for heap allocation.

hierarchical menu: A menu that includes, among its various menu choices, the ability to display a submenu. In most cases the submenu appears to the right of the menu item used to select it, and is marked with a filled triangle indicator.

highlight: To display an object on the screen in a distinctive visual way, such as inverting it.

hotSpot: The point in a cursor that's aligned with the mouse location.

icon: A 32-by-32 bit image that graphically represents an object, concept, or message.

icon list: A resource consisting of a list of icons.

icon number: A digit from 1 to 255 to which the Menu Manager adds 256 to get the resource ID of an icon associated with a menu item.

inactive control: A control that won't respond to the user's actions with the mouse. An inactive control is highlighted in some special way, such as dimmed.

inactive window: Any window that isn't the frontmost window on the desktop.

indicator: The moving part of a dial that displays its current setting.

insertion point: An empty selection range; the character position where text will be inserted (usually marked with a blinking caret).

interface routine: A routine called from Pascal whose purpose is to trap to a certain Toolbox or Operating System routine.

International Utilities Package: A Macintosh package that gives you access to country-dependent information such as the formats for numbers, currency, dates, and times.

invalidation: When a color table is modified, its inverse table must be rebuilt, and the screen should be redrawn to take advantage of this new information. Rather than being reconstructed when the color table is changed, the inverse table is marked invalid, and is automatically rebuilt when next accessed.

inverse table: A special Color Manager data structure arranged in such a manner that, given an arbitrary RGB color, the pixel value can be very rapidly looked up.

invert: To highlight by changing white pixels to black and vice versa.

invisible control: A control that's not drawn in its window.

invisible window: A window that's not drawn in its plane on the desktop.

item: In dialog and alert boxes, a control, icon, picture, or piece of text, each displayed inside its own display rectangle. See also **menu item**.

item list: A list of information about all the items in a dialog or alert box.

item number: The index, starting from 1, of an item in an item list.

IWM: "Integrated Woz Machine"; the custom chip that controls the $3\frac{1}{2}$ inch disk drives.

job dialog: A dialog that sets information about one printing job; associated with the Print command.

jump table: A table that contains one entry for every routine in an application and is the means by which the loading and unloading of segments is implemented.

key code: An integer representing a key on the keyboard or keypad, without reference to the character that the key stands for.

key-down event: An event generated when the user presses a character key on the keyboard or keypad.

key-up event: An event generated when the user releases a character key on the keyboard or keypad.

keyboard equivalent: The combination of the Command key and another key, used to invoke a menu item from the keyboard.

keyboard event: An event generated when the user presses, releases, or holds down a character key on the keyboard or keypad; any key-down, key-up, or auto-key event.

leading: The amount of blank vertical space between the descent line of one line of text and the ascent line of the next line of single-spaced text.

ligature: A character that combines two letters.

line-height table: A TextEdit data structure that holds vertical spacing information for an edit record's text.

List Manager: The part of the Operating System that provides routines for creating, displaying, and manipulating lists.

local coordinate system: The coordinate system local to a grafPort, imposed by the boundary rectangle defined in its bit map.

local ID: A number that refers to an icon list or file reference in an application's resource file and is mapped to an actual resource ID by a bundle.

localization: The process of adapting an application to different languages, including converting its user interface to a different script.

lock: To temporarily prevent a relocatable block from being moved during heap compaction.

lock bit: A bit in the master pointer to a relocatable block that indicates whether the block is currently locked.

locked file: A file whose data cannot be changed.

locked volume: A volume whose data cannot be changed. Volumes can be locked by either a software flag or a mechanical setting.

logical end-of-file: The position of one byte past the last byte in a file; equal to the actual number of bytes in the file.

luminance: The intensity of light. Two colors with different luminances will be displayed at different intensities.

main event loop: In a standard Macintosh application program, a loop that repeatedly calls the Toolbox Event Manager to get events and then responds to them as appropriate.

main screen: On a system with multiple display devices, the screen with the menu bar is called the main screen.

main segment: The segment containing the main program.

master pointer: A single pointer to a relocatable block, maintained by the Memory Manager and updated whenever the block is moved, purged, or reallocated. All handles to a relocatable block refer to it by double indirection through the master pointer.

Memory Manager: The part of the Operating System that dynamically allocates and releases memory space in the heap.

memory block: An area of contiguous memory within a heap zone.

menu: A list of menu items that appears when the user points to a menu title in the menu bar and presses the mouse button. Dragging through the menu and releasing over an enabled menu item chooses that item.

menu bar: The horizontal strip at the top of the Macintosh screen that contains the menu titles of all menus in the menu list.

menu definition procedure: A procedure called by the Menu Manager when it needs to perform type-dependent operations on a particular type of menu, such as drawing the menu.

menu entry: An entry in a menu color table that defines color values for the menu's title, bar, and items.

menu ID: A number in the menu record that identifies the menu.

menu item: A choice in a menu, usually a command to the current application.

menu item number: The index, starting from 1, of a menu item in a menu.

menu list: A list containing menu handles for all menus in the menu bar, along with information on the position of each menu.

Menu Manager: The part of the Toolbox that deals with setting up menus and letting the user choose from them.

menu record: The internal representation of a menu, where the Menu Manager stores all the information it needs for its operations on that menu.

menu title: A word or phrase in the menu bar that designates one menu.

modal dialog: A dialog that requires the user to respond before doing any other work on the desktop.

modeless dialog: A dialog that allows the user to work elsewhere on the desktop before responding.

modifier key: A key (Shift, Caps Lock, Option, or Command) that generates no keyboard events of its own, but changes the meaning of other keys or mouse actions.

mounted volume: A volume that previously was inserted into a disk drive and had descriptive information read from it by the File Manager.

mouse-down event: An event generated when the user presses the mouse button.

mouse-up event: An event generated when the user releases the mouse button.

network event: An event generated by the AppleTalk Manager.

newline character: Any character, but usually Return (ASCII code $0D), that indicates the end of a sequence of bytes.

nonbreaking space: The character with ASCII code $CA; drawn as a space the same width as a digit, but interpreted as a nonblank character for the purposes of word wraparound and selection.

nonrelocatable block: A block whose location in the heap is fixed and can't be moved during heap compaction.

null event: An event reported when there are no other events to report.

null-style record: A TextEdit data structure used to store the style information for a null selection.

offspring: For a given directory, the set of files and directories for which it is the parent.

on-line volume: A mounted volume with its volume buffer and descriptive information contained in memory.

open file: A file with an access path. Open files can be read from and written to.

open permission: Information about a file that indicates whether the file can be read from, written to, or both.

Operating System: The lowest-level software in the Macintosh. It does basic tasks such as I/O, memory management, and interrupt handling.

Operating System Event Manager: The part of the Operating System that reports hardware-related events such as mouse-button presses and keystrokes.

Operating System Utilities: Operating System routines that perform miscellaneous tasks such as getting the date and time, finding out the user's preferred speaker volume and other preferences, and doing simple string comparison.

page rectangle: The rectangle marking the boundaries of a printed page image. The boundary rectangle, portRect, and clipRgn of the printing grafPort are set to this rectangle.

palette: A collection of small symbols, usually enclosed in rectangles, that represent operations that can be selected by the user. Also, a collection of colors provided and used by your application according to your needs.

Palette Manager: The part of the Toolbox that establishes and monitors the color environment of the Macintosh II. It gives preference to the color needs of the front window, making the assumption that the front window is of greatest interest to the user.

pane: An independently scrollable area of a window, for showing a different part of the same document.

panel: An area of a window that shows a different interpretation of the same part of a document.

parameter RAM: In the clock chip, 20 bytes where settings such as those made with the Control Panel desk accessory are preserved.

part code: An integer between 1 and 253 that stands for a particular part of a control (possibly the entire control).

partial pathname: A pathname beginning from any directory other than the root directory.

path reference number: A number that uniquely identifies an individual access path; assigned when the access path is created.

pathname: A series of concatenated directory and file names that identifies a given file or directory. See also **partial pathname** and **full pathname.**

pattern: An 8-by-8 bit image, used to define a repeating design (such as stripes) or tone (such as gray).

pattern transfer mode: One of eight transfer modes for drawing lines or shapes with a pattern.

physical end-of-file: The position of one byte past the last allocation block of a file; equal to 1 more than the maximum number of bytes the file can contain.

physical size: The actual number of bytes a memory block occupies within its heap zone.

picture: A saved sequence of QuickDraw drawing commands (and, optionally, picture comments) that you can play back later with a single procedure call; also, the image resulting from these commands.

picture frame: A rectangle, defined as part of a picture, that surrounds the picture and gives a frame of reference for scaling when the picture is played back.

pixel: A dot on a display screen. Pixel is short for picture element.

pixel map: Color QuickDraw's extended data structure, containing the dimensions and content of a pixel image, plus information on the image's storage format, depth, resolution, and color usage.

pixel pattern: The pattern structure used by Color QuickDraw, one of three types: old-style pattern, full color pixel pattern, or RGB pattern.

pixel value: The bits in a pixel, taken together, form a number known as the pixel value. Color QuickDraw represents each pixel on the screen using one, two, four, or eight bits in memory.

plane: The front-to-back position of a window on the desktop.

point: The intersection of a horizontal grid line and a vertical grid line on the coordinate plane, defined by a horizontal and a vertical coordinate; also, a typographical term meaning approximately 1/72 inch.

polygon: A sequence of connected lines, defined by QuickDraw line-drawing commands.

pop-up menu: A menu not located in the menu bar, which appears when the user presses the mouse button in a particular place.

port: See **grafPort.**

portBits: The bit map of a grafPort.

portRect: A rectangle, defined as part of a grafPort, that encloses a subset of the bit map for use by the grafPort.

post: To place an event in the event queue for later processing.

print record: A record containing all the information needed by the Printing Manager to perform a particular printing job.

Printer Driver: The device driver for the currently installed printer.

printer resource file: A file containing all the resources needed to run the Printing Manager with a particular printer.

Printing Manager: The routines and data types that enable applications to communicate with the Printer Driver to print on any variety of printer via the same interface.

printing grafPort: A special grafPort customized for printing instead of drawing on the screen.

purge: To remove a relocatable block from the heap, leaving its master pointer allocated but set to NIL.

purge bit: A bit in the master pointer to a relocatable block that indicates whether the block is currently purgeable.

purge warning procedure: A procedure associated with a particular heap zone that's called whenever a block is purged from that zone.

purgeable block: A relocatable block that can be purged from the heap.

queue: A list of identically structured entries linked together by pointers.

QuickDraw: The part of the Toolbox that performs all graphic operations on the Macintosh screen.

radio button: A standard Macintosh control that displays a setting, either on or off, and is part of a group in which only one button can be on at a time.

RAM: The Macintosh's random access memory, which contains exception vectors, buffers used by hardware devices, the system and application heaps, the stack, and other information used by applications.

reallocate: To allocate new space in the heap for a purged block, updating its master pointer to point to its new location.

reference number: A number greater than 0, returned by the Resource Manager when a resource file is opened, by which you can refer to that file. In Resource Manager routines that expect a reference number, 0 represents the system resource file.

region: An arbitrary area or set of areas on the QuickDraw coordinate plane. The outline of a region should be one or more closed loops.

relative handle: A handle to a relocatable block expressed as the offset of its master pointer within the heap zone, rather than as the absolute memory address of the master pointer.

release: To free an allocated area of memory, making it available for reuse.

release timer: A timer for determining when an exactly-once response buffer can be released.

relocatable block: A block that can be moved within the heap during compaction.

resource: Data or code stored in a resource file and managed by the Resource Manager.

resource attribute: One of several characteristics, specified by bits in a resource reference, that determine how the resource should be dealt with.

resource data: In a resource file, the data that comprises a resource.

resource file: The resource fork of a file.

resource fork: The part of a file that contains data used by an application (such as menus, fonts, and icons). The resource fork of an application file also contains the application code itself.

resource header: At the beginning of a resource file, data that gives the offsets to and lengths of the resource data and resource map.

resource ID: A number that, together with the resource type, identifies a resource in a resource file. Every resource has an ID number.

Resource Manager: The part of the Toolbox that reads and writes resources.

resource map: In a resource file, data that is read into memory when the file is opened and that, given a resource specification, leads to the corresponding resource data.

resource name: A string that, together with the resource type, identifies a resource in a resource file. A resource may or may not have a name.

resource reference: In a resource map, an entry that identifies a resource and contains either an offset to its resource data in the resource file or a handle to the data if it's already been read into memory.

resource specification: A resource type and either a resource ID or a resource name.

resource type: The type of a resource in a resource file, designated by a sequence of four characters (such as 'MENU' for a menu).

result code: An integer indicating whether a routine completed its task successfully or was prevented by some error condition (or other special condition, such as reaching the end of a file).

resume procedure: A procedure within an application that allows the application to recover from system errors.

RGB space: How Color QuickDraw represents colors. Each color has a red, a green, and a blue component, hence the name RGB.

RGB value: Color QuickDraw represents color using the RGBColor record type, which specifies the red, green, and blue components of the color. The RGB color record used by an application specifies the colors it needs. The translation from the RGB value to the pixel value is performed at the time the color is drawn.

ROM: The Macintosh's permanent read-only memory, which contains the routines for the Toolbox and Operating System, and the various system traps.

root directory: The directory at the base of a file catalog.

Scrap Manager: The part of the Toolbox that enables cutting and pasting between applications, desk accessories, or an application and a desk accessory.

scrap: A place where cut or copied data is stored.

scrap file: The file containing the desk scrap (usually named "Clipboard File").

screen buffer: A block of memory from which the video display reads the information to be displayed.

SCSI: See **Small Computer Standard Interface**.

SCSI Manager: The part of the Operating System that controls the exchange of information between a Macintosh and peripheral devices connected through the Small Computer Standard Interface (SCSI).

segment: One of several parts into which the code of an application may be divided. Not all segments need to be in memory at the same time.

selection range: The series of characters (inversely highlighted), or the character position (marked with a blinking caret), at which the next editing operation will occur.

signature: A four-character sequence that uniquely identifies an application to the Finder.

Small Computer Standard Interface (SCSI): A specification of mechanical, electrical, and functional standards for connecting small computers with intelligent peripherals such as hard disks, printers, and optical disks.

solid shape: A shape that's filled in with any pattern.

Sound Driver: The device driver that controls sound generation in an application.

sound procedure: A procedure associated with an alert that will emit one of up to four sounds from the Macintosh's speaker. Its integer parameter ranges from 0 to 3 and specifies which sound.

source transfer mode: One of eight transfer modes for drawing text or transferring any bit image between two bit maps.

stack: The area of memory in which space is allocated and released in LIFO (last-in-first-out) order.

Standard File Package: A Macintosh package for presenting the standard user interface when a file is to be saved or opened.

startup screen: When the system is started up, one of the display devices is selected as the startup screen, the screen on which the "happy Macintosh" icon appears.

structure region: An entire window; its complete "structure."

style: See **character style**.

style dialog: A dialog that sets options affecting the page dimensions; associated with the Page Setup command.

style record: A TextEdit data structure that specifies the styles for the edit record's text.

style scrap: A new TextEdit scrap type, 'styl' is used for storing style information in the desk scrap along with the old "TEXT" scrap.

style table: A TextEdit data structure that contains one entry for each distinct style used in an edit record's text.

subdirectory: Any directory other than the root directory.

submenu delay: The length of time before a submenu appears as a user drags through a hierarchical main menu; it prevents rapid flashing of submenus.

System Error Handler: The part of the Operating System that assumes control when a fatal system error occurs.

system error alert: An alert box displayed by the System Error Handler.

system error ID: An ID number that appears in a system error alert to identify the error.

system event mask: A global event mask that controls which types of events get posted into the event queue.

system font: The font that the system uses (in menus, for example). Its name is Chicago.

system font size: The size of text drawn by the system in the system font; 12 points.

system heap: The portion of the heap reserved for use by the Operating System.

system heap zone: The heap zone provided by the Memory Manager for use by the Operating System; equivalent to the system heap.

system resource: A resource in the system resource file.

system resource file: A resource file containing standard resources, accessed if a requested resource wasn't found in any of the other resource files that were searched.

system window: A window in which a desk accessory is displayed.

target device: An SCSI device (typically an intelligent peripheral) that receives a request from an initiator device to perform a certain operation.

text styles: TextEdit records used for communicating style information between the application program and the TextEdit routines.

TextEdit: The part of the Toolbox that supports the basic text entry and editing capabilities of a standard Macintosh application.

TextEdit scrap: The place where certain TextEdit routines store the characters most recently cut or copied from text.

theGDevice: When drawing is being performed on a device, a handle to that device is stored as a global variable **theGDevice.**

thumb: The Control Manager's term for the scroll box (the indicator of a scroll bar).

tick: A sixtieth of a second.

Toolbox: Same as **User Interface Toolbox**.

Toolbox Event Manager: The part of the Toolbox that allows your application program to monitor the user's actions with the mouse, keyboard, and keypad.

Toolbox Utilities: The part of the Toolbox that performs generally useful operations such as fixed-point arithmetic, string manipulation, and logical operations on bits.

transfer mode: A specification of which Boolean operation Quick-Draw should perform when drawing or when transferring a bit image from one bit map to another.

trap dispatch table: A table in RAM containing the addresses of all Toolbox and Operating System routines in encoded form.

trap dispatcher: The part of the Operating System that examines a trap word to determine what operation it stands for, looks up the address of the corresponding routine in the trap dispatch table, and jumps to the routine.

trap number: The identifying number of a Toolbox or Operating System routine; an index into the trap dispatch table.

trap word: An unimplemented instruction representing a call to a Toolbox or Operating System routine.

type coercion: Many compilers feature type coercion (also known as typecasting), which allows a data structure of one type to be converted to another type. In many cases, this conversion is simply a relaxation of type-checking in the compiler, allowing the substitution of a differently-typed but equivalent data structure.

unimplemented instruction: An instruction word that doesn't correspond to any valid machine-language instruction but instead causes a trap.

unlock: To allow a relocatable block to be moved during heap compaction.

unmounted volume: A volume that hasn't been inserted into a disk drive and had descriptive information read from it, or a volume that previously was mounted and has since had the memory used by it released.

unpurgeable block: A relocatable block that can't be purged from the heap.

update event: An event generated by the Window Manager when a window's contents need to be redrawn.

update region: A window region consisting of all areas of the content region that have to be redrawn.

User Interface Toolbox: The software in the Macintosh ROM that helps you implement the standard Macintosh user interface in your application.

version data: In an application's resource file, a resource that has the application's signature as its resource type; typically a string that gives the name, version number, and date of the application.

vertical blanking interval: The time between the display of the last pixel on the bottom line of the screen and the first one on the top line.

view rectangle: In TextEdit, the rectangle in which the text is visible.

virtual key codes: The key codes that appear in keyboard events. (See also **raw key codes.**)

visible control: A control that's drawn in its window (but may be completely overlapped by another window or other object on the screen).

visible window: A window that's drawn in its plane on the desktop (but may be completely overlapped by another window or object on the screen).

visRgn: The region of a grafPort, manipulated by the Window Manager, that's actually visible on the screen.

volume: A piece of storage medium formatted to contain files; usually a disk or part of a disk. A $3\frac{1}{2}$ inch Macintosh disk is one volume.

volume attributes: Information contained on volumes and in memory indicating whether the volume is locked, whether it's busy (in memory only), and whether the volume control block matches the volume information (in memory only).

volume name: A sequence of up to 27 printing characters that identifies a volume; followed by a colon (:) in File Manager routine calls, to distinguish it from a file name.

window: An object on the desktop that presents information, such as a document or a message.

window class: In a window record, an indication of whether a window is a system window, a dialog or alert window, or a window created directly by the application.

window definition function: A function called by the Window Manager when it needs to perform certain type-dependent operations on a particular type of window, such as drawing the window frame.

window definition ID: A number passed to window-creation routines to indicate the type of window. It consists of the window definition function's resource ID and a variation code.

window frame: The structure region of a window minus its content region.

window list: A list of all windows ordered by their front-to-back positions on the desktop.

Window Manager: The part of the Toolbox that provides routines for creating and manipulating windows.

Window Manager port: A grafPort that has the entire screen as its portRect and is used by the Window Manager to draw window frames.

window record: The internal representation of a window, where the Window Manager stores all the information it needs for its operations on that window.

window template: A resource from which the Window Manager can create a window.

word wraparound: Keeping words from being split between lines when text is drawn.

working directory: An alternative way of referring to a directory. When opened as a working directory, a directory is given a working directory reference number that's used to refer to it in File Manager calls.

working directory control block: A data structure that contains the directory ID of a working directory, as well as the volume reference number of the volume on which the directory is located.

working directory reference number: A temporary reference number used to identify a working directory. It can be used in place of the volume reference number in all File Manager calls; the File Manager uses it to get the directory ID and volume reference number from the working directory control block.

Appendix B

Code
Listings

The following pages contain complete listings of all the source code presented in this book. The listings are presented in order by Chapter. Remember, you can send in the coupon in the back of the book for a disk containing the complete set of Macintosh Programming Primer, Volume II *projects.*

Chapter 3, ShowINIT.c

```
/**************************-
  Filename: CShowINIT_PROC.c
  Color ShowINIT, for use with LightspeedC
  This translation by Ken McLeod (thecloud@dhw68k.cts.com)
  Version of: Thursday, April 6, 1989 3:30:00 PM

  INIT notification routine by Paul Mercer, Darin Adler,
        and Paul Snively from an idea by Steve Capps
  Version of: Friday, July 15, 1988 12:08:09 AM (1.1B1)
    -revved back to previous calling interface.
    -you only need to call ShowINIT now and due
        to popular demand, deltaX is back!
    -also due to popular demand, color icons are
        now done automatically.
    -note that the color icon is only used if 4
        bits or more is available on
      the main graphics device; the normal #ICN
        is used for all other cases.

  Build & save this file as a 'PROC' resource, and include it
in your INIT's resource file.  Use the following code within
your INIT to load the 'PROC' and call CShowINIT:

    Handle procH;

    if ((procH = GetResource('PROC', PROC_ID)) != OL)
    {
        HLock(procH);
        CallPascal(ICON_ID, -1, *procH);
        HUnlock(procH);
    }

  ***********************-*/

#include <Color.h>

typedef struct QuickDraw
{        /* struct to hold QuickDraw globals */
  char private[76];
  long randSeed;
  BitMap screenBits;
```

```
    Cursor arrow;
    Pattern dkGray;
    Pattern ltGray;
    Pattern gray;
    Pattern black;
    Pattern white;
    GrafPtr thePort;
} QuickDraw;

extern short myH : 0x92C;              /* CurApName+28   */
extern short myCheck: 0x92E;           /* CurApName+30   */


#define    firstX          8
                /* left margin - offset to first icon */
#define    bottomEdge      8
                /* this far from bottom of screen */
#define    iconWidth       32
                /* size of icon (square normally) */
#define    defaultMoveX    40
                /* default amount to move icons */
#define    checksumConst   0x1021
                /* constant used for computing checksum */
#define    minColorDepth   4
                /* min. bits/pixel for drawing color icons */
#define    maskOffset      128
                /* offset to mask in ICN# resource */
#define    iconRowBytes    32/8
                /* 32/8 bits */
#define    hasCQDBit       6
                /* bit in ROM85 cleared if CQD available */


/************************-
Display the ICN# (cicn when in 4 bit mode or higher) specified
by iconID and move the pen horizontally by moveX.  Pass a -1
in moveX to move the standard amount (40 pixels).

pascal void ShowINIT(iconID, moveX)
    short iconID, moveX;
    extern;


************************-*/
```

```
pascal void main(iconID, moveX)
short iconID, moveX;
{
   Handle  theIconHdl;
            /* handle to the icon (or cicn) */
   short    dh;
            /* for calculating horizontal offset */
   short   colorFlag;
            /* set if drawing a color icon */
   short    theDepth;
            /* depth of main screen; used for CQD only */
   GDHandle theMainDevice;
            /* handle to main screen device; CQD only */
   Rect srcRect, destRect;
            /* source & destination rectangles */
   BitMap myBitMap;
            /* icon bitmap; used for b/w icon only */
   GrafPort myPort;
            /* port we draw into */
   QuickDraw qdGlobals;
            /* our own personal QD globals... */
   Ptr localA5;
            /* pointer to qdGlobals.thePort */
   Ptr   savedA5;
            /* storage for saved contents of A5 */

asm
{
    move.l  A5,savedA5
            /* save "real" QD globals ptr */
    lea        localA5,A5
            /* set up A5 to point to our globals */
    move.l  A5,CurrentA5
}
    InitGraf(&qdGlobals.thePort);
            /* initialize our qdGlobals structure */
    OpenPort(&myPort);
    colorFlag = 0;
            /* default: no color */

    if (!(BitTst(&ROM85, 7-hasCQDBit)))
    {   /* does CQD exist? */
        theMainDevice = MainDevice;
```

```
                /* yes; get handle to main device */
                theDepth = (*(*theMainDevice)->gdPMap)->pixelSize;
                if (theDepth >= minColorDepth)
                {   /* deep enough to draw in color? */
                    if ((theIconHdl = (Handle)GetCIcon(iconID)) != OL)
                        colorFlag = 1;
                    /* found a color icon; set flag */
                }
            }

    if (!(colorFlag))
    {   /* no CQD, insufficient depth, or lack of 'cicn' */
        if (!(theIconHdl = GetResource('ICN#',iconID)))
        {
            SysBeep(3);
            /* can't get b/w icon  */
            /* signal error and bail out */
            goto out;
        }
    }
    dh = (myH << 1) ^ checksumConst;
        /* checksum to find dh */
    myH = ((dh == myCheck) ? (myH):(firstX));
        /* reset if necessary */
```

/* notice that we stored the new horizontal value directly back into the low-memory 'myH' location, rather than using a temporary variable.

   This is the way the original ShowINIT works, and IconWrap relies on it. */

```
    destRect.bottom = myPort.portRect.bottom - bottomEdge;
    destRect.left = myPort.portRect.left + myH;
    destRect.top = destRect.bottom - iconWidth;
    destRect.right = destRect.left + iconWidth;

    if (colorFlag)
    {   /* draw color icon */
        PlotCIcon(&destRect,(CIconHandle)theIconHdl);
        DisposCIcon((CIconHandle)theIconHdl);
    }
    else
    {   /* draw b/w icon */
        HLock(theIconHdl);
```

```
        srcRect.top = srcRect.left = 0;
        srcRect.bottom = srcRect.right = iconWidth;
        myBitMap.rowBytes = iconRowBytes;
        myBitMap.bounds = srcRect;
        myBitMap.baseAddr = *theIconHdl + maskOffset;
        /* punch hole with mask */
        CopyBits(&myBitMap, &myPort.portBits,
            &srcRect, &destRect, srcBic, 0L);
        myBitMap.baseAddr = *theIconHdl;
        /* now draw the icon */
        CopyBits(&myBitMap, &myPort.portBits,
            &srcRect, &destRect, srcOr, 0L);
        HUnlock(theIconHdl);
        ReleaseResource(theIconHdl);
    }
    myH += ((moveX == -1) ? (defaultMoveX):(moveX));
            /* advance for next time */
    myCheck = (myH << 1) ^ checksumConst;
                /* calc new checksum */

out:
    ClosePort(&myPort);
    asm
    {
        move.l    savedA5,A5
        move.l    A5,CurrentA5
    }
}
```

Chapter 3, AFI.c

```
#define BASE_ICON_ID    128
#define LAST_ICON_ID    -4064
#define PROC_ID  128
#define WORD_RES_ID     -4048
#define NUM_ICONS       8
#define NORMAL_APP_FONT        applFont
#define DELAY     30L

main()
{
    Handle  procH, wHandle;
```

```
int     i, fontNumber;
long    dummy;

if ( ( wHandle = GetResource( 'word', WORD_RES_ID ) ) !=
    0L )
{
    fontNumber = *( (short *)(*wHandle) );

    *( (short *) 0x0204 ) = fontNumber - 1;

    WriteParam();

    if ( ( procH = GetResource( 'PROC', PROC_ID ) ) != 0L )
    {
        HLock(procH);

        if ( fontNumber == NORMAL_APP_FONT )
        {
            CallPascal( BASE_ICON_ID + NUM_ICONS, -1,
                    *procH);
        }
        else
        {
            CallPascal( BASE_ICON_ID, 0, *procH);

            Delay( DELAY, &dummy );

            for ( i=1; i<NUM_ICONS-1; i++ )
                CallPascal( BASE_ICON_ID + i, 0, *procH);

            CallPascal( LAST_ICON_ID, -1, *procH);
        }

        HUnlock(procH);
    }
}
}
```

Chapter 3, cdev.c

```c
#define DEFAULT_ITEM    1
#define USER_ITEM       2

#define RUN_ON_ALL_MACHINES 1L
#define ERROR_STATE     0L
#define WORD_RES_ID     -4048
#define FONT_MENU_ID    -4048

#define NORMAL_APP_FONT         applFont

typedef struct
{
    short           curFontNum;
} FontNumInfo,      **FontNumH;


pascal longmain( message, item, numItems, cPanelID, e,
            cDevValue, cpDialog )
int             message, item, numItems, cPanelID;
EventRecord*e;
long            cDevValue;
DialogPtr       cpDialog;
{
    int         itemType, fontNumber, choice;
    Handle      itemH, tempHandle;
    Rect        itemRect;
    MenuHandle  fontMenu;
    Str255      tempStr;

    if ( message == macDev )
        return( RUN_ON_ALL_MACHINES );
    else if ( message == initDev )
    {
        tempHandle = NewHandle( sizeof( FontNumInfo ) );
        fontNumber = FindFontNumber();
        (**((FontNumH)tempHandle)).curFontNum = fontNumber;
        return( (long)tempHandle );
    }

    if ( (cDevValue != cdevUnset) && (cDevValue != ERROR_STATE) )
    {
```

```
switch( message )
{
    case hitDev:
        if ( item == DEFAULT_ITEM + numItems )
        {
            GetDItem( cpDialog, USER_ITEM + numItems,
                    &itemType, &itemH, &itemRect );
            fontNumber = NORMAL_APP_FONT;
            SetAppFont( fontNumber );
            DrawFontName( fontNumber, &itemRect );
            (**((FontNumH)cDevValue)).curFontNum = |
                fontNumber;
            FixResource( fontNumber );
        }
        else if ( item == USER_ITEM + numItems )
        {
            GetDItem( cpDialog, USER_ITEM + numItems,
                    &itemType, &itemH, &itemRect );
            fontMenu = GetMenu( FONT_MENU_ID );
            InsertMenu( fontMenu, -1 );
            AddResMenu( fontMenu, 'FONT' );
            itemRect.right += 1;
            choice = DoPopup( &itemRect, fontMenu );

            if ( choice != 0 )
            {
                GetItem( fontMenu, choice, &tempStr );
                GetFNum( tempStr, &fontNumber );
                SetAppFont( fontNumber );
                DrawFontName( fontNumber, &itemRect );
                (**((FontNumH)cDevValue)).curFontNum =
                    fontNumber;
                FixResource( fontNumber );
            }

            DeleteMenu( FONT_MENU_ID );
            ReleaseResource( fontMenu );
        }
        break;
    case closeDev:
        DisposHandle( (Handle)cDevValue );
        break;
    case nulDev:
        break;
```

```
                case updateDev:
                    GetDItem( cpDialog, USER_ITEM+numItems,
                            &itemType, &itemH, &itemRect );
                    FrameRect( &itemRect );
                    MoveTo( itemRect.left + 1, itemRect.bottom );
                    LineTo( itemRect.right, itemRect.bottom );
                    LineTo( itemRect.right, itemRect.top + 1 );
                    fontNumber = (**((FontNumH)cDevValue)).curFontNum;
                    DrawFontName( fontNumber, &itemRect );
                    break;
                case activDev:
                    break;
                case deactivDev:
                    break;
                case keyEvtDev:
                    break;
                case macDev:
                    return( 1L );
                    break;
                case undoDev:
                    break;
                case cutDev:
                    break;
                case copyDev:
                    break;
                case pasteDev:
                    break;
                case clearDev:
                    break;
            }
        }

    return( cDevValue );
}


/***************************** FixResource ******/

FixResource( fontNumber )
short   fontNumber;
{
    Handle  wHandle;
```

```
    if ( ( wHandle = GetResource( 'word', WORD_RES_ID ) ) !=
0L )
    {
        *( (short *)(*wHandle) ) = fontNumber;
        ChangedResource( wHandle );
        WriteResource( wHandle );
    }
}


/***************************** DoPopup ******/

int         DoPopup( popupRectPtr, theMenu )
Rect        *popupRectPtr;
MenuHandle  theMenu;
{
    Point   popupUpperLeft;
    long    theChoice = 0x0000;

    popupUpperLeft.h = popupRectPtr->left + 2;
    popupUpperLeft.v = popupRectPtr->bottom;

    LocalToGlobal( &popupUpperLeft );

    InvertRect( popupRectPtr );
    theChoice = PopUpMenuSelect( theMenu, popupUpperLeft.v,
                                 popupUpperLeft.h, 0 );
    InvertRect( popupRectPtr );
    return( LoWord( theChoice ) );
}


/************************************* FindFontNumber */

short FindFontNumber()
{
    Handle  wHandle;
    short   fontNumber;

    if ( ( wHandle = GetResource( 'word', WORD_RES_ID ) ) != 0L )
    {
        fontNumber = *( (short *)(*wHandle) );
        return( fontNumber );
    }
```

```
    else
        return( NORMAL_APP_FONT );
}


/********************************************  SetAppFont  */

SetAppFont( fontNum )
short    fontNum;
{
    *( (short *) 0x0204 ) = fontNum - 1;

    WriteParam();
}


/********************************************  DrawFontName  */

DrawFontName( fontNum, rPtr )
short        fontNum;
Rect         *rPtr;
{
    Str255       tempStr;
    int          w;
    Rect         tempRect;

    tempRect = *rPtr;
    InsetRect( &tempRect, 2, 2 );
    EraseRect( &tempRect );
    if ( fontNum == 1 )
        GetFontName( geneva, &tempStr );
    else
        GetFontName( fontNum, &tempStr );
    w = rPtr->right - rPtr->left - StringWidth( tempStr );
    MoveTo( rPtr->left + w/2, rPtr->bottom - 4 );
    DrawString( tempStr );
}
```

Chapter 3, MDEF.c (With scrolling)

```
#include "ColorToolbox.h"

#define MARGIN      2
#define UP          1
#define DOWN        2
```

```
/************************************************ main ***/

pascal void      main( message, theMenu, menuRectPtr, hitPt,
                     whichItemPtr )
int              message;
MenuHandle       theMenu;
Rect             *menuRectPtr;
Point            hitPt;
int              *whichItemPtr;
{
    short        PICTResID, numPicts, maxH, maxV, i, sWidth,
                     sHeight;
    PicHandle    myPicture;
    Rect         r, tempRect;
    int          cellNum, cellsBelowMenu, cellsOnScreen,
                     cellsVisible, itemNum, numScrolled;
    Boolean      hasUpArrow, hasDownArrow;
    RgnHandle    updateRgn;

    switch( message )
    {
        case mDrawMsg:
            GetNumPicts( theMenu, &PICTResID, &numPicts );
            CalcMaxHV( PICTResID, numPicts, &maxH, &maxV );
            cellsVisible = (menuRectPtr->bottom - menuRectPtr-
                            >top) / (maxV + MARGIN);

            r.top = menuRectPtr->top + MARGIN/2;
            r.left = menuRectPtr->left + MARGIN;
            r.bottom = r.top + maxV;
            r.right = r.left + maxH;

            for ( i=0; i<cellsVisible-1; i++ )
            {
                myPicture = GetPicture( PICTResID + i );
                tempRect = r;
                CenterPict( myPicture, &tempRect );
                DrawPicture( myPicture, &tempRect );
                OffsetRect( &r, 0, maxV + MARGIN );
            }

            if ( cellsVisible < numPicts )
                DrawArrow( &r, DOWN );
```

```
            else
            {
                PlotPicture( PICTResID + i, &r );
                OffsetRect( &r, 0, maxV + MARGIN );
            }
            TopMenuItem = menuRectPtr->top;
            AtMenuBottom = TopMenuItem + ((maxV + MARGIN) *
                                         numPicts);
            break;
    case mChooseMsg:
            GetNumPicts( theMenu, &PICTResID, &numPicts );
            CalcMaxHV( PICTResID, numPicts, &maxH, &maxV );
            cellsVisible = (menuRectPtr->bottom - menuRectPtr-
                        >top)
                        / (maxV + MARGIN);
            hasUpArrow = (TopMenuItem < menuRectPtr->top);
            hasDownArrow = (AtMenuBottom > menuRectPtr->bottom);
            cellNum = ( (hitPt.v - menuRectPtr->top) / (maxV +
                    MARGIN) ) + 1;/*  cells are 1-based  */

            if ( PtInRect( hitPt, menuRectPtr ) )
            {
                if ( (cellNum == 1) && hasUpArrow )  /*   then
                    scroll down 1 item  */
                {
                    TopMenuItem += maxV + MARGIN;
                    AtMenuBottom += maxV + MARGIN;
                    itemNum = (hitPt.v - TopMenuItem) / (maxV +
                            MARGIN);/*  items are 0-based */

                    if ( *whichItemPtr > 0 )  /*  Is there a
                        selected cell?  If so, deselect it  */
                    {
                        numScrolled = (menuRectPtr->top -
                                    TopMenuItem) / (maxV +
                                    MARGIN);
                        r = *menuRectPtr;
                        r.top += ( (*whichItemPtr - numScrolled -
                                2) * (MARGIN + maxV) );
                        r.bottom = r.top + maxV + MARGIN;
                        InvertRect( &r );
                        *whichItemPtr = 0;
                    }
```

```
            r = *menuRectPtr;
            if ( ! hasDownArrow )
            {
                r.top = r.bottom - maxV - MARGIN;
                EraseRect( &r );
                DrawArrow( &r, DOWN );
            }
            r.top = menuRectPtr->top + maxV + MARGIN;
            r.bottom = menuRectPtr->bottom - maxV -
                MARGIN;
            updateRgn = NewRgn();
            ScrollRect( &r, 0, maxV + MARGIN, updateRgn );
            DisposeRgn( updateRgn );

            r.top = menuRectPtr->top + maxV + MARGIN;
            r.bottom = r.top + maxV + MARGIN;
            PlotPicture( PICTResID + itemNum + 1, &r );

            if ( itemNum == 0 ) /*  replace up-arrow with
                first pict  */
            {
                r = *menuRectPtr;
                r.bottom = r.top + maxV + MARGIN;
                PlotPicture( PICTResID + itemNum, &r );
            }
        }
        else if ( (cellNum == cellsVisible) &&
                hasDownArrow ) /* then scroll up 1 item */
        {
            TopMenuItem -= maxV + MARGIN;
            AtMenuBottom -= maxV + MARGIN;
            itemNum = (hitPt.v - TopMenuItem) / (maxV +
                    MARGIN);/*  items are 0-based */

            if ( *whichItemPtr > 0 )  /*  Is there a
                selected cell?  If so, deselect it  */
            {
                numScrolled = (menuRectPtr->top -
                            TopMenuItem) / (maxV +
                            MARGIN);
                r = *menuRectPtr;
                r.top += ( (*whichItemPtr - numScrolled) *
                        (MARGIN + maxV) );
```

```
            r.bottom = r.top + maxV + MARGIN;
            InvertRect( &r );
            *whichItemPtr = 0;
        }

        r = *menuRectPtr;
        if ( ! hasUpArrow )
        {
            r.bottom = r.top + maxV + MARGIN;
            EraseRect( &r );
            DrawArrow( &r, UP );
        }
        r.top = menuRectPtr->top + maxV + MARGIN;
        r.bottom = menuRectPtr->bottom - maxV -
            MARGIN;
        updateRgn = NewRgn();
        ScrollRect( &r, 0, -maxV - MARGIN, updateRgn );
        DisposeRgn( updateRgn );

        r.top = menuRectPtr->bottom - 2 * (maxV +
            MARGIN);
        r.bottom = r.top + maxV + MARGIN;
        PlotPicture( PICTResID + itemNum - 1, &r );

        if ( itemNum == numPicts - 1 ) /*  replace
            down-arrow with last pict  */
        {
            OffsetRect( &r, 0, maxV + MARGIN );
            PlotPicture( PICTResID + itemNum, &r );
        }
    }
    else
    {
        itemNum = (hitPt.v - TopMenuItem) / (maxV +
                    MARGIN);/*  items are 0-based */
        numScrolled = (menuRectPtr->top - TopMenuItem)
                    / (maxV + MARGIN);
        if ( ( *whichItemPtr > 0 ) && ( *whichItemPtr
            != itemNum + 1 ) )
        {
            r = *menuRectPtr;
            r.top += ( (*whichItemPtr - numScrolled -1)
                    * (MARGIN + maxV) );
```

```
                    r.bottom = r.top + maxV + MARGIN;
                    InvertRect( &r );
                }

                if ( *whichItemPtr != itemNum + 1 )
                {
                    *whichItemPtr = itemNum + 1;
                    r = *menuRectPtr;
                    r.top += ( (*whichItemPtr - numScrolled -1)
                                * (MARGIN + maxV) );
                    r.bottom = r.top + maxV + MARGIN;
                    InvertRect( &r );
                }
            }
        }
        else if ( *whichItemPtr > 0 )
        {
            numScrolled = (menuRectPtr->top - TopMenuItem)
                            / (maxV + MARGIN);
            r = *menuRectPtr;
            r.top += ( (*whichItemPtr - numScrolled -1) *
                        (MARGIN + maxV) );
            r.bottom = r.top + maxV + MARGIN;
            InvertRect( &r );
            *whichItemPtr = 0;
        }
        break;
    case mSizeMsg:
        GetNumPicts( theMenu, &PICTResID, &numPicts );
        CalcMaxHV( PICTResID, numPicts, &maxH, &maxV );
        GetScreenSize( &sHeight, &sWidth );
        cellsOnScreen = (sHeight - MBarHeight) / (maxV +
                        MARGIN);
        HLock( theMenu );
        (**theMenu).menuWidth = maxH + 2 * MARGIN;
        if ( cellsOnScreen > numPicts )
            (**theMenu).menuHeight = (maxV + MARGIN) *
            numPicts;
        else
            (**theMenu).menuHeight = (maxV + MARGIN) *
            cellsOnScreen;
        HUnlock( theMenu );
        break;
    case mPopUpMsg:
```

```
/*  cellsBelowMenu is the number of cells that will fit
below the menu. cellsOnScreen is the number of cells
that will fit between the bottom of the menu bar and
the bottom of the screen. Note that the Toolbox (for
very arcane reasons) switches hitPt.h and hitPt.v on
the popup message only.  Don't worry, this code is
correct...
   */
   GetNumPicts( theMenu, &PICTResID, &numPicts );
   CalcMaxHV( PICTResID, numPicts, &maxH, &maxV );
   GetScreenSize( &sHeight, &sWidth );
   cellsBelowMenu = (sHeight - hitPt.h) / (maxV +
                      MARGIN);
   cellsOnScreen = (sHeight - MBarHeight) / (maxV +
                      MARGIN);

   if ( cellsOnScreen > numPicts )
   {
       if ( cellsBelowMenu > numPicts )
       {
           menuRectPtr->top = hitPt.h;
           menuRectPtr->bottom = hitPt.h + ( (maxV +
               MARGIN) * numPicts );
       }
       else
       {
           menuRectPtr->bottom = sHeight;
           menuRectPtr->top = menuRectPtr->bottom -
               ( (maxV + MARGIN) * numPicts );
       }
   }
   else    /*  We have to scroll, use entire screen  */
   {
       menuRectPtr->bottom = sHeight;
       menuRectPtr->top = menuRectPtr->bottom -
           ( (maxV + MARGIN) * cellsOnScreen );
   }
   menuRectPtr->left = hitPt.v;
   menuRectPtr->right = hitPt.v + maxH + 2 * MARGIN;
   *whichItemPtr = 0;
   break;
   }
}
```

```
/***************************** PlotPicture *********/

PlotPicture( resID, rPtr )
int     resID;
Rect    *rPtr;
{
    PicHandle  pic;
    Rect       tempRect;

    pic = GetPicture( resID );
    tempRect = *rPtr;
    EraseRect( &tempRect );
    CenterPict( pic, &tempRect );
    DrawPicture( pic, &tempRect );
}



/***************************** DrawArrow *********/

DrawArrow( rPtr, upOrDown )
Rect        *rPtr;
int         upOrDown;
{
    int     top, mid, i;

    top = (rPtr->bottom - rPtr->top) / 2 + rPtr->top - 3;
    mid = (rPtr->right - rPtr->left) / 2 + rPtr->left;

    if ( upOrDown == UP )
    {
        for ( i=0; i<6; i++ )
        {
            MoveTo( mid - i - 1, top + i );
            LineTo( mid + i, top + i );
        }
    }
    else
    {
        for ( i=0; i<6; i++ )
        {
            MoveTo( mid - (6-i), top + i );
            LineTo( mid + (5-i), top + i );
        }
    }
```

```
/***************************** CenterPict *********/

CenterPict( thePicture, myRectPtr )
PicHandle  thePicture;
Rect       *myRectPtr;
{
    Rect    windRect, pictureRect;

    windRect = *myRectPtr;
    pictureRect = (**( thePicture )).picFrame;
    myRectPtr->top = (windRect.bottom - windRect.top -
                    (pictureRect.bottom - pictureRect.top))
        / 2 + windRect.top;
    myRectPtr->bottom = myRectPtr->top + (pictureRect.bottom -
                                    pictureRect.top);
    myRectPtr->left = (windRect.right - windRect.left -
                    (pictureRect.right - pictureRect.left))
                    / 2 + windRect.left;
    myRectPtr->right = myRectPtr->left + (pictureRect.right -
                                    pictureRect.left);
}


/******************************************** CalcMaxHV ***/

CalcMaxHV( PICTResID, numPicts, hPtr, vPtr )
short       PICTResID, numPicts, *hPtr, *vPtr;
{
    short      i;
    Rect       r;
    PicHandle  myPicture;

    *hPtr = 0;
    *vPtr = 0;
    for ( i=0; i<numPicts; i++ )
    {
        myPicture = GetPicture( PICTResID + i );
        r = (**myPicture).picFrame;

        if ( r.bottom - r.top > *vPtr )
            *vPtr = r.bottom - r.top;
        if ( r.right - r.left > *hPtr )
            *hPtr = r.right - r.left;
    }
}
```

```
/***************************************  GetScreenSize  ***/

GetScreenSize( heightPtr, widthPtr )
short       *heightPtr, *widthPtr;
{
    SysEnvRec       mySE;
    GDHandle        mainDev;
    Rect            dummyRect;
    WindowPtr       dummyWindow;

    SysEnvirons( 2, &mySE );
    if ( mySE.hasColorQD )
    {
        mainDev = GetMainDevice();
        HLock( mainDev );
        *heightPtr = (**mainDev).gdRect.bottom -
                        (**mainDev).gdRect.top;
        *widthPtr =  (**mainDev).gdRect.right -
                        (**mainDev).gdRect.left;
    }
    else
    {
        SetRect( &dummyRect, 0, 0, 100, 100 );
        dummyWindow = NewWindow( 0L, &dummyRect, "\p", FALSE,
                            0, -1L, FALSE, 0L );
        *heightPtr = dummyWindow->portBits.bounds.bottom -
                        dummyWindow->portBits.bounds.top;
        *widthPtr =  dummyWindow->portBits.bounds.right -
                        dummyWindow->portBits.bounds.left;
        DisposeWindow( dummyWindow );
    }
}



/*********************************************  GetNumPicts  ***/

GetNumPicts( theMenu, baseIDPtr, numPictsPtr )
MenuHandle theMenu;
short       *baseIDPtr, *numPictsPtr;
{
    HLock( theMenu );
    *baseIDPtr = HiWord((**theMenu).enableFlags);
    *numPictsPtr = LoWord((**theMenu).enableFlags);
    HUnlock( theMenu );
}
```

Chapter 3, Tester.c (For MDEF)

```
#define BASE_RES_ID          400
#define APPLE_MENU_ID        400
#define NIL_POINTER          0L
#define MOVE_TO_FRONT        -1L
#define REMOVE_ALL_EVENTS    0

#define WNE_TRAP_NUM         0x60
#define UNIMPL_TRAP_NUM      0x9F
#define MIN_SLEEP            60L
#define NIL_MOUSE_REGION     0L

#define FILE_MENU_ID         401
#define F_QUIT_ITEM          1

#define PICT_MENU_ID         403


Boolean        gDone, gWNEImplemented;
EventRecord    gTheEvent;
MenuHandle     gAppleMenu;
PicHandle      gCurPicture;
WindowPtr      gTheWindow;


main()
{
    ToolBoxInit();
    MenuBarInit();

    gTheWindow = GetNewWindow( BASE_RES_ID, NIL_POINTER,
                                MOVE_TO_FRONT );
    SetPort( gTheWindow );
    ShowWindow( gTheWindow );

    gCurPicture = GetPicture( BASE_RES_ID );

    MainLoop();
}
```

```
/******************************* ToolBoxInit */

ToolBoxInit()
{
    InitGraf( &thePort );
    InitFonts();
    FlushEvents( everyEvent, REMOVE_ALL_EVENTS );
    InitWindows();
    InitMenus();
    TEInit();
    InitDialogs( NIL_POINTER );
    InitCursor();
}


/******************************** MenuBarInit*/

MenuBarInit()
{
    Handle      myMenuBar;

    myMenuBar = GetNewMBar( BASE_RES_ID );
    SetMenuBar( myMenuBar );
    gAppleMenu = GetMHandle( APPLE_MENU_ID );
    AddResMenu( gAppleMenu, 'DRVR' );
    DrawMenuBar();
}


/****************************** MainLoop ********/

MainLoop()
{
    gDone = FALSE;
    gWNEImplemented = ( NGetTrapAddress( WNE_TRAP_NUM,
                        ToolTrap ) !=
                        NGetTrapAddress( UNIMPL_TRAP_NUM,
                        ToolTrap ) );
    while ( gDone == FALSE )
    {
        HandleEvent();
    }
}
```

```
/*********************************** HandleEvent   */

HandleEvent()
{
    char    theChar;

    if ( gWNEImplemented )
        WaitNextEvent( everyEvent, &gTheEvent, MIN_SLEEP,
                    NIL_MOUSE_REGION );
    else
    {
        SystemTask();
        GetNextEvent( everyEvent, &gTheEvent );
    }

    switch ( gTheEvent.what )
    {
        case mouseDown:
            HandleMouseDown();
            break;
        case keyDown:
        case autoKey:
            theChar = gTheEvent.message & charCodeMask;
            if (( gTheEvent.modifiers & cmdKey ) != 0)
                HandleMenuChoice( MenuKey( theChar ) );
            break;
        case updateEvt:
            BeginUpdate( gTheEvent.message );
            DrawMyPicture( gCurPicture, gTheWindow );
            EndUpdate( gTheEvent.message );
            break;
    }
}


/*********************************** HandleMouseDown */

HandleMouseDown()
{
    WindowPtr  whichWindow;
    short int  thePart;
    long int   menuChoice, windSize;
```

```
        thePart = FindWindow( gTheEvent.where, &whichWindow );
        switch ( thePart )
        {
            case inMenuBar:
                menuChoice = MenuSelect( gTheEvent.where );
                HandleMenuChoice( menuChoice );
                break;
            case inSysWindow :
                SystemClick( &gTheEvent, whichWindow );
                break;
            case inDrag :
                DragWindow( whichWindow, gTheEvent.where,
                            &(screenBits.bounds) );
                break;
        }
}


/********************************** HandleMenuChoice */

HandleMenuChoice( menuChoice )
long int     menuChoice;
{
    int theMenu;
    int theItem;

    if ( menuChoice != 0 )
    {
        theMenu = HiWord( menuChoice );
        theItem = LoWord( menuChoice );
        switch ( theMenu )
        {
            case FILE_MENU_ID :
                if ( theItem == F_QUIT_ITEM )
                    gDone = TRUE;
                break;
            case PICT_MENU_ID :
                EraseRect( &gTheWindow->portRect );
                InvalRect( &gTheWindow->portRect );
                gCurPicture = GetPicture( BASE_RES_ID + theItem - 1 );
                break;
        }
        HiliteMenu( 0 );
    }
}
```

```
/*************************** DrawMyPicture ********/

DrawMyPicture( thePicture, pictureWindow )
PicHandle   thePicture;
WindowPtr   pictureWindow;
{
    Rect     myRect;

    myRect = pictureWindow->portRect;
    CenterPict( thePicture, &myRect );
    DrawPicture( thePicture, &myRect );
}



/**************************** CenterPict ********/

CenterPict( thePicture, myRectPtr )
PicHandle   thePicture;
Rect        *myRectPtr;
{
    Rect     windRect, pictureRect;

    windRect = *myRectPtr;
    pictureRect = (**( thePicture )).picFrame;
    myRectPtr->top = (windRect.bottom - windRect.top -
                    (pictureRect.bottom - pictureRect.top))
        / 2 + windRect.top;
    myRectPtr->bottom = myRectPtr->top + (pictureRect.bottom -
                                        pictureRect.top);
    myRectPtr->left = (windRect.right - windRect.left -
                    (pictureRect.right - pictureRect.left))
        / 2 + windRect.left;
    myRectPtr->right = myRectPtr->left + (pictureRect.right -
                                        pictureRect.left);

}
```

Chapter 3, DLOG.c

```
#define BASE_RES_ID          400
#define NIL_POINTER          0L
#define MOVE_TO_FRONT        -1L
#define REMOVE_ALL_EVENTS    0
```

```
#define OK_ITEM               1
#define CANCEL_ITEM           2
#define TEXT_ITEM             4

#define TE_ENTER_KEY          3
#define TE_TAB_CHAR           9
#define TE_CARRIAGE_RETURN    13

pascal   Boolean   DLOGFilter();

main()
{
    DialogPtr    theDialog;
    Boolean      done;
    int          itemHit, itemType;
    Handle       OKHandle, textHandle;
    Rect         itemRect;
    Str255       theText;

    ToolBoxInit();

    theDialog = GetNewDialog( BASE_RES_ID, NIL_POINTER,
                              MOVE_TO_FRONT );
    GetDItem( theDialog, OK_ITEM, &itemType, &OKHandle,
            &itemRect );
    GetDItem( theDialog, TEXT_ITEM, &itemType, &textHandle,
            &itemRect );

    CenterDialog( theDialog );
    ShowWindow( theDialog );
    SetPort( theDialog );
    DrawOKButton( theDialog );

    done = FALSE;
    while ( ! done )
    {
        GetIText( textHandle, &theText );
        if ( theText[ 0 ] == 0 )
            HiliteControl( OKHandle, 255 );
        else
            HiliteControl( OKHandle, 0 );
        ModalDialog( DLOGFilter, &itemHit );
```

```
            done = ( (itemHit == OK_ITEM) || (itemHit ==
                CANCEL_ITEM) );
    }
}


/********************************** ToolBoxInit */

ToolBoxInit()
{
    InitGraf( &thePort );
    InitFonts();
    FlushEvents( everyEvent, REMOVE_ALL_EVENTS );
    InitWindows();
    InitMenus();
    TEInit();
    InitDialogs( NIL_POINTER );
    InitCursor();
}


/******************************************* DLOGFilter  *****/

pascal          Boolean DLOGFilter( theDialog, e, iPtr )
DialogPtr       theDialog;
EventRecord     *e;
int             *iPtr;
{
    int         itemType;
    Rect        itemRect;
    Handle      item;
    Str255      tempStr;
    char        theChar;

    GetDItem( theDialog, TEXT_ITEM, &itemType, &item,
            &itemRect );
    GetIText( item, &tempStr );

    if (e->what == keyDown)
    {
        theChar = (e->message & charCodeMask);
        if ( (theChar == TE_CARRIAGE_RETURN) || (theChar ==
            TE_ENTER_KEY) )
```

```
      {
          if ( tempStr[ 0 ] != 0 )
          {
              *iPtr = OK_ITEM;
              GetDItem( theDialog, OK_ITEM, &itemType, &item,
                        &itemRect );
              HiliteControl( item, 1 );
              return( TRUE );
          }
          else
          {
              *iPtr = TEXT_ITEM;
              return( TRUE );
          }
      }
   }
   return( FALSE );
}


/*************************************  DrawOKButton  *****/

DrawOKButton( theDialog )
DialogPtr   theDialog;
{
    int       itemType;
    Rect      itemRect;
    Handle    item;
    GrafPtr   oldPort;

    GetDItem( theDialog, OK_ITEM, &itemType, &item, &itemRect );
    GetPort( &oldPort );
    SetPort( theDialog );

    PenSize( 3, 3 );
    InsetRect( &itemRect, -4, -4 );
    FrameRoundRect( &itemRect, 16, 16 );
    PenNormal();

    SetPort( oldPort );
}
```

```
/******************************** CenterDialog *****/

CenterDialog( theDialog )
DialogPtr   theDialog;
{
    Rect        r;
    int         width, height, sWidth, sHeight, h, v;

    r = theDialog->portRect;

    width = r.right - r.left;
    height = r.bottom - r.top;

    sWidth = screenBits.bounds.right - screenBits.bounds.left;
    sHeight = screenBits.bounds.bottom - screenBits.bounds.top;

    h = (sWidth - width) / 2;
    v = (sHeight - height) / 2;

    MoveWindow( theDialog, h, v, FALSE );
}
```

Chapter 4, ColorInfo.c

```
#include "ColorToolbox.h"

#define BASE_RES_ID         400
#define NIL_POINTER         0L
#define NIL_STRING          "\p"
#define INVISIBLE           FALSE
#define NO_GOAWAY           FALSE
#define MOVE_TO_FRONT       (WindowPtr)-1L
#define REMOVE_ALL_EVENTS   0
#define INDEX_DEVICE        TRUE
#define DIRECT_DEVICE       FALSE


Boolean IsColor();
```

```
main()
{
    int        pixDepth;
    GDHandle   curDev;
    Rect       bounds;

    ToolBoxInit();

    if ( IsColor() )
    {
        curDev = GetDeviceList();

        while( curDev != NIL_POINTER )
        {
            bounds = (**curDev).gdRect;

            pixDepth = GetPixelDepth( curDev );
            switch( pixDepth )
            {
                case 1:
                    DisplayColors( &bounds, 1, 2, 128, INDEX_DEVICE );
                    break;
                case 2:
                    DisplayColors( &bounds, 2, 2, 128, INDEX_DEVICE );
                    break;
                case 4:
                    DisplayColors( &bounds, 4, 4, 64, INDEX_DEVICE );
                    break;
                case 8:
                    DisplayColors( &bounds, 16, 16, 24, INDEX_DEVICE );
                    break;
                default:
                    DisplayColors( &bounds, 48, 48, 8,
                                    DIRECT_DEVICE );
                    break;
            }
            curDev = GetNextDevice( curDev );
        }
        while( ! Button() ) ;
    }
    else
        DoAlert( "\pThis machine does not support Color QuickDraw!" );
}
```

```
/********************************* ToolBoxInit */

ToolBoxInit()
{
    InitGraf( &thePort );
    InitFonts();
    FlushEvents( everyEvent, REMOVE_ALL_EVENTS );
    InitWindows();
    InitMenus();
    TEInit();
    InitDialogs( NIL_POINTER );
    InitCursor();
}


/******************************** GetPixelDepth *********/

int GetPixelDepth( theDevice )
GDHandle    theDevice;
{
    PixMapHandle    screenPMapH;
    int             pixelDepth;

    screenPMapH = (**theDevice).gdPMap;
    pixelDepth = (**screenPMapH).pixelSize;
    return( pixelDepth );
}


/******************************** IsColor *********/

Boolean IsColor()
{
    SysEnvRec   mySE;

    SysEnvirons( 1, &mySE );
    return( mySE.hasColorQD );
}
```

```
/*********************************** DisplayColors */

DisplayColors( boundsPtr, width, height, pixPerBox, isIndex )
Rect        *boundsPtr;
int         width, height, pixPerBox;
Boolean     isIndex;
{
    Rect        r;
    int         row, col;
    WindowPtr   cWindow;
    RGBColor    curColor;
    HSVColor    hsvColor;
    long        colorNum;

    hsvColor.value = hsvColor.saturation = 65535;

    r.top = 0;
    r.left = 0;
    r.right = width * pixPerBox;
    r.bottom = height * pixPerBox;

    cWindow = NewCWindow( NIL_POINTER, &r, "\pDevice Colors",
            INVISIBLE, noGrowDocProc, MOVE_TO_FRONT,
            NO_GOAWAY, NIL_POINTER );

    CenterWindow( cWindow, boundsPtr );
    ShowWindow( cWindow );
    SetPort( cWindow );

    for ( row=0; row<height; row++ )
    {
        for ( col=0; col<width; col++ )
        {
            r.top = row * pixPerBox;
            r.left = col * pixPerBox;
            r.bottom = r.top + pixPerBox;
            r.right = r.left + pixPerBox;

            if ( isIndex )
                Index2Color( (long)(row*width + col), &curColor );
            else
            {
                colorNum = (long)(row*width + col);
```

```
                        hsvColor.hue = 65535 * colorNum / (width * height );
                        HSV2RGB( &hsvColor, &curColor );
                    }
                    RGBForeColor( &curColor );
                    PaintRect( &r );
                }
            }
        }


/******************************** CenterWindow */

CenterWindow( w, boundsPtr )
Rect        *boundsPtr;
WindowPtr   w;
{
    Rect    r;
    int     width, height, sWidth, sHeight, h, v;

    r = w->portRect;

    width = r.right - r.left;
    height = r.bottom - r.top;

    sWidth = boundsPtr->right - boundsPtr->left;
    sHeight = boundsPtr->bottom - boundsPtr->top;

    h = boundsPtr->left + ((sWidth - width) / 2);
    v = boundsPtr->top + ((sHeight - height) / 2);

    MoveWindow( w, h, v, FALSE );
}


/******************************** DoAlert */

DoAlert( s )
Str255      s;
{
    ParamText( s, NIL_STRING, NIL_STRING, NIL_STRING );
    NoteAlert( BASE_RES_ID, NIL_POINTER );
}
```

Chapter 4, Palette.c

```c
#include "ColorToolbox.h"

#define BASE_RES_ID          400
#define NIL_POINTER          0L
#define NIL_STRING           "\p"
#define VISIBLE              TRUE
#define HAS_GOAWAY           TRUE
#define MOVE_TO_FRONT        -1L
#define REMOVE_ALL_EVENTS    0
#define MIN_SLEEP            0L
#define NIL_MOUSE_REGION     0L

#define PRECISE_TOLERANCE    0x0000
#define NUM_SQUARES          150


Boolean        IsColor();
WindowPtr      CreateColorWindow();
PaletteHandle  MakeRedPalette(), MakeBrightPalette(),
               MakeGrayPalette();


main()
{
    Point          corner;
    WindowPtr      window;
    PaletteHandle  pal;

    ToolBoxInit();

    if ( ! IsColor() )
        DoAlert( "\pThis machine does not support Color QuickDraw!" );
    else
    {
        corner.h = 10;
        corner.v = 40;
        window = CreateColorWindow( corner, "\pRed Palette" );
        pal = MakeRedPalette();
        SetPalette( window, pal, TRUE );
```

```
            corner.h = 170;
            corner.v = 177;
            window = CreateColorWindow( corner, "\pBright Palette"
);

            pal = MakeBrightPalette();
            SetPalette( window, pal, TRUE );

            corner.h = 330;
            corner.v = 40;
            window = CreateColorWindow( corner, "\pGray Palette" );
            pal = MakeGrayPalette();
            SetPalette( window, pal, TRUE );

            DoEventLoop();
    }
}


/********************************* ToolBoxInit */

ToolBoxInit()
{
    InitGraf( &thePort );
    InitFonts();
    FlushEvents( everyEvent, REMOVE_ALL_EVENTS );
    InitWindows();
    InitMenus();
    TEInit();
    InitDialogs( NIL_POINTER );
    InitCursor();
}


/********************************* DoEventLoop */

DoEventLoop()
{
    Boolean         done;
    EventRecord     e;
    short           part;
    WindowPtr       window;
```

```
    done = FALSE;
    while ( ! done )
    {
        WaitNextEvent( everyEvent, &e, MIN_SLEEP,
                       NIL_MOUSE_REGION );

        switch( e.what )
        {
            case mouseDown:
                part = FindWindow( e.where, &window );
                if ( part == inGoAway )
                    done = TRUE;
                else if ( part == inDrag )
                    DragWindow( window, e.where,
                                &screenBits.bounds );
                else if ( part == inContent )
                {
                    if ( window != FrontWindow() )
                        SelectWindow( window );
                }
                break;
            case updateEvt:
                BeginUpdate( (WindowPtr)e.message );
                SetPort( (WindowPtr)e.message );
                DrawBullseye();
                EndUpdate( (WindowPtr)e.message );
                break;
        }
    }
}


/********************************* DrawBullseye */

DrawBullseye()
{
    int     i, center;
    Rect    r;

    center = NUM_SQUARES;

    for ( i=1; i<=NUM_SQUARES; i++ )
    {
```

```
                    PmForeColor( i - 1 );
                    r.top = center - i;
                    r.left = center - i;
                    r.bottom = center + i;
                    r.right = center + i;

                    FrameRect( &r );
            }
    }


/****************************** IsColor ********/

Boolean IsColor()
{
    SysEnvRec   mySE;

    SysEnvirons( 1, &mySE );
    return( mySE.hasColorQD );
}


/****************************** MakeRedPalette ********/

PaletteHandle  MakeRedPalette()
{
    RGBColor        c;
    long            i;
    PaletteHandle   redPalette;

    redPalette = NewPalette( NUM_SQUARES, NIL_POINTER,
                             pmTolerant, PRECISE_TOLERANCE );

    c.green = 0;
    c.blue = 0;

    for ( i=0; i<NUM_SQUARES; i++ )
    {
        c.red = (i * 65535) / NUM_SQUARES;
        SetEntryColor( redPalette, i, &c );
    }

    return( redPalette );
}
```

```
/****************************** MakeBrightPalette *********/

PaletteHandle  MakeBrightPalette()
{
    PaletteHandle  brightPalette;
    long           i;
    RGBColor       rgbColor;
    HSVColor       hsvColor;

    brightPalette = NewPalette( NUM_SQUARES, NIL_POINTER,
                                pmTolerant, PRECISE_TOLERANCE );

    hsvColor.value = 65535;
    hsvColor.saturation = 65535;

    for ( i=0; i<NUM_SQUARES; i++ )
    {
        hsvColor.hue = (i * 65535) / NUM_SQUARES;
        HSV2RGB( &hsvColor, &rgbColor );
        SetEntryColor( brightPalette, i, &rgbColor );
    }

    return( brightPalette );
}


/****************************** MakeGrayPalette *********/

PaletteHandle  MakeGrayPalette()
{
    PaletteHandle  grayPalette;
    long           i;
    RGBColor       rgbColor;

    grayPalette = NewPalette( NUM_SQUARES, NIL_POINTER,
                              pmTolerant, PRECISE_TOLERANCE );

    for ( i=0; i<NUM_SQUARES; i++ )
    {
        rgbColor.red = (i * 65535) / NUM_SQUARES;
        rgbColor.green = rgbColor.red;
        rgbColor.blue = rgbColor.red;
```

```
            SetEntryColor( grayPalette, i, &rgbColor );
    }

    return( grayPalette );
}



/******************************** CreateColorWindow */

WindowPtr   CreateColorWindow( corner, title )
Point       corner;
Str255      title;
{
    WindowPtr   cWindow;
    Rect        r;

    SetRect( &r, corner.h, corner.v, corner.h + (2 * NUM_SQUARES),
                    corner.v + (2 * NUM_SQUARES) );

    cWindow = NewCWindow( NIL_POINTER, &r, title,
            VISIBLE, noGrowDocProc, MOVE_TO_FRONT,
            HAS_GOAWAY, NIL_POINTER );

    return( cWindow );
}



/******************************** DoAlert */

DoAlert( s )
Str255      s;
{
    ParamText( s, NIL_STRING, NIL_STRING, NIL_STRING );
    NoteAlert( BASE_RES_ID, NIL_POINTER );
}
```

Chapter 4, ColorTutor.c

```
#include "ColorToolbox.h"

#define BASE_RES_ID     400
#define NIL_POINTER     0L
#define NIL_STRING      "\p"
#define VISIBLE         TRUE
```

```
#define HAS_GOAWAY           TRUE
#define MOVE_TO_FRONT        -1L
#define REMOVE_ALL_EVENTS  0
#define MIN_SLEEP            OL
#define NIL_MOUSE_REGION    OL
#define NOT_A_NORMAL_MENU  -1

#define PRECISE_TOLERANCE  0x0000

#define BLACK_PATTERN        1
#define GRAY_PATTERN         2
#define COLOR_RAMP           4
#define GRAY_RAMP            5
#define SINGLE_COLOR         6

#define SRC_AND_BACK_MENU 400
#define MODE_MENU           401


Boolean        IsColor(), PickColor();

Rect           gSrcRect, gBackRect, gDestRect,
               gSrcMenuRect, gBackMenuRect, gModeMenuRect,
               gOpColorRect;
int            gSrcPattern, gBackPattern, gCopyMode,
               gSrcType, gBackType;
RGBColor       gSrcColor, gBackColor, gOpColor;
MenuHandle     gSrcMenu, gBackMenu, gModeMenu;
WindowPtr      gColorWindow;



main()
{
    Point          corner;
    PaletteHandle  pal;

    ToolBoxInit();

    if ( ! IsColor() )
        DoAlert( "\pThis machine does not support Color QuickDraw!" );
    else
```

```
    {
        SetUpWindow();
        SetUpGlobals();

        DoEventLoop();
    }
}


/******************************** ToolBoxInit */

ToolBoxInit()
{
    InitGraf( &thePort );
    InitFonts();
    FlushEvents( everyEvent, REMOVE_ALL_EVENTS );
    InitWindows();
    InitMenus();
    TEInit();
    InitDialogs( NIL_POINTER );
    InitCursor();
}


/******************************** SetUpWindow */

SetUpWindow()
{
    Rect        r;

    SetRect( &r, 5, 40, 225, 275 );

    gColorWindow = NewCWindow( NIL_POINTER, &r, "\pColorTutor",
            VISIBLE, noGrowDocProc, MOVE_TO_FRONT,
            HAS_GOAWAY, NIL_POINTER );

    SetRect( &r, 15, 207, 95, 225 );
    NewControl( gColorWindow, &r, "\pOpColor...",
            VISIBLE, 0, 0, 1, pushButProc, NIL_POINTER );

    SetPort( gColorWindow );
    TextFont( systemFont );
}
```

```
/********************************* SetUpGlobals */

SetUpGlobals()
{
    SetRect( &gSrcRect, 15, 6, 95, 86 );
    SetRect( &gBackRect, 125, 6, 205, 86 );
    SetRect( &gDestRect, 125, 122, 205, 202 );
    SetRect( &gOpColorRect, 15, 122, 95, 202 );

    SetRect( &gSrcMenuRect, 7, 90, 103, 108 );
    SetRect( &gBackMenuRect, 117, 90, 213, 108 );
    SetRect( &gModeMenuRect, 117, 206, 213, 226 );

    gSrcPattern = BLACK_PATTERN;
    gBackPattern = BLACK_PATTERN;

    gCopyMode = srcCopy;

    gSrcColor.red = 65535;
    gSrcColor.green = gSrcColor.blue = 0;
    gSrcType = SINGLE_COLOR;

    gBackColor.blue = 0xFFFF;
    gBackColor.red = gBackColor.green = 0;
    gBackType = SINGLE_COLOR;

    gOpColor.green = 32767;
    gOpColor.red =  32767;
    gOpColor.blue = 32767;
    OpColor( &gOpColor );

    gSrcMenu = GetMenu( SRC_AND_BACK_MENU );
    InsertMenu( gSrcMenu, NOT_A_NORMAL_MENU );

    gBackMenu = GetMenu( SRC_AND_BACK_MENU );
    InsertMenu( gBackMenu, NOT_A_NORMAL_MENU );

    gModeMenu = GetMenu( MODE_MENU );
    InsertMenu( gModeMenu, NOT_A_NORMAL_MENU );
}
```

```
/******************************* DoEventLoop */

DoEventLoop()
{
    Boolean         done;
    EventRecord     e;
    short           part;
    WindowPtr       window;
    Point           p;

    done = FALSE;
    while ( ! done )
    {
        WaitNextEvent( everyEvent, &e, MIN_SLEEP, NIL_MOUSE_REGION );

        switch( e.what )
        {
            case mouseDown:
                part = FindWindow( e.where, &window );
                if ( part == inGoAway )
                    done = TRUE;
                else if ( part == inDrag )
                    DragWindow( window, e.where,
                                &screenBits.bounds );
                else if ( part == inContent )
                {
                    p = e.where;
                    GlobalToLocal( &p );
                    DoContent( p );
                }
                break;
            case updateEvt:
                BeginUpdate( (WindowPtr)e.message );
                SetPort( (WindowPtr)e.message );
                DrawWindow();
                DrawControls( (WindowPtr)e.message );
                EndUpdate( (WindowPtr)e.message );
                break;
        }
    }
}
```

```
/********************************** DoContent */

DoContent( p )
Point    p;
{
    int            choice;
    ControlHandle  control;
    RGBColor       rgbColor;

    if ( FindControl( p, gColorWindow, &control ) )
    {
        if ( TrackControl( control, p, NIL_POINTER ) )
        {
            rgbColor = gOpColor;
            if ( PickColor( &rgbColor ) )
            {
                gOpColor = rgbColor;
                InvalRect( &gOpColorRect );
                InvalRect( &gDestRect );
                OpColor( &gOpColor );
            }
        }
    }
    else if ( PtInRect( p, &gSrcMenuRect ) )
    {
        UpdateSrcMenu();
        choice = DoPopup( gSrcMenu, &gSrcMenuRect );
        if ( choice > 0 )
        {
            DoSrcChoice( choice );
            InvalRect( &gSrcRect );
            InvalRect( &gDestRect );
        }
    }
    else if ( PtInRect( p, &gBackMenuRect ) )
    {
        UpdateBackMenu();
        choice = DoPopup( gBackMenu, &gBackMenuRect );
        if ( choice > 0 )
        {
            DoBackChoice( choice );
            InvalRect( &gBackRect );
            InvalRect( &gDestRect );
        }
    }
```

```
        else if ( PtInRect( p, &gModeMenuRect ) )
        {
            UpdateModeMenu();
            choice = DoPopup( gModeMenu, &gModeMenuRect );
            if ( choice > 0 )
            {
                DoModeChoice( choice );
                InvalRect( &gDestRect );
            }
        }
    }
}


/********************************** DrawWindow */

DrawWindow()
{
    RGBColor    rgbBlack;
    Rect        source, dest;

    rgbBlack.red = rgbBlack.green = rgbBlack.blue = 0;

    if ( gSrcPattern == BLACK_PATTERN )
        PenPat( black );
    else
        PenPat( gray );

    if ( gSrcType == COLOR_RAMP )
        DrawColorRamp( &gSrcRect );
    else if ( gSrcType == GRAY_RAMP )
        DrawGrayRamp( &gSrcRect );
    else
    {
        RGBForeColor( &gSrcColor );
        PaintRect( &gSrcRect );
    }

    if ( gBackPattern == BLACK_PATTERN )
        PenPat( black );
    else
        PenPat( gray );

    if ( gBackType == COLOR_RAMP )
```

```
        DrawColorRamp( &gBackRect );
    else if ( gBackType == GRAY_RAMP )
        DrawGrayRamp( &gBackRect );
    else
    {
        RGBForeColor( &gBackColor );
        PaintRect( &gBackRect );
    }
    PenPat( black );

    RGBForeColor( &gOpColor );
    PaintRect( &gOpColorRect );

    RGBForeColor( &rgbBlack );
    DrawLabel( &gSrcMenuRect, "\pSource" );
    DrawLabel( &gBackMenuRect, "\pBackground" );
    DrawLabel( &gModeMenuRect, "\pMode" );

    PenSize( 2, 2 );
    FrameRect( &gSrcRect );
    FrameRect( &gBackRect );
    FrameRect( &gDestRect );
    FrameRect( &gOpColorRect );

    PenNormal();

    source = gBackRect;
    InsetRect( &source, 2, 2 );

    dest = gDestRect;
    InsetRect( &dest, 2, 2 );

    CopyBits( &((CGrafPtr)gColorWindow)->portPixMap,
        &((CGrafPtr)gColorWindow)->portPixMap,
        &source, &dest, srcCopy, NIL_POINTER );

    source = gSrcRect;
    InsetRect( &source, 2, 2 );

    CopyBits( &((CGrafPtr)gColorWindow)->portPixMap,
        &((CGrafPtr)gColorWindow)->portPixMap,
        &source, &dest, gCopyMode, NIL_POINTER );
}
```

```
/******************************** DrawColorRamp */

DrawColorRamp( rPtr )
Rect    *rPtr;
{
    long        numColors, i;
    HSVColor    hsvColor;
    RGBColor    rgbColor;
    Rect        r;

    r = *rPtr;
    InsetRect( &r, 2, 2 );
    numColors = (rPtr->right - rPtr->left - 2) / 2;
    hsvColor.value = hsvColor.saturation = 65535;

    for ( i=0; i<numColors; i++ )
    {
        hsvColor.hue = i * 65535 / numColors;
        HSV2RGB( &hsvColor, &rgbColor );
        RGBForeColor( &rgbColor );
        FrameRect( &r );
        InsetRect( &r, 1, 1 );
    }
}


/******************************** DrawGrayRamp */

DrawGrayRamp( rPtr )
Rect    *rPtr;
{
    long        numColors, i;
    RGBColor    rgbColor;
    Rect        r;

    r = *rPtr;
    InsetRect( &r, 2, 2 );
    numColors = (rPtr->right - rPtr->left - 2) / 2;

    for ( i=0; i<numColors; i++ )
    {
        rgbColor.red = i * 65535 / numColors;
        rgbColor.green = rgbColor.red;
```

```
            rgbColor.blue = rgbColor.red;
            RGBForeColor( &rgbColor );
            FrameRect( &r );
            InsetRect( &r, 1, 1 );
        }
    }


/******************************* DrawLabel */

DrawLabel( rPtr, s )
Rect        *rPtr;
Str255      s;
{
    Rect    tempRect;
    int     size;

    tempRect = *rPtr;
    tempRect.bottom -= 1;
    tempRect.right -= 1;
    FrameRect( &tempRect );

    MoveTo( tempRect.left + 1, tempRect.bottom );
    LineTo( tempRect.right, tempRect.bottom );
    LineTo( tempRect.right, tempRect.top + 1 );

    size = rPtr->right - rPtr->left - StringWidth( s );
    MoveTo( rPtr->left + size/2, rPtr->bottom - 6 );
    DrawString( s );
}


/******************************** UpdateSrcMenu */

UpdateSrcMenu()
{
    int i;

    for ( i=1; i<=6; i++ )
        CheckItem( gSrcMenu, i, FALSE );

    if ( gSrcPattern == BLACK_PATTERN )
        CheckItem( gSrcMenu, BLACK_PATTERN, TRUE );
```

```
        else
            CheckItem( gSrcMenu, GRAY_PATTERN, TRUE );

        if ( gSrcType == COLOR_RAMP )
            CheckItem( gSrcMenu, COLOR_RAMP, TRUE );
        else if ( gSrcType == GRAY_RAMP )
            CheckItem( gSrcMenu, GRAY_RAMP, TRUE );
        else if ( gSrcType == SINGLE_COLOR )
            CheckItem( gSrcMenu, SINGLE_COLOR, TRUE );
}


/********************************** UpdateBackMenu */

UpdateBackMenu()
{
    int i;

    for ( i=1; i<=6; i++ )
        CheckItem( gBackMenu, i, FALSE );

    if ( gBackPattern == BLACK_PATTERN )
        CheckItem( gBackMenu, BLACK_PATTERN, TRUE );
    else
        CheckItem( gBackMenu, GRAY_PATTERN, TRUE );

    if ( gBackType == COLOR_RAMP )
        CheckItem( gBackMenu, COLOR_RAMP, TRUE );
    else if ( gBackType == GRAY_RAMP )
        CheckItem( gBackMenu, GRAY_RAMP, TRUE );
    else if ( gBackType == SINGLE_COLOR )
        CheckItem( gBackMenu, SINGLE_COLOR, TRUE );
}


/********************************** UpdateModeMenu */

UpdateModeMenu()
{
    int i;

    for ( i=1; i<=17; i++ )
        CheckItem( gModeMenu, i, FALSE );
```

```
    if ( ( gCopyMode >=0 ) && ( gCopyMode <= 7 ) )
        CheckItem( gModeMenu, gCopyMode + 1, TRUE );
    else
        CheckItem( gModeMenu, gCopyMode - 22, TRUE );
}


/******************************* DoSrcChoice */

DoSrcChoice( item )
int     item;
{
    RGBColor        rgbColor;

    switch( item )
    {
        case BLACK_PATTERN:
            gSrcPattern = BLACK_PATTERN;
            break;
        case GRAY_PATTERN:
            gSrcPattern = GRAY_PATTERN;
            break;
        case COLOR_RAMP:
            gSrcType = COLOR_RAMP;
            break;
        case GRAY_RAMP:
            gSrcType = GRAY_RAMP;
            break;
        case SINGLE_COLOR:
            gSrcType = SINGLE_COLOR;
            rgbColor = gSrcColor;
            if ( PickColor( &rgbColor ) )
                gSrcColor = rgbColor;
            break;
    }
}


/******************************* DoBackChoice */

DoBackChoice( item )
int     item;
{
```

```
        RGBColor        rgbColor;

    switch( item )
    {
        case BLACK_PATTERN:
            gBackPattern = BLACK_PATTERN;
            break;
        case GRAY_PATTERN:
            gBackPattern = GRAY_PATTERN;
            break;
        case COLOR_RAMP:
            gBackType = COLOR_RAMP;
            break;
        case GRAY_RAMP:
            gBackType = GRAY_RAMP;
            break;
        case SINGLE_COLOR:
            gBackType = SINGLE_COLOR;
            rgbColor = gBackColor;
            if ( PickColor( &rgbColor ) )
                gBackColor = rgbColor;
            break;
    }
}


/******************************** DoModeChoice */

DoModeChoice( item )
int     item;
{
    if ( ( item >= 1 ) && ( item <= 8 ) )
        gCopyMode = item - 1;
    else
        gCopyMode = item + 22;
}


/***************************** DoPopup *******/

int         DoPopup( menu, rPtr )
MenuHandle  menu;
Rect        *rPtr;
{
```

```
    Point    corner;
    long     theChoice = 0L;

    corner.h = rPtr->left;
    corner.v = rPtr->bottom;

    LocalToGlobal( &corner );

    InvertRect( rPtr );
    theChoice = PopUpMenuSelect( menu, corner.v - 1, corner.
                                 h + 1, 0 );

    InvertRect( rPtr );

    return( LoWord( theChoice ) );
}


/****************************** PickColor ********/

Boolean PickColor( colorPtr )
RGBColor    *colorPtr;
{
    Point   where;

    where.h = -1;
    where.v = -1;

    return( GetColor( where, "\pChoose a color...", colorPtr,
            colorPtr ) );
}


/****************************** IsColor ********/

Boolean IsColor()
{
    SysEnvRec   mySE;

    SysEnvirons( 1, &mySE );
    return( mySE.hasColorQD );
}
```

```
/******************************* DoAlert */

DoAlert( s )
Str255      s;
{
    ParamText( s, NIL_STRING, NIL_STRING, NIL_STRING );
    NoteAlert( BASE_RES_ID, NIL_POINTER );
}
```

Chapter 4, QuickDraw32Bit.h

```
/*************************************************************

Created: Thursday, March 23, 1989 at 7:25 PM by Jean-Charles
         Mourey
    QuickDraw32Bit.h
    C Interface to the Macintosh Libraries


    Copyright Apple Computer, Inc.   1985-1989
    All rights reserved

*************************************************************/


#ifndef __QuickDraw32Bit__
#define __QuickDraw32Bit__

#ifndef __QUICKDRAW__

#endif

/* New Constants for 32-Bit QuickDraw */

#define ditherCopy 64
    /* Dither mode for Copybits */
#define RGBDirect 16
    /* 16 & 32 bits/pixel pixelType value */


/* New error codes */
```

```
#define rgnOverflowErr -147
    /* Region accumulation failed.
        Resulting region may be currupt */
#define pixmapTooDeepErr -148
    /* Pixmap is not 1-bit/pixel for
        BitmapToRegion */
#define insufficientStackErr -149
    /* QuickDraw could not complete
        the operation */
#define cDepthErr -157
    /* invalid pixel depth passed to NewGWorld
        or UpdateGWorld */


/* Flag bits passed to or returned by Offscreen routines */

enum {
    pixPurgeBit = 0,
    noNewDeviceBit = 1,
    pixelsPurgeableBit = 6,
    pixelsLockedBit = 7,

    mapPixBit = 16,
        /* set if color table mapping occurred */
    newDepthBit = 17,
        /* set if pixels were scaled to a
            different depth */
    alignPixBit = 18,
        /* set if pixels were realigned to
            screen alignment */
    newRowBytesBit = 19,
        /* set if pixmap was reconfigured
            in a new rowBytes */
    reallocPixBit = 20,
        /* set if offscreen buffer had to be
            reallocated */
    clipPixBit = 28,
        /* set if pixels were or are to be
            clipped */
    stretchPixBit = 29,
        /* set if pixels were or are to be
            stretched/shrinked */
    ditherPixBit = 30,
    gwFlagErrBit = 31
};
```

```
typedef enum {
    pixPurge = 1 << pixPurgeBit,
    noNewDevice = 1 << noNewDeviceBit,
    pixelsPurgeable = 1 << pixelsPurgeableBit,
    pixelsLocked = 1 << pixelsLockedBit,
    mapPix = 1 << mapPixBit,
    newDepth = 1 << newDepthBit,
    alignPix = 1 << alignPixBit,
    newRowBytes = 1 << newRowBytesBit,
    reallocPix = 1 << reallocPixBit,
    clipPix = 1 << clipPixBit,
    stretchPix = 1 << stretchPixBit,
    ditherPix = 1 << ditherPixBit,
    gwFlagErr = 1 << gwFlagErrBit
}GWorldFlag;

typedef long GWorldFlags;

/* Type definition of a GWorldPtr */

typedef CGrafPtr GWorldPtr;


#ifdef __safe_link
extern "C" {
#endif

pascal OSErr BitmapToRegion(RgnHandle region, BitMap *bMap)
    = {0xA8D7};


pascal QDErr NewGWorld (GWorldPtr *offscreenGWorld, short
                          pixelDepth,
        Rect *boundsRect, CTabHandle cTable, GDHandle aGDevice,
  GWorldFlags flags)
    = {0x7000,0xAB1D};
pascal Boolean LockPixels (PixMapHandle pm)
    = {0x7001,0xAB1D};
pascal void UnlockPixels (PixMapHandle pm)
    = {0x7002,0xAB1D};
pascal GWorldFlags UpdateGWorld (GWorldPtr *offscreenGWorld,
short pixelDepth,
```

```
        Rect *boundsRect, CTabHandle cTable, GDHandle aGDevice,
GWorldFlags flags)
    = {0x7003,0xAB1D};
pascal void DisposeGWorld (GWorldPtr offscreenGWorld)
    = {0x7004,0xAB1D};
pascal void GetGWorld (CGrafPtr *port, GDHandle *gdh)
    = {0x7005,0xAB1D};
pascal void SetGWorld (CGrafPtr port, GDHandle gdh)
    = {0x7006,0xAB1D};
pascal void CTabChanged (CTabHandle ctab)
    = {0x7007,0xAB1D};
pascal void PixPatChanged (PixPatHandle ppat)
    = {0x7008,0xAB1D};
pascal void PortChanged (GrafPtr port)
    = {0x7009,0xAB1D};
pascal void GDeviceChanged (GDHandle gdh)
    = {0x700A,0xAB1D};
pascal void AllowPurgePixels (PixMapHandle pm)
    = {0x700B,0xAB1D};
pascal void NoPurgePixels (PixMapHandle pm)
    = {0x700C,0xAB1D};
pascal GWorldFlags GetPixelsState (PixMapHandle pm)
    = {0x700D,0xAB1D};
pascal void SetPixelsState (PixMapHandle pm, GWorldFlags
state)
    = {0x700E,0xAB1D};
pascal Ptr GetPixBaseAddr (PixMapHandle pm)
    = {0x700F,0xAB1D};
pascal QDErr NewScreenBuffer (Rect *globalRect, Boolean
purgeable, GDHandle *gdh,
        PixMapHandle *offscreenPixMap)
    = {0x7010,0xAB1D};
pascal void DisposeScreenBuffer (PixMapHandle offscreenPixMap)
    = {0x7011,0xAB1D};
pascal GDHandle GetGWorldDevice (GWorldPtr offscreenGWorld)
    = {0x7012,0xAB1D};
#ifdef __safe_link
}
#endif


#endif
```

Chapter 4, GWorld.c

```c
#include "ColorToolbox.h"
#include "QuickDraw32Bit.h"

#define BASE_RES_ID         400
#define NIL_POINTER         0L
#define NIL_STRING          "\p"
#define VISIBLE             TRUE
#define NO_GOAWAY           FALSE
#define MOVE_TO_FRONT       -1L
#define REMOVE_ALL_EVENTS   0


#define MAX_PIXEL_DEPTH     32
#define WORLD_WIDTH         100
#define WORLD_HEIGHT        100
#define NO_FLAGS            0L


#define QD32TRAP            0xAB03
#define UNIMPL_TRAP         0xA89F



Boolean         Is32Bit();
GWorldPtr       MakeGWorld();
WindowPtr       CreateColorWindow();


main()
{
    WindowPtr   window;
    GWorldPtr   world;
    Rect        worldBounds, windowRect, destRect;

    ToolBoxInit();

    if ( ! Is32Bit() )
        DoAlert( "\pThis machine does not support 32-Bit QuickDraw!" );
    else
    {
        SetRect( &worldBounds, 0, 0, WORLD_HEIGHT, WORLD_WIDTH );
        world = MakeGWorld( &worldBounds );
        window = CreateColorWindow();
```

```
            SetRect( &destRect, 0, 0, 4 * WORLD_WIDTH, 4 *
                    WORLD_HEIGHT );
            CopyWorldBits( world, window, &destRect );

            SetRect( &destRect, 0, 0, 2 * WORLD_WIDTH, 2 *
                    WORLD_HEIGHT );
            CopyWorldBits( world, window, &destRect );

            SetRect( &destRect, 0, 0, WORLD_WIDTH, WORLD_HEIGHT );
            CopyWorldBits( world, window, &destRect );

            SetRect( &destRect, 0, 0, WORLD_WIDTH / 2, WORLD_HEIGHT
                    / 2 );
            CopyWorldBits( world, window, &destRect );

            SetRect( &destRect, 0, 0, WORLD_WIDTH / 4, WORLD_HEIGHT
                    / 4 );
            CopyWorldBits( world, window, &destRect );

            while ( ! Button() ) ;
        }
}


/********************************** ToolBoxInit */

ToolBoxInit()
{
    InitGraf( &thePort );
    InitFonts();
    FlushEvents( everyEvent, REMOVE_ALL_EVENTS );
    InitWindows();
    InitMenus();
    TEInit();
    InitDialogs( NIL_POINTER );
    InitCursor();
}


/********************************** CreateColorWindow */

WindowPtr  CreateColorWindow()
{
```

```
    WindowPtr   cWindow;
    Rect        r;

    SetRect( &r, 10, 40, 10 + (4 * WORLD_WIDTH),
             40 + (4 * WORLD_HEIGHT) );

    cWindow = NewCWindow( NIL_POINTER, &r, "\pColor Test",
            VISIBLE, noGrowDocProc, MOVE_TO_FRONT,
            NO_GOAWAY, NIL_POINTER );

    SetPort( cWindow );

    return( cWindow );
}



/********************************** MakeGWorld */

GWorldPtr MakeGWorld( boundsPtr )
Rect    *boundsPtr;
{
    GDHandle    oldGD;
    GWorldPtr   oldGW, newWorld;
    HSVColor    hsvColor;
    RGBColor    rgbColor;
    long        i;
    Rect        r;
    QDErr       errorCode;

    GetGWorld( &oldGW, &oldGD );

    errorCode = NewGWorld( &newWorld, MAX_PIXEL_DEPTH,
                           boundsPtr, NIL_POINTER,
                           NIL_POINTER, NO_FLAGS );
    if ( errorCode != noErr )
    {
        DoAlert( "\pMy call to NewGWorld died!  Bye..." );
        ExitToShell();
    }

    LockPixels( newWorld->portPixMap );
    SetGWorld( newWorld, NIL_POINTER );
```

```
    hsvColor.value = 65535;
    hsvColor.saturation = 65535;

    for( i=boundsPtr->left; i<=boundsPtr->right; i++ )
    {
        hsvColor.hue = i * 65535 / ( boundsPtr->right - 1 );
        HSV2RGB( &hsvColor, &rgbColor );
        RGBForeColor( &rgbColor );
        MoveTo( i, boundsPtr->bottom / 2 );
        LineTo( i, boundsPtr->bottom );

        rgbColor.red = i * 65535 / ( boundsPtr->right - 1 );
        rgbColor.green = rgbColor.red;
        rgbColor.blue = rgbColor.red;

        RGBForeColor( &rgbColor );
        MoveTo( i, 0 );
        LineTo( i, boundsPtr->bottom / 2 );
    }

    SetGWorld(oldGW,oldGD);
    UnlockPixels( newWorld->portPixMap );

    return( newWorld );
}


/*********************************** CopyWorldBits */

CopyWorldBits( world, window, destRectPtr )
GWorldPtr   world;
WindowPtr   window;
Rect        *destRectPtr;
{
    RGBColor    rgbBlack;

    rgbBlack.red = rgbBlack.green = rgbBlack.blue = 0;
    RGBForeColor( &rgbBlack );

    LockPixels( world->portPixMap );
    CopyBits( &world->portPixMap, &thePort->portBits,
            &world->portRect, destRectPtr, ditherCopy, 0 );
    UnlockPixels( world->portPixMap );
}
```

```
/****************************** Is32Bit ********/

Boolean Is32Bit()
{
    SysEnvRec   mySE;

    SysEnvirons( 1, &mySE );

    if ( ! mySE.hasColorQD )
        return( FALSE );

    return( NGetTrapAddress( QD32TRAP, ToolTrap ) !=
        NGetTrapAddress( UNIMPL_TRAP, ToolTrap ) );
}


/********************************** DoAlert */

DoAlert( s )
Str255      s;
{
    ParamText( s, NIL_STRING, NIL_STRING, NIL_STRING );
    NoteAlert( BASE_RES_ID, NIL_POINTER );
}
```

Chapter 5, FormEdit.c

```
/******************/
/*     MENUs      */
/******************/

#define APPLE_MENU_ID           400
#define A_ABOUT_ITEM            1

#define FILE_MENU_ID            401
#define F_NEW_ITEM              1
#define F_CLOSE_ITEM            2
#define F_QUIT_ITEM             3

#define EDIT_MENU_ID            402
#define E_UNDO_ITEM             1
#define E_CUT_ITEM              3
```

```
#define E_COPY_ITEM            4
#define E_PASTE_ITEM           5
#define E_CLEAR_ITEM           6


/******************/
/*   Window Types  */
/******************/

#define NIL_WINDOW             0
#define UNKNOWN_WINDOW         1
#define DA_WINDOW              2
#define FORM_WINDOW            3


/******************/
/*      ALRTs      */
/******************/

#define ABOUT_ALERT            400
#define ERROR_ALERT_ID         401


/******************/
/*   Error STRs    */
/******************/

#define NO_MBAR                BASE_RES_ID
#define NO_MENU                BASE_RES_ID+1
#define NO_WIND                BASE_RES_ID+2


/******************/
/*     TextEdit    */
/******************/

#define TE_NAME_AREA           0
#define TE_MISC_AREA           1

#define TE_ENTER_KEY           3
#define TE_DELETE_CHAR         8
#define TE_TAB_CHAR            9
#define TE_CARRIAGE_RETURN     13
```

```
/***********************/
/*   General Defines        */
/***********************/


#define BASE_RES_ID             400
#define NIL_POINTER             0L
#define MOVE_TO_FRONT           -1L
#define REMOVE_ALL_EVENTS       0

#define DRAG_THRESHOLD          30

#define WINDOW_HOME_LEFT        5
#define WINDOW_HOME_TOP         45
#define NEW_WINDOW_OFFSET       20

#define MIN_SLEEP               0L
#define NIL_MOUSE_REGION        0L

#define LEAVE_WHERE_IT_IS       FALSE

#define WNE_TRAP_NUM            0x60
#define UNIMPL_TRAP_NUM         0x9F
#define SUSPEND_RESUME_BIT      0x0001
#define RESUMING                1

#define NIL_STRING              "\p"
#define UNTITLED_STRING         "\p<Untitled>"
#define VISIBLE                 TRUE
#define HOPELESSLY_FATAL_ERROR  "\pGame over, man!"



/***********************/
/*     Useful Macros        */
/***********************/

#define TopLeft( myRect )       (* (Point *) &(myRect.top) )
#define BotRight( myRect )      (* (Point *) &(myRect.bottom) )
```

```
/***********************/
/*      Typedefs       */
/***********************/

typedef struct
{
    WindowRecord    w;
    int             wType;
    ControlHandle   vScroll;
    TEHandle        nameTE, miscTE, curTE;
} FormRecord,       *FormPeek;


/***********************/
/*        Globals      */
/***********************/

Boolean         gDone, gWNEImplemented, gInBackground;
EventRecord     gTheEvent;
MenuHandle      gAppleMenu,
                gFileMenu,
                gEditMenu;
int             gNewWindowLeft = WINDOW_HOME_LEFT,
                gNewWindowTop = WINDOW_HOME_TOP;
Rect            gNameRect = { 3, 43, 19, 250 },
                gMiscRect = { 22, 43, 150, 231 },
                gScrollBarRect = { 22, 234, 150, 250 };


/***********************/
/*       Routines      */
/***********************/

void            AdjustCursor( Point mouse, RgnHandle region );
void            AdjustMenus( void );
void            AdjustScrollBar( FormPeek form );
void            CommonAction( ControlHandle   control, short
                    *amount );
void            CreateWindow( void );
void            DoActivate( WindowPtr window, Boolean
                    becomingActive );
void            DoCloseWindow( WindowPtr window );
void            DoContentClick( WindowPtr window, Point mouse );
```

```
void            DoIdle( void );
void            DoTEKey( char c );
void            DoUpdate( WindowPtr window );
void            DrawForm( WindowPtr window );
void            ErrorHandler( int stringNum );
void            HandleAppleChoice( int theItem );
void            HandleEditChoice( int theItem );
void            HandleEvent( void );
void            HandleFileChoice( int theItem );
void            HandleMenuChoice( long int menuChoice );
void            HandleMouseDown( void );
void            MainLoop( void );
void            MenuBarInit( void );
pascal Boolean  NewClikLoop( void );
void            StartTextEdit( FormPeek form );
void            SwitchToNewArea( FormPeek form, int newArea );
void            ToolBoxInit( void );
void            TurnOffTextArea( FormPeek form, int whichArea );
void            TurnOnTextArea( FormPeek form, int whichArea );
pascal void     VActionProc( ControlHandle control, int part );
int             WindowType( WindowPtr window );



/***************************** main *********/

main()
{
    ToolBoxInit();
    MenuBarInit();

    MainLoop();
}



/******************************** ToolBoxInit */

void    ToolBoxInit()
{
    InitGraf( &thePort );
    InitFonts();
    FlushEvents( everyEvent, REMOVE_ALL_EVENTS );
    InitWindows();
```

```
        InitMenus();
        TEInit();
        InitDialogs( NIL_POINTER );
        InitCursor();
    }


/******************************** MenuBarInit*/

void    MenuBarInit()
{
    Handle      myMenuBar;

    if ( ( myMenuBar = GetNewMBar( BASE_RES_ID ) ) ==
        NIL_POINTER )
          ErrorHandler( NO_MBAR );
    SetMenuBar( myMenuBar );

    if ( ( gAppleMenu = GetMHandle( APPLE_MENU_ID ) ) ==
        NIL_POINTER )
          ErrorHandler( NO_MENU );
    AddResMenu( gAppleMenu, 'DRVR' );

    if ( ( gFileMenu = GetMHandle( FILE_MENU_ID ) ) ==
        NIL_POINTER )
          ErrorHandler( NO_MENU );

    if ( ( gEditMenu = GetMHandle( EDIT_MENU_ID ) ) ==
        NIL_POINTER )
          ErrorHandler( NO_MENU );

    DrawMenuBar();
}


/****************************** MainLoop ********/

void    MainLoop()
{
    RgnHandle   cursorRgn;
    Boolean     gotEvent;

    gDone = FALSE;
```

```
        gInBackground = FALSE;

        cursorRgn = NewRgn();

        gWNEImplemented = ( NGetTrapAddress( WNE_TRAP_NUM,
                            ToolTrap ) !=
                            NGetTrapAddress( UNIMPL_TRAP_NUM,
                                    ToolTrap ) );
        while ( gDone == FALSE )
        {
            if ( gWNEImplemented )
                gotEvent = WaitNextEvent( everyEvent, &gTheEvent,
                                    MIN_SLEEP, cursorRgn );
            else
            {
                SystemTask();
                gotEvent = GetNextEvent( everyEvent, &gTheEvent );
            }

            AdjustCursor( gTheEvent.where, cursorRgn );

            if ( gotEvent )
                HandleEvent();
            else
                DoIdle();
        }
}


/*********************************** HandleEvent   */

void    HandleEvent()
{
    char        c;

    switch ( gTheEvent.what )
    {
        case nullEvent:
            DoIdle();
            break;
        case mouseDown:
            HandleMouseDown();
            break;
```

```
        case keyDown:
        case autoKey:
            c = gTheEvent.message & charCodeMask;
            if (( gTheEvent.modifiers & cmdKey ) != 0)
            {
                AdjustMenus();
                HandleMenuChoice( MenuKey( c ) );
            }
            else
                DoTEKey( c );
            break;
        case activateEvt:
            DoActivate( (WindowPtr)gTheEvent.message,
                        (gTheEvent.modifiers & activeFlag) != 0 );
            break;
        case updateEvt:
            DoUpdate( (WindowPtr)gTheEvent.message );
            break;
        case app4Evt:
            if ( ( gTheEvent.message & SUSPEND_RESUME_BIT ) ==
                RESUMING )
            {
                gInBackground = (gTheEvent.message & 0x01) == 0;
                DoActivate(FrontWindow(), !gInBackground);
            }
            else
                DoIdle();
            break;
    }
}


/*********************************** DoTEKey    */

void    DoTEKey( c )
char    c;
{
    WindowPtr       window;
    FormPeek        form;
    int             wType, length, i;
    CharsHandle     text;
    Str255          tempStr;
```

```
window = FrontWindow();
wType = WindowType( window );

if ( wType == FORM_WINDOW )
{
    form = (FormPeek)window;

    if ( c == TE_TAB_CHAR )
    {
        if ( form->curTE == form->nameTE )
            SwitchToNewArea( form, TE_MISC_AREA );
        else
        {
            SwitchToNewArea( form, TE_NAME_AREA );
            TESetSelect( 0, 32767, form->curTE );
        }
    }
    else
    {
        TEKey( c, form->curTE );
        if ( form->curTE == form->nameTE )
        {
            length = (*form->nameTE)->teLength;
            if ( length == 0 )
                SetWTitle( window, UNTITLED_STRING );
            else
            {
                text = TEGetText( form->nameTE );
                tempStr[ 0 ] = length;
                for ( i=0; ( (i<length) && (i<256) ); i++ )
                {
                    tempStr[ i+1 ] = (*text)[ i ];
                }
                SetWTitle( window, tempStr );
            }
        }
        else
            AdjustScrollBar( form );
    }
}
}
```

```
/*********************************** DoIdle      */

void    DoIdle()
{
    WindowPtr   window;
    int         wType;

    window = FrontWindow();
    wType = WindowType( window );

    if ( wType == FORM_WINDOW )
        TEIdle( ((FormPeek)window)->curTE );
}


/*********************************** HandleMouseDown */

void    HandleMouseDown()
{
    WindowPtr   window;
    short int   thePart;
    long int    menuChoice, windSize;

    thePart = FindWindow( gTheEvent.where, &window );
    switch ( thePart )
    {
        case inMenuBar:
            AdjustMenus();
            menuChoice = MenuSelect( gTheEvent.where );
            HandleMenuChoice( menuChoice );
            break;
        case inSysWindow:
            SystemClick( &gTheEvent, window );
            break;
        case inContent:
            if ( window != FrontWindow() )
            {
                SelectWindow(window);
            }
            else
                DoContentClick( window, gTheEvent.where );
            break;
        case inDrag:
```

```
                    DragWindow( window, gTheEvent.where,
                            &(screenBits.bounds) );
                break;
            case inGoAway:
                if ( TrackGoAway(window, gTheEvent.where) )
                    DoCloseWindow( window );
                break;
        }
}


/*********************************** DoCloseWindow */

void    DoCloseWindow( window )
WindowPtr   window;
{
    HideWindow( window );
    DisposeControl( ((FormPeek)window)->vScroll );
    TEDispose( ((FormPeek)window)->nameTE );
    TEDispose( ((FormPeek)window)->miscTE );
    CloseWindow( window );
    DisposPtr( window );
}


/*********************************** AdjustMenus */

void    AdjustMenus()
{
    WindowPtr   window;
    int         wType;
    int         offset;
    TEHandle    te;

    window = FrontWindow();
    wType = WindowType( window );

    if ( window == NIL_POINTER )
    {
        DisableItem( gFileMenu, F_CLOSE_ITEM );

        DisableItem( gEditMenu, E_UNDO_ITEM );
        DisableItem( gEditMenu, E_CUT_ITEM );
```

```
            DisableItem( gEditMenu, E_COPY_ITEM );
            DisableItem( gEditMenu, E_PASTE_ITEM );
            DisableItem( gEditMenu, E_CLEAR_ITEM );
    }
    else if ( wType == DA_WINDOW )
    {
            DisableItem( gFileMenu, F_CLOSE_ITEM );

            EnableItem( gEditMenu, E_UNDO_ITEM );
            EnableItem( gEditMenu, E_CUT_ITEM );
            EnableItem( gEditMenu, E_COPY_ITEM );
            EnableItem( gEditMenu, E_PASTE_ITEM );
            EnableItem( gEditMenu, E_CLEAR_ITEM );
    }
    else if ( wType == FORM_WINDOW )
    {
            EnableItem( gFileMenu, F_CLOSE_ITEM );

            DisableItem( gEditMenu, E_UNDO_ITEM );
            DisableItem( gEditMenu, E_CUT_ITEM );
            DisableItem( gEditMenu, E_COPY_ITEM );
            DisableItem( gEditMenu, E_PASTE_ITEM );
            DisableItem( gEditMenu, E_CLEAR_ITEM );

            te = ((FormPeek)window)->curTE;
            if ( (*te)->selStart < (*te)->selEnd )
            {
                EnableItem( gEditMenu, E_CUT_ITEM );
                EnableItem( gEditMenu, E_COPY_ITEM );
                EnableItem( gEditMenu, E_CLEAR_ITEM );
            }
            if ( GetScrap( NIL_POINTER, 'TEXT', &offset)  > 0 )
                EnableItem( gEditMenu, E_PASTE_ITEM );
    }
}


/*********************************** WindowType */

int WindowType( window )
WindowPtr   window;
{
    if ( window == NIL_POINTER )
        return( NIL_WINDOW );
```

```
    if ( ((WindowPeek)window)->windowKind < 0 )
        return( DA_WINDOW );

    if ( ((FormPeek)window)->wType == FORM_WINDOW )
        return( FORM_WINDOW );

    return( UNKNOWN_WINDOW );
}


/*********************************** HandleMenuChoice */

void    HandleMenuChoice( menuChoice )
long int    menuChoice;
{
    int theMenu;
    int theItem;

    if ( menuChoice != 0 )
    {
        theMenu = HiWord( menuChoice );
        theItem = LoWord( menuChoice );
        switch ( theMenu )
        {
            case APPLE_MENU_ID :
                HandleAppleChoice( theItem );
                break;
            case FILE_MENU_ID :
                HandleFileChoice( theItem );
                break;
            case EDIT_MENU_ID :
                HandleEditChoice( theItem );
        }
        HiliteMenu( 0 );
    }
}


/****************************** HandleAppleChoice *******/

void    HandleAppleChoice( theItem )
int theItem;
{
```

```
    Str255      accName;
    int         accNumber;

    switch ( theItem )
    {
        case A_ABOUT_ITEM :
            NoteAlert( ABOUT_ALERT, NIL_POINTER );
            break;
        default :
            GetItem( gAppleMenu, theItem, accName );
            accNumber = OpenDeskAcc( accName );
            break;
    }
}


/********************************* HandleFileChoice   *******/

void    HandleFileChoice( theItem )
int theItem;
{
    WindowPtr  window;
    switch ( theItem )
    {
        case F_NEW_ITEM :
            CreateWindow();
            break;
        case F_CLOSE_ITEM :
            if ( ( window = FrontWindow() ) != NIL_POINTER )
                DoCloseWindow( window );
            break;
        case F_QUIT_ITEM :
            gDone = TRUE;
            break;
    }
}


/********************************* HandleEditChoice   *******/

void    HandleEditChoice( theItem )
int theItem;
{
```

```
TEHandle     te;
WindowPtr    window;
int          wType, length, i;
CharsHandle  text;
Str255       tempStr;
FormPeek     form;

if ( ! SystemEdit( theItem - 1 ) )
{
    window = FrontWindow();
    wType = WindowType( window );

    if ( wType == FORM_WINDOW )
    {
        form = (FormPeek)window;
        te = form->curTE;
        switch ( theItem )
        {
            case E_UNDO_ITEM:
                break;
            case E_CUT_ITEM:
                if ( ZeroScrap() == noErr )
                {
                    TECut(te);
                    AdjustScrollBar( form );
                    if ( TEToScrap() != noErr )
                        ZeroScrap();
                }
                break;
            case E_COPY_ITEM:
                if ( ZeroScrap() == noErr )
                {
                    TECopy(te);
                    if ( TEToScrap() != noErr )
                        ZeroScrap();
                }
                break;
            case E_PASTE_ITEM:
                if ( TEFromScrap() == noErr )
                {
                    TEPaste(te);
                    AdjustScrollBar( form );
                }
```

```
                                break;
                        case E_CLEAR_ITEM:
                            TEDelete(te);
                            AdjustScrollBar( form );
                            break;
                }

                if ( te == form->nameTE )
                {
                    length = (*form->nameTE)->teLength;
                    if ( length == 0 )
                        SetWTitle( window, UNTITLED_STRING );
                    else
                    {
                        text = TEGetText( form->nameTE );
                        tempStr[ 0 ] = length;
                        for ( i=0; ( (i<length) && (i<256) ); i++ )
                        {
                            tempStr[ i+1 ] = (*text)[ i ];
                        }
                        SetWTitle( window, tempStr );
                    }
                }

            }
        }
}


/***************************** DoContentClick ******/

void        DoContentClick( window, mouse )
WindowPtr   window;
Point       mouse;
{
    int             wType, value;
    int             thePart;
    Boolean         shiftDown;
    Point           locMouse;
    ControlHandle   control;
    FormPeek        form;

    wType = WindowType( window );
```

```
if ( wType == FORM_WINDOW )
{
    form = (FormPeek)window;
    locMouse = mouse;
    GlobalToLocal( &locMouse );

    if ( ( thePart = FindControl( locMouse, window,
        &control ) ) != 0 )
    {
        switch( thePart )
        {
            case inUpButton:
            case inDownButton:
            case inPageUp:
            case inPageDown:
                value = TrackControl( control, locMouse,
                                    (ProcPtr) VActionProc );

                break;
            case inThumb:
                value = GetCtlValue( control );
                thePart = TrackControl( control, locMouse,
                                    NIL_POINTER );
                if ( thePart != 0 )
                {
                    value -= GetCtlValue( control );
                    if ( value != 0 )
                        TEScroll(0, value * (*form->curTE)-
                                >lineHeight, form->miscTE );
                }
                break;
        }
    }
    else if ( PtInRect( locMouse, &gNameRect ) )
    {
        if ( form->curTE == form->nameTE )
        {
            shiftDown = ( gTheEvent.modifiers & shiftKey) != 0;
            TEClick( locMouse, shiftDown, form->nameTE );
        }
        else
        {
            SwitchToNewArea( form, TE_NAME_AREA );
            TEClick( locMouse, FALSE, form->nameTE );
```

```
            }
        }
        else if ( PtInRect( locMouse, &gMiscRect ) )
        {
            if ( form->curTE == form->miscTE )
            {
                shiftDown = ( gTheEvent.modifiers & shiftKey) != 0;
                TEClick( locMouse, shiftDown, form->miscTE );
            }
            else
            {
                SwitchToNewArea( form, TE_MISC_AREA );
                TEClick( locMouse, FALSE, form->miscTE );
            }
        }
    }
}


/********************************** VActionProc */

pascal voidVActionProc(control, part)
ControlHandle  control;
int            part;
{
    short        amount;
    WindowPtr    window;
    TEPtr        te;

    if ( part != 0 )
    {
        window = (*control)->contrlOwner;
        te = *((FormPeek)window)->miscTE;
        switch ( part ) {
            case inUpButton:
            case inDownButton:     /* one line */
                amount = 1;
                break;
            case inPageUp:         /* one page */
            case inPageDown:
                amount = (te->viewRect.bottom - te-
>viewRect.top) / te->lineHeight;
                break;
        }
```

```
                if ( (part == inDownButton) || (part == inPageDown) )
                    amount = -amount;
                CommonAction(control, &amount);
                if ( amount != 0 )
                    TEScroll( 0, amount * te->lineHeight,
                            ((FormPeek)window)->miscTE );
        }
}


/*********************************** CommonAction */

void            CommonAction( control, amount )
ControlHandle   control;
short           *amount;
{
    short       value, max;

    value = GetCtlValue( control );    /* get current value */
    max = GetCtlMax( control );        /* and maximum value */
    *amount = value - *amount;
    if ( *amount < 0 )
        *amount = 0;
    else if ( *amount > max )
        *amount = max;
    SetCtlValue( control, *amount );
    *amount = value - *amount;         /* calculate the real change */
}


/*********************************** DoActivate   */

void        DoActivate( window, becomingActive )
WindowPtr   window;
Boolean     becomingActive;
{
    FormPeek    form;
    int         wType;

    wType = WindowType( window );

    if ( wType == FORM_WINDOW )
    {
```

```
        form = (FormPeek)window;
        if ( becomingActive )
        {
            SetPort( window );
            if ( form->curTE == form->miscTE )
                TurnOnTextArea( form, TE_MISC_AREA );
            else
                TurnOnTextArea( form, TE_NAME_AREA );
            HiliteControl( form->vScroll, 0 );
        }
        else
        {
            if ( form->curTE == form->miscTE )
                TurnOffTextArea( form, TE_MISC_AREA );
            else
                TurnOffTextArea( form, TE_NAME_AREA );
            HiliteControl( form->vScroll, 255 );
        }
    }
}


/****************************** AdjustCursor ********/

void        AdjustCursor( mouse, region )
Point       mouse;
RgnHandle   region;
{
    WindowPtr       window;
    RgnHandle       arrowRgn, iBeamRgn, tempRgn;
    Rect            tempRect;
    int             wType;
    GrafPtr         oldPort;

    window = FrontWindow();
    wType = WindowType( window );

    if ( gInBackground || ( wType != FORM_WINDOW ) )
    {
        SetCursor( &arrow );
        return;
    }
```

```
    GetPort( &oldPort );
    SetPort( window );

    arrowRgn = NewRgn();
    iBeamRgn = NewRgn();
    tempRgn = NewRgn();

    SetRectRgn( arrowRgn, -32700, -32700, 32700, 32700 );

    tempRect = gNameRect;
    LocalToGlobal( &TopLeft(tempRect) );
    LocalToGlobal( &BotRight(tempRect) );
    RectRgn( tempRgn, &tempRect );
    UnionRgn( iBeamRgn, tempRgn, iBeamRgn );

    tempRect = gMiscRect;
    LocalToGlobal( &TopLeft(tempRect) );
    LocalToGlobal( &BotRight(tempRect) );
    RectRgn( tempRgn, &tempRect );
    UnionRgn( iBeamRgn, tempRgn, iBeamRgn );

    DiffRgn( arrowRgn, iBeamRgn, arrowRgn );

    if ( PtInRgn( mouse, iBeamRgn ) )
    {
        SetCursor( *GetCursor( iBeamCursor ) );
        CopyRgn( iBeamRgn, region );
    }
    else
    {
        SetCursor( &arrow );
        CopyRgn( arrowRgn, region );
    }
    DisposeRgn( arrowRgn );
    DisposeRgn( iBeamRgn );
    DisposeRgn( tempRgn );

    SetPort( oldPort );
}
```

```
/******************************** DoUpdate  */

void        DoUpdate( window )
WindowPtr   window;
{
    FormPeek    form;
    int         wType;
    GrafPtr     oldPort;

    GetPort( &oldPort );
    SetPort( window );

    wType = WindowType( window );

    if ( wType == FORM_WINDOW )
    {
        BeginUpdate( window );
        EraseRect( &window->portRect );
        DrawForm( window );
        EndUpdate( window );
    }

    SetPort( oldPort );
}


/********************************* DrawForm  */

void    DrawForm( window )
WindowPtr   window;
{
    FrameRect( &gNameRect );
    FrameRect( &gMiscRect );
    DrawControls( window );

    TextFont( geneva );
    TextFace( bold );

    MoveTo( gNameRect.left - 34, gNameRect.top + 12 );
    DrawString( "\pName" );
    MoveTo( gMiscRect.left - 34, gMiscRect.top + 12 );
    DrawString( "\pMisc." );
```

```
    TextFont( monaco );
    TextFace( 0 );

    TEUpdate( &window->portRect, ((FormPeek)window)->nameTE );
    TEUpdate( &window->portRect, ((FormPeek)window)->miscTE );
}


/********************************** CreateWindow */

void    CreateWindow()
{
    WindowPtr    theNewestWindow;
    Ptr          wStorage;
    FormPeek     form;

    wStorage = NewPtr( sizeof(FormRecord) );

    if ( ( theNewestWindow = GetNewWindow( BASE_RES_ID,
        wStorage,
            MOVE_TO_FRONT ) ) == NIL_POINTER )
        ErrorHandler( NO_WIND );
    if ( ( (screenBits.bounds.right - gNewWindowLeft) <
            DRAG_THRESHOLD ) ||
        ( ( screenBits.bounds.bottom - gNewWindowTop) <
            DRAG_THRESHOLD ) )
    {
        gNewWindowLeft = WINDOW_HOME_LEFT;
        gNewWindowTop = WINDOW_HOME_TOP;
    }

    MoveWindow( theNewestWindow, gNewWindowLeft,
                gNewWindowTop, LEAVE_WHERE_IT_IS );
    gNewWindowLeft += NEW_WINDOW_OFFSET;
    gNewWindowTop += NEW_WINDOW_OFFSET;

    form = (FormPeek)theNewestWindow;
    form->wType = FORM_WINDOW;

    form->vScroll = NewControl( theNewestWindow,
                                &gScrollBarRect, NIL_STRING,
            VISIBLE, 0, 0, 0, scrollBarProc, 0L);
```

```
    ShowWindow( theNewestWindow );
    SetPort( theNewestWindow );
    TextFont( monaco );
    TextFace( 0 );
    TextSize( 9 );
    StartTextEdit( form );
}



/***************************** StartTextEdit ********/

void        StartTextEdit( form )
FormPeek    form;
{
    Rect    r;

    r = gNameRect;
    InsetRect( &r, 2, 2 );
    form->nameTE = TENew( &r, &r );

    r = gMiscRect;
    InsetRect( &r, 2, 2 );
    form->miscTE = TENew( &r, &r );
    SetClikLoop( NewClikLoop, form->miscTE );

    TEAutoView( TRUE, form->miscTE );

    form->curTE = form->nameTE;
}



/****************************** NewClikLoop ********/

pascal Boolean NewClikLoop()
{
    WindowPtr    window;
    FormPeek     form;
    TEHandle     te;
    Rect         tempRect;
    Point        mouse;
    GrafPtr      oldPort;
    int          amount;
    RgnHandle    oldClip;
```

```
    window = FrontWindow();
    if ( WindowType( window ) != FORM_WINDOW )
        return( FALSE );

    form = (FormPeek)window;
    te = form->curTE;

    GetPort( &oldPort );
    SetPort( window );
    oldClip = NewRgn();
    GetClip( oldClip );

    SetRect( &tempRect, -32767, -32767, 32767, 32767 );
    ClipRect( &tempRect );

    GetMouse( &mouse );

    if ( mouse.v < gMiscRect.top )
    {
        amount = 1;
        CommonAction( form->vScroll, &amount );
        if ( amount != 0 )
            TEScroll( 0, amount * ((*te)->lineHeight), te );
    }
    else if ( mouse.v > gMiscRect.bottom )
    {
        amount = -1;
        CommonAction( form->vScroll, &amount );
        if ( amount != 0 )
            TEScroll( 0, amount * ((*te)->lineHeight), te );
    }

    SetClip( oldClip );
    DisposeRgn( oldClip );
    SetPort( oldPort );
    return( TRUE );
}


/****************************** SwitchToNewArea ********/

void        SwitchToNewArea( form, newArea )
FormPeek    form;
int         newArea;
{
```

```
        if ( form->curTE == form->nameTE )
        {
            TurnOffTextArea( form, TE_NAME_AREA );
            TurnOnTextArea( form, TE_MISC_AREA );
        }
        else
        {
            TurnOffTextArea( form, TE_MISC_AREA );
            TurnOnTextArea( form, TE_NAME_AREA );
        }
}


/******************************* TurnOnTextArea *********/

void        TurnOnTextArea( form, whichArea )
FormPeek    form;
int         whichArea;
{
    TEPtr   te;

    if ( whichArea == TE_MISC_AREA )
    {
        te = *form->miscTE;
        te->viewRect.bottom = (((te->viewRect.bottom - te-
                        >viewRect.top) / te->lineHeight)
                        * te->lineHeight) + te->viewRect.top;
        te->destRect.bottom = te->viewRect.bottom;
        AdjustScrollBar( form );
        form->curTE = form->miscTE;
    }
    else
        form->curTE = form->nameTE;

    TEActivate( form->curTE );
}


/******************************* TurnOffTextArea *********/

void        TurnOffTextArea( form, whichArea )
FormPeek    form;
int         whichArea;
```

```
{
    if ( whichArea == TE_MISC_AREA )
        TEDeactivate( form->miscTE );
    else
        TEDeactivate( form->nameTE );
}



/****************************** AdjustScrollBar ********/

void        AdjustScrollBar( form )
FormPeek    form;
{
    short   value, lines, max;
    short   oldValue, oldMax;
    TEPtr   te;

    oldValue = GetCtlValue( form->vScroll );
    oldMax = GetCtlMax( form->vScroll );
    te = *(form->miscTE);

    lines = te->nLines;
    if ( *(*te->hText + te->teLength - 1) == TE_CARRIAGE_RETURN )
        lines += 1;
    max = lines - ((te->viewRect.bottom - te->viewRect.top) /
            te->lineHeight);

    if ( max < 0 ) max = 0;
    SetCtlMax( form->vScroll, max);

    te = *(form->miscTE);
    value = (te->viewRect.top - te->destRect.top) / te-
            >lineHeight;

    if ( value < 0 ) value = 0;
    else if ( value >  max ) value = max;

    SetCtlValue( form->vScroll, value);

    TEScroll( 0, (te->viewRect.top - te->destRect.top) -
            (GetCtlValue( form->vScroll ) * te-
            >lineHeight), form->miscTE );
}
```

```
/****************************** ErrorHandler *********/

void    ErrorHandler( stringNum )
int     stringNum;
{
    StringHandle    errorStringH;

    if ( ( errorStringH = GetString( stringNum ) ) ==
        NIL_POINTER )
        ParamText( HOPELESSLY_FATAL_ERROR, NIL_STRING,
                NIL_STRING, NIL_STRING );
    else
    {
        HLock( errorStringH );
        ParamText( *errorStringH, NIL_STRING, NIL_STRING,
                NIL_STRING );
        HUnlock( errorStringH );
    }
    StopAlert( ERROR_ALERT_ID, NIL_POINTER );
    ExitToShell();
}
```

Chapter 6, BuildWindow(), (from CStarterDoc.c)

```
/***
 * BuildWindow
 *
 * Replace the old BuildWindow with this one...
 *
 ***/

void CStarterDoc::BuildWindow (Handle theData)
{
    CScrollPane     *theScrollPane;
    CStarterPane    *thePanorama;
    Rect            panFrame;

    itsWindow = new( CWindow );
    itsWindow->IWindow( WINDStarter, FALSE,
                    gDesktop, this );

    theScrollPane = new( CScrollPane );
```

```
theScrollPane->IScrollPane( itsWindow, this,
        0, 0, 0, 0,
        sizELASTIC, sizELASTIC,
        TRUE, TRUE, TRUE );

theScrollPane->FitToEnclFrame( TRUE, TRUE );
theScrollPane->SetSteps( 10, 10 );

thePanorama = new( CStarterPane );
thePanorama->IStarterPane( theScrollPane, this,
        0, 0, 0, 0,
        sizELASTIC, sizELASTIC );

thePanorama->FitToEnclosure( TRUE, TRUE );
theScrollPane->InstallPanorama( thePanorama );

itsMainPane = thePanorama;
itsGopher = thePanorama;

itsWindow->Zoom(inZoomOut);
thePanorama->GetFrame(&panFrame);
thePanorama->SetBounds(&panFrame);

gDecorator->PlaceNewWindow( itsWindow );

}
```

Chapter 6, CDragPane.c

```
#include "CStarterPane.h"
#include "CDragPane.h"

Boolean     gIsScrolling = FALSE;


/***************************** IDragPane ********/

void CDragPane::IDragPane( corner, height, width,
        patNum, anEnclosure, aSupervisor )
Point           corner;
int             height;
int             width;
```

```
int            patNum;
CView          *anEnclosure;
CBureaucrat    *aSupervisor;
{
    Rect r;

    ((CPanorama *)anEnclosure)->GetBounds( &r );

    if ((corner.h + width) > r.right)
        corner.h -= corner.h + width - r.right;

    if ((corner.v + height) > r.bottom)
        corner.v -= corner.v + height - r.bottom;

    IPane( anEnclosure, aSupervisor,
           width, height,
           corner.h, corner.v,
           sizFIXEDSTICKY, sizFIXEDSTICKY );

    patNumber = patNum;

    SetWantsClicks( TRUE );
    Refresh();
}


/******************************* Draw ********/

void CDragPane::Draw( rPtr )
Rect    *rPtr;
{
    if ( ! gIsScrolling )
    {
        Prepare();

        switch( patNumber )
        {
            case 0:
                PenPat( ltGray );
                break;
            case 1:
                PenPat( gray );
                break;
```

```
            case 2:
                PenPat( dkGray );
                break;
            default:
                PenPat( black );
                break;
        }

        PaintRect( rPtr );
    }
}


/***************************** DoClick ********/

void    CDragPane::DoClick( hitPt, modifierKeys, when )
Point   hitPt;
short   modifierKeys;
long    when;
{
    Rect    r;
    Rect    endLocation;

    r = frame;
    EraseRect( &r );

    FrameToEnclR(&r);

    ((CStarterPane *)itsEnclosure)->DoDrag( width,
            height, hitPt, r, &endLocation );

    Place( endLocation.left, endLocation.top, TRUE );
}
```

Chapter 6, CDragPane.h

```
#define _H_CDragPane

#include "CPane.h"

extern Boolean    gIsScrolling;
```

```
struct CDragPane : CPane
{
    int       patNumber;

    void      IDragPane( Point corner, int height,
                  int width, int patNum,
                  CView *anEnclosure,
                  CBureaucrat *aSupervisor );

    void      Draw( Rect *area );

    void      DoClick( Point hitPt,
                  short modifierKeys, long when );
};
```

Chapter 6, CMouse.c

```
#include "CMouse.h"


/******************************** IMouse ********/

void CMouse::IMouse( strID, objWidth, objHeight,
                  hitPt, theLoc, theRama )
int         strID;
int         objWidth;
int         objHeight;
Point       hitPt;
Rect        theLoc;
CPanorama   *theRama;
{
    Rect r;

    IMouseTask( strID );

    thePanorama = theRama;
    theLocation = theLoc;

    thePanorama->GetBounds( &r );
    r.left += hitPt.h;
    r.top += hitPt.v;
    r.right -= ( objWidth - hitPt.h );
```

```
        r.bottom -= ( objHeight - hitPt.v );
        theBounds = r;
}


/******************************** BeginTracking *********/

void CMouse::BeginTracking( startPt )
Point *startPt;
{
    Rect    r;

    PenMode( patXor );
    PenPat( gray );

    r = theLocation;
    FrameRect( &r );
}


/******************************** KeepTracking *********/

void CMouse::KeepTracking( currPt, prevPt, startPt )
Point *currPt;
Point *prevPt;
Point *startPt;
{
    Rect        r, f;
    long        curTicks;
    Point       startPosit, newPosit, cp, pp;
    RgnHandle   clipRgn;

    thePanorama->GetPosition( &startPosit );

    clipRgn = NewRgn();

    if ( thePanorama->AutoScroll( *currPt )
            || ! EqualPt( *currPt, *prevPt ) )
    {
        thePanorama->GetPosition( &newPosit );

        GetClip( clipRgn );
        r = (**clipRgn).rgnBBox;
```

```
        OffsetRect( &r, startPosit.h - newPosit.h,
                startPosit.v - newPosit.v );

        thePanorama->GetFrame(&f);
        PinInRect(&f, &(r.top));
        PinInRect(&f, &(r.bottom));

        ClipRect( &r );

        r = theLocation;

        curTicks = TickCount();
        while ( curTicks == TickCount() ) ;
        FrameRect( &r );

        cp = *currPt;
        pp = *prevPt;
        PinInRect(&theBounds, &cp);
        PinInRect(&theBounds, &pp);

        OffsetRect(&r, cp.h - pp.h, cp.v - pp.v);

        SetClip( clipRgn );

        curTicks = TickCount();
        while ( curTicks == TickCount() ) ;
        FrameRect( &r );

        theLocation = r;
    }

    DisposeRgn( clipRgn );
}


/****************************** EndTracking ********/

void CMouse::EndTracking( currPt, prevPt, startPt )
Point *currPt;
Point *prevPt;
Point *startPt;
{
    Rect    r;
```

```
    r = theLocation;
    FrameRect( &r );
    PenNormal();
}


/***************************** GetLocation ********/

void CMouse::GetLocation( theLoc )
Rect    *theLoc;
{
    *theLoc = theLocation;
}
```

Chapter 6, CMouse.h

```
#define _H_CMouse

#include "CMouseTask.h"
#include <CPanorama.h>

struct CMouse : CMouseTask
{
    CPanorama    *thePanorama;
    Rect         theLocation, theBounds;

    void    IMouse( int strID,
            int objWidth, int objHeight,
            Point hitPt, Rect theLoc,
            CPanorama *theRama );

    void    BeginTracking( Point *startPt );

    void    KeepTracking( Point *currPt,
            Point *prevPt, Point *startPt );

    void    EndTracking( Point *currPt,
            Point *prevPt, Point *startPt );

    void    GetLocation(Rect*);
};
```

Chapter 6, CStarterPane.c

```
#include "CStarterPane.h"
#include "CDragPane.h"
#include "CMouse.h"


/*********************************** IStarterPane */

void CStarterPane::IStarterPane( anEnclosure,
                    aSupervisor,
                    aWidth, aHeight,
                    aHEncl, aVEncl,
                    aHSizing, aVSizing )
CView           *anEnclosure;
CBureaucrat     *aSupervisor;
short           aWidth, aHeight, aHEncl, aVEncl;
SizingOption    aHSizing, aVSizing;
{
    CPanorama::IPanorama( anEnclosure, aSupervisor,
                    aWidth, aHeight,
                    aHEncl, aVEncl,
                    aHSizing, aVSizing );

    GetDateTime( &randSeed );

    SetWantsClicks( TRUE );
}


/****************************** DoClick ********/

void CStarterPane::DoClick( hitPt, modifierKeys, when )
Point   hitPt;
short   modifierKeys;
long    when;
{
    int         width, height, patNum;
    CDragPane   *myDragPane;

    width = Randomize( MAX_PANE_SIZE );
    height = Randomize( MAX_PANE_SIZE );
    patNum = Randomize( NUM_PATS );
```

```
    myDragPane = new( CDragPane );
    myDragPane->IDragPane( hitPt, height, width,
                    patNum, this, this );
}




/****************************** AdjustCursor *********/

void CStarterPane::AdjustCursor( where, mouseRgn )
Point       where;
RgnHandle   mouseRgn;
{
    SetCursor( *GetCursor( plusCursor ) );
}




/****************************** DoDrag *********/

void CStarterPane::DoDrag( objWidth, objHeight,
            hitPt, startLocation, endLocation )
int     objWidth, objHeight;
Point   hitPt;
Rect    startLocation, *endLocation;
{
    CMouse  *aMouseTask;
    Rect    boundsRect;
    Point   p;

    gIsScrolling = TRUE;

    boundsRect = bounds;

    aMouseTask = new( CMouse );

    aMouseTask->IMouse( NO_UNDO_STRING, objWidth,
            objHeight, hitPt, startLocation, this );

    Prepare();

    GetMouse( &p );
    TrackMouse( aMouseTask, p, &boundsRect );

    gIsScrolling = FALSE;
```

```
        aMouseTask->GetLocation( endLocation );

        Refresh();
}


/****************************** Randomize *********/

Randomize( range )
int      range;
{
        long    rawResult;

        rawResult = Random();
        if ( rawResult < 0 ) rawResult *= -1;
        return( (rawResult * range) / 32768 );
}
```

Chapter 6, CStarterPane.h

```
#define _H_CStarterPane
#include <CPanorama.h>

#define MAX_PANE_SIZE    200
#define NUM_PATS         4
#define NO_UNDO_STRING   0

struct CStarterPane : CPanorama
{
    void    IStarterPane( CView *anEnclosure,
                CBureaucrat *aSupervisor,
                short aWidth, short aHeight,
                short aHEncl, short aVEncl,
                SizingOption aHSizing,
                SizingOption aVSizing);

    void    DoClick( Point hitPt,
                short modifierKeys, long when );

    void    AdjustCursor( Point where,
                RgnHandle mouseRgn );
```

```
    void    DoDrag( int objWidth, int objHeight,
            Point hitPt, Rect frame,
            Rect *endLocation );
};
```

Index

Working with THINK C 5.0

When Symantec introduced version 5.0 of THINK C, they really made some changes. In fact, they practically rewrote the whole thing. Needless to say, you'll need to make some changes to your source code to keep up with these changes. For starters, read Appendix A in the THINK C *User Manual*. This will give you a good sense of what basic changes have occurred.

As you type in each of the Primer's programs, find the corresponding entry in the following pages. For example, the first entry discusses the changes you'll need to make to the source code file cdev.c, to make the program compatible with THINK C 5.0. Most of the book's programs are fairly easy to modify. By far, the largest percentage of changes must be made to the object programming example in Chapter 6. This is because of the extensive changes made to the THINK Class Library between versions 4.0 and 5.0 of THINK C.

You can find an electronic version of these changes on America Online, in the Macintosh Developer's library and on CompuServe, in the Macintosh Developer's library (GO MACDEV) in section 11 (Learn Programming). Good luck...

cdev.c:
1) (p. 67) Insert line, just after the last #define:
```
        short    FindFontNumber();
```

Tester.c:
1) (p. 95) Replace #define MOVE_TO_FRONT from
```
        -1L
    to
        (WindowPtr)-1L
```

2) (p. 97) Change BeginUpdate(gTheEvent.message) to
```
        BeginUpdate( (WindowPtr)gTheEvent.message )
```

3) (p. 97) Change EndUpdate(gTheEvent.message) to
```
        EndUpdate( (WindowPtr)gTheEvent.message )
```

DLOG.c:
1) (p. 111) Replace #define MOVE_TO_FRONT from
```
        -1L
    to
        (WindowPtr)-1L
```

ColorInfo.c:
1) (p. 136) Replace the line:
```
        #include "ColorToolbox.h"
    with
        #include "Picker.h"
```

Palette.c:
1) (p. 153) Replace the line:
```
        #include "ColorToolbox.h"
    with the two lines:
        #include "Palettes.h"
        #include "Picker.h"
```

2) (p. 153) Replace #define MOVE_TO_FRONT from
```
        -1L
    to
        (WindowPtr)-1L
```

508

ColorTutor.c:
1) (p. 171) Replace the line:
```
#include "ColorToolbox.h"
```
　　　with the two lines:
```
#include "Palettes.h"
#include "Picker.h"
```

2) (p. 171) Replace #define MOVE_TO_FRONT from
```
-1L
```
　　　to
```
(WindowPtr)-1L
```

GWorld.c:
1) (p. 203) Replace the two lines:
```
#include "ColorToolbox.h"
#include "QuickDraw32Bit.h"
```
　　　with the two lines:
```
#include "Picker.h"
#include "QDOffscreen.h"
```

2) (p. 203) Replace #define MOVE_TO_FRONT from
```
-1L
```
　　　to
```
(WindowPtr)-1L
```

FormEdit.c:
1) (p. 244) Replace #define MOVE_TO_FRONT from
```
-1L
```
　　　to
```
(WindowPtr)-1L
```

2) (p. 251) In the function DoTEKey(), replace the line:
```
tempStr[ i+1 ] = (*text)[ i ];
```
　　　with the line:
```
tempStr[ i+1 ] = (*(char **)text)[ i ];
```

3) (p. 257) In the function HandleEditChoice(), replace the line:
```
tempStr[ i+1 ] = (*text)[ i ];
```
　　　with the line:
```
tempStr[ i+1 ] = (*(char **)text)[ i ];
```

4) (p. 266) In the function NewClikLoop(), replace the declaration:
```
int             amount;
```
　　　with the line:
```
short           amount;
```

Starter.π (p. 341):
1) Make a copy of the "Starter Folder" found in the "TCL 1.1 Demos" folder in your "Development" folder. Next, copy the following files from your old "MyStarter" folder into this new folder:
  - CDragPane.c
  - CDragPane.h
  - CMouse.c
  - CMouse.h
  - CStarterDoc.c
  - CStarterDoc.h
  - CStarterPane.c
  - CStarterPane.h
  - Starter.c

You should be copying 9 files, replacing their counterparts in the new folder. Do **NOT copy** the files **CStarterApp.c** and **CStarterApp.h**!!!!!
Start up THINK C by double-clicking the file Starter.π in this new folder.

2) Select **Add...** from the Source menu and add the files CDragPane.c and CMouse.c to the project. Make sure you add the two files to the first segment in the project window. To select the first segment, click on the file name CStarterApp.c (in the project window) before you select **Add...**

3) Select **Options...** from the Edit menu.
   - Select "Language Settings" from the popup menu.
   - Make sure that the "Language Extensions" check box is checked.
   - Select the "THINK C + Objects" radio button.
   - Make sure the "Strict Prototype Enforcement" check box is checked.
   - Select the "Infer Prototypes" radio button.

4) Edit each of the functions in the files CDragPane.c, CMouse.c, and CStarterPane.c. Change each function's parameter declarations from the old style to the new style of parameter declaration. Make sure you edit every single function!!! Old style declarations look like this:

```
void CDragPane::DoClick( hitPt, modifierKeys, when )
Point    hitPt;
short    modifierKeys;
long     when;
{
}
```

New style declarations look like this:

```
void CDragPane::DoClick( Point hitPt,
        short modifierKeys, long when )
{
}
```

5) (p. 348) In the file CDragPane.c, in the function `IDragPane()`, change the declaration:
```
Rect r;
```
to
```
LongRect r;
```

6) (p. 349-350) Also in CDragPane.c, in the function `DoClick()`, change the first five lines from:
```
Rect       r;
Rect       endLocation;

r = frame;
EraseRect( &r );

FrameToEnclR(&r);
```
to these eight lines:
```
Rect       r;
Rect       endLocation;
LongRect   longR;

FrameToQDR( &frame, &r );
EraseRect( &r );

QDToLongRect(&r,&longR);
FrameToEnclR(&longR);
LongToQDRect( &longR, &r );
```

7) (p. 354) In the file CMouse.h, change the three lines:
```
void     BeginTracking( Point *startPt );
void     KeepTracking( Point *currPt, Point *prevPt,
             Point *startPt );
void     EndTracking( Point *currPt, Point *prevPt,
             Point *startPt );
```
to:
```
void     BeginTracking( struct LongPt *startPt );
void     KeepTracking( struct LongPt *currPt, struct LongPt
             *prevPt, struct LongPt *startPt );
```

```
        voidEndTracking( struct LongPt  *currPt, struct LongPt  *prevPt,
                         struct LongPt  *startPt );
```

8) (p. 351) In the file CMouse.c, in the function I Mouse ( ), change the declaration:
```
        Rect r;
```
   to
```
        LongRect r;
```

9) (p. 351) Also in the file CMouse.c, in the function I Mouse ( ), change:
```
        theBounds = r;
```
   to
```
        LongToQDRect( &r, &theBounds );
```

10) (p. 351) Also in the file CMouse.c, in the function BeginTracking(), change the function declaration from:
```
        void CMouse::BeginTracking( Point *startPt )
```
   to
```
        void CMouse::BeginTracking( struct LongPt *startPt )
```

11) (p. 352-353) Also in the file CMouse.c, replace the function KeepTracking() with the following:

```
        void CMouse::KeepTracking( struct LongPt
                 *currPt, struct LongPt *prevPt,
                 struct LongPt *startPt )
{
    LongRect     r, f;
    Rect         shortR;
    long         curTicks;
    LongPt       startPosit, newPosit, cp, pp;
    RgnHandle    clipRgn;

    thePanorama->GetPosition( &startPosit );

    clipRgn = NewRgn();

    if ( thePanorama->AutoScroll( currPt )
            || ! EqualLongPt( currPt, prevPt ) )
        {
        thePanorama->GetPosition( &newPosit );

        GetClip( clipRgn );
        QDToLongRect( &((**clipRgn).rgnBBox), &r );
        OffsetLongRect( &r, startPosit.h - newPosit.h,
                startPosit.v - newPosit.v );

        thePanorama->GetFrame(&f);
        PinInRect(&f, (LongPt *)(&(r.top)));
        PinInRect(&f, (LongPt *)(&(r.bottom)));

        LongToQDRect( &r, &shortR );
        ClipRect( &shortR );

        shortR = theLocation;   /* Erase old gray rect */

        curTicks = TickCount();
        while ( curTicks == TickCount() ) ;
        FrameRect( &shortR );
        QDToLongRect( &shortR, &r );


        cp = *currPt;
        pp = *prevPt;
        QDToLongRect( &theBounds, &f );
        PinInRect(&f, &cp);
        PinInRect(&f, &pp);
```

```
        OffsetLongRect(&r, cp.h - pp.h, cp.v - pp.v);

        SetClip( clipRgn );

        curTicks = TickCount();
        while ( curTicks == TickCount() ) ;

        LongToQDRect( &r, &shortR );
        FrameRect( &shortR );   /* Draw new gray rect */
        theLocation = shortR; /* update theLocation
            instance var */
    }
    DisposeRgn( clipRgn );
}
```

12) (p. 353) Also in the file CMouse.c, Replace the declaration of the function
    EndTracking() with:
```
    void CMouse::EndTracking( struct LongPt  *currPt,
        struct LongPt  *prevPt, struct LongPt  *startPt )
```

13) Add these three lines to the list of include files in the file CStarterDoc.c:
```
    #include "TBUtilities.h"
    #include "CWindow.h"
    #include <Packages.h>
```

14) In the file CStarterDoc.c, in the function OpenFile(), replace the line:
```
        theError = theFile->Open(fsRdWrPerm);
```
    with the line
```
        theFile->Open(fsRdWrPerm);
```

15) In the file CStarterDoc.c, in the function OpenFile(), comment out each of the lines:
```
        gApplication->RequestMemory(FALSE, TRUE);
        theFile->ReadAll(&theData);
```
    and
```
        gApplication->RequestMemory(FALSE, FALSE);
```

16) (p. 343) In the file CStarterDoc.c, in the function BuildWindow(), change the line:
```
    Rect            panFrame;
```
    to
```
    LongRect        panFrame;
```

17) (p. 346) In the file CStarterPane.c, in the function DoDrag(), change the declaration:
```
    Rect        boundsRect;
```
    to
```
    LongRect boundsRect;
```

18) (p. 346) In the file CStarterPane.c, in the function DoDrag(), add the new declaration:
```
    LongPt          longP;
```

19) (p. 346) In the file CStarterPane.c, in the function DoDrag(), change the line:
```
    TrackMouse( aMouseTask, p, &boundsRect );
```
    to
```
    QDToLongPt( p, &longP );
    TrackMouse( aMouseTask, &longP, &boundsRect );
```

ShowINIT.c:
1) (p. 397) Delete the line:
```
    #include <Color.h>
```

Macintosh C Programming Primer, Volume II: The Disk!

If you'd like to receive a complete set of source code, projects, and resources from Volume II of the Mac Primer:

1) Fill out the coupon. Print clearly.

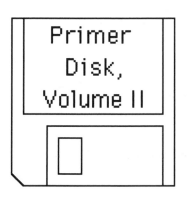

2) Attach a check for $30. Make the check out to **Intelligence at Large**. Make sure that the check is in **U.S. dollars**, drawn on a U.S. or Canadian bank. If you'd like the disk shipped outside the United States, please add $5.

3) Send the check and the coupon to:

> Intelligence at Large
> 3624 Market Street
> Philadelphia, PA 19104

> Call 215-387-6002 to order by VISA or MasterCard.

Here's my $30!
Send me the Primer Disk II,
quick!!! Mail the disk to:

Name_____

Company_____

Address _____

City _____ State____ Zip _____